HUMAN DEVELOPMENT IN IN[

HUMAN
DEVELOPMENT

HUMAN DEVELOPMENT IN INDIA

CHALLENGES FOR A SOCIETY IN TRANSITION

Sonalde B. Desai
Amaresh Dubey
Brij Lal Joshi
Mitali Sen
Abusaleh Sharif
Reeve Vanneman

OXFORD
UNIVERSITY PRESS

OXFORD
UNIVERSITY PRESS

YMCA Library Building, Jai Singh Road, New Delhi 110001

Oxford University Press is a department of the University of Oxford. It furthers the
University's objective of excellence in research, scholarship, and education
by publishing worldwide in

Oxford New York

Auckland Cape Town Dar es Salaam Hong Kong Karachi
Kuala Lumpur Madrid Melbourne Mexico City Nairobi
New Delhi Shanghai Taipei Toronto

With offices in
Argentina Austria Brazil Chile Czech Republic France Greece
Guatemala Hungary Italy Japan Portugal Singapore
South Korea Switzerland Thailand Turkey Ukraine Vietnam

Oxford is a registered trade mark of Oxford University Press
in the UK and in certain other countries

Published in India
by Oxford University Press, New Delhi

© Oxford University Press 2010

The moral rights of the author have been asserted
Database right Oxford University Press (maker)

First published 2010

All rights reserved. No part of this publication may be reproduced,
stored in a retrieval system, or transmitted, in any form or by any means, without the
prior permission in writing of Oxford University Press, or as expressly permitted by
law, or under terms agreed with the appropriate reprographics rights organization.
Enquiries concerning reproduction outside the scope of the above should be sent to
the Rights Department, Oxford University Press, at the address above

You must not circulate this book in any other binding or cover
and you must impose this same condition on any acquirer

ISBN-13: 978-0-19-806512-8
ISBN-10: 0-19-806512-4

Typeset in Adobe Garamond Pro 10.5/12.7
by Excellent Laser Typesetters, Pitampura, Delhi 110 034
Printed in India at Pragati Offset Pvt. Ltd., Hyderabad 500 004
Published by Oxford University Press
YMCA Library Building, Jai Singh Road, New Delhi 110 001

To

*The 41,554 households who participated in
India Human Development Survey
for allowing us to take a peek at their daily lives*

Contents

List of Tables, Figures, and Boxes — ix
Foreword — xv
Preface — xvii
Acknowledgements — xviii
List of Research Team and Advisors — xxi
List of Partner NGOs, Institutions, and Individuals — xxiii
List of Abbreviations — xxiv

Approach

1. Introduction — 3

Economic Well-being

2. Income, Poverty, and Inequality — 11
3. Agriculture — 28
4. Employment — 39
5. Household Assets and Amenities — 60

Education and Health

6. Education — 75
7. Health and Medical Care — 97

Vulnerable Population

8. Child Well-being — 125
9. Well-being of the Older Population — 138
10. Gender and Family Dynamics — 148

Social Changes

11. Social Integration and Exclusion — 171
12. Villages in a Global World — 182

Policy Responses

13. Social Safety Nets in India — 197
14. Conclusion — 207

Appendix I—IHDS: The Design — 213
Appendix II—Chapter Organization and Definition of Variables — 223

Bibliography — 229

Tables, Figures, and Boxes

TABLES

2.1	Household Income (Rs) Distribution	12
2.2	Median Household and Per Capita Incomes by State (Annual)	13
2.3	Structure of Income: Urban, Rural, and All India	16
2.4	Per cent of Households Drawing Income from Various Sources	17
2.5	Mean and Median Annual Income and Consumption	20
2.6	Headcount Ratio of Population below Poverty (NSS and IHDS)	21
2.7	Income and Consumption Inequality	22
A.2.1a	Mean and Median Household Incomes, Consumption, and Poverty	24
A.2.1b	Statewise Household Incomes, Consumption, and Poverty	25
A.2.2a	Proportion of Household Incomes by Source	26
A.2.2b	Statewise Proportion of Household Income by Source	27
A.3.1a	Cultivation and Farm Conditions	37
A.3.1b	Statewise Cultivation and Farm Ownership	38
A.4.1a	Work Participation Rates for Men and Women Aged 15–59 Years	49
A.4.1b	Statewise Work Participation Rates for Men and Women Aged 15–59 Years	50
A.4.2a	Number of Days Worked for Employed Men and Women Aged 15–59 Years	51
A.4.2b	Statewise Number of Days Worked for Employed Men and Women Aged 15–59 Years	52
A.4.3a	Type of Employment for Employed Men and Women Aged 15–59 Years (Urban and Rural)	53
A.4.3b	Statewise Distribution of Type of Employment for Employed Men and Women Aged 15–59 Years	55
A.4.4a	Distribution of Rural Workers between Farm and Non-farm Sector	56
A.4.4b	Statewise Distribution of Rural Workers between Farm and Non-farm Sector	57
A.4.5a	Daily Income for Wage and Salary Workers Aged 15–59 Years	58
A.4.5b	Statewise Daily Income for Wage and Salary Workers Aged 15–59 Years	59
5.1	Household Fuel Used for Different Fuels	63
5.2	Mode of Payment for Electricity by Place of Residence (for households with electricity)	66
A.5.1a	Household Access to Assets and Amenities	70
A.5.1b	Household Access to Assets and Amenities by State	71

6.1	Enrolment by School Type for Children Aged 6–14	82
6.2	Private Schooling Costs for Children Aged 6–14 by State	84
A.6.1a	Literacy Rates for Population Age 7 and above	88
A.6.1b	Statewise Literacy Rates for Population Age 7 and above	88
A.6.2a	Discontinuation Rates for Men and Women by Educational Level	89
A.6.2b	Statewise Discontinuation Rates for Men and Women by Educational Level	90
A.6.3a	Schooling Experiences of Children Aged 6–14	91
A.6.3b	Schooling Experiences of Children Aged 6–14 by State	92
A.6.4a	Reading, Writing, and Arithmetic Skills of Children Aged 8–11 by School Type	93
A.6.4b	Reading, Writing, and Arithmetic Skills of Children Aged 8–11 by School Type and State	94
A.6.5a	Skill Levels of Men and Women Aged 15–49	95
A.6.5b	Statewise Skill Levels of Men and Women Aged 15–49	96
7.1	Illness Types and Source of Treatment	100
A.7.1a	Prevalence Rates and Days Lost Due to Different Types of Illnesses	117
A.7.1b	Statewise Prevalence Rates and Days Lost Due to Different Types of Illnesses	118
A.7.2a	Utilization of Medical Care and Expenditure for Illnesses and Delivery	119
A.7.2b	Statewise Utilization of Medical Care and Expenditure for Illnesses and Delivery	120
A.7.3a	Health Knowledge: Ever-married Women Aged 15–49 Years	121
A.7.3b	Health Knowledge: Ever-married Women Aged 15–49 Years by State	121
A.8.1a	Infant and Child Mortality Rate (Per 1,000 Births) for Births in Preceding 10 Years	133
A.8.1b	Statewise Infant and Child Mortality Rate (Per 1,000 Births) for Births in Preceding 10 Years	133
A.8.2a	Vaccination Rate for Children Aged 12–59 Months	134
A.8.2b	Statewise Vaccination Rate for Children Aged 12–59 Months	135
A.8.3a	School Enrolment and Work for Children Aged 10–14 Years	136
A.8.3b	Statewise School Enrolment and Work for Children Aged 10–14 Years	137
9.1	Labour Force Participation and Type of Work Among Older Men and Women	140
9.2	Sources of Income Among Households with Elderly	142
A.9.1a	Distribution of Elderly Population and Selected Characteristics	146
A.9.1b	Statewise Distribution of Elderly Population and Selected Characteristics	147
A.10.1a	Marriage and Family Patterns	156
A.10.1b	Marriage and Family Patterns by State	157
A.10.2a	Women's Social Support Networks	158
A.10.2b	Women's Social Support Networks by State	159
A.10.3a	Average Expected Marriage Expenses and Dowry	160
A.10.3b	Average Expected Marriage Expenses and Dowry Across States	161
A.10.4a	Expectation of Old Age Support from Sons and Daughters	162
A.10.4b	Statewise Expectation of Old Age Support from Sons and Daughters	163
A.10.5a	Women's Control Over Resources and Physical Mobility	164
A.10.5b	Statewise Women's Control Over Resources and Physical Mobility	165
A.10.6a	Common Perception of Domestic Violence in the Community	166
A.10.6b	Statewise Common Perception of Domestic Violence in the Community	167
A.11.1a	Social Integration, Social Networks, and Crime Victimization	180
A.11.1b	Social Integration, Social Networks, and Crime Victimization by State	181
12.1	Village Infrastructure by State	183
12.2	Primary Water Source in Village by State	184
12.3	Availability of PDS Shops, Banks, Post Offices, Buses, and Phones in the Village	185

12.4	Access to Government Educational Institutions in the Village	187
12.5	Distance to Nearest Educational Institution (Government or Private)	188
12.6	Index of Government and Private School Access in the Village	189
12.7	Per cent of Sample Villages with Different Types of Medical Facilities	191
12.8	Per cent of Sample Villages with Access to Different Government Programmes	192
13.1	Use of PDS Shops for Rice, Wheat, Sugar, and Kerosene by Income and Card Type	200
13.2	Targeting and Coverage of Government Benefits	202
A.13.1a	Access to Social Safety Net Programmes	204
A.13.1b	Statewise Access to Social Safety Net Programmes	206
AI.1	Statewise Distribution of IHDS Sample	217
AI.2	Comparison of New and Re-interview Rural Sample in Districts Where Any Re-interviews Took Place	218
AI.3	Comparison of IHDS Estimates with Other Data Sources	220
AII.1	Sample Distribution Along Individual and Household Background Characteristics	224

FIGURES

2.1	Annual Household Income Distribution	12
2.2	Median Household Income by Number of Adults in the Household	14
2.3	Median Household Income (Rs) for Different Social Groups	14
2.4	Agricultural and Non-Agricultural Source of Income for Rural Households by Income Quintile	18
2.5	Statewise Median Incomes and Average Proportion of Income from Salaried Work	19
2.6	Statewise Median Incomes and Income Inequality	22
3.1	Distribution of Owned and Cultivated Land	29
3.2a	Pattern of Renting Land by Land Owned	30
3.2b	Pattern of Renting Land by Land Cultivated	31
3.3	Agricultural Income by Land Ownership	32
3.4	Statewise Median Agricultural Income (Cultivation + Livestock)	32
3.5	Per cent Rural Households Owning Livestock by Cultivation Status	35
3.6	Farm Expenses and Assets for Cultivating Households	35
4.1	Employment Rates by Age for Men and Women	40
4.2	Type of Employment for Working Men and Women	42
4.3	Type of Employment for Employed Men by Social Group (Urban and Rural)	43
4.4	Distribution of Rural Workers between Farm and Non-farm Sector	44
4.5	Distribution of Salaried Workers between Public and Private Sector (in per cent)	45
4.6	Salaries of Workers in Private and Public Sector and the Ratio by Education	46
4.7	Daily Income (Wage/Salary) by Education for Men and Women (Urban and Rural)	47
5.1	Water Source by Place of Residence	61
5.2	Indoor Piped Water by Income and Place of Residence	61
5.3	Availability of Toilet by Place of Residence	62
5.4	Fuel Use by Place of Residence	64
5.5	LPG Use by Income and Place of Residence	65
5.6	Household Access to Electricity by Place of Residence	65
5.7	Electricity by Income Levels and Place of Residence	66
5.8	Household Possessions	67
5.9	Distribution of Household Possessions Index by Place of Residence	68
5.10	Household Possessions Index by Number of Adults in the Household	68

6.1a	Literacy Rates for Males by Age	77
6.1b	Literacy Rates for Females by Age	77
6.2a	Reading Skills of Children Aged 8–11 (in per cent)	80
6.2b	Arithmetic Skills of Children Aged 8–11 (in per cent)	80
6.3	Educational Costs by Current Standard (Children Aged 6–14)	81
6.4	Total Educational Costs by Sex (Children Aged 6–14)	81
6.5	Per Child Educational Expenditure by Household Income Quintiles (Children Aged 6–14)	82
7.1	Short-term Morbidity by Age and Sex	99
7.2	Short-term Morbidity by Housing Characteristics	101
7.3	Diagnosed Long-term Illnesses	101
7.4	Long-term Morbidity by Age and Sex	102
7.5	Disabilities in Activities of Daily Living	103
7.6	Disabilities in Activities of Daily Living by Age	103
7.7	Pregnancy Problems for Last Birth between the Period 2000–5	104
7.8	Self-reported Health Being Good or Very Good for Women Aged 15–49 by Number of Children	105
7.9	Use of Public and Private Care by Availability in Village	107
7.10	Statewise Availability and Use of Public Health Centres	108
7.11	Prenatal and Postnatal Care	110
7.12	Physician-assisted Births by Birth Order	110
7.13	Medical Spending for Short-term and Long-term Illness	111
7.14	Medical Spending by Household Income (for all members)	112
7.15	Minor Illness Expenses by Source of Treatment	112
7.16	Major Medical Expenses by Source of Treatment	113
7.17	Distribution of Short-term Medical Expenses by Category (in per cent)	113
7.18	Health Knowledge Ever-married Women Aged 15–49 Years	114
8.1	Mortality Rates for Children by Age and Sex	126
8.2	Mortality Rate by Birth Order and Age	127
8.3	Home Visit by Health Worker During Pregnancy and Full Immunization Coverage by Place of Residence	128
8.4	Sex Ratio at Birth	129
8.5	Sex Ratio at Birth by Birth Order and Number of Children	129
8.6	Percentage of Women Getting Ultrasound/Amniocentesis by Birth Order and Number of Sons	130
8.7	Comparison of Brothers' and Sisters' Mortality by Age (Sister=1)	130
8.8	Participation in the Labour Force for Children Aged 10–14 (in per cent)	131
9.1	Statewise Distribution of the Population Above Age 60 (per cent)	139
9.2a	Living Arrangements of Elderly Men (in per cent)	143
9.2b	Living Arrangements of Elderly Women (in per cent)	143
9.3	Landholding and Joint Family Living for Men and Women Aged 60 and Older	144
9.4	Widowhood by Age for Men and Women Aged 60 and Older	145
9.5	Relationship with Household Head for Elderly Men and Women (in per cent)	145
10.1	Gap Between Marriage and Cohabitation by Age at Marriage	149
10.2	Length of Acquaintance Before Marriage by Education	150
11.1	Membership in Different Organizations (in per cent)	172
11.2	Organizational Membership by State	173
11.3	Amount of Village/Neighbourhood Conflict by State	174
11.4	Crime Victimization in the Preceding Year by State	175
11.5	Households' Social Networks by Type of Contact	176

11.6	Social Networks by State	177
11.7	Social Networks by Caste and Religion	178
12.1	Number of Infrastructure Items Available by Distance to District Headquarters	186
12.2	Distribution of Sample Villages by Health Facilities	190
12.3	Presence of NGO Programmes by Infrastructure Development of the Village	193
13.1	BPL Cards by Household Income and Assets	199
AI.1	India Human Development Survey 2005, District Coverage—Urban and Rural	214
AI.2	India Human Development Survey 2005, District Coverage—Rural Sample	215
AI.3	India Human Development Survey 2005, District Coverage—Urban Sample	216
AI.4	Sample Distribution	219
A.II.1	Socio-religious Group Categorization (in percentage)	228

BOXES

1.1	IHDS 2005	7
3.1	Cascading Effect of Many Inequalities in the Agricultural Sector between Social Groups	34
4.1	Education Does Not Always Lead to Greater Levels of Employment for Women	41
5.1	Gender and Domestic Drudgery	62
5.2	Contextual Impacts on Households' Access to Water and Sanitation	63
5.3	Have Televisions, Will Watch	69
6.1	Private Tutoring Increases Work Burden for Children	83
6.2	Characteristics of Government and Private Elementary Schools	84
6.3	Growing English Medium Enrolment	86
7.1	Alcohol and Tobacco Use	99
7.2	Government and Private Health Facilities	106
7.3	Television and HIV/AIDS Education	115
10.1	Women's Freedom of Physical Movement and Access to Health Care	154
11.1	Trust and Confidence in Institutions	179
14.1	Regional Differences Are Often Larger Than Other Differences	210

Foreword

India has been fortunate as our understanding of the development processes in the country has been based on insights that emanated from ground realities assessed through empirical evidence. It is one of the first countries in the world to put an elaborate mechanism in place to collect hard information on various indicators of development through household surveys. Indeed, for much of the past century, this set of information was perhaps the only source available to academics and policymakers for assessing development options and outcomes empirically.

However, over time, there has been a significant increase in demand for data that support analytical studies and address multiple aspects of development within a consistent framework. The public data systems have not been able to keep up with this demand and non-governmental agencies stepped in to fill the breach. This monograph is the result of one such endeavour. The six authors of the monograph led by Sonalde B. Desai embarked on a challenging task of creating an information base from a survey of over 41,500 Indian households providing indicators required to assess human development. Using these new data, this volume expands and deepens the policy discourse. The National Council of Applied Economic Research (NCAER) was one of the first institutions in India to address human development as far back as the 1990s. In the current volume, reflecting collaboration between researchers from the University of Maryland and NCAER, this agenda has been expanded to incorporate both human and social development issues. It provides fresh evidence to address some of the central challenges of our times.

The monograph broadly covers five thematic areas. Some of these have already become synonymous with human development through the efforts of the *Human Development Reports* published by the UN, while others are only just beginning to receive importance. These are income and employment, education and health, well-being of the vulnerable populations, social development, and policy challenges and responses. In each area, the discussion tries to deepen the human development discourse. For example, when discussing income and consumption, the volume explores the underlying processes that create the observed patterns of levels of living and attempts to assess the magnitude of income inequality. Similarly, the analyses of education go beyond the enrolment statistics to assess quality as well as costs of education.

The key message that emerges is that even in an era of rapid economic growth, the processes that have shaped inequalities in the country along gender, caste, and religious lines continue to persist. For some outcomes, for example, regional and urban–rural inequalities are even more important than other forms of social inequality. Addressing these inequalities is going to be a crucial policy challenge in the coming decade and the data in this volume will provide a useful supplementary input for policy dialogue.

I have been associated with this work from a very early stage as Chairperson of the Advisory Group that consisted of eminent academicians and policymakers. Having seen this project grow from conceptualization to a dataset that is being widely used by Indian and international research communities, it gives me immense satisfaction in acknowledging that

Sonalde B. Desai and her colleagues have produced a valuable and well-conceived primary data base which can become a foundation for future initiatives. In addition, they have also provided some important insights into the dynamics of household well-being in this monograph. The information base created by the team is now a public resource and I hope it will be used for a more rigorous analysis of the dynamics of the household well-being in days to come.

Dr Pronab Sen
Chief Statistician of India

January 2010

Preface

On account of the size of its population, its cultural and religious diversity, and its wager on universal suffrage at the time of Independence in 1947, India has always been central to the debate on growth poverty, inequality, and human development.

India's rapid economic growth since the 1980s has stimulated further global interest in understanding its complex society. The story about contemporary India is deeper than a story of simple economic expansion. To understand how that expansion has touched the daily lives of ordinary Indians, this report highlights the way in which poverty and affluence intersect with age-old divisions of regional inequalities, gender, caste, and religion that have long structured human development in India. Together, these economic and social forces shape each facet of Indians' lives—their livelihoods, their children's education, their health and medical care, the creation of new families and the care of older generations, and their entry into or exclusion from important social connections.

The strength of this report is its analysis of a survey of 41,554 households jointly undertaken by researchers from the National Council of Applied Economic Research (NCAER) and the University of Maryland. The India Human Development Survey (IHDS) builds on a long tradition of household surveys at NCAER and has been designed to assess human development in a way that expands and deepens the definition of human development. The chapters in this volume use statistics from the survey to paint a nuanced portrait of contemporary India and address a wide range of debates and policy challenges.

Financial support for this data collection was provided by the US National Institute of Child Health and Human Development with supplemental support from The World Bank. Intellectual leadership of this project was provided by Sonalde B. Desai, Amaresh Dubey, Abusaleh Shariff, and Reeve Vanneman with guidance from an eminent advisory board chaired by Pronab Sen, Chief Statistician of India.

As India continues to experience rapid economic growth, the challenge to ensure this growth carries forward to benefit even the country's poorest citizens, will remain at the heart of political discourse in the years to come. The NCAER is committed to providing unbiased data for policy dialogue. This report represents only a fraction of the information available in IHDS. Data from this are now available free of cost to all researchers. We hope they will continue to be used to provide the groundwork for policy analysis and debates in the coming decade.

Suman K. Bery
Director-General
National Council of Applied Economic Research, Delhi

January 2010

Acknowledgements

This volume is the culmination of six years of work, including organization of a household survey entitled India Human Development Survey and its analysis. In retrospect, we are astounded by the scope of this work. The survey involved interviews of 41,554 households in about 1,500 villages and 800 urban blocks, in 13 languages. This would not have been feasible without the collaboration of networking agencies in different parts of India. They recruited the field investigators who knew the local language and customs and undertook field operations on our behalf. The effort put in by each one of them is gratefully acknowledged.

This vast project was carried out under the guidance from an Advisory Committee headed by Pronab Sen, Chief Statistician of India and Secretary, Department of Statistics, Government of India. Members of this committee included some of the most prominent academics and policymakers in India as well as representatives of a variety of governmental and non-governmental organizations. At every stage of the project, they helped us with critical comments, responded to our findings, and also provided us with valuable insights and suggestions about how to move forward. Like all true academics, however, they never imposed their ideas on us. We thank the anonymous reviewers as well as Professor Sundaram for his comments on the initial version of this monograph.

Our team also included a large number of Research Assistants, Research Associates, Consultants, and support staff at NCAER and the University of Maryland. We acknowledge their support during the course of this work that lasted over six years. O.P. Sharma at NCAER deserves special thanks for field management as does Douglas Barnes from The World Bank for advice and collaboration.

We appreciate the support from our home institutions, the University of Maryland and NCAER, for encouraging and facilitating this work. Among the many who worked behind the scenes, two persons, Suman Bery and Shashank Bhide, Director General and Senior Research Councillor, respectively, at NCAER, deserve special thanks. Without their understanding and support we would not have been able to complete this work.

We received invaluable support from different ministries and departments of the Government of India throughout this project. The Planning Commission helped us frame the broad research themes while providing logistical support. The Registrar General helped with drawing urban samples and several state and district officials facilitated the data collection process. We are grateful for their generosity.

Financial support for this research was provided by the US National Institute of Child Health and Human Development through two grants (R01HD04155 and R01HD046166). Supplementary funding was provided by The World Bank. Their support is gratefully acknowledged. We would like to thank two National Institutes of Health (NIH) Programme Officers, Jeffrey Evans and Michael Spittel, who encouraged us to pursue an ambitious agenda while helping us overcome practical hurdles.

While space does not permit here in naming all the field investigators, supervisors, research staff, consultants, and the networking agencies, a complete list has been given.

Finally, it must be added here that we alone take responsibility for any shortcoming or error in this research or data.

SONALDE B. DESAI
AMARESH DUBEY
BRIJ LAL JOSHI
MITALI SEN
ABUSALEH SHARIFF
REEVE VANNEMAN

January 2010

Research Team and Advisors

RESEARCH TEAM

Abhilasha Sharma	Associate Fellow, NCAER
Abhinav Alakshendra	Research Associate, NCAER
Abhishek Kumar	Research Associate, NCAER
Abusaleh Shariff	Senior Research Fellow, International Food Policy Research Institute
Amaresh Dubey	Professor, JNU
Anamika Sinha	Research Associate, NCAER
Anand Verma	Research Trainee, NCAER
Anupam Tyagi	Consultant, NCAER
Brij Lal Joshi	Fellow (retired), NCAER
Biswarupa Ghosh	Consultant, NCAER
Cecily Adams	Research Assistant, University of Maryland
Deepak Varshney	Research Associate, NCAER
Devendra Kumar Bajpai	Research Associate, NCAER
Gheda Temsah	Research Assistant, University of Maryland
Hemanta Hazarika	Research Associate, NCAER
James Noon	Research Assistant, University of Maryland
Jaya Koti	PC Operator, NCAER
Joydeep Goswami	Consultant, NCAER
K.C. Shyam	Research Assistant, University of Maryland
Koyal Roy	Research Associate, NCAER
Lekha Subaiya	Research Assistant, University of Maryland
Lester Andrist	Research Assistant, University of Maryland
Lijuan Wu	Research Assistant, University of Maryland
Lipika Das Gupta	Research Associate, NCAER
M.K. Arora	Consultant, NCAER
Manjistha Banerji	Research Associate, NCAER
Mitali Sen	US Census Bureau
Monisha Grover	Research Associate, NCAER
Moumita Das Gupta	Research Associate, NCAER
Nish Varghese	Research Trainee, NCAER

O.P. Sharma	Associate Fellow, NCAER
P.K. Ghosh	Associate Fellow, NCAER
P.K. Panda	Consultant, NCAER
Rahmat Khan	Research Associate, NCAER
Rajendra Singh Bargali	Research Associate, NCAER
Rakesh Kumar Shrivastava	Senior Executive IT, NCAER
Rakesh Kumari Jaswal	Research Trainee, NCAER
Reema Gupta	Research Associate, NCAER
Reeve Vanneman	Professor, University of Maryland
Ruchi Jain	Research Associate, NCAER
Rupali Subudhi	Research Associate, NCAER
S.M. Shadab	Research Trainee, NCAER
Sonalde B. Desai	Professor, University of Maryland and Senior Fellow, NCAER
Sonya Rastogi	Research Assistant, University of Maryland
Varsha Soni	Research Trainee, NCAER
Vidyasagar	Research Trainee, NCAER

ADVISORS

Rukmini Banerjee	PRATHAM
Douglas Barnes	The World Bank

Partner NGOs, Institutions, and Individuals

PARTNER NGOs AND INSTITUTIONS

AMS Consulting (P) Limited, Lucknow

Centre for Research Evaluation Analysis Training and Education, Lucknow

Centre for Survey Research and Management Services, Kochi

Coalition of Population Activities and Research, Kolkata

Department of Communication and Behavioural Sciences, J&K Institute of Management, Public Administration and Rural Development, Srinagar

Development & Research Pvt. Ltd., New Delhi

Economic Information Technology, Kolkata

Indian Institute of Development Management, Bhopal

Indian Society for Applied Research & Development, Delhi

Indian Socio Economic Research Unit, Pune

Institute of Environmental Research Entrepreneurship Education & Development India, Lucknow

Institute of Objective Studies, New Delhi

Institute of Regional Analysis, Bhopal

Janhit-Kala Sansthan, Patna

Maroof Socio-Economic & Educational Welfare Trust, Bangalore

Research and Analysis Consultants, Bhubaneswar

Sandhan Society for Study of Education and Development, Jaipur

S V Enterprises, Ghaziabad

TNS India Pvt Ltd., New Delhi

Trend Setters, Kolkata

United Research Organization, Vadodra

VIMARSH, New Delhi

Zenith Corporate Services Pvt. Ltd., Hyderabad

INDIVIDUALS

Anil Kumar Joshi
Punjab

A.R. Lokrey
Hyderabad

Umme Zakira
Bangalore

Kanmani Chandran
Chennai

Veronica Pala
Meghalaya

S. Krishnamoorthy
Coimbatore

Abbreviations

ASER	Annual Status of Educational Report
BPL	Below Poverty Line
CHC	Community Health Centre
DPT	Diptheria, Pertussis, and Tetanus
FPS	Fair Price Shop
HCR	Head Count Ratio
HDI	Human Development Index
HDPI	Human Development Profile of India
HIV/AIDS	Human Immunodeficiency Virus/Acquired Immunodeficiency Syndrome
ICDS	Integrated Child Development Services
IHDS	India Human Development Survey
LPG	Liquefied Petroleum Gas
MDM	Midday Meal
NCAER	National Council of Applied Economic Research
NCERT	National Council of Education Research and Training
NFHS	National Family Health Survey
NGO	Non-governmental Organization
NOAPS	National Old Age Pension Scheme
NSS	National Sample Survey
OBC	Other Backward Class
PDS	Public Distribution System
PHC	Primary Health Centre
PL	Poverty Line
PSU	Primary Sampling Unit
SGRY	Sampoorna Grameen Rozgar Yojana
STDs	Sexually Transmitted Diseases
TPDS	Targeted Public Distribution System
UNDP	United Nations Development Programme

Approach

Introduction

Long years ago we made a tryst with destiny, and now the time comes when we shall redeem our pledge, not wholly or in full measure, but very substantially. At the stroke of the midnight hour, when the world sleeps, India will awake to life and freedom. A moment comes, which comes but rarely in history, when we step out from the old to the new, when an age ends, and when the soul of a nation, long suppressed, finds utterance. It is fitting that at this solemn moment we take the pledge of dedication to the service of India and her people and to the still larger cause of humanity…. That future is not one of ease or resting but of incessant striving so that we may fulfil the pledges we have so often taken and the one we shall take today. The service of India means the service of the millions who suffer. It means the ending of poverty and ignorance and disease and inequality of opportunity. The ambition of the greatest man of our generation has been to wipe every tear from every eye. That may be beyond us, but as long as there are tears and suffering, so long our work will not be over. (Nehru 2003[1])

With these evocative words, an independent India began her tryst with destiny. It is fitting that we celebrate the awakening of the Indian economy and an era of faster annual growth by remembering this pledge of service to the 1.2 billion-plus population in diverse corners of India. This book is dedicated to exploring the contours of the day to day lives of Indians in 2004 and 2005, nearly 60 years after this pledge was made. This search must acknowledge the achievements of the last century as well as anticipate the challenges of the twenty-first century. It must document the lived experiences of Indian families in cities and villages from Kashmir to Kanyakumari as they go about negotiating their daily lives in a globalizing India. In documenting the way they live, work, educate their children, care for their aged parents, and deal with ill health, we seek to infuse the development discourse with the lived experiences of ordinary people.

We begin by thanking the 41,554 families in the India Human Development Survey (IHDS) 2005, who opened their hearts and homes to strangers and shared details of their daily lives. The diversity of India demands that experiences of Indians from remote parts of the North-East be heard along with those in the crowded streets of old Delhi, and those of Adivasi and Dalit labourers be heard side by side with those of the upwardly mobile middle class. A search for a human face for the nation demands that individuals not be reduced to growth rates or poverty rates but that, instead, their lives be seen in holistic terms. This study attempts to balance competing goals of painting a broad panorama, without ignoring the details, by relying on interviews with men, women, and children in the IHDS.

Our narrative relies on the IHDS for empirical support. This survey was organized by the authors of this book, as a part of the collaboration between University of Maryland and National Council of Applied Economic Research (NCAER), New Delhi, with assistance from 24 organizations located throughout India. The survey, which involved 41,554 household interviews in 1,503 villages and 971 urban blocks in 33 states and union territories of India (Figure AI.1 in Appendix I), was designed to be nationally representative. This survey builds on a prior survey conducted by NCAER in 1993–4. This survey is unique in that it was designed to measure different dimensions of human development, with a particular emphasis on understanding social inequalities. Unlike single-topic surveys of health, labour market behaviour, or consumption patterns, it emphasized a variety of

---

[1] Jawaharlal Nehru's midnight address to the Constituent Assembly, 14–15 August 1947.

topics of interest to a study of human development under a single rubric, providing us with a rich array of data for our study.

What does it mean to take a holistic perspective on peoples' lives? Past *Human Development Reports* have expanded development discourse beyond its focus on economic growth to consider human development and people's basic needs, such as their standard of living, education, and health care. It is now universally accepted that these different dimensions of human development—livelihood, education, and health—play important roles in shaping personal well being. However, these markers of individual well being are embedded in wider networks of family and kin groups, castes, tribes, and religious identities, the political economy of villages and towns, and the direct and indirect actions of the state and civic society.

In this book, we seek to deepen this development discourse in four ways. First, while building on past discourse on human development, we seek to expand it by looking beyond basic indicators to more complex evaluations of human development. For example, we look not just at levels of school enrolments, but at assessments of what is being learned. Second, recognizing the diversity of Indian society across gender, caste, ethnicity, religion, income, education, and region, we consistently disaggregate the human development outcomes by each of these characteristics and try to ground our discussion within these differences. Third, we emphasize that individuals exist in a web of social networks and expand our discussion to examine how individuals are linked to the world around them. Contexts are important for each of the human development outcomes we consider. Finally, a holistic perspective on people's lived experiences must recognize how the separate dimensions of human development are interrelated. Employment, education, health, and social networks must be addressed in separate chapters, but they do not exist as independent segments in people's lives. A major advantage of a comprehensive survey like the IHDS is the ability to investigate these interrelationships.

COMPLEXITY

We seek to document patterns of human development at its most basic level in Indian society. In accomplishing this task, we try to refocus the rhetoric of development from basic indicators of welfare to the new challenges facing India in the coming decades. For example, much has been attained in the field of education since Independence. Although the literacy rate for elderly individuals aged 60 and older is barely 59 per cent for men and 19 per cent for women, their grandchildren aged between ten to fourteen boast of 92 per cent literacy among boys and 88 per cent among girls. It is time to set a higher bar, and focus on school quality and functional skills. So, in addition to asking about enrolment rates, IHDS also gave the eight to eleven olds simple tests of reading, arithmetic, and writing. We also asked about English fluency and computer skills.

A second example is found in our analysis of employment. Rates of employment and sectoral location remain important indicators of individual and family position. But to understand how Indian families manage the opportunities and risks of the modern economy, we need to look also at how families, and even individuals, diversify their employment patterns across sectors, combining agricultural and non-agricultural labour or cultivation with private business.

A final example of the need to expand past approaches to human development is the IHDS measurement of economic position. Excellent measures of consumption levels have been available from the National Sample Survey (NSS) for years. More abbreviated measures of economic standing, based on household possessions, have been well developed by the *National Family Health Survey* (*NFHS*). The IHDS included adaptations of both these measures. But while consumption expenditures and household possessions can provide good estimates of levels of economic well being, they say little about how households came to their current economic position. Income measures are necessary for a better understanding of the sources of poverty or economic success. The IHDS provides the most comprehensive data, yet, available on Indian incomes.

INEQUALITY

Variations in all these markers of well being are consistently mapped across cleavages in Indian society, based on gender, caste, religion, class, and place of residence. Similar tables at the end of each chapter show variations in each type of human development.

While amelioration of these inequalities has been at the core of the nationalist agenda in twentieth century India, the success of these efforts has often been disappointing. Even well meaning policies often fail due to poor implementation. For example, in spite of increasing efforts at reducing educational inequalities in school enrolments, IHDS data documents substantial differences in reading, writing, and arithmetic skills between children of various socio-religious groups. Dalit, Adivasi, and Muslim children read at lower levels and can complete fewer basic arithmetic tasks than their forward caste brothers and sisters, even those with identical school attainments.

Additionally, external forces in a now global world pose challenges that risk unintentional widening of inequalities. Analyses, presented in the chapter on employment, indicate that Adivasis are far more likely to be employed in agriculture than other socio-religious communities. Consequently, the agricultural stagnation of the 1990s has had a far greater impact on Adivasis than on other communities, contributing to the income disparities reported in Chapter 2. Disproportionate regional growth further exacerbates these inequalities because Adivasis are far more likely to be rural and live in poorer states like Chhattisgarh, Jharkhand, and Madhya Pradesh, than in the prosperous Punjab or Haryana.

Nevertheless, an important theme that emerges from the chapters that follow is how deep regional cleavages are, even compared with caste and income inequalities. While it is well known that some states are far more economically developed than others, this general economic observation misses much of the nature of interstate disparities. Chapter 7 shows that a poor, illiterate Dalit labourer in Cochi or Chennai is likely to be healthier, and certainly has better access to medical care than a college graduate, forward caste, large landowner in rural Uttar Pradesh. Social inequalities matter, but their importance is overwhelmed for many aspects of human development by state and rural–urban differences.

Contexts

The extent of these regional inequalities justifies the attention that the IHDS placed on investigating the social and economic contexts in which the 41,554 households found themselves. The IHDS recognized that individuals exist in a web and sought to examine how individuals, families, and communities are linked to the world around them. Consequently, we focused on gender roles and norms when trying to understand gender disparities in Indian society; explore the way in which different families are linked to social networks and institutions when studying inequalities between diverse social groups; and tried to focus on institutional structures and linkages shaping the relationship of villages and states in an increasingly global world.

INTERRELATIONSHIPS

We argue that it is time for the development discourse to pay greater attention to the politics of culture and the culture of politics. The politics of culture is perhaps most clearly seen in the discourse surrounding gender in Indian society. Gender inequality, in different markers of human development, particularly the imbalance in the juvenile sex ratio, is well recognized in literature. However, role of cultural traditions, in creating a climate within which these inequalities emerge, have received little attention. In this study, we examine differences in intra-family relationships across different parts of India and different communities, and observe far greater egalitarian gender relations among Adivasis and a greater willingness of parents in southern India to rely on daughters for social and financial support. We argue that it would be surprising if more favourable gender ratios among Adivasis and in south India were not related to these differences in gender roles. We also suggest that instead of thinking of culture as being immutably fossilized, it would make sense to see it as a process that is being constantly modified and to understand that public policies have a broad impact on how traditions are interpreted and modified. Results on women's employment provide an interesting example by showing that gender inequalities in salaries are far greater in the private than in the public sector. The culture of politics and the differential ability of states to ensure a climate within which their residents live healthy and productive lives is a recurring theme throughout this study.

In addition to introduction and conclusion, this monograph is divided into four sections. The first section focuses on livelihoods, with chapters exploring the level and composition of household income and poverty; agriculture and access to means of production; employment patterns and wages; and standard of living. The second section focuses on education and health, with a focus on assessing current status as well as the availability and cost of educational and health services. The third section focuses on the well-being of vulnerable populations: children, the elderly, and women. The fourth section is unique in its focus on the linkages between individuals and households and the broader social structures. Chapters in this section include analysis of social integration of the households into broader community networks; the level of village development in an increasingly global world; and the policy responses in the form of social safety net provisions. Our survey methodology and sample are discussed in Appendices I and II. Some highlights are discussed in Box 1.1.

In trying to provide a holistic view of the daily lives of Indian families, this monograph covers a broad terrain. However, many chapters contain similar themes. Chapters on income, agriculture, and employment suggest that while India remains overwhelmingly rural, with nearly 72 per cent of the Indian population still residing in villages, stagnation in agricultural productivity has found an echo in the declining importance of farming in the household economy. Although 53 per cent of the rural households engage in farming and 57 per cent engage in raising livestock, only 20 per cent of the households draw all their income from agriculture. Nearly 27 per cent of rural males work in the non-farm sector and a further 21 per cent combine own-account farming/care of live stock/agricultural wage labour with non-farm work. Salaried work, particularly in the public sector, remains at the top of the job ladder. Salaried public sector workers earn an average of Rs 6,980 per month as compared with salaried workers in the private sector who barely earn Rs 4,569 per month, if in a permanent job and Rs 2,365, if in a temporary job. All of them are better off than the manual labourers, who earn only Rs 50–80 per day and are lucky if they can find about 200 days of employment in a year.

Education remains the key to obtaining this coveted *sarkari naukari* (government job), but access to education is socially structured. Although school enrolment has been rising at a rapid rate and about 85 per cent of children aged six to fourteen are enrolled in school, only 54 per cent of eight to eleven year olds are able to read a simple paragraph and barely 48 per cent are able to do two-digit subtraction. There is wide divergence in the three R's (reading, writing, and arithmetic) by social and religious background, with children from Dalit, Adivasi, and Muslim families falling substantially behind other communities. Not surprisingly, this educational deficiency is reflected in lower access to salaried jobs among these communities. Chapter 6 also records high rates of private school enrolment among both urban and rural children, with children of the rich being far more likely to attend private schools than those from poor households. Private schools seem to offer higher quality education, as seen in skills obtained by children. With 51 per cent of the urban children attending private schools, this trend seems more or less irreversible in urban areas. Growth of private schools in rural India is a relatively recent phenomenon; and with only 20 per cent of the rural children in private schools, there is still a chance to improve the quality of rural government schools and keep middle class as well as poor children in the same school, somewhat levelling the playing field.

In contrast, social inequalities in health seem far less important than regional inequalities. Individuals in the north central plains are more likely to suffer from minor as well as major illnesses than those in southern states. If education is undergoing rapid privatization, medical care seems to be already dominated by private providers. In spite of an extensive network of government clinics, four times as many Indian households rely on private care as on public medical-care. Out-of-pocket expenses for public services remain high, and a perception of better quality in private care seems to drive many people—even poor people—towards using private medical care.

As Section 3 documents, households continue to be primary determinants of the well-being of members who reside within them—and the sites within which inequalities between boys and girls, and men and women are articulated. An overwhelming preference for sons continues to result in fewer girls being born than boys and a lower survival rate for girls than for boys. In spite of the ban against prenatal sex determination, 25–30 per cent of the women respondents acknowledge receiving an ultrasound or amniocentesis during their pregnancy, and women with no sons are far more likely to undergo an ultrasound or amniocentesis than those with a son. Moreover, nearly 34 per cent of those who underwent these tests seemed to know the sex of the child, although it is illegal for a medical provider to tell them. Not surprisingly, considerably fewer girls than boys are born in many parts of India. At the same time, households also continue to be primarily responsible for the welfare of the elderly. Nearly 87 per cent of the elderly we studied live in extended families and while a few receive pensions or benefits from government schemes such as the National Old Age Pension Scheme, this income is rarely adequate for support.

However, these households are located in a rapidly globalizing world, and their linkages to this world receive attention in Section 4. The analysis of linkages between households and the broader social fabric paints an interesting picture of diversity across states and regions but greater homogeneity within states. Who individuals know, and more importantly who knows them, often determines the success they have in obtaining jobs, health care, and better quality education. Consequently, social and religious background plays an important role in whether anyone in the household knows a government worker, teacher or school employee, or medical personnel. Dalits, Adivasis, and Muslims have access to fewer networks than other social and religious groups. In contrast, participation in non-governmental organizations (NGOs) or other organizations is a function of whether an organization exists in a community, and we find sharp differences in organizational memberships across states but few differences between households in a state. Throughout our analysis, we consistently find differences in human development outcomes for individuals by place of residence, with those living in rural areas being the most disadvantaged. However, a deeper analysis of village development reported in Chapter 12 paints an interesting picture of both progress and isolation. Although some pockets of isolation remain, roads and primary schools are available in most villages, and even electric connections are available in a large number of villages. However, when we focus on higher level services as well as quality of services, differences between states become vast, to some extent explaining the differences in human development outcomes across states. The findings in this chapter also point to an ironic observation: the development discourse has tended to see civil society institutions, particularly the NGO sector, as filling the vacuum when the state is weak or ineffective. We find that many of the community-based programmes, which are run directly by NGOs or as an intermediary of the state, are far more prevalent in areas where infrastructure is better developed. Thus, instead of being a substitute for state action, these organizations complement state inputs.

As we assess different dimensions of human development in a rapidly evolving social and economic context, the role of public policy assumes paramount importance. By all accounts, Indian economic growth is accompanied by rising inequality between different social groups, between urban and rural India, and between states. As the chapter on income points out, most statistics on inequality in India are based on consumption expenditure which understates income inequality, and it may well be that inequality is rising at a faster pace than is conventionally acknowledged.

Readers of the *Human Development Reports* may find a lack of attention to the Human Development Index (HDI) in this monograph puzzling. *Human Development Reports*, developed by the United Nations Development Programme (UNDP), have pioneered the HDI relying on components that include life expectancy at birth, adult literacy; gross enrolment in primary, secondary, and tertiary education, and gross domestic product per capita. This index allows for a ranking of countries in order to provide a quick feedback to policy makers. The *National Human Development Report 2001* prepared by the Planning Commission uses somewhat different indicators but follows a similar approach. The value of these indices lies in their simplicity and the focus on a limited number of variables. However, given our interest in broadening this discourse by focusing on the complexity of different aspects of well being in India, and attention to inequality by caste, tribe, religion, class, gender, and place of residence, we eschew the construction of indices and instead focus on a variety of markers of human development that are included in the literature and that we consider important for addressing the challenges that India will face in the era of transition.

This introduction began with an allusion to the high hopes with which India's tryst with destiny began at Independence. As we conclude, we remain cognizant of the parallels between India at Independence and at the start of the twenty-first century. The lethargy of the middle years, in which the normative expectation of the Hindu rate of growth was 3–4 per cent per year, has been banished by the rapid economic strides of the past decade. It is time to set a higher bar for the kind of human development we strive for.

To quote Amartya Sen,[2]

It would be a great mistake to concentrate on the Human Development Index. These are useful indicators in rough and ready work: but the real merit of the human development approach lies in the plural attention it brings to bear on development evaluation, not in the aggregative measures it presents as an aid to diverse statistics.

Box 1.1   IHDS 2005

The IHDS was carried out by researchers from the University of Maryland and the NCAER between December 2004 and November 2005. The data collection was funded by the US National Institutes of Health. The survey involved face-to-face interviews with members of 41,554 households located in urban and rural areas of 33 states and union territories and was designed to provide a nationally representative sample. The survey collected information on income, consumption, employment, education, health, and different aspects of gender and family relationships from both male and female respondents and provides information about the lives of 2,15,754 individuals. It also collected information on schools, medical facilities, and village infrastructure. The survey was administered in 13 languages and was carried out by 25 organizations with interviewers fluent in local customs and language. These data are now in the public domain and are freely available for analysis by interested researchers. More information is available at www.ihds.umd.edu

Source: IHDS 2004–5 data.

---

[2] Sen (2000).

Economic Well-being

2

Income, Poverty, and Inequality

As we discuss different dimensions of human development—such as access to education, health care, and the well-being of vulnerable populations like children and the elderly—in the following chapters, we will document considerable differences by household income. While financial resources themselves are insufficient to ensure health, educational attainment, or gender equality within households, a lack of financial resources is frequently an important constraint. Access to financial resources has been defined as an instrumental freedom in the broad discourse on human development. Hence, we begin this report with an analysis of household incomes, poverty, and inequality.

This chapter highlights several themes that foreshadow the discussion in the remaining chapters. It documents tremendous diversity in incomes and expenditures across different segments of the Indian society, with some households facing substantial vulnerability and others forming a part of the burgeoning middle class. Access to livelihoods that offer more or less year round work is the crucial determinant of household income. As Chapter 4 on employment documents, access to year-round work is far more likely for people in salaried jobs or for those who are self-employed in business than for farmers, farm workers, or other manual labourers. Consequently, areas where salaried work or work in business has greater availability—such as in urban areas or states like Gujarat, Maharashtra, Himachal Pradesh, and Haryana—are better off than the rest of the country. Farm size and irrigation also affect household incomes, increasing average incomes in areas like Haryana and Punjab (see Chapter 3). Education is strongly related to access to salaried work, and vast differences in education across different social groups are at least partly responsible for the income differentials across socio-religious communities (see Chapter 6).

While income levels are associated with the availability of work, the productivity of land, and individual human capital, consumption levels are further affected by household composition. The income advantages of urban households are further amplified by lower dependency burdens. This chapter also documents that income based inequalities are far greater than consumption based inequalities.

The rest of the chapter is organized as follows. The next section discusses the way in which the IHDS collected data on income and consumption, as well as the limitations of these data. The following section discusses household income, both at the aggregate level and by different household characteristics. This is followed by a discussion of the IHDS data on consumption and incidence of poverty, and the last section focuses on inequality. The main findings are summarized in the final section.

MEASURING INCOME AND CONSUMPTION

Incomes are not usually measured in developing-country surveys, and rarely in India. Instead, surveys have measured consumption expenditures or counts of household assets because they are less volatile over time, and are said to be more reliably measured. Survey measures of consumption expenditures have their own problems (for example, respondent fatigue) and volatility (marriages, debts, and health crises can create unrepresentative spikes for some households). The IHDS also measured consumption and household assets, but went to some effort to measure income. By measuring income and its sources, we know not merely the level of a household's standard of living but also how it achieved that level and, thus, we obtain a better understanding of why it is poor, average, or affluent.

Measuring income along with household expenditures and possessions also reveals aspects of income volatility and provides an additional measure of inequality. However, obtaining precise estimates of household incomes is complicated because few households have regular sources of income. Where incomes are irregular, such as in agriculture or business, considerable effort is required to obtain estimates of revenue and expenditure before net income can be calculated. Measurement errors may be particularly large in agricultural incomes, since seasonal variation in agricultural incomes is much greater than that in other incomes. These limitations are described in greater detail in Appendix II. Given these limitations, it is important to use the income data to form our understanding of the livelihoods of Indian households, rather than to use them to pinpoint the exact positions of different population groups, or states.

STRUCTURE OF INCOME AND INCOME DISPARITIES

The typical Indian household earned Rs 27,856 in 2004; half of all households earned less, and half earned more.[1] Some households, however, earned much more. Almost 11 per cent earned over Rs 1,00,000. The mean household income, therefore, is considerably higher than the median. Figure 2.1 shows the household income distribution.

Urban households dominate the higher income categories. Urban households compose only 9 per cent of the lowest income quintile, but represent the majority (56 per cent) of the top income quintile. As shown in Table 2.1 the typical (median) urban household earns more than twice the income of the typical rural household.

Table 2.1 Household Income (Rs) Distribution
(by Rural/Urban Residence)

	Rural	Urban	Total	U/R Ratio
1st percentile	−2,338	1,200	−1,229	—
5th percentile	3,300	11,500	4,400	3.48
10th percentile	6,580	17,000	8,000	2.58
25th percentile	12,845	28,873	15,034	2.25
Median	22,400	51,200	27,857	2.29
75th percentile	41,027	94,800	56,400	2.31
90th percentile	76,581	152,000	103,775	1.98
95th percentile	110,633	210,000	149,000	1.90
99th percentile	235,144	396,000	300,000	1.68
Mean	36,755	75,266	47,804	2.05
No. of Households	26,734	14,820	41,554	

Source: IHDS 2004–5 data.

It is not just the urban rich who benefit from living in cities. The poorest urban households are considerably richer than

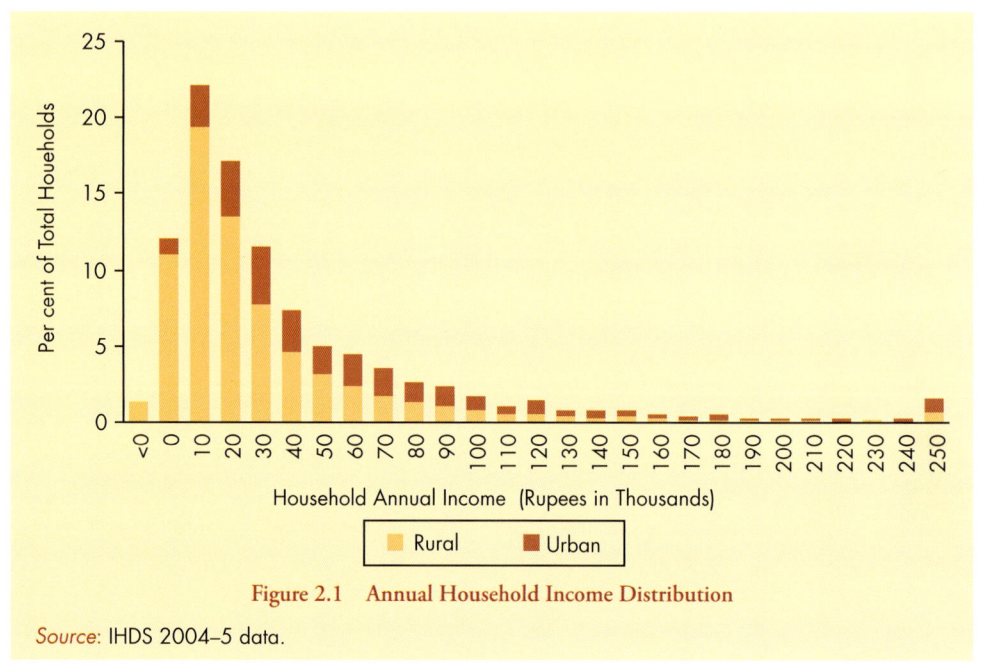

Figure 2.1 Annual Household Income Distribution
Source: IHDS 2004–5 data.

[1] Some households reported negative incomes. These are usually farm households with partially failed production whose value did not fully cover the reported expenses. Other analyses show that these households do not appear especially poor: their consumption expenditures and household possessions resemble average households more than they do to other low-income households. Because of this anomaly, for income calculations in the remainder of the study, we exclude all households with income below Rs 1,000 (N = 837). The median income after this exclusion is Rs 28,721.

the poorest rural households. The 10th percentile of income in urban areas is 2.6 times that of rural areas, although this advantage declines slightly at higher levels; the 90th percentile of urban incomes is only twice that of rural areas.

Table 2.2 reports large regional variations in both rural and urban incomes. While the IHDS samples are too small to fix the position of any one state precisely, the general pattern of results is clear.

States in the north have the highest household incomes. Punjab and Haryana in the plains are doing quite well as are Himachal Pradesh and Jammu and Kashmir in the hills. The lowest regional household incomes are in the central region, in Bihar, Uttar Pradesh, and Madhya Pradesh. The lowest incomes are in Orissa. Households in these central states and Orissa have only half the income of those in the northern plains. These statewise differences are especially pronounced for rural areas and somewhat narrow for urban incomes.

The composition and education of households are the primary determinants of its income. Individuals with higher education are more likely to obtain salaried jobs than others, resulting in higher incomes in households with educated adults. Among the 24 per cent of households in our sample that do not have even a single literate adult, the median income is only Rs 17,017. In contrast, among the 13 per cent of households with at least one college graduate, the median income is Rs 85,215—five times the median income of illiterate households (see Table A.2.1a).

As shown in Figure 2.2, household income also rises regularly with the number of adults in the household, regardless of their education.

Table 2.2 Median Household and Per Capita Incomes by State (Annual)

States	Household Income (Rs) Rural	Household Income (Rs) Urban	Household Income (Rs) Total	Per Capita Income (Rs) Rural	Per Capita Income (Rs) Urban	Per Capita Income (Rs) Total
All India	22,400	51,200	27,857	4,712	11,444	5,999
Jammu and Kashmir	47,325	75,000	51,458	7,407	13,460	8,699
Himachal Pradesh	43,124	72,000	46,684	9,440	15,662	9,942
Uttarakhand	28,896	60,000	32,962	6,000	12,800	6,857
Punjab	42,021	60,000	48,150	7,622	12,120	9,125
Haryana	44,000	72,000	49,942	8,000	14,647	9,443
Delhi	88,350	66,400	68,250	NA	15,000	15,000
Uttar Pradesh	20,544	46,000	24,000	3,605	8,285	4,300
Bihar	19,235	39,600	20,185	3,339	6,857	3,530
Jharkhand	20,700	70,000	24,000	4,175	13,654	4,833
Rajasthan	29,084	45,600	32,131	5,732	9,000	6,260
Chhattisgarh	21,900	59,000	23,848	4,800	12,000	5,306
Madhya Pradesh	18,025	33,700	20,649	3,530	6,328	4,125
North-East	49,000	90,000	60,000	11,153	22,700	13,352
Assam	22,750	48,000	25,000	5,567	10,342	6,000
West Bengal	21,600	59,700	28,051	4,928	14,571	6,250
Orissa	15,000	42,000	16,500	3,096	9,000	3,450
Gujarat	21,000	56,500	30,000	4,494	12,240	6,300
Maharashtra, Goa	24,700	64,600	38,300	5,337	14,000	7,975
Andhra Pradesh	20,642	48,000	25,600	5,250	11,250	6,241
Karnataka	18,900	54,000	25,600	4,333	12,000	5,964
Kerala	40,500	48,000	43,494	9,563	10,413	9,987
Tamil Nadu	20,081	35,000	26,000	5,297	9,000	7,000

Note: Sample of all 41,554 households.
Source: IHDS 2004–5 data.

14 HUMAN DEVELOPMENT IN INDIA

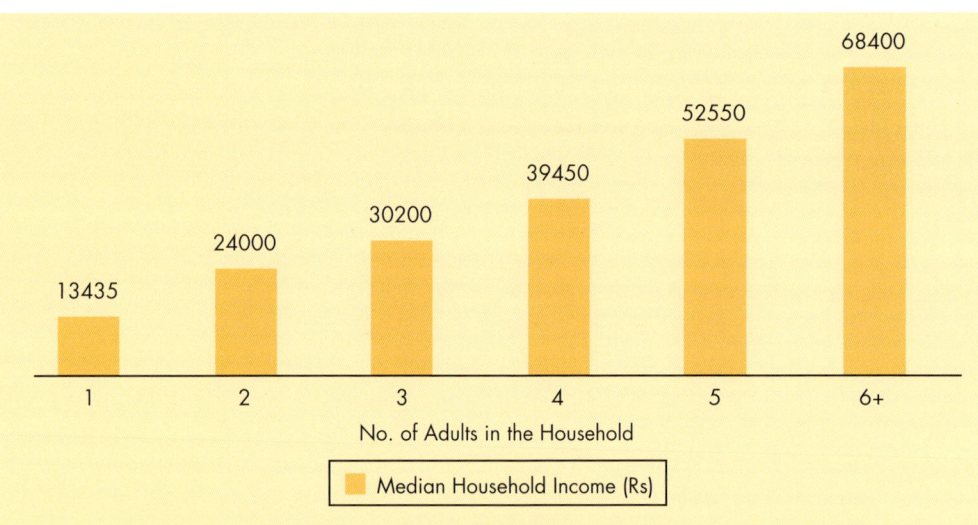

Figure 2.2 Median Household Income by Number of Adults in the Household
Source: IHDS 2004–5 data.

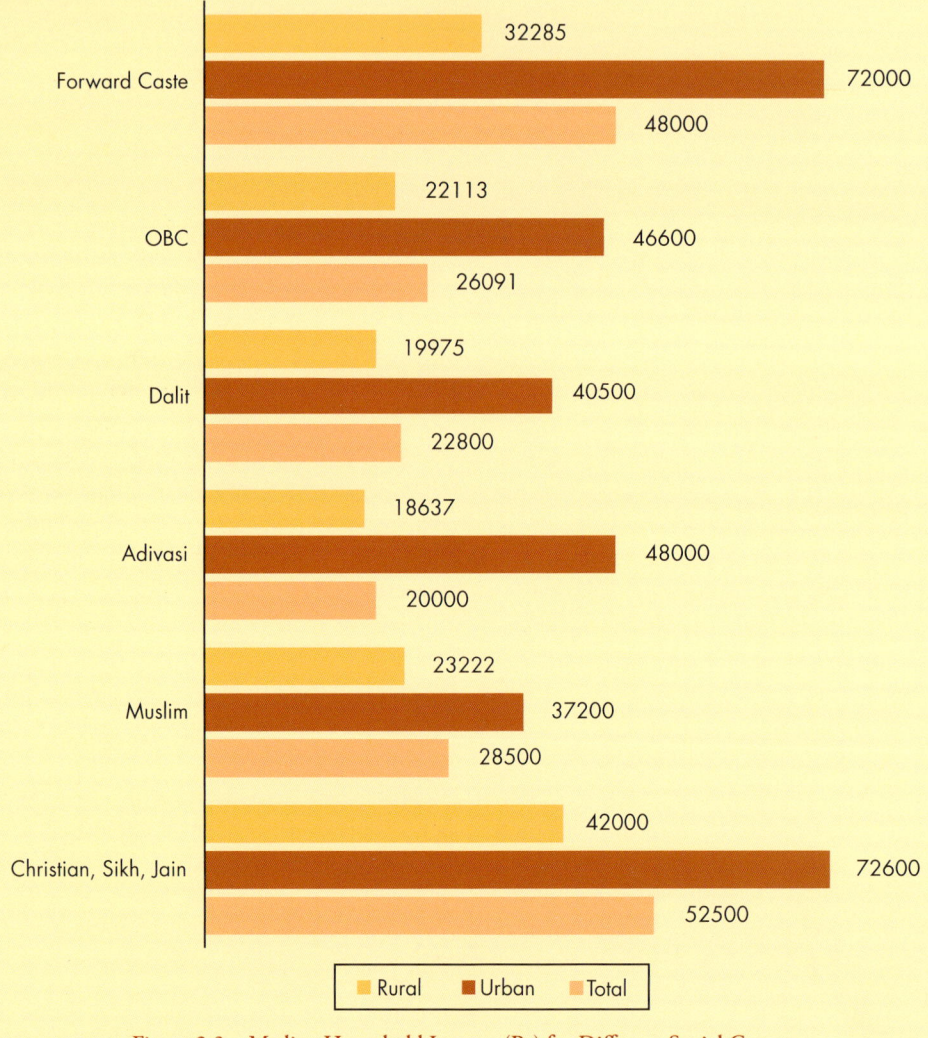

No. of Adults	Median Household Income (Rs)
1	13435
2	24000
3	30200
4	39450
5	52550
6+	68400

Figure 2.3 Median Household Income (Rs) for Different Social Groups
Source: IHDS 2004–5 data.

Social Group	Rural	Urban	Total
Forward Caste	32285	72000	48000
OBC	22113	46600	26091
Dalit	19975	40500	22800
Adivasi	18637	48000	20000
Muslim	23222	37200	28500
Christian, Sikh, Jain	42000	72600	52500

About half of all Indian households have two adults, and their median income (Rs 24,000) is near the national median. But almost a quarter of Indian households have four or more adults. With four adults, the median household income rises to Rs 39,450, and with six or more, it rises to Rs 68,400. Not surprisingly, the 8 per cent of households, with only one adult, are the poorest with a median annual income of only Rs 13,435. Since larger households also contain more children, per capita income is not as clearly associated with larger household size. However, given the economies of scale, as we will document in Chapter 5, larger households often have a better standard of living than smaller households.

Life cycle patterns also influence household income, especially in urban areas. Incomes rise steadily as the adults in the household age from the twenties onwards to a peak in the fifties. The median income of urban households with a man in his fifties is twice that of urban households in which the oldest man is only in his twenties. After adults reach their fifties, household incomes are fairly constant. These lifecycle differences matter, even though the young tend to be better educated (see Chapter 6). These educational disadvantages of older households are somewhat offset by the larger size of older households.

Despite changes in access to education and affirmative action by the Indian government, social groups that were traditionally at the lowest rung of the social hierarchy are still economically worse off.

Adivasi and Dalit households have the lowest annual incomes: Rs 20,000 and Rs 22,800, respectively. The Other Backward Classes (OBCs) and Muslim households are slightly better off, with incomes of Rs 26,091 and Rs 28,500, respectively. The forward castes and other minorities (Jains, Sikhs, and Christians) have the highest median annual incomes: Rs 48,000 and Rs 52,500, respectively. A variety of factors combine to contribute to these differences, and looking at urban and rural residents separately is useful. Adivasis are disadvantaged in rural areas, but not as much in urban areas. However, since nearly 90 per cent of the Adivasis in our sample live in rural areas, the higher income of urban Adivasis has little overall influence.

Other religious minorities are located at the top position of rural household incomes, largely because so many Sikhs live in fertile Punjab. These rankings are similar in the urban sector, but urban Adivasis are doing as well as OBCs and it is the Muslims who are at the bottom. In addition, the advantages of minority religions over forward caste Hindus in rural areas are reduced to a negligible difference in towns and cities. Our classification may also play some role. Dalit and Adivasi Christians, who are poorer than other Christians, are classified with Dalits and Adivasis, as are the poor Sikhs. Consequently, the poorest among the minority religions are included elsewhere, thereby inflating the incomes for these religious groups.

SOURCES OF LIVELIHOOD

A great advantage of using income data is our ability to examine the sources of livelihoods, to identify the way in which these sources are related to income and poverty. In India, as in most developing economies, households derive income from a wider range of sources than is typically true in advanced industrial economies. Besides wages and salaries, farms and other businesses are important for more families in India than in developed countries. Transfers, from other family members working across the country or even abroad, are also important for many areas. The IHDS recorded incomes from more than fifty separate sources. These are grouped into a more manageable set of eight categories in Table 2.3.

Because some of these income sources are more reliable and more generous, they determine the level of income that these households can attain. Most Indian households (71 per cent) receive wage and salary income. This accounts for more than half (54 per cent) of all income.[2] By far the most remunerative incomes are salaries received by employees paid monthly, as opposed to casual work at daily wages. More than a quarter of households (28 per cent) receive some salary income, and these salaries account for 36 per cent of all income. Businesses owned by the household are also fairly widespread and rewarding. About 20 per cent of households engage in some form of business, and this income accounts for 19 per cent of all income. Income from property, dividends, and pensions is less common (only 10 per cent of households receive this kind of income), but the amounts received can be significant (the typical receipt is Rs 14,400 per year), composing 5 per cent of all household income.

In contrast, both agricultural and non-agricultural daily wage labour, while widespread, accounts for a relatively small portion of total household income because the wages are so low (see Chapter 4). More than a quarter (29 per cent) of households are engaged in agricultural labour, but this work tends to be seasonal and the income accounts for only 7 per cent of total income. Similarly, 27 per cent of households engage in non-agricultural wage labour, but it accounts for only 11 per cent of total income.

Farm incomes are even more common. More than half (53 per cent) of all Indian households have some agricultural income. The income returns from farms, however, are modest so agricultural income constitutes only 19 per cent of total income. Even in rural areas, where agricultural income plays a more important role, total income from cultivation is only

---

[2] Note that the proportion of rural, urban, and total income reported by income source in Table 2.3 is based on all sectoral income and, hence, higher-income households contribute disproportionately to these percentages. However, Table 2.5, which we discuss later, averages across households.

Table 2.3 Structure of Income: Urban, Rural, and All India

	Rural				Urban				Total			
	Mean (Rs)	Per cent hh with Income from Source	Per cent of Total Rural Income	Median if any Income from Source (Rs)	Mean (Rs)	Per cent hh with Income from Source	Per cent of Total Urban Income	Median if any Income from Source (Rs)	Mean (Rs)	Per cent hh with income from souce	Per cent of total Rural income	Median if any income from source (Rs)
Total Income	36,755	100	100	22,500	75,266	100	100	51,712	47,804	100	100	28,000
Total Wage and Salary	16,944	70	46	15,900	48,332	74	64	45,600	25,949	71	54	21,000
Salaries	7,632	18	21	24,100	40,583	52	54	60,000	17,085	28	36	42,400
Agricultural Wages	4,507	39	12	9,000	900	5	1	14,500	3,472	29	7	9,000
Non-Agricultural Wages	4,805	29	13	12,700	6,849	24	9	24,300	5,391	27	11	15,000
Total Self-employment	16,672	73	45	9,389	20,508	35	27	36,000	17,772	62	37	11,759
Business	4,807	17	13	18,000	19,042	28	25	40,000	8,891	20	19	25,000
Farming/Animal Care/Agr. Prop.	12,285	69	33	5,944	1,816	12	2	4,000	9,282	53	19	5,825
Family Remittances	1,042	6	3	10,000	782	3	1	12,000	968	5	2	10,000
Properties and Pensions	1,473	8	4	9,500	5,091	16	7	20,400	2,511	10	5	14,400
Government Benefits	204	16	1	650	203	6	0	1,200	204	13	0	750

Notes: Per cent of sectoral income is disproportionately affected by high income households (hh); Agr. Prop. refers to agricultural property.

Source: IHDS 2004–5 data.

33 per cent of the total, with agricultural wage work adding an additional 12 per cent. However, given the difficulties of measuring agricultural income, these results should be treated with caution.

Finally, private and public transfers are important for many Indian households. Remittances from family members working away from home account for 2 per cent of all household incomes, but 5 per cent of Indian households receive at least some income from absent family members. Government support is even more common: 13 per cent of Indian households receive some form of direct income supplement from the government. The most common source of government support comes in the form of old-age and widows' pensions. This government assistance is usually quite small (the typical reported payment is only Rs 750 per year), so it accounts for less than half a per cent (0.4 per cent) of household income. For poor households, however, this help can be significant.

Multiple Income Sources

Although much of the discussion on income sources tends to assume that households rely predominantly on one source of income, the IHDS data suggest that more than 50 per cent of Indian households receive income from multiple sources.

Table 2.4 shows the proportion of households that draw income from various sources of income.

For example, more than four out of five farm households also have income from some other source, more often from agricultural and non-agricultural wage labour and salaried work (40 per cent) but also from private businesses (17 per cent). Similarly, 71 per cent of households with a private family business also receive other types of income, for instance, from family farms (37 per cent). This diversification implies significant interconnections between different sectors of the Indian economy and suggests that policies that affect one sector of the economy could have widespread impact on a large number of households.

Some of these sources of income are highly interconnected. It is quite common for farmers to work on other people's fields when their own fields do not require attention. However, as we show in Figure 2.4, a substantial proportion of farm households rely on non-agricultural income, particularly in higher income categories.

Income Disparities and Sources of Income

How much income a household earns is closely related to the source of income (see Table A.2.2a). Wealthy households receive much of their income from monthly salaries.

Table 2.4 Per cent of Households Drawing Income from Various Sources

Cultivation	Wage Work	Business	Other	Rural	Urban	Total	Median Income
☑	☑	☑	☑	1.14	0.26	0.89	35,755
☑	☑	☑	–	2.78	0.61	2.16	32,938
☑	☑	–	☑	8.69	1.12	6.52	25,507
☑	☑	–	–	23.55	3.83	17.89	23,536
☑	–	☑	☑	1.4	0.51	1.15	54,850
☑	–	☑	–	3.9	1.28	3.15	36,000
☑	–	–	☑	5.48	0.56	4.07	31,265
☑	–	–	–	11.27	1.03	8.33	20,964
–	☑	☑	☑	0.81	1.61	1.04	47,400
–	☑	☑	–	2.43	5.98	3.45	40,900
–	☑	–	☑	6.33	12.1	7.98	33,600
–	☑	–	–	24.23	48.46	31.18	27,000
☑	–	☑	☑	0.99	3.71	1.77	52,000
–	–	☑	–	3.39	14.1	6.47	40,000
–	–	–	☑	1.98	4.15	2.6	18,000
Negative or no income	–	–	–	1.61	0.69	1.35	–985
Grand Total				100	100	100	

Notes: Wage work includes agricultural and non-agricultural wage, and salaried work.
Other sources include pensions, family transfers, and income from government programmes.
Source: IHDS 2004–5 data.

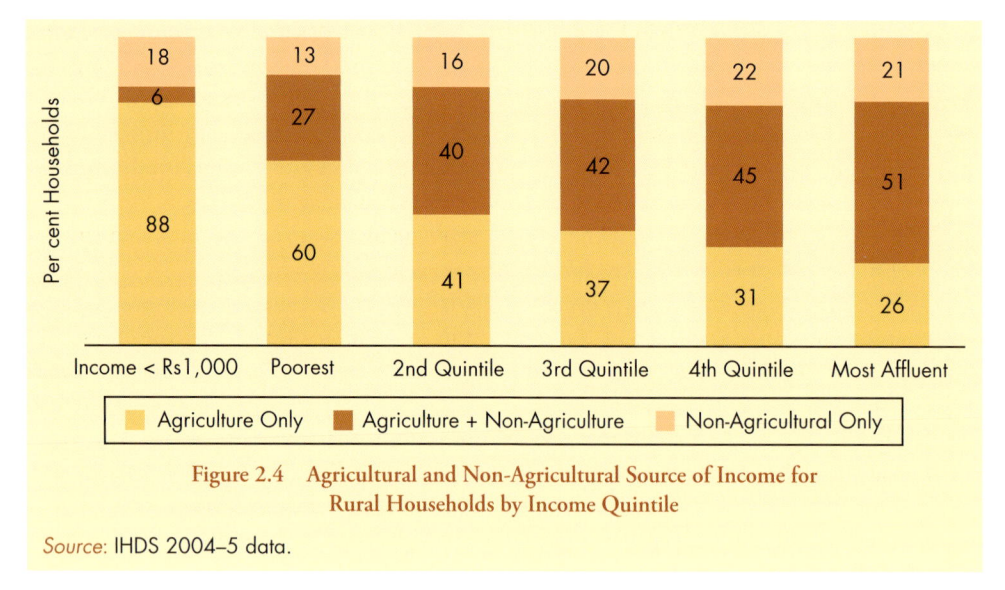

Figure 2.4 Agricultural and Non-Agricultural Source of Income for Rural Households by Income Quintile

Income Group	Agriculture Only	Agriculture + Non-Agriculture	Non-Agricultural Only
Income < Rs 1,000	88	6	18
Poorest	60	27	13
2nd Quintile	41	40	16
3rd Quintile	37	42	20
4th Quintile	31	45	22
Most Affluent	26	51	21

Source: IHDS 2004–5 data.

The poor depend on unskilled labour. Agricultural labour incomes are especially concentrated in the poorest quintile of households. Non-Agricultural labour is most important for the next-to-lowest quintile.

Interestingly, farm incomes are well represented in all five quintiles, although slightly more important for the lower and middle income quintiles (21 per cent of all income) than for the richest (17 per cent). Animal products, especially, make the difference for increased agricultural incomes among this middle income quintile. Private businesses are also important for all income levels but, like salaries, are more important for the wealthiest households. Government assistance is primarily useful for the poorest income quintile, as it should be, although some near-poor and middle-income households also benefit. Private transfers from other family members, however, benefit households at all income levels, even the wealthiest who receive 3 per cent of their income from these remittances.

Restricting our examination to rural households provides an interesting snapshot of the importance of agricultural and non-agricultural sources of income. Here, we combine cultivation and agricultural wage work and compare the households that rely solely on agricultural incomes with those that rely solely on non-agricultural incomes, and those that draw incomes from agricultural as well as non-agricultural sector. As Figure 2.4 shows, at the lower income quintiles, households rely solely on agricultural incomes; at higher income levels, however, both farm and non-farm sources of income become important. Table 2.3 indicates that non-agricultural incomes (salaries or businesses) are higher than agricultural incomes: median incomes from cultivation are about Rs 6,000 and median agricultural wage incomes are Rs 9,000, compared with a median of Rs 18,000 for business and more than Rs 24,000 for salaries. This suggests that access to these better paying sources of income increases levels of household income far above those of households relying solely on agriculture. However, even rural households with higher incomes continue to engage in agricultural work. Some engage in dairy or poultry farming, others in cultivation, and still others in seasonal agricultural labour. Thus, external forces that influence agriculture also influence nearly 80 per cent of the households in any income quintile.

Vulnerabilities of Agricultural Households

Inequalities in household income are presented in Appendix Tables A.2.1a and A.2.1b. This table documents substantial inequalities by urban/rural residence, household education, and social group. Here, we explore the linkages between these differences and the reliance on various sources of income. Not surprisingly, privileged groups depend more on salaried incomes, while less privileged groups tend to depend on cultivation and agricultural, and non-agricultural wage work).

Rural residents, not surprisingly, depend more on agriculture for their incomes than do urban residents. This dependence is partly to blame for the lower incomes in rural areas, since agriculture usually provides lower incomes (see Table 2.3). However, villages which are more developed, with better infrastructure and transportation, appear to rely less on cultivation. As Table A.2.2a documents, only 22 per cent of the household incomes in more developed villages come from cultivation, compared with 31 per cent in less developed villages. A higher level of village development seems to offer more opportunities for salaried work as well as work in business. As a result, the median of household incomes in developed villages is Rs 24,722 compared with Rs 20,297 for less developed villages. Since some households in developed villages have fairly high incomes, mean differences are even larger: mean household income is

Rs 41,595 in developed villages and Rs 32,230 in less developed villages.

Access to salaried work is also an important determinant of differences across states. As Figure 2.5 indicates, states in which a greater proportion of incomes come from salaries have higher median incomes than those in which access to salaried incomes is low.

Thus, the surprisingly high incomes in the North-East are a result of over half of all incomes coming from regular salaried positions (see Table A.2.2b). These positions are mostly in the organized sector—either directly employed by the government or in state-owned economic activities. In contrast, only 12 per cent of income in Bihar comes from salaries, placing it near the bottom of the income rankings. This relationship is not totally uniform, however. States like Kerala draw a substantial proportion of their incomes from remittances sent by migrant workers and have high median incomes, whereas Punjab benefits from high agricultural productivity in addition to access to salaried incomes.

Advantaged groups earn more of their income from salaries, while disadvantaged groups earn more from wage labour, or remittances and public support. Households with a college graduate get 50 per cent of their income from salaries; illiterate households get only 8 per cent from salaries but 60 per cent from daily wages (see Table A.2.2a). This is also reflected in differences across social groups. Figure 2.3 documents substantial differences in median incomes across socio-religious communities, with Dalit and Adivasi households having the lowest median incomes. Although their low income is partly associated with rural residence, even within rural areas, they remain the lowest income groups. As we look at the structure of incomes across different social groups, it is apparent that forward castes and minority religious groups like Christians, Sikhs, and Jains have greater access to salaried incomes. In contrast, Dalits and Adivasis are far more likely to draw income from agricultural and non-agricultural wage work (see Table A.2.2a). Muslims are the most likely to receive income from small family businesses, partly because of educational differences across communities (documented in detail in Chapter 6). Education, however, does not totally explain the concentration of socio-religious groups in certain types of work. Moreover, regardless of the reasons for concentration in business or farming, when faced with sectoral shifts in incomes or prices, groups that are concentrated in certain sectors, such as family businesses, may face greater vulnerability.

BEYOND INCOME: CONSUMPTION AND POVERTY

What Income Statistics Hide

Beginning with the pioneering work of the National Sample Survey (NSS) in 1950–1, Indian social scientists and policy makers have long relied on expenditures to measure household welfare. There are good reasons for this approach. First, income is difficult to measure. Second, incomes tend to be far more variable, because of seasonal fluctuations and external shocks, than are expenditures. Data collection that relies on a single calendar year or one agricultural year may not coincide with the income cycle. In contrast, consumption tends to be more stable. In low-income years, households can engage in consumption smoothing by selling some

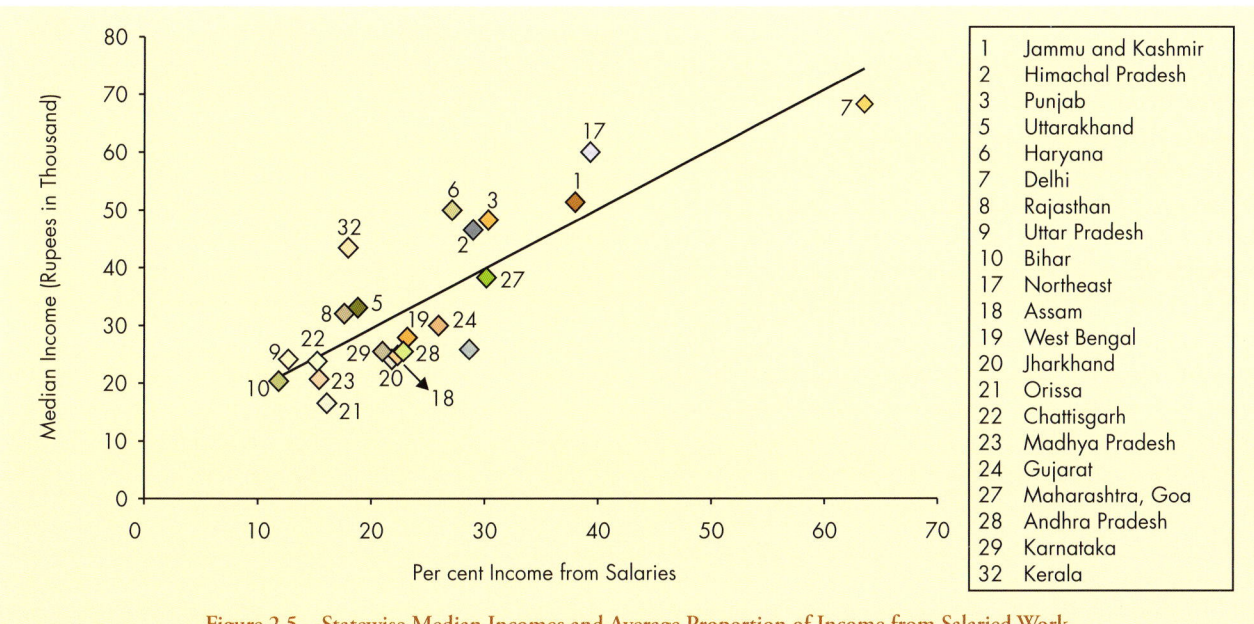

Figure 2.5 Statewise Median Incomes and Average Proportion of Income from Salaried Work
Source: IHDS 2004–5 data.

assets, consuming savings, or borrowing. In high-income years, they tend to save. This reasoning has led to a focus on permanent income, reflected in consumption expenditures, as a more stable measure of well-being.

Since the IHDS is one of the few surveys to collect both income and consumption data, we can compare household incomes with expenditures. Table 2.5 shows mean and median household incomes and expenditures in urban and rural areas. In urban areas, income exceeds expenditure, as might be expected; in rural areas, both mean and median incomes seem to be below expenditures, suggesting greater measurement errors there or greater variability in incomes from year to year.[3]

Table 2.5 Mean and Median Annual Income and Consumption

	Income (Rs)		Consumption (Rs)	
	Mean	Median	Mean	Median
Household				
Rural	38,018	23,100	42,167	31,883
Urban	75,993	52,000	64,935	50,922
All India	49,073	28,721	48,795	36,476
U/R Ratio	2.00	2.25	1.54	1.60
Per Capita				
Rural	7,101	4,462	7,877	6,115
Urban	15,649	10,284	13,372	10,149
All India	9,421	5,500	9,368	6,934
U/R Ratio	2.20	2.30	1.70	1.66

Note: Households with Total Income < = Rs 1,000 (N= 40,717)
Source: IHDS 2004–5 data.

Table 2.5 shows both household and per capita income, and consumption. The difference between urban and rural areas is much greater for per capita measures than for household measures, reflecting the benefits of smaller households in urban areas.

Who is Poor?

While the income and expenditure data discussed above focus on average levels of income and consumption, they fail to provide much information about the vulnerability of the individuals and households at the bottom of the income distribution. In this section, we examine the composition of these economically vulnerable groups by focusing on poverty.

Estimating poverty requires two essentials: a comparable welfare profile and a predetermined poverty norm. A household is classified as poor if its consumption level is below the poverty norm. In India, the welfare profile is usually measured using consumption expenditures of the households because income represents potential, but not actual, consumption. The IHDS uses the official rural and urban statewise poverty lines for 2004–5 that are available from the Planning Commission, Government of India. The average poverty line is Rs 356 per person per month in rural areas, and Rs 538 in urban areas. Statewise poverty lines range from Rs 292 to Rs 478 for rural areas and Rs 378 to Rs 668 in urban areas.[4] The poverty line was established in 1973[5] based on the consumption expenditure required to obtain the necessary caloric intake, and has been continuously adjusted for inflation.

The most commonly used measure of income poverty is the headcount ratio (HCR), which is simply the ratio of the number of persons who fall below the poverty line to the total population. Table 2.6 presents three national poverty estimates from NSS data using different data collection methods based on recall periods, and whether a long or an abridged expenditure schedule was canvassed. It also presents poverty calculations from the IHDS using the same norms.

The national estimate based on the IHDS, 25.7 per cent, is quite close to the estimates available from the NSS sources for the reference years 2004–5. Depending on the data collection method used, the NSS estimates range from 28.3 per cent to 21.8 per cent for rural India and 25.7 per cent to 21.7 per cent for urban India. The IHDS estimates fall in between, with rural poverty at 26.5 per cent and urban poverty at 23.7 per cent.

It is important to note that the similarities in urban and rural poverty rates are a function of the nearly Rs 150 per month higher poverty norm in urban areas. This does not imply that urban and rural residents have equally comfortable lives. As Chapter 5 documents, rural households have substantially less access to household amenities than urban households.

The IHDS sample is considerably smaller than the NSS sample and, consequently, cannot offer state-level point estimates of poverty that are as reliable as those generated by the NSS. However, for most states, the IHDS poverty estimates are similar to the NSS estimates. Punjab, Himachal Pradesh, and Jammu and Kashmir have low poverty while

---

[3] Note that the reference periods for income and expenditure data differ. Expenditure data are collected using a mixed recall period with data for commonly used items restricted to the preceding 30 days. The income data are collected for the preceding year. As has been observed with NSS, shorter recall periods lead to higher consumption estimates (Deaton and Kozel 2005). Thus, income and consumption data in IHDS are not strictly comparable and income is likely to be underestimated compared to consumption.

[4] We have converted these into yearly poverty line using the conversion factor, Yearly PL_{iu} = (Monthly PL_{iu} * 365)/30, where, PL_{iu} is the poverty line for u, urban/rural area, in the ith state.

[5] Dandekar and Rath (1971).

Table 2.6 Headcount Ratio of Population below Poverty (NSS and IHDS)

	NSS 61 Round			IHDS***
	CES*		EUS**	
	Mixed Recall	Uniform Recall	Abridged	
Andhra Pradesh	11.1	15.8	12.3	6.8
Assam	15.0	19.7	18.0	24.6
Bihar	32.5	41.4	35.0	17.0
Chhattisgarh	32.0	40.9	30.1	63.3
Delhi	10.2	14.7	12.3	13.9
Gujarat	12.5	16.8	12.6	13.1
Haryana	9.9	14.0	12.1	11.3
Himachal Pradesh	6.7	10.0	7.7	4.3
Jammu & Kashmir	4.2	5.4	3.6	3.4
Jharkhand	34.8	40.3	34.4	49.0
Karnataka	17.4	25.0	21.7	18.3
Kerala	11.4	15.0	13.2	26.8
Madhya Pradesh	32.4	38.3	34.0	45.5
Maharashtra	25.2	30.7	27.9	27.9
Orissa	39.9	46.4	42.9	41.3
Punjab	5.2	8.4	8.2	4.9
Rajasthan	17.5	22.1	19.6	26.7
Tamil Nadu	17.8	22.5	19.2	18.3
Uttar Pradesh	25.5	32.8	29.4	33.2
Uttarakhand	31.8	39.6	34.8	35.7
West Bengal	20.6	24.7	25.1	23.1
All India	21.8	27.5	24.2	25.7

Notes: *Government of India (2007), Poverty Estimates for 2004–5, Planning Commission, Press Information Bureau, March and **Author's calculations using NSS 61st round employment and unemployment surveys unit record data.
Source: ***IHDS 2004–5.

Orissa, Jharkhand, and Madhya Pradesh have high poverty. Exceptions include Bihar, which has a lower IHDS than the NSS poverty rate, and Chhattisgarh and Kerala, which have higher IHDS than NSS poverty rates.

Table A.2.1a shows differences in poverty across different strata of Indian society. Adivasis are the most vulnerable group, with nearly 50 per cent below the poverty line. Dalits and Muslims, with poverty rates of 32 per cent and 31 per cent, are also above the national average. The HCR is lowest at 12 per cent for other minority religions and, similarly low for forward caste Hindus at 12.3 per cent.

Poverty diminishes substantially with household education. Only 7 per cent of the households in which an adult has a college degree are in poverty range, compared to 38 per cent for those with education below primary school. Combined with the high incomes for the well educated households, reported earlier, this observation reinforces the importance of education in providing livelihoods and raising families out of poverty.

While poverty rates are associated with household income and consumption, unlike them they take into account household size. Hence, although poverty is concentrated in households in the lowest income and expenditure quintiles, 9 per cent of individuals living in households in the highest income quintile and 2 per cent in households in the highest consumption quintile are poor. Adjustment for household size also changes the social group position. For example, Muslims appear to be closer to OBCs in terms of median income and consumption, but poverty rates, which are adjusted for household size, bring them closer to Dalits.

CONTOURS OF INCOME INEQUALITY

Throughout this report, we will discuss inequality in income, health, education, and other dimensions of human development, with a particular focus on inequality between different states, urban and rural areas, and different social groups. However, one of the reasons these inequalities become so striking is the overall inequality in income distribution in India. We discuss the broad outlines of these income inequalities below. When discussing human development in India, a focus on inequality is particularly important because the gap between the top and bottom is vast. The top 10 per cent of households (that is the 90th percentile) earn more than Rs 1,03,775, whereas the bottom 10 per cent (that is, the 10th percentile) earn Rs 8,000 or less (Table 2.1), an elevenfold difference. This gap is not simply the result of a few billionaires who have appropriated a vast amount of Indian wealth. It reflects inequalities at various levels in the Indian society. The income gap between the top and bottom 10 per cent is almost equally a result of the gap between the middle and the poor (3.5 times) and that between the rich and the middle (3.7 times).

Table 2.7 reports Gini statistics, the most common overall indicator of income inequality. Gini coefficients can range from 0.0 (perfect equality) to 1.0 (total inequality).

Much of the discussion regarding inequality in India has focused on consumption-based inequality. With Gini coefficients of about 0.37, India is considered to be a moderately unequal country by world standards. For example, the Gini coefficient for Scandinavia and Western Europe is generally below 0.30, while that for middle-income developing countries tends to range from 0.40 to 0.50, and that in some of the poorest nations exceeds 0.55.

22 HUMAN DEVELOPMENT IN INDIA

Table 2.7 Income and Consumption Inequality

	NSS 61 Round*			IHDS**	
	CES		EUS Abridged	Consumption	Income***
	Mixed Recall	Uniform Recall			
Rural	0.28	0.31	0.27	0.36	0.49
Urban	0.36	0.38	0.36	0.37	0.48
All India	0.35	0.36	0.34	0.38	0.52

Notes: *Author's calculation using consumer expenditure and employment and unemployment survey unit record data.
***Income inequality calculations exclude households with negative incomes and income < Rs 1000.
Source: **IHDS 2004–5

However, this ranking is substantially affected by whether the inequality is measured by income or consumption. When inequality in income is measured, the United States looks moderately unequal, with a Gini of about 0.42. But when inequality in consumption is measured, it looks much better, with a Gini of about 0.31. The difference occurs mainly because households at upper income levels do not spend all that they earn, and those at lower income levels often consume more than they earn. Hence, consumption looks more equal than income.

The IHDS data show similar differences between income and consumption inequality. The Gini index for consumption inequality, based on the IHDS in Table 2.7, is about 0.38 for India, comparable to results from the NSS. However, the Gini index based on income is considerably higher, at 0.52.[6] This difference suggests that income inequality in India may be greater than hitherto believed. While consumption inequalities reflect inequalities in well-being for societies in transition, income inequalities provide a useful additional way of tracking emerging inequalities. For example, some studies in the United States have found that when inequality is rising, income inequalities tend to rise at a faster pace than consumption inequalities.[7]

Although urban incomes are higher than rural incomes, they are not more unequal. In fact, rural incomes tend to be more unequal (Gini = 0.49) than urban incomes (Gini = 0.48). Rural incomes are especially unequal near the bottom of the income distribution, where the poorest 10 per cent in villages are further from average incomes than are the poorest 10 per cent in towns and cities. And despite the recent growth of high incomes in some urban areas, inequality at the top is no worse in towns and cities than in villages.

The Kuznets curve suggests that for poor countries, inequality will rise with development.[8] In India, however, states with higher median incomes tend to have somewhat lower inequality than poorer states (see Figure 2.6), but this relationship is not very strong.

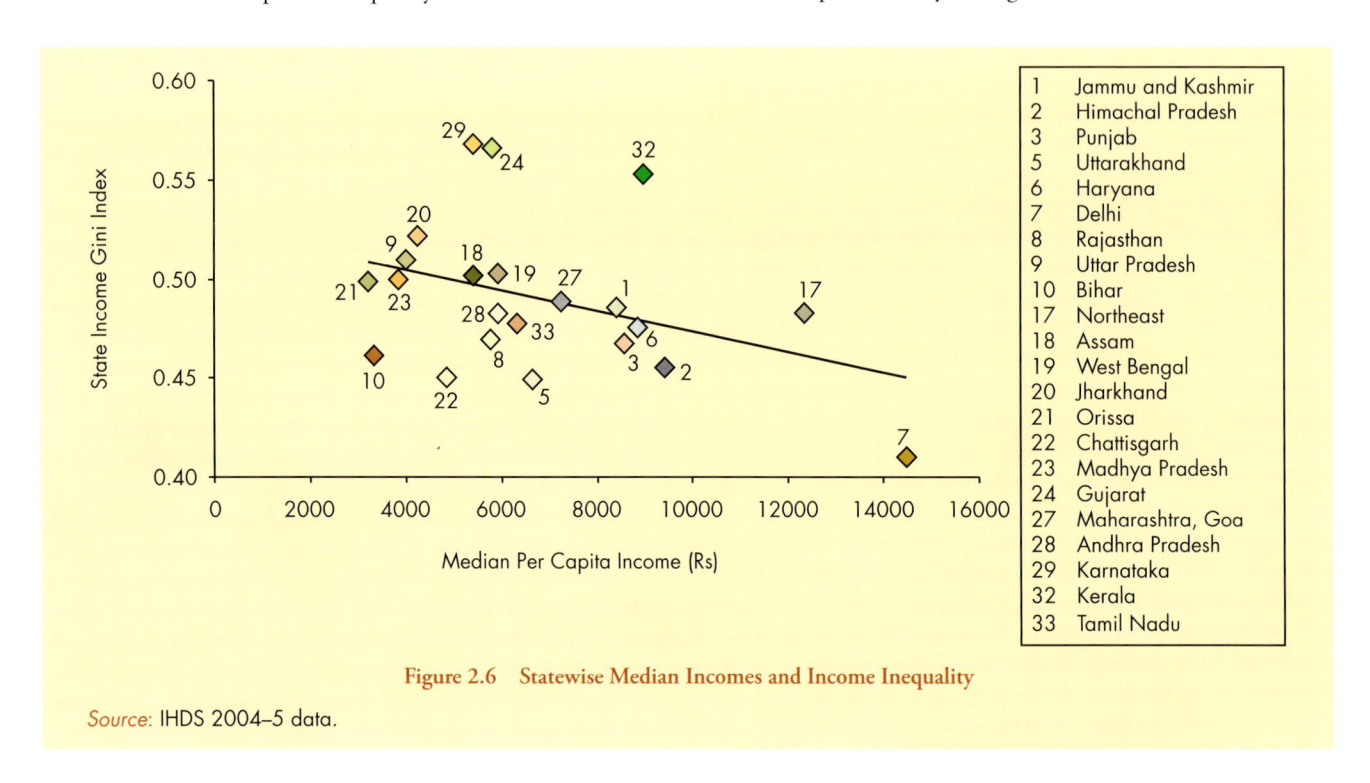

Figure 2.6 Statewise Median Incomes and Income Inequality

Source: IHDS 2004–5 data.

---

[6] The Gini index of 0.52 excludes households with negative incomes and those with incomes less than Rs 1,000. If they are included, the Gini index rises to 0.53.
[7] Johnson et al. (2005).
[8] Kuznets (1955).

DISCUSSION

This chapter has focused on the livelihoods of Indian families and identified some sources of vulnerability. Some of the findings presented echo well articulated themes. Poverty and low incomes are concentrated among Dalits and Adivasis, followed by Muslims and OBCs. Poverty also tends to be geographically concentrated in the central states.

However, our examination of income and income sources emphasizes some dimensions of economic well-being that have received less attention. Access to salaried income is one of the primary axes that divides Indian households. Households in which at least one adult has a job with a monthly salary are considerably better off than households that rely solely on farming, petty business, or casual daily labour. Unfortunately, only 28 per cent of households can claim access to salaried jobs. This suggests that access to salaried jobs and education (a prerequisite for salaried work) is a major source of inequality in household income—a topic addressed in detail in Chapter 4 and 6.

One of the most striking findings presented in this chapter is the great diversity of income sources within Indian households. Nearly 50 per cent of the households receive income from more than one source. Implications of this diversification require careful consideration. On the one hand, income diversification provides a cushion from such risks as crop failure or unemployment. On the other hand, the role of income diversification may depend on the nature of diversification. Where households are able to obtain better paying salaried jobs, diversification may be associated with higher incomes. Where poor agricultural productivity pushes household members into manual wage work, such as construction, the income benefits may be limited. This is a topic to which we return when we discuss different employment patterns of individuals in Chapter 4. However, these data also indicate that regardless of the share of agricultural incomes, a vast majority of the rural households are engaged in agriculture, resulting in a high degree of sectoral interdependence.

This chapter also shows that inequality in income is far greater than inequality in consumption. The higher inequality for incomes than expenditures is a common finding in other countries, but has been insufficiently appreciated in India. It will be important to track income inequality over time because with rising incomes, inequality in incomes may grow faster than inequality in consumption.

HIGHLIGHTS

- Median household income in urban areas is twice that in rural areas.
- Dalit and Adivasi households have the lowest incomes, followed by OBC and Muslim households.
- Salaried work provides the highest level of income.
- Although 35 per cent of households engage in farming or animal care, cultivation accounts for only 19 per cent of the total income.
- About 25.7 per cent of the population lives below the poverty line.
- Inequality in income is considerably higher than that in consumption.

Table A.2.1a Mean and Median Household Incomes, Consumption, and Poverty

	Income (Rs) Mean	Income (Rs) Median	Consumption (Rs) Mean	Consumption (Rs) Median	% Poor
All India	47,804	27,857	48,706	36,457	25.7
Education					
None	21,734	17,017	29,595	24,502	38.1
1–4 Std	25,984	18,800	33,365	27,876	37.2
5–9 Std	35,718	25,920	41,803	34,338	29.7
10–11 td	53,982	39,961	55,341	45,040	18.7
12 Std/Some College	69,230	48,006	65,717	52,494	14.8
Graduate/Diploma	1,14,004	85,215	89,186	70,897	6.8
Place of Residence					
Metro city	93,472	72,000	71,260	56,864	13.4
Other urban	68,747	45,800	62,629	48,448	27.0
Developed village	41,595	24,722	45,513	34,338	20.9
Less developed village	32,230	20,297	39,081	29,722	31.5
Household Income					
Income < 1,000 Rs	–4,476	–333	45,039	34,803	17.3
Lowest Quintile	8,833	9,305	29,117	23,356	36.1
2nd Quintile	18,241	18,040	32,430	27,200	36.8
3rd Quintile	28,959	28,721	40,063	33,686	31.1
4th Quintile	50,158	48,929	51,643	44,660	21.5
Highest Quintile	1,40,098	1,05,845	91,122	72,958	9.0
Household Consumption					
Lowest Quintile	18,338	14,947	14,965	15,860	70.5
2nd Quintile	26,799	20,800	26,075	26,040	42.2
3rd Quintile	36,217	28,504	36,645	36,458	24.3
4th Quintile	52,639	41,426	52,927	52,140	10.4
Highest Quintile	1,05,032	79,400	1,12,926	92,980	2.2
Social Groups					
Forward Caste Hindu	72,717	48,000	65,722	50,170	12.3
OBC	42,331	26,091	46,750	36,105	23.3
Dalit	34,128	22,800	39,090	30,288	32.3
Adivasi	32,345	20,000	29,523	22,738	49.6
Muslim	44,158	28,500	50,135	37,026	30.9
Other religion	1,01,536	52,500	72,787	54,588	12.0

Notes: Sample of all 41,554 households. The quintiles were generated taking into account all the households in the sample, and with weights. Therefore, higher income quintiles would be having higher proportion from the urban sector not only because the urban incomes, on an average, are higher but also because of rural–urban price differential, which is about 15 per cent or more. Std refers to Standard. Henceforth, Std.
Source: IHDS 2004–5 data.

Table A.2.1b Statewise Household Incomes, Consumption, and Poverty

	Income (Rs) Mean	Income (Rs) Median	Consumption (Rs) Mean	Consumption (Rs) Median	% Poor
All India	47,804	27,857	48,706	36,457	25.7
Jammu and Kashmir	78,586	51,458	1,02,397	81,232	3.4
Himachal Pradesh	68,587	46,684	78,387	56,672	4.3
Uttarakhand	49,892	32,962	50,422	40,544	35.7
Punjab	73,330	48,150	71,876	60,004	4.9
Haryana	74,121	49,942	78,641	59,280	11.3
Delhi	87,652	68,250	77,791	62,096	13.9
Uttar Pradesh	40,130	24,000	50,313	35,896	33.2
Bihar	30,819	20,185	47,731	39,017	NA
Jharkhand	42,022	24,000	36,579	24,610	49.0
Rajasthan	50,479	32,131	51,149	39,396	26.7
Chhattisgarh	39,198	23,848	27,972	16,941	63.4
Madhya Pradesh	36,152	20,649	39,206	27,604	45.5
North-East	82,614	60,000	60,612	43,752	9.8
Assam	42,258	25,000	39,268	31,020	24.6
West Bengal	46,171	28,051	41,958	31,714	23.1
Orissa	28,514	16,500	32,834	22,990	41.3
Gujarat	54,707	30,000	53,616	43,832	13.1
Maharashtra, Goa	59,930	38,300	50,372	39,502	27.9
Andhra Pradesh	39,111	25,600	46,996	37,520	6.8
Karnataka	51,809	25,600	53,490	38,074	18.3
Kerala	72,669	43,494	52,470	39,952	26.8
Tamil Nadu	40,777	26,000	43,966	34,146	18.3

Note: NA—not available due to potential measurement errors and/or small sample sizes.
Source: IHDS 2004–5 data.

Table A.2.2a Proportion of Household Incomes by Source

(in percentage)

	\multicolumn{6}{c}{Proportion of Household Income From}
	Salary	Agricultural Wages	Non-Farm Wages	Family Business	Cultivation	Other
All India	22	18	19	14	20	8
Education						
None	8	34	26	7	18	8
1–4 Std	10	30	23	11	21	6
5–9 Std	17	17	24	15	22	6
10–11 Std	30	10	15	18	20	8
12 Std/Some college	33	7	10	21	20	9
Graduate/Diploma	50	3	4	18	14	12
Place of Residence						
Metro city	57	2	13	20	1	7
Other urban	40	4	21	23	3	9
Developed village	15	25	18	13	22	8
Less developed village	11	22	20	9	31	7
Household Income						
Lowest Quintile	7	36	19	8	21	10
2nd Quintile	9	28	28	11	20	5
3rd Quintile	17	17	25	15	20	6
4th Quintile	28	8	17	18	20	8
Highest Quintile	49	1	5	19	17	9
Social Groups						
Forward Caste Hindu	32	8	9	18	24	10
OBC	21	17	17	14	23	7
Dalit	19	29	27	8	11	7
Adivasi	15	30	22	7	23	4
Muslim	19	11	27	21	16	7
Other religion	30	10	12	16	21	12

Source: IHDS 2004–5 data.

Table A.2.2b Statewise Proportion of Household Income by Source

(in percentage)

	\multicolumn{6}{c}{Proportion of Household Income From}
	Salary	Agricultural Wages	Non-Farm Wages	Family Business	Cultivation	Other
All India	22	18	19	14	20	8
Jammu and Kashmir	38	3	17	12	22	8
Himachal Pradesh	29	8	17	9	21	17
Uttarakhand	19	6	27	10	22	16
Punjab	30	12	16	16	18	8
Haryana	27	13	15	13	22	9
Delhi	64	1	14	16	1	4
Uttar Pradesh	13	9	23	16	31	9
Bihar	12	23	16	16	24	10
Jharkhand	22	6	34	18	17	4
Rajasthan	18	4	29	13	27	9
Chhattisgarh	15	21	18	8	33	4
Madhya Pradesh	15	23	20	11	27	4
North-East	39	8	11	16	21	5
Assam	22	2	28	13	30	4
West Bengal	23	18	17	17	18	7
Orissa	16	17	19	13	25	9
Gujarat	26	26	11	17	16	5
Maharashtra, Goa	30	18	10	16	19	7
Andhra Pradesh	23	35	16	11	9	7
Karnataka	21	30	15	14	14	6
Kerala	18	16	29	10	14	14
Tamil Nadu	29	24	23	12	3	8

Source: IHDS 2004–5 data.

Forward castes cultivate land more often (65 per cent) than OBC households (58 per cent); rural Dalit households are the least likely (37 per cent) to cultivate (although, calculations not reported here show that 35 per cent earn agricultural wages without cultivating any land themselves). However, Adivasi households have higher than average farming rates (59 per cent). Farming has a curvilinear relationship with rural incomes: it is most common in the poorest and wealthiest quintiles, but least common in the middle quintile.

LAND AND WATER: PRECIOUS RESOURCES

One of the most striking developments of the second half of the twentieth century is a decline in average farm size and an increase in small farms. The NSS records that between 1961 and 2002–3, the proportion of farms that were classified as marginal (less than one hectare) increased from 39 per cent of all farms to nearly 70 per cent of all farms; medium and large farms (four or more hectares) decreased from about 19 per cent of all farms to 5 per cent.[4] Some of the early decline in large farms occurred with land reforms immediately following independence. But in recent years, much of the change has occurred due to land fragmentation associated with population growth. As Figure 3.1 indicates, about 43 per cent of households own no land, while about 22 per cent farm plots that are less than half a hectare.

Most farmers cultivate less than a hectare; only 20 per cent of farmers work two or more hectares. Farm size varies widely across India (see Table A.3.1b). The average landholding in Punjab is 2.65 hectares, twice the national average (1.35 hectares). Other states with large average farms include Rajasthan, Madhya Pradesh, the North-East, Gujarat, Maharashtra, and Karnataka. On the other hand, mean farm sizes in West Bengal, Himachal Pradesh, Uttarakhand, and Kerala are the smallest in the nation.

The difference between land owned and land cultivated is due to the renting in or renting out of land. Modern tenancy differs from the tenancy arrangements inherited by India at independence. Under the British rule, tenancy arrangements originated from a complex system of revenue farming in which tenancy arrangements were long term and often hereditary, and in many instances, a long line of intermediaries operated between the tenant farmer and the land title holder. Tenancy reforms following independence eliminated these arrangements and often transferred the title of the land to the tenant farmer, or provided for effective possession. In modern India, the tenancy arrangements tend to be short term, and the NSS documents that the proportion of holdings under tenancy have declined sharply from over 23 per cent in 1960–1 to about 10 per cent in 2002–3. The IHDS records a slightly higher percentage of cultivators renting in: about 15 per cent using a slightly different reference period.[5]

Rental arrangements vary across the country. In some cases, the landowner takes half the produce; in other instances, a fixed rent is paid. Households with larger farms are more likely to rent out some of the land, and those with smaller farms are more likely to rent in (see Figure 3.2a).

Cultivating households are less likely to rent out the land than those who have no adult member who can farm (see Figure 3.2b).

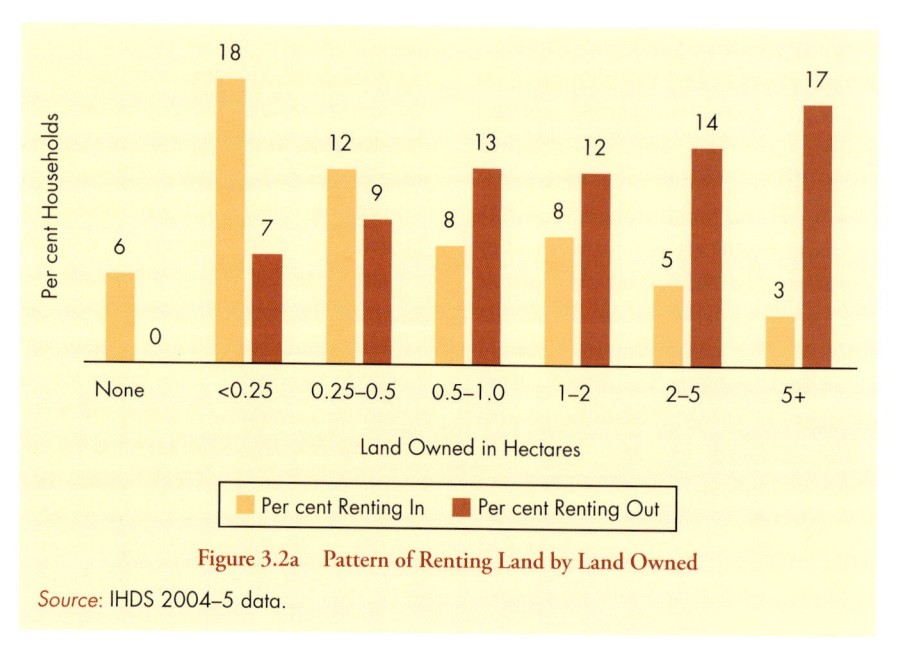

Figure 3.2a Pattern of Renting Land by Land Owned
Source: IHDS 2004–5 data.

---

[4] National Sample Survey Organization (2003).
[5] NSS data refer to single season, kharif or monsoon crops. The IHDS data refer to all three cropping seasons in a year and, hence, record a slightly higher incidence of tenancy (NSSO 2003).

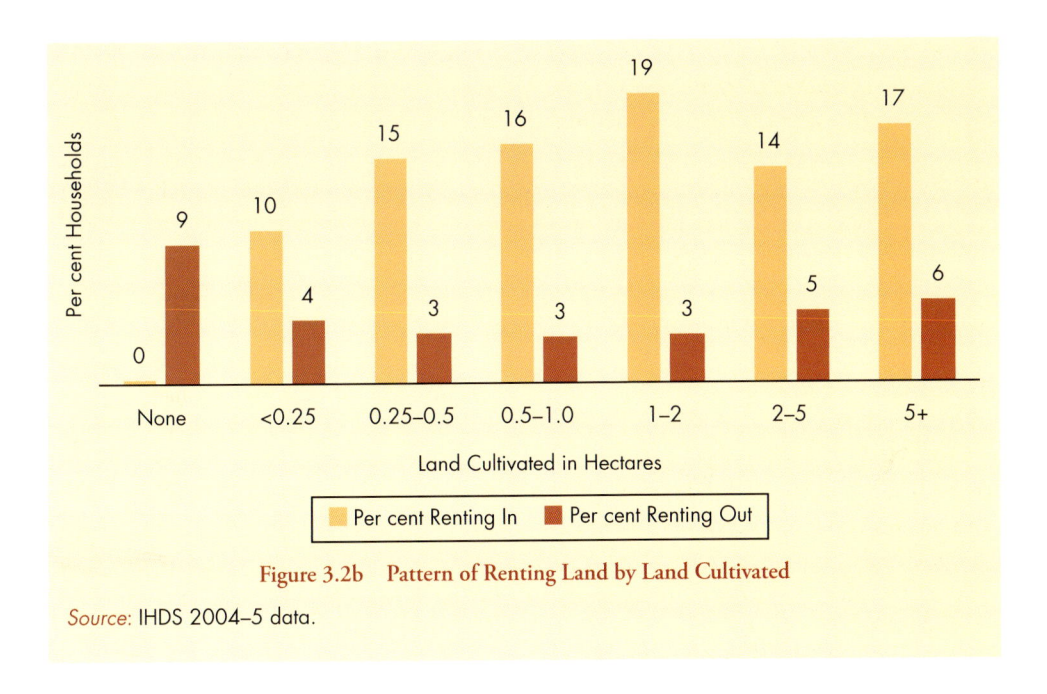

Figure 3.2b Pattern of Renting Land by Land Cultivated
Source: IHDS 2004–5 data.

Educated households are more likely to rent out land and look for other sources of income; less educated households are more likely to rent in. The renting in of land is more common in the east than elsewhere in India. More than one-fourth of cultivators in Bihar, West Bengal, and Orissa rent at least some land (see Table A.3.1b).

AGRICULTURAL INCOME

Arguably, one of the most striking features of the IHDS is the low incomes reported by agricultural households. Farmers rarely maintain accounts of expenditures on various farm inputs and, consequently, agricultural incomes remain subject to substantial measurement error. Nonetheless, most researchers involved in rural data collection came away from the interviewing process with a keen appreciation for low incomes and uncertainties faced by the farm households they studied. Fifty per cent of rural cultivating households earned Rs 8,475 or less from the crops and animals they raised (see Table A.3.1b).[6] But some households earned much more. So the average (mean) agricultural earnings were Rs 21,609. Analysis not included here shows that about 11 per cent of farms reported higher expenses than gross farm income and, thus, suffered a net loss in agriculture for the year.

Farm income depends on land and water. Large farms have large incomes. Irrigation typically doubles a farm's income mainly because irrigated farms are more often multiple cropped (80 per cent) than un-irrigated farms (34 per cent). The benefits from irrigation are even greater for large farms (see Figure 3.3).

Almost all types of farm incomes increase with land size and irrigation. Crop, crop residue, animal, and rental incomes all rise with more land and greater access to water. Expenses, also, are greater in large irrigated farms, but these are more than offset by the larger gross incomes. Yields per hectare, however, decline with farm size. Small farms—especially small, irrigated farms—are more intensively cultivated.

Because farm size and access to irrigation vary across India (Table A.3.1b), farm incomes also show enormous statewise variations. As is well known, farms in Punjab and Haryana are more prosperous than elsewhere in India. Figure 3.4 dramatizes how big this difference is.

The typical farm in Punjab or Haryana earns four to six times the national median. Farms in Jharkhand and Orissa, and more surprisingly in Andhra Pradesh and Karnataka are far less prosperous.

More advantaged groups have higher agricultural incomes. The average farm with a college graduate adult earns three times from agriculture what a farm with only illiterate adults earns (see Table A.3.1a). Similarly, forward caste farms earn more than OBC farms, which in turn earn more than Dalit farms. The ratio of forward caste farm incomes to Dalit farm incomes is about 2.75 to 1. Adivasis also do not earn much from their farms, although they earn somewhat more than the typical Dalit. Muslim farms earn about as much as OBC farms. By far the most prosperous farms belong to

[6] In some states average income of the households from cultivation and live stock appears low. This could be either due to general low productivity of land in the states, or a lower proportion of the households engaged in cultivation, or both. But, since there are a large proportion of households who have multiple sources of income, in rankings based on total household, these states could be ranked higher than the states which report higher mean income from agriculture and live stock.

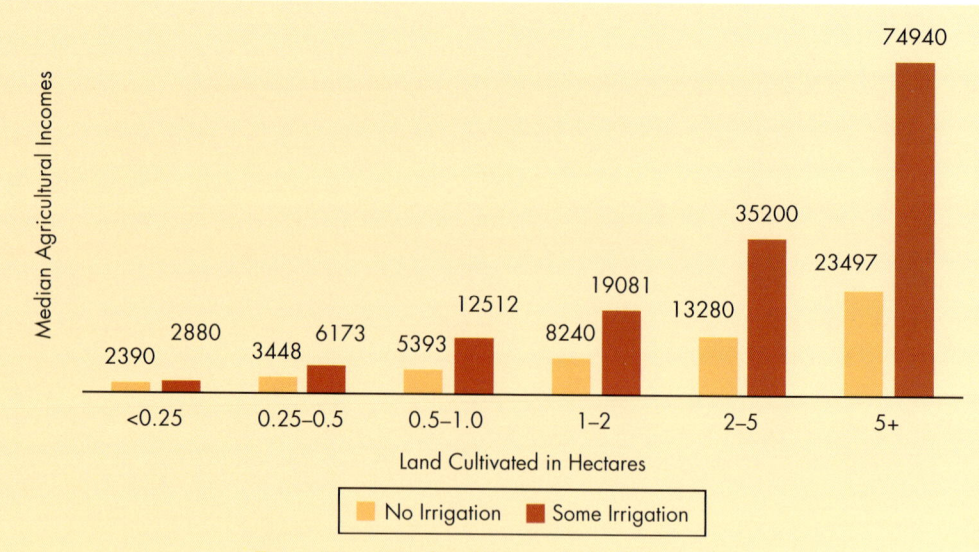

Figure 3.3 Agricultural Income by Land Ownership

Source: IHDS 2004–5 data.

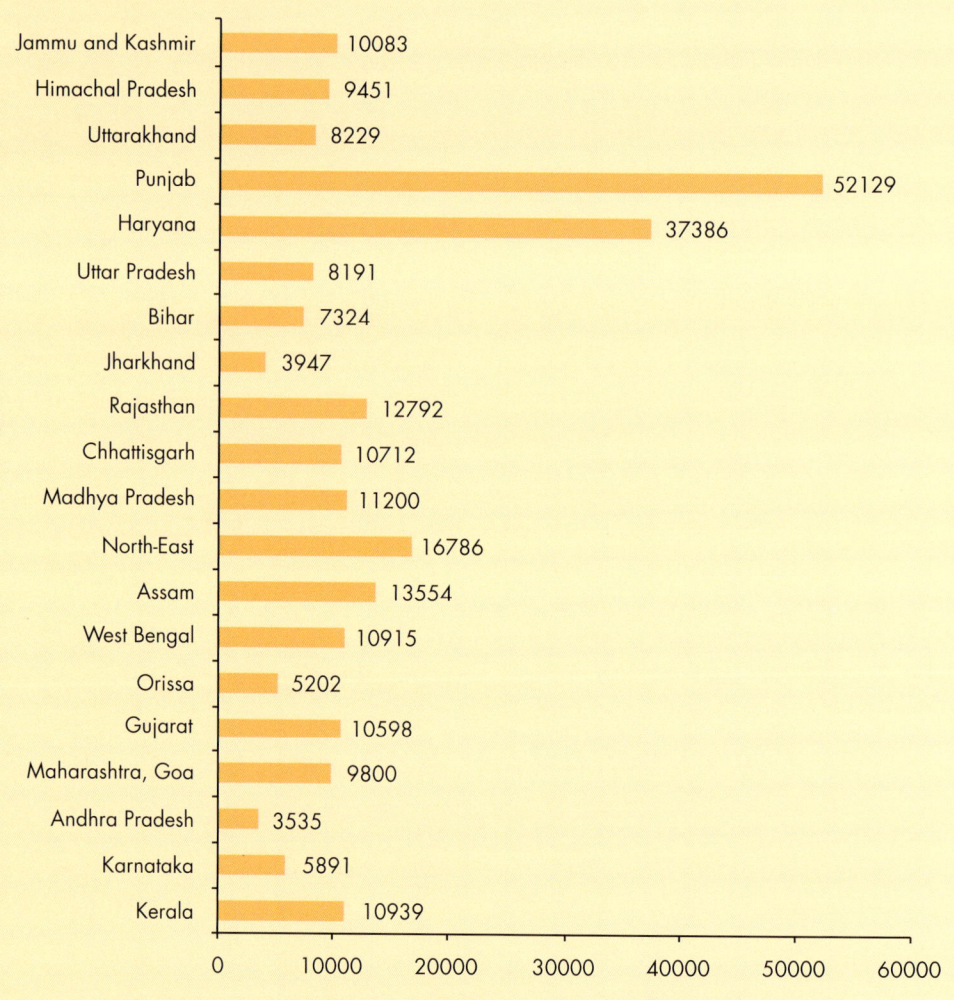

Figure 3.4 Statewise Median Agricultural Income (Cultivation + Livestock)

Source: IHDS 2004–5 data.

other religious minorities. The typical farm owned by any of the minority religious groups (Sikh, Christian, or Jain) earns twice as much as even a forward caste farm (Table A.3.1a). Here, socio-religious affiliation is often a proxy for geographic location, with Sikh farmers located in prosperous Punjab and Haryana regions, and Christian farmers located in Kerala. Adivasi farmers are often found in poorer states like Chhattisgarh. The different ways in which a variety of inequalities in access to land, irrigation, mechanization, and geographic location cascade into large inequalities in agricultural incomes between different social groups are elaborated in Box 3.1.

The IHDS also collected some information on crops grown. Analysis of this crop data shows that over half (56 per cent) of farms grew some rice, and more than two-fifths (42 per cent) grew wheat. Other cereals (for example, *jowar*, *bajra*, maize), pulses, and oilseeds were also grown by more than 20 per cent of Indian farms. Fewer farms grew high value crops such as fruits and vegetables (14 per cent), sugarcane (5 per cent), spices (4 per cent), cotton (7 per cent), and other non-food crops, such as rubber, jute, coffee, and tobacco (8 per cent). But these crops yield high returns and, thus, accounted for a substantial share of Indian farm income.[7]

While Indian agriculture as a whole is well diversified across these various types of crops, many individual crops are quite localized. Thus, spices and rubber are important in Kerala, cotton in Gujarat, and vegetables and fruits in the hills of Jammu and Kashmir and Himachal Pradesh. While wheat is still not grown much in the east and south, rice cultivation is spread across most states, leaving only dry areas in the west, such as Rajasthan, not growing significant amounts of rice.

Land and water determine not only how much Indian farms grow but often what kinds of crops are grown. Large farms more often grow cotton and oilseeds. Small and medium sized plots have relatively more non-food crops. The proportion of income from rice also diminishes for larger farms. Irrigation is even more important in determining what is grown. Sugarcane almost always requires irrigated land and wheat also does now, even more than rice which was traditionally considered the more water dependent crop. Non-food crops, especially coffee and rubber, are grown more on un-irrigated lands; to a lesser extent, so are coarse cereals (for example, jowar) and some pulses (that is, *moong* and *tur dal*s).

Types of crops are also correlated with the economic and social status of the households that grow them. Food grains are grown by all farmers, but relatively more by the poor and illiterate. Wealthy, educated farm households tend to specialize in commercial crops like spices, sugar, and non-food crops. Caste and religious hierarchies follow this specialization to some extent. Cotton and sugar are dominated by forward castes. Spices and other non-food crops are dominated by minority religions. Disadvantaged groups like Dalits and Adivasis get relatively more of their incomes from food grains. The exception is the Sikhs, who owe their affluence to their success in growing rice and wheat. Once again, the geographic concentration of various socio-religious communities plays an important role. Adivasis are located in remote areas where commercial crops are not generally found and farmers from minority religions are located in areas with high productivity, such as Punjab, and in Kerala, where spices are often found.

ANIMAL HUSBANDRY

Most rural farming households (80 per cent) own animals. A quarter (24 per cent) of rural households that do not cultivate any land keep animals that produce income. Figure 3.5 shows that milch cows or buffaloes dominate animal ownership.

The importance of animals for agricultural production varies widely across India. Animal ownership is almost universal on farms in the hill states of the north. These farms earn better than average income from animals, so animal income is a significant portion of agricultural incomes. The rich states of Punjab and Haryana also have high rates of animal ownership. They earn extremely high returns on these animals, but all agriculture is productive there so the proportion of animal income is only slightly above average. Rajasthan has only slightly lower rates of animal ownership and average animal incomes, and because crop production is lower there, animal income is especially important for Rajasthan farms. In contrast to the north-west, animal production is less common in the south. Returns here are only modest, so animal husbandry is relatively unimportant for agricultural incomes. In the east, animal ownership is fairly common, but returns are very low. So animal production is also a small part of agricultural incomes.

FARM INPUTS

More Indian farms are using modern farm inputs than ever before. More than half use chemical herbicides and a quarter have irrigation pumps. Tractors are still uncommon (4 per cent of Indian farms) but in Punjab almost half (43 per cent) of the farms own their own tractor.

The spread of these modern inputs is very uneven. Large farms are far more likely to use these modern inputs than small farms (see Table A.3.1a). Moreover, farms that have

---

[7] We do not present detailed analysis of crop data because the interviewers were asked to write down exact crops and then code them. The coding remains subject to considerable error and results should be treated with caution.

Box 3.1 Cascading Effect of Many Inequalities in the Agricultural Sector between Social Groups

Inequalities in Mean Income from Cultivation and Animal Husbandry (Rupees Per Household)
- Forward Caste Hindu: 22065
- OBC: 11772
- Dalit: 4506
- Adivasi: 8332
- Muslim: 10018
- Other Religion: 62060

Who Earns Most?

Inequalities in Likelihood of Cultivation (Households, %)
- Forward Caste Hindu: 65
- OBC: 58
- Dalit: 37
- Adivasi: 59
- Muslim: 47
- Other Religion: 50

Who Farms?

Inequalities in Farm Size (Hectare Per Household)
- Forward Caste Hindu: 1.981
- OBC: 1.37
- Dalit: 0.771
- Adivasi: 1.404
- Muslim: 0.783
- Other Religion: 1.386

Who Owns Large Farms?

Inequalities in Tenancy (Households Renting in Land)
- Forward Caste Hindu: 8
- OBC: 17
- Dalit: 23
- Adivasi: 11
- Muslim: 16
- Other Religion: 7

Is it Owned by the Farmer? What are the Rental Costs?

Inequalities in Mechanization (Per cent) — Irrigation | Diesel or Electric Pump | Tractors
- Forward Caste Hindu: 65 | 34 | 8
- OBC: 63 | 23 | 5
- Dalit: 61 | 14 | 1
- Adivasi: 28 | 11 | 1
- Muslim: 74 | 16 | 3
- Other Religion: 60 | 63 | 17

Is it Irrigated? Is It Mechanized?

Inequalities in Net Agricultural Income Per Hectare (Mean Income from Cultivation & Animals)
- Forward Caste Hindu: 31340
- OBC: 26640
- Dalit: 21652
- Adivasi: 14002
- Muslim: 35510
- Other Religion: 148058

How Productive is the Land? Where is it Located?

Source: IHDS 2004–5 data.

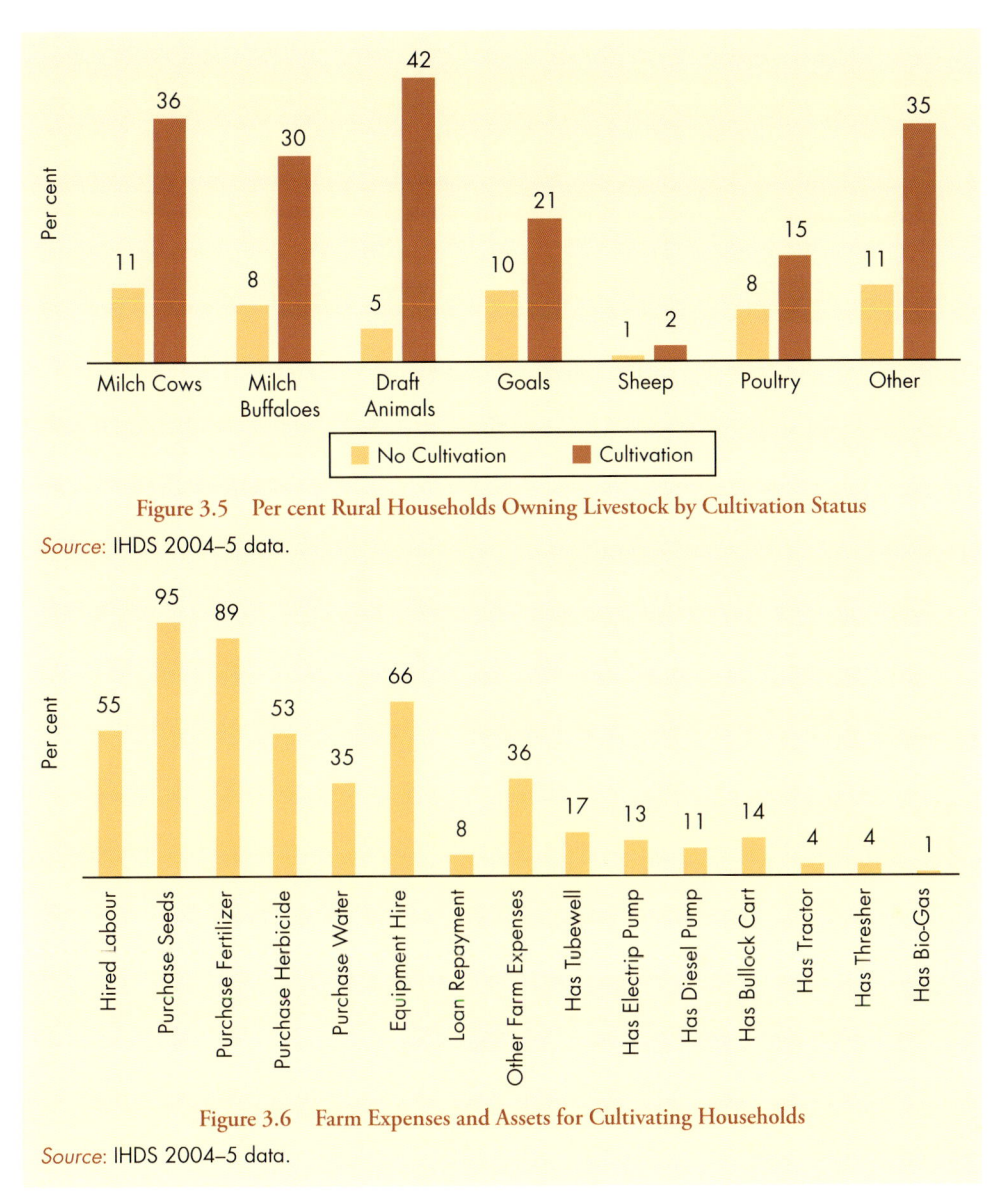

Figure 3.5 Per cent Rural Households Owning Livestock by Cultivation Status
Source: IHDS 2004–5 data.

Figure 3.6 Farm Expenses and Assets for Cultivating Households
Source: IHDS 2004–5 data.

irrigation also appear to have access to other modern inputs. For example, two-thirds of irrigated farms use herbicides, compared with only 28 per cent of un-irrigated farms (tables not included). Over half (54 per cent) of farms greater than five hectares own their own diesel or electric pump while only 8 per cent of farms with less than a quarter hectare do. Consequently, the distribution of these inputs follows all the well established social and economic hierarchies. Wealthy farms with educated adults, especially forward caste farms or farms belonging to households from minority religions, are far more likely to use these modern inputs. All inputs are more common in Punjab. The typical farmer in Jharkhand is unlikely to have any of these benefits.

DISCUSSION

To sum up, with the rural population composing almost three-fourths of the population of India, agriculture remains at the core of the Indian economy, and most Indian families are not far from their farming roots. In rural areas, nearly 74 per cent households receive some income from farming or agricultural wage labour. If income from animal husbandry is included, nearly 83 per cent have some engagement with agriculture and allied activities. Thus, farming forms an integral part of the vast Indian rural panorama. It is important to emphasize this even as we discuss the diversification of incomes and activities in Chapters 2 and 4.

It is for this reason that low levels of incomes from agriculture and animal husbandry come as such a surprise. Measurement errors in agricultural incomes may play some part in this. However, after interviewing numerous agricultural families in diverse parts of India, we have developed a striking awareness of the fragility and vulnerability of these farm households. Agricultural inputs such as seeds, fertilizers, and farm implements can be expensive. Labour demand in peak harvesting periods may outstrip available family labour and require hired labour, and water shortages may restrict multiple cropping. Most importantly, vagaries of weather may increase vulnerabilities of farmers if the crops fail.

These vulnerabilities are not evenly distributed across different segments of Indian society. Farms in Punjab are large and irrigated and, hence, are prosperous, and able to invest in new technologies. Farms in Jharkhand are small and un-irrigated, and farmers in many areas grow traditional crops with traditional methods. Some states or some communities are able to find high yielding niches that offset small farm sizes or lack of water. Spices and non-food crops in Kerala are an example of this exception and so Kerala agriculture is richer than one might expect from its land and water endowments. Fruits and vegetables in Himachal Pradesh and in Jammu and Kashmir are similar exceptions. Animal husbandry is especially productive for Rajasthan. However, in spite of these pockets of high productivity, a majority of Indian farmers earn less than Rs 9,000 (US$ 200) per year—far less than they would if the labour devoted to farming were used in alternative manual work at minimum wages.

This review highlights three challenges for Indian public policy. First, it highlights the vulnerability of Indian farmers. Given their low incomes, few farmers have savings that would allow them to tide over droughts, floods, or crop failures without catastrophic consequences. Hence, a focus on insurance against catastrophes may provide a much needed safety net for farm households. Second, landownership, access to irrigation facilities, and access to farm equipment seem to differ between different socio-religious communities. Given the inequalities in non-agricultural employment (Chapter 4), education (Chapter 6) and urbanization along the same fault lines, marginalized communities, particularly Dalits and Adivasis, deserve particular attention in agricultural extension programmes and policies. Third, with low farm incomes, non-farm activities and employment are of increasing importance in the survival of farm households. The importance of non-farm activities is highlighted in our discussion on income (Chapter 2) and employment (Chapter 4). However, much of the policy discourse surrounding the growth of the non-farm sector tends to highlight the pull of the non-farm sector while ignoring the push due to low farm productivity. This subtle change in emphasis has substantial policy implications, both for the demands that might be generated for such programmes as under the National Rural Employment Guarantee Act (NREGA), and for the kind of impact a change in agricultural input or output prices may be expected to have.

HIGHLIGHTS

- About 53 per cent of rural households cultivate land. About 83 per cent of the rural households have some involvement with agriculture.
- Most farms are small; about 80 per cent cultivate two or fewer hectares.
- Farm incomes vary tremendously across India, with farmers in Punjab and Haryana far outpacing the farmers in the central plains.
- Access to land, land size, agricultural inputs, and farm incomes vary substantially between social groups.

Table A.3.1a Cultivation and Farm Condition

	Any Cultivation (per cent)	For Cultivating Households								
		Median Agricultural Income (Rs)	Mean Land Own (ha)	Rent in Land (per cent)	Rent out Land (per cent)	Any Irrigation (per cent)	Hired Labour (per cent)	Use Herbicide (per cent)	Diesel or Elec. Pump (per cent)	Has Tractor (per cent)
All India	53	8,475	1.345	15	4	60	55	53	23	4
Land Owned (Hectares)										
None	6	5,868	0	100	0	73	51	46	5	1
<0.25	85	3,471	0.148	21	1	65	39	46	8	0
0.25–0.5	90	4,857	0.374	14	2	58	46	49	15	1
0.5–1.0	86	8,721	0.73	9	4	58	58	53	20	2
1–2	90	12,340	1.346	9	5	56	63	57	29	5
2–5	90	23,660	2.893	6	6	59	68	63	40	12
5+	93	42,300	9.159	4	11	68	73	64	54	29
Education										
None	42	5,182	0.93	21	3	55	45	44	14	1
1–4 Std	52	5,851	1.013	19	3	55	51	54	16	1
5–9 Std	56	8,580	1.262	16	3	60	51	52	21	3
10–11 Std	56	13,550	1.7	12	3	65	64	62	32	9
12 Std/Some college	64	12,027	1.813	9	6	64	65	59	32	9
Graduate/Diploma	64	17,197	2.048	7	7	68	76	65	35	12
Place of Residence										
Developed village	44	8,921	1.475	13	4	61	60	55	28	6
Less developed village	60	8,243	1.256	17	4	60	52	52	19	4
Household Income										
Income < 1000 Rs	75	−2,346	1.391	29	1	65	70	54	25	3
Lowest Quintile	53	3,448	0.792	18	3	53	49	46	13	1
2nd Quintile	47	7,100	0.903	18	3	54	47	45	14	1
3rd Quintile	50	13,368	1.175	15	4	62	52	55	21	2
4th Quintile	53	23,073	1.588	12	4	65	59	59	30	6
Highest Quintile	63	48,270	2.885	8	6	71	74	69	44	17
Social Groups										
Forward Caste Hindu	65	14,210	1.981	8	6	65	65	59	34	8
OBC	58	8,571	1.37	17	4	63	57	53	23	5
Dalit	37	5,166	0.771	23	3	61	43	48	14	1
Adivasi	59	6,203	1.404	11	3	28	43	39	11	1
Muslim	47	9,101	0.783	16	4	74	58	67	16	3
Other religion	50	28,850	1.386	7	2	60	76	69	63	17

Note: Elec. refers to electric.
Source: IHDS 2004–5 data.

Table A.3.1b Statewise Cultivation and Farm Ownership

	Any Cultivation (per cent)	For Cultivating Households								
		Median Agricultural Income (Rs)	Mean Land Own (ha)	Rent in Land (per cent)	Rent out Land (per cent)	Any Irrigation (per cent)	Hired Labour (per cent)	Use Herbicide (per cent)	Diesel or Elec. Pump (per cent)	Has Tractor (per cent)
All India	53	8,475	1.345	15	4	60	55	53	23	4
Jammu and Kashmir	83	10,083	0.553	0	2	65	49	61	5	2
Himachal Pradesh	85	9,451	0.587	2	1	18	9	23	0	1
Uttarakhand	71	8,229	0.485	5	2	45	14	28	7	6
Punjab	29	52,129	2.654	14	4	99	78	97	83	43
Haryana	38	37,386	1.67	19	7	78	39	79	29	21
Uttar Pradesh	66	8,191	0.925	20	6	94	48	56	24	7
Bihar	56	7,324	0.715	36	4	94	62	47	14	4
Jharkhand	50	3,947	0.966	7	2	15	39	23	9	1
Rajasthan	67	12,792	2.326	8	1	50	37	31	28	5
Chhattisgarh	75	10,712	1.347	11	3	37	62	43	11	1
Madhya Pradesh	60	11,200	2.172	12	3	64	44	39	37	6
North-East	43	16,786	3.373	16	21	45	69	64	4	4
Assam	46	13,554	0.768	14	3	54	31	89	3	0
West Bengal	43	10,915	0.554	28	5	79	81	91	18	2
Orissa	65	5,202	0.862	27	5	35	74	54	6	2
Gujarat	52	10,598	2.251	6	2	48	47	67	13	7
Maharashtra, Goa	64	9,800	2.182	7	2	45	41	49	41	3
Andhra Pradesh	29	3,535	1.29	16	3	47	81	72	24	2
Karnataka	55	5,891	1.9	9	4	26	82	44	18	2
Kerala	38	10,939	0.579	2	1	41	69	53	49	0
Tamil Nadu	25	NA	1.277	10	2	64	91	52	42	2

Note: NA—not available due to possible measurement errors and/or small sample sizes.
Source: IHDS 2004–5 data.

4

Employment

Chapter 2 noted tremendous inequality in the economic well-being of households and observed that much of this inequality is associated with sources of livelihoods. Households that rely only on agriculture are considerably poorer than those in which some members have a steady salaried job. Chapter 3 amplified this theme by documenting low average agricultural incomes for farmers. In this chapter, we focus on employment and examine the characteristics of workers who are able to obtain non-farm jobs and the nature of their work.

A focus on employment is particularly important in the context of rapid changes in the Indian economy in which rewards to formal sector work have rapidly outstripped rewards to other activities. For a barely literate manual worker, a monthly salaried job as a waiter in a roadside restaurant is far more remunerative, on an average, than seasonal agricultural work. However, if the same worker is able to find a job as a waiter in a government run canteen or cafe, his salary will most likely outstrip his earnings in a privately owned cafe. Two forces are at work here. First, movements from agricultural work to non-farm regular employment increase income by reducing underemployment. Second, employment in government or the public sector further boosts salaries. This chapter will explore some of these processes.

Another important theme of this chapter is gender differences in employment. Women are less likely to participate in the work force than men. When women work, they are largely concentrated in agriculture and the care of the livestock. Even when they engage in wage work, they work fewer days per year and at a considerably lower pay than men. Even education fails to bridge the gender gap in labour force participation. Educated women seem to be *less* likely to be employed than their less educated sisters. The progressive decline in labour force participation with higher levels of education stops only at college graduation. However, college graduates form a very small segment of the female population.

Finally, regional inequalities in employment are pervasive. Both employment opportunities and wage rates vary dramatically by state. In some cases, state variations in employment mirror state development levels. There are informative exceptions in the hill states for rural non-farm work that demonstrate the potential for combining agricultural and non-agricultural employment. And the vast statewise variations in gender inequalities in employment are not at all related to state levels of development.

MEASURING EMPLOYMENT

This chapter exploits several special features of the IHDS. As already noted, the IHDS is one of the rare surveys in India to collect information on income as well as employment. The survey questions began by asking about different sources of household income. They then immediately asked which household members participated in each of those work activities and the level of their participation. For example, the IHDS asked whether the household owned any animals and, if so, who took care of these animals. Whether the household engaged in farming or gardening in the past year and, if so, who worked on these farms, and how many days and hours they worked. Whether any members of the household worked for payment, in cash or kind, and details about the work. Whether the household owned or operated a small or large business, and if so, the names of the household members who participated and the days and hours of work in the past year. Interviewers were specially trained to ask about the participation of women and children as well as adult men in each of these activities. This combination of information from different streams of activity draws a holistic picture of the work undertaken by all individuals in the household in the preceding year.

The IHDS line of questioning provides results that are broadly similar, although not identical, to the work participation rates given by the 'usual status' employment questions used by the NSS or Census. The most important exception is that the IHDS questions on caring for livestock yield higher rates of rural female labour force participation. A second definitional difference is how the IHDS and NSS exclude work undertaken for fewer than thirty days. Under the IHDS definition, those working two hours per day would have to work 120 days in a year to be considered employed, while those working four hours per day would need to work sixty days. This definitional difference leads to a slight reduction in work participation rates using the IHDS definition.[1]

WORK FORCE PARTICIPATION

People are considered working if they were engaged for at least 240 hours during the preceding year in one or more gainful activities. Those working in household farms or businesses, or for a wage or salary are considered as workers. Additionally, persons who usually take care of animals are counted as workers. Tables A.4.1a and A.4.1b present these employment rates for different population groups and states.

The most striking differences in employment are those by age and sex (see Figure 4.1).

For both men and women, employment rates increase with age in the early part of the life cycle, although they increase somewhat later in urban areas, where an increasing number of adolescents stay in school. After age sixty employment rates decline for all groups, with the largest decline for urban men, who often face compulsory retirement from formal sector jobs between the ages of fifty-five and sixty. Nevertheless, work participation rates between ages sixty to sixty-four are high, at nearly 77 per cent among rural men, a theme explored in more detail in Chapter 9. Child labour is discussed in greater detail in Chapter 8.

The striking difference between men and women is also evident in Figure 4.1. Most males work, the exception being boys and young men in school, or just entering the labour

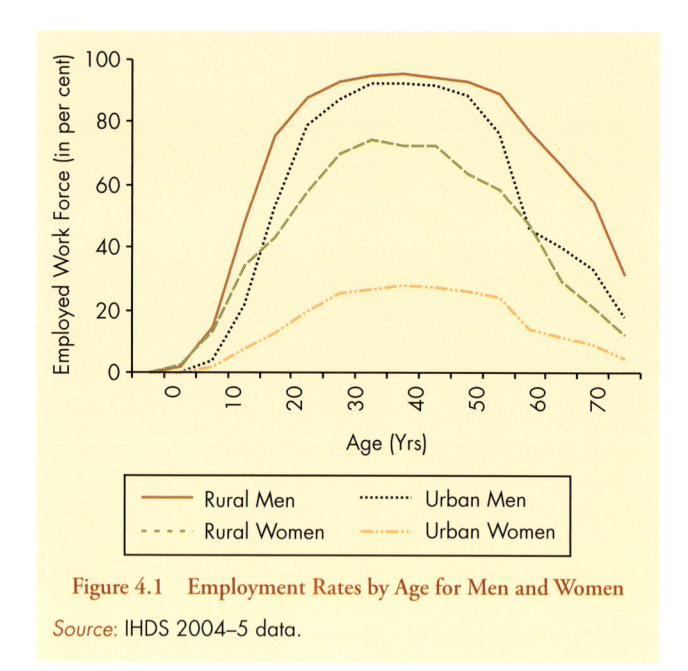

Figure 4.1 Employment Rates by Age for Men and Women
Source: IHDS 2004–5 data.

force, and the elderly, who are slowly withdrawing from the labour force. For men, the important difference among social groups and regions depends on their ability to find year-round work, as discussed in the following section. For women, work participation varies by their social background and place of residence, with urban women being the least likely to participate in the work force.

Women's labour force participation is concentrated at the lower end of the socioeconomic distribution (see Table A.4.1a). Women from households in the bottom income quintile are more likely to work than women higher up the income scale. Adivasi women are more likely to work than forward caste or other minority religion women, with Dalit and OBC women falling in the middle. Women in metro cities are the least likely to work, while women living in the least developed villages are the most likely to work. Some of these differences are quite large: for example, only 15 per cent of women in metro cities are employed, compared with 62 per cent in the least developed villages.

Even women's education has a generally negative association with work participation rates despite the incentives provided by higher earnings for the well educated. Women who have finished the 10th standard are less likely to be employed than illiterate women. The negative effect of low to moderate levels of education for women can be seen even when other family income is controlled (see Box 4.1).

State differences in women's work participation rates presented in Table A.4.1b are also interesting. Unlike house-

---

[1] For males, the IHDS work participation rates are 53.9 and 48.2 in rural and urban areas, respectively, compared with NSS rates of 54.6 and 54.9, respectively. For females, IHDS rates are 38.4 and 14.1 in rural and urban areas, respectively, compared with NSS rates of 32.6 and 16.7 (NSSO 2005a). For those who are employed for cash remuneration (that is, wage or salary), the daily income measured by the IHDS is about Rs 92 per day compared to Rs 96 per day as measured by the NSS.

Box 4.1 Education Does Not Always Lead to Greater Levels of Employment for Women

Women's Employment by Education and Household Income (Rural)

Women's Employment by Education and Household Income (Urban)

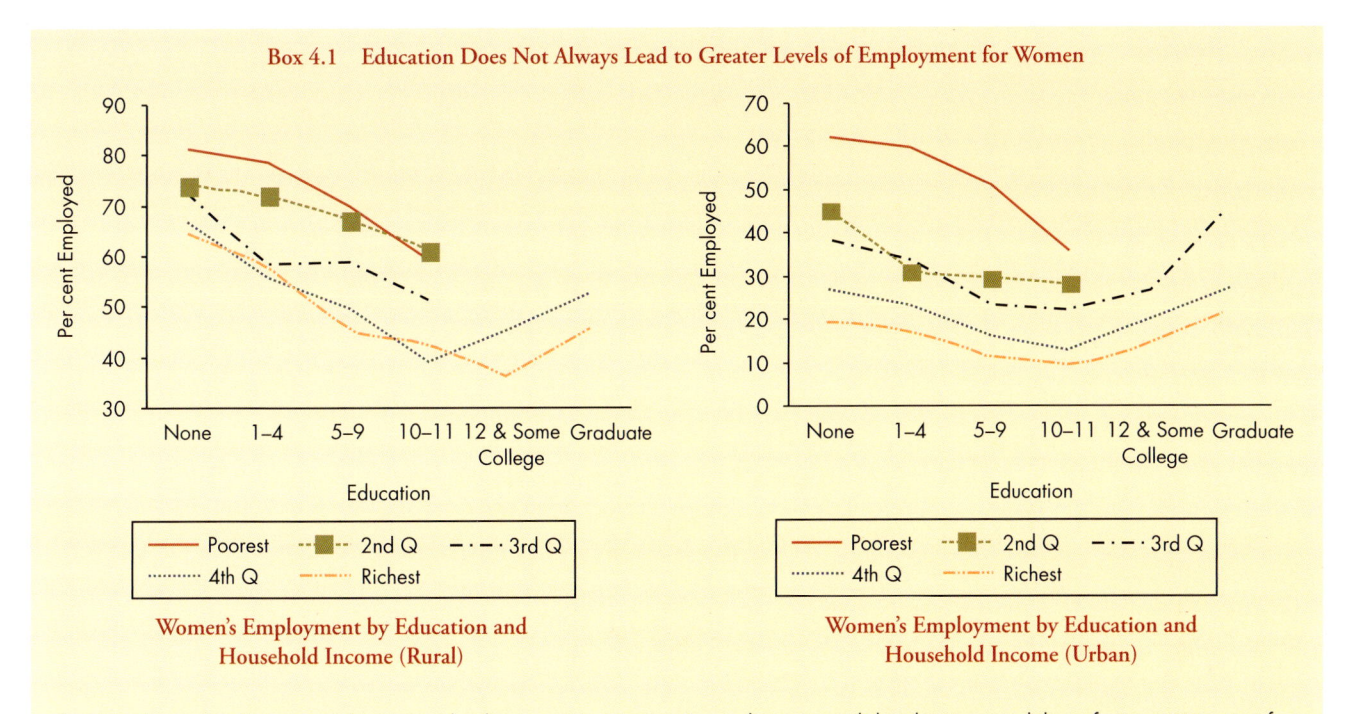

In general one would expect education to lead to greater opportunities and wages and thereby increase labour force participation for women. However, educated women may also come from higher income families which would reduce the incentive for employment among educated women. Figures in this box plot levels of women's work participation by their own education levels and quintiles of other family income (that is, family income minus the woman's own earnings from wage or salary employment).

Higher levels of other family income show the expected disincentive for women's labour force participation. But regardless of family income, women's work participation declines as their education increases from none to 10th standard.

Only schooling beyond 10th standard has any positive incentive for women's work participation. The absence of skilled work preferred by educated women may be partially responsible for this negative relationship. The increase in employment for women with higher secondary and college education, especially in urban areas, suggests that a greater availability of suitable white-collar and salaried employment could lead to increased female labour force participation.

Source: IHDS 2004–5 data.

hold differences, state differences do not follow state income differences. Some affluent states like Himachal Pradesh have high rates of women's labour force participation while others like Punjab have very low rates. Some poor states like Chhattisgarh have high rates while others like Jharkhand have low rates. Regional differences in women's work participation appear to follow more historical and cultural trajectories than differences in household wealth. Inferring macro-level changes from the cross sectional household differences is especially hazardous, given these state differences.

LEVEL OF EMPLOYMENT

Most adult men are in the labour force and their well-being is governed by their ability to gain year-round work. Tables A.4.2a and A.4.2b report the number of days worked during the preceding year—whether family farm labour, other farm labour, non-farm labour, salaried work, or time devoted to family businesses.[2]

The results paint an interesting picture. There is much less employment available in rural India than in urban areas. The average rural man works only 206 days per year, compared with 282 days for the average urban man. The average rural working woman works 106 days per year, compared with 180 days for the average urban working woman.

Table A.4.2a reports differences in days of employment by educational and social characteristics. Although men's employment varies less by population groups than across states, some results are noteworthy. Adivasi men are significantly less likely to be employed (200 days) than other forward castes, Muslims, and other minority groups, who range from 236 days to 265 days. The disadvantages for Adivasis come in part from their rural location, but even in urban populations Adivasi men work fewer days.

[2] Since the IHDS did not collect information on time spent in animal care, this type of labour is omitted from the table. Only people who were employed more than 120 hours in the previous year are reported in Tables A.4.2a and A.4.2b. Days of employment are calculated as full day equivalents, where a full day is assumed to be eight hours of work. Many employees who worked as drivers or domestic servants, or who held two jobs, reported working more than 365 full day equivalents in a year; thus, total days are capped at 365.

Poor states, such as Uttar Pradesh, Bihar, Chattisgarh, and Orissa have the lowest overall days employed by men (about 190–5 days; see Table A.4.2b); wealthier Punjab, Haryana, Delhi, and Maharashtra have the highest number of days employed (about 260–300 days). The state differences for women are also striking, ranging from eighty to eighty six days in Bihar and Jharkhand, to 196 in Maharashtra, and 204 in Delhi. These large differences in days worked are at least partly responsible for the many differences in well-being across the states. Some of these state differences are associated with greater urbanization, but most are based on the availability of work in rural areas. On the whole, differences in rural employment, across state boundaries, are larger than those in urban employment.[3] On an average, employed men in rural Maharashtra work about 235 days per year, compared with only 172 days in Uttar Pradesh. Similarly, large differences in days worked are found for rural women.

The inability to gain year-round work is one of the most important markers of economic vulnerability. Jobs that provide year-round work increase incomes by reducing underemployment. Year-round work is usually associated with salaried employment at monthly wages, non-farm work in rural areas in sectors such as construction, and increased availability of agricultural work due to multiple cropping seasons in a year.

TYPES OF EMPLOYMENT

The preceding sections suggest a need to look beyond the simple availability of work to explore the sectors of employment, since this determines the level of underemployment as well as income. In this section, work activities are classified into six categories grouped into farm and non-farm work (see Figure 4.2). Each individual can be employed in more than one of these six types of work. Indeed, this section focuses on who has multiple types of employment.

This figure highlights the differences between men and women, and between urban and rural areas. When employed, rural women are likely to work in farm related activities. Rural men also have access to some non-farm work, such as non-farm casual labour (24 per cent), salaried work (13 per cent), and business (12 per cent). More urban men engage in salaried work and business than do rural men, although non-agricultural wage work as daily labourers remains important for both. Interestingly, even among employed women

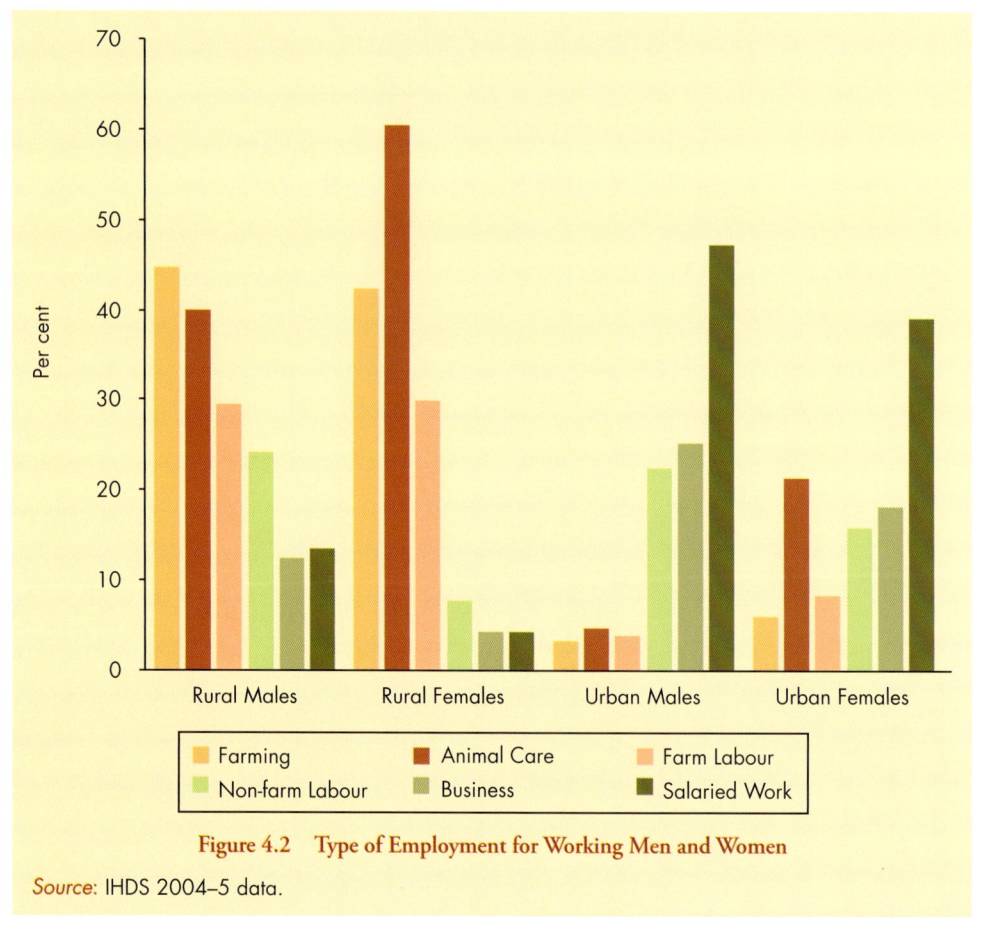

Figure 4.2 Type of Employment for Working Men and Women
Source: IHDS 2004–5 data.

[3] The coefficient of variation, which reflects the amount of variation in days worked across states, is twelve for rural and seven for urban male employment.

in urban areas, animal care remains an important activity. Taken in conjunction with the fact that rural women are far more likely to work than urban women, it is not surprising that an overwhelming majority of employed Indian women rely solely on agricultural work.

Table A.4.3a shows how different population groups engage in various types of employment.

Although there is some decline in farming and animal care among women who are college graduates, men and women generally continue to engage in farming and animal husbandry, regardless of their educational level. In contrast, education is associated with substantial declines in the likelihood of working as an agricultural or non-agricultural wage labourer.

As Figure 4.3 shows, social group differences in employment types are striking.

Adivasis are most likely to be cultivators, reflecting their rural residence, followed by OBCs and forward castes. In contrast, Dalits, Muslims, and other religious minorities are the least likely to be cultivators. While lower levels of farming for Muslims and other religious minorities stem from urban residence, those for Dalits are associated with a lower probability of landownership (as documented in Chapter 3). Dalits and Adivasis are far more likely than other groups to be agricultural wage labourers. Dalits, Adivasis, and Muslims are more likely than other groups to be non-agricultural wage labourers. As shown in Table A.4.3a, social group differences are most visible in salaried work. More than 30 per cent of men from forward castes, and from Christian and other religious minorities are employed in salaried jobs, while only 13 per cent of Adivasi men are so employed. Muslims are the most likely to be in business, particularly in rural areas, with many working as home-based artisans. When we examine social group differences among women, it is particularly striking that among employed women, forward caste and OBC womens' agricultural wage labour participation is considerably lower than that for Dalit and Adivasi women (13 per cent and 26 per cent for forward caste and OBC women, respectively, compared to 39 per cent for Dalit women and 45 per cent for Adivasi women).

Differences in economic activity across states are shown in Table A.4.3b. Relatively few individuals in southern states like Andhra Pradesh, Kerala, and Tamil Nadu engage in own account farming, partly reflecting the high urban concentrations in those areas. However, urbanization is only part of the story. Agricultural wage work exceeds own account cultivation in each of these states, pointing to the

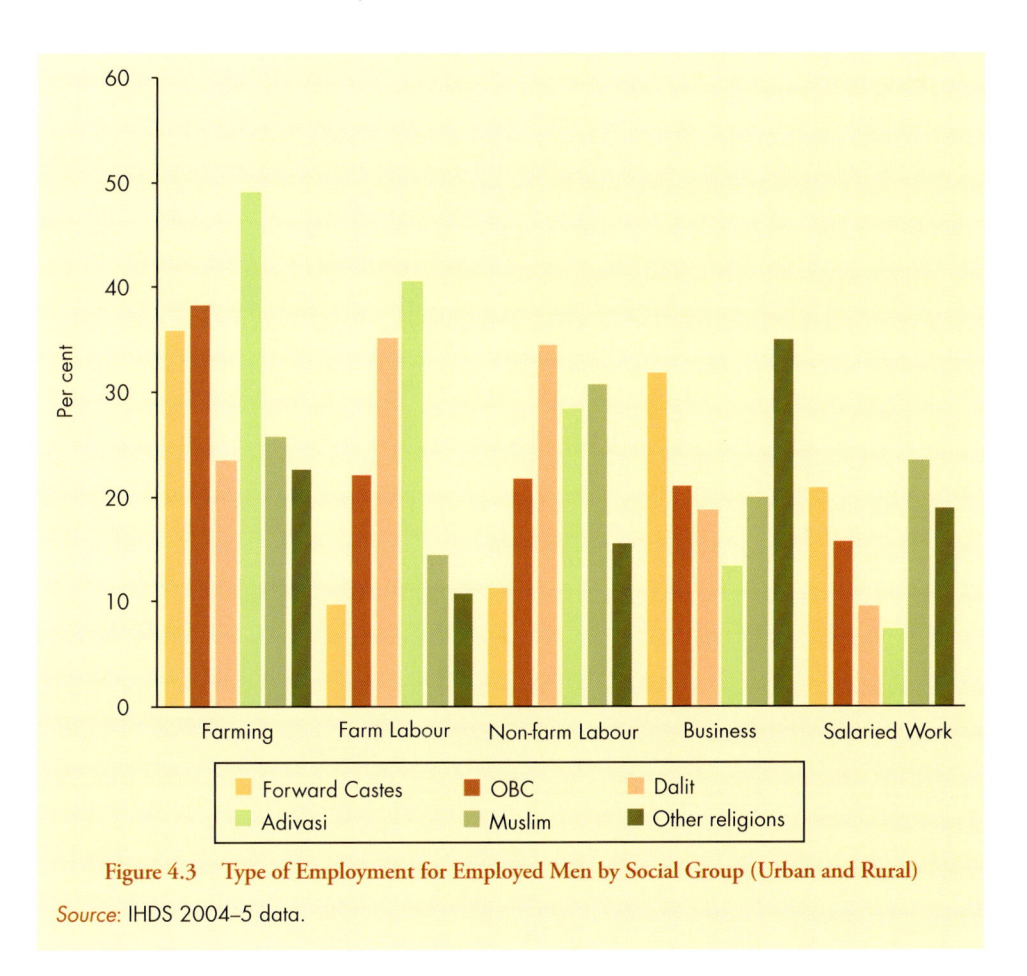

Figure 4.3 Type of Employment for Employed Men by Social Group (Urban and Rural)
Source: IHDS 2004–5 data.

importance of commercial farming there. Not surprisingly, the urban state of Delhi tops the list of states in rates of salaried employment. Other wealthier states with a large prevalence of salaried work include Jammu and Kashmir, Punjab, the North-East, and Tamil Nadu. In contrast, salaried work is least available in the poorer states of Uttar Pradesh, Bihar, Chhattisgarh, Madhya Pradesh, and Orissa.

Piecing Together a Livelihood: Combining Farm and Non-farm Work

Table A.4.2b suggests that rural workers have difficulty finding year-round work. Without year-round work, rural households are faced with tremendous challenges to make ends meet. The IHDS results suggest that one household strategy may be to take on more than one activity. Chapter 2 documents that more than 50 per cent of the Indian households receive income from multiple sources. Although having different household members specialize such that one member farms, while another works as nonagricultural labourer, and a third takes up a salaried job may be a good way of mitigating risk. It is also interesting that a substantial proportion of rural workers hold more than one job. While farming normally goes hand in hand with animal care and should not be treated as a separate job, a substantial proportion of individuals engage in secondary activities that are diverse. These multiple activities are far more common in villages (34 per cent for men and 22 per cent for women) than in towns (5 per cent for men and 6 per cent for women).

In rural areas, one tends to imagine small and marginal farmers who work as casual wage labourers on other farms when their own farms do not need work. However, only 11 per cent of rural men fall in this category, and they do not represent the majority of multiple job holders in rural areas. Many men combine farm oriented activities with non-farm activities: while they manage their own farms, they also work as non-agricultural labourers. Similarly, casual wage labourers work in both the agriculture and non-agricultural sectors. When agricultural work is available—for example, during the harvesting period—they may work in agriculture. During the off season, they may work as construction or transportation workers.

Stagnating agricultural productivity heightens our interest in the nature of multiple activities in rural areas. Although the existence of the non-farm sector, even in rural areas, has been recognized for some time, estimates of non-farm work continue to underestimate its importance by ignoring the fact that many individuals combine farm and non-farm work. Figure 4.4 shows that 51 per cent of employed rural men engage solely in farm oriented activities,

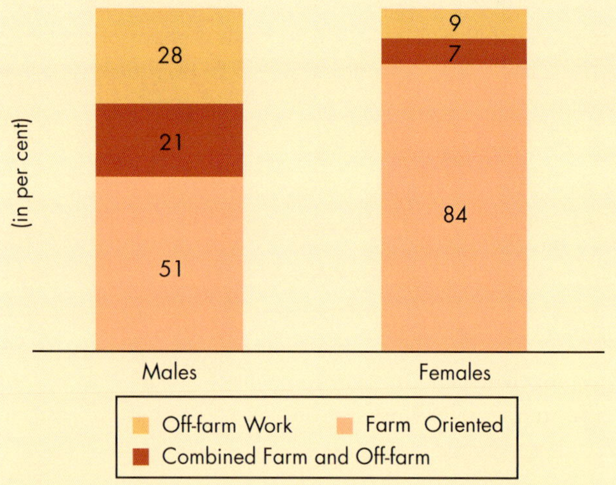

Figure 4.4 Distribution of Rural Workers between Farm and Non-farm Sector

Source: IHDS 2004–5 data.

including own account cultivation, animal care, and farm labour; 28 per cent engage solely in off-farm work, including non-agricultural labour, salaried employment, and own business, and 21 per cent engage in both.

There has been some debate among researchers[4] about whether non-farm employment for rural residents reflects the pull of better paying jobs, or whether it reflects a push away from the poorly paid farm sector. Table A.4.4a suggests that individuals who rely solely on non-farm employment are located in the more privileged sectors of society. They tend to live in more developed villages, have higher education, and live in households that are at the upper end of the income distribution.

In contrast, combining farm and non-farm activities has little relationship with individuals' own characteristics and depends far more on agricultural productivity. Table A.4.4b indicates that the combination of farm and non-farm activities is most common in states like Himachal Pradesh and Uttarakhand, where the weather restricts year round cultivation, or in states like Uttar Pradesh, Bihar, Chhattisgarh, Madhya Pradesh, and Orissa, where agricultural productivity is low.

In contrast, in the agriculturally prosperous states of Punjab, Haryana, and Gujarat, few working men combine farm and off-farm activities. Similarly, a combination of farm and off-farm work is most common in less developed villages. In more developed villages, most individuals engage either solely in farm oriented activities, or solely in non-farm activities. It is also important to note that since Adivasis are far more likely to live in less developed villages and in states with low agricultural productivity like Chhattisgarh, it is

---

[4] For recent work in this area, see Lanjouw and Murgai (2009).

not surprising that Table A.4.4a indicates that Adivasis are the most likely to engage in the combination of activities, and the least likely to concentrate solely on non-agricultural work.

These observations point to the diversity within the rural non-farm sector. The non-farm sector involves regular salaried work, family business, and casual wage work at a daily rate. Salaried work requires a far longer and more stable time commitment than casual wage work and is difficult to combine with farm demands. In contrast, non-agricultural wage work at a daily rate, often in construction, is easier to combine with agricultural demands. However, as we will show in the following section, salaried work is far more remunerative than daily wage work.

Salaried Work

In keeping with the conventional definition, the IHDS defines salaried workers as those who are paid monthly rather than daily.[5] The IHDS asked whether the employer is in the government/public sector or is a private employer, and whether employment arrangements were permanent or casual. Salaried workers in India represent a small portion of the workforce. Tables A.4.3a and A.4.3b indicate that 22 per cent of employed men and 9 per cent of employed women are salaried workers. Nevertheless, salaried work is the most remunerative and deserves a more detailed analysis.

Figure 4.5 shows that 36 per cent of salaried workers are employed in the public sector, while the remaining 64 per cent are in the private sector.

Among private sector salaried workers, most are employed as casual workers, and relatively few classify themselves as permanent employees (52 verses 12 per cent). Many of these casual workers are employed as drivers, domestic servants, salespersons in small shops, and similar occupations, in which they are unlikely to benefit from labour legislation.

Actual salary differences among these sectors conflict with a common belief that private sector salaries are soaring and that the public sector is unable to keep pace. The average salary for casual workers is Rs 2,303 per month in the private sector; Rs 4,640 for permanent workers in the private sector; and Rs 6,974 for public sector employees.[6]

Figure 4.6 presents private and public sector salaries by education as well as the ratio between them.

At each level, private sector salaries are below public sector salaries, with the public sector benefit being the greatest at the lowest educational levels. These advantages for public sector workers are not inconsistent with extremely high salaries in the private sector for a few highly skilled workers, but the results suggest that the small number of well paid MBAs or technical workers fail to counterbalance the overall disparities between public and private sector salaries. The results also demonstrate the importance of public sector employment for individuals with low levels of education. Due to a guaranteed minimum salary in government service, a cleaning worker in a government office is likely to earn far more than a domestic servant doing the same work in a private home or business.

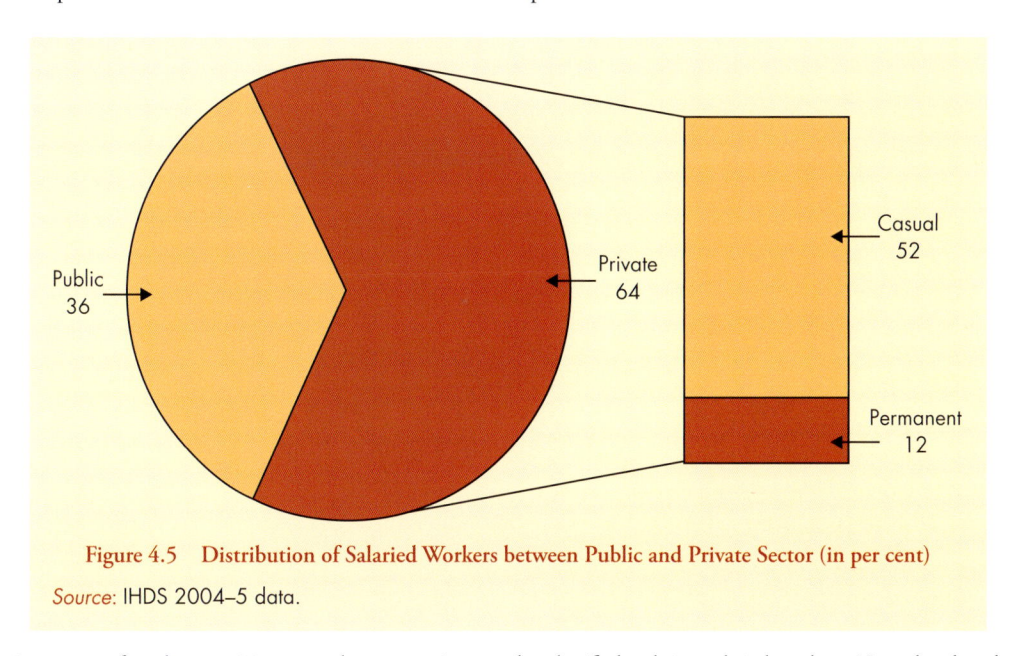

Figure 4.5 Distribution of Salaried Workers between Public and Private Sector (in per cent)
Source: IHDS 2004–5 data.

---

[5] Less than 1 per cent of workers receiving annual remuneration are also classified as being salaried workers. Note also that the IHDS contains employee-level data, in contrast to the enterprise statistics often presented in national data that are limited to enterprises of ten workers or more.

[6] In calculating monthly salary, we have included bonuses as well as imputed values for housing and meals. This imputed value for housing is assumed to be 10 per cent of the salary for rural areas and 15 per cent for urban areas. The value of meals is assumed to be Rs 5 per day for rural areas and Rs 10 per day for urban areas.

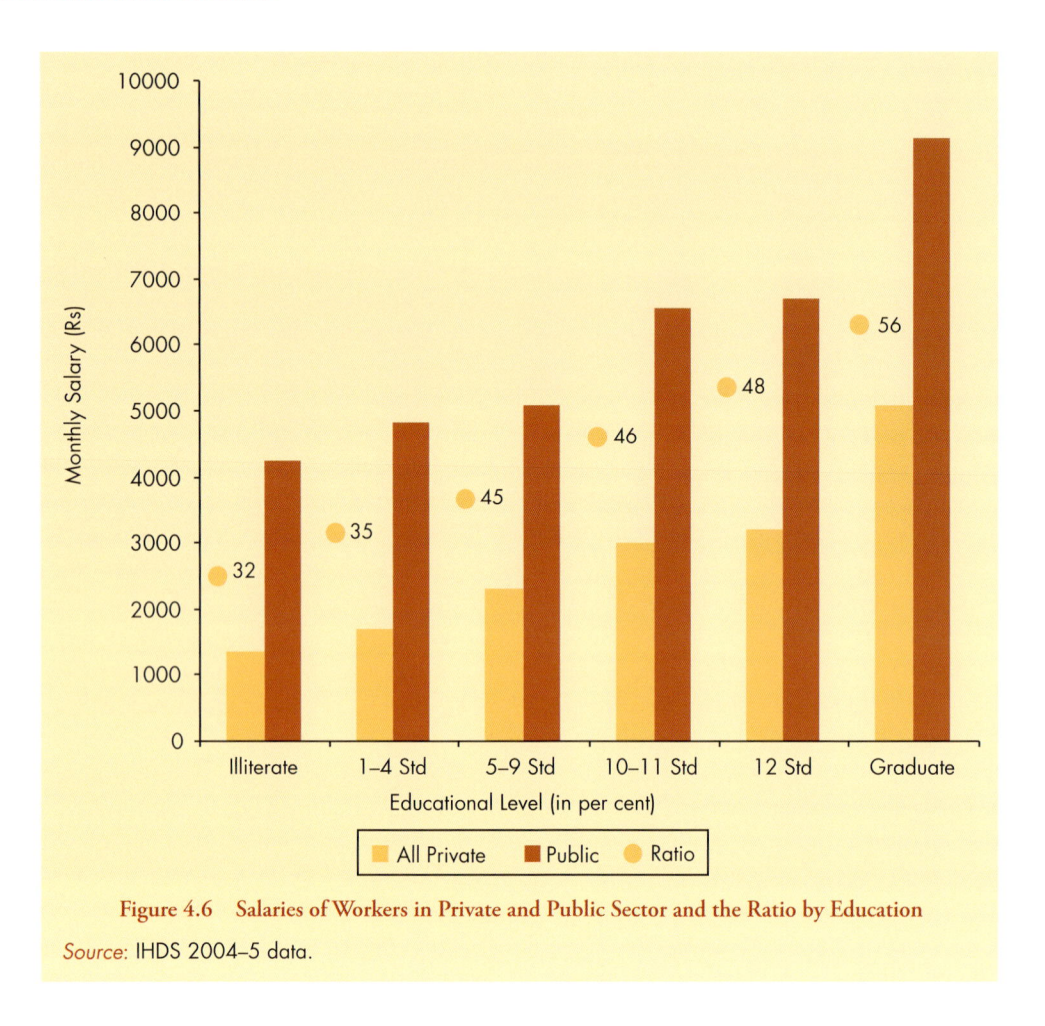

Figure 4.6 Salaries of Workers in Private and Public Sector and the Ratio by Education
Source: IHDS 2004–5 data.

Government or public sector employment also serves as a moderating influence on other forms of social inequalities. While women earn lower salaries in both the public and private sector, the ratio of female to male salaries is considerably higher in the public sector (0.73) than in the private sector (0.53). Similarly, salary inequalities among various social groups are larger in the private sector than in the public sector. Regardless of the sector, forward castes and other minority religions have higher salaries than OBCs, Dalits, Adivasis, and Muslims. As Chapter 6 on education points out, these groups have higher educational attainment, so they should be expected to be in the upper rungs of the bureaucracy and have higher salaries. But it is also interesting to note that the disadvantages of caste, tribe, and religion are moderated in public sector salaries, partly because of better government salaries for low skill workers. Even for higher skill levels, however, differences in government salaries by social background are lower than those in the private sector.

Wage Work
Wage workers are paid at a daily rate. Their income depends on both the amount of work they are able to find and the prevailing wage rate. The average all India agricultural wage rate recorded by the IHDS was Rs 50 per day for men and Rs 33 for women (see Table A.4.5a). The average non-agricultural wage rate was Rs 76 for men and Rs 43 for women.

Beyond gender, there is little individual variation in the agricultural wage rates by education or social background. The main differences are geographic. Less developed villages have lower agricultural wages than more developed ones. In wealthier states, such as Himachal Pradesh, Punjab, Haryana, and Kerala, agricultural labourers average Rs 75 per day or more. In poorer states, such as Chhattisgarh, Madhya Pradesh, and Orissa, the daily agricultural wages are less than Rs 40 (see Table A.4.5b). Some of the social differences we observe result from these geographic differences. Thus, Adivasis, who are located more often in the least developed villages in poor states, receive lower wages.

In contrast, non-agricultural wages vary more widely by age, level of education, and social background and somewhat less by location. Dalits and Adivasis are particularly disadvantaged in non-agricultural wages. Increased returns to education are not especially noticeable until secondary school for both men and women.

These agricultural and non-agricultural wage rates must be viewed in conjunction with the rampant underemployment discussed earlier. With only 206 days of average work available to rural men compared to 282 days for urban men, a rural agricultural wage labourer can expect to earn about Rs 10,242 per year, while the urban non-agricultural labourer can expect to earn about Rs 22,395. All of these wages are a far cry from the average annual earnings of over Rs 50,000 per year for an illiterate male working in a salaried government job. Thus, it is not surprising that salaried jobs in the government sector are so coveted.

An earlier section in this chapter identified that a substantial proportion of individuals, about 20 per cent of male workers in rural areas, engage in both farm and off-farm activities. These workers are more disadvantaged than their brothers who engage in only one type of work. For agricultural wages, rural men who work only in the farm oriented sector receive Rs 50 per day, compared with Rs 43 for those who combine farm and non-farm activities. On the other hand, for non-agricultural work, men who undertake only non-agricultural work receive Rs 83 per day, compared to Rs 63 per day for those who engage in both farm and non-farm work. This suggests that the phenomenon of combining work in different sectors may be due more to a lack of other options than to a preference by individuals.

EARNINGS

Differences in total earnings[7] result from a combination of better jobs (especially salaried work), more work days, and a higher wage rate. These advantages accumulate across educational level, age, social group, gender, and especially, urban location. Thus, employed rural women earn an average of Rs 42 per day, that is, Rs 4,491 earnings per year. Rural men work more days and at a higher average rate (Rs 79) and, thus, earn 3.6 times as much (Rs 16,216) as rural women in a year. Employed urban women work about as many days as rural men but at a much higher average rate (Rs 118), and so they earn more in a year (Rs 21,263) than rural men or women. Finally, urban men work the most days and at a higher rate (Rs 173), and so they have the highest annual earnings (Rs 48,848).

These daily wage rates are strongly affected by investments in human capital, especially education. Figure 4.7 shows returns to years of schooling, separately for men and women in urban and rural areas.

Urban wage rates are higher than rural wage rates at every educational level and men's wage rates are higher than women's for every educational level except urban secondary school completion, for which there is little difference. Only a small proportion of urban women work. It may be that among the high education category, only women who can obtain high salaries work, reducing the difference between males and females for this select category. The educational differences, at least for secondary school and beyond, are larger than even the gender or rural–urban differences. However, there appear to be negligible economic returns to primary school. Primary school graduates earn little more than illiterates.

Other group differences are smaller than the underlying educational, rural–urban location, and gender differences, and are, in part, attributable to these underlying differences (see Table A.4.5a). For example, Dalits and rural Adivasis have low wages and annual earnings, while forward castes and other minority religions have higher wages and earnings. These earnings differences mirror the educational differences among these social groups reported in Chapter 6. State variations are again substantial.

DISCUSSION

This chapter has examined the broad shape of employment in India. Chapter 2 identified the inequalities in economic well-being along the lines of caste, educational status, and region. This chapter has focused on employment as the key mechanism through which these inequalities emerge. Lack of access to an adequate quantity of work, coupled with inequalities in remuneration, based on occupation and industry, as well as individual characteristics generate the inequalities in income recorded earlier. Several dimensions of this phenomenon deserve attention. Access to employment remains limited for many sectors of society. Female labour force participation rates are low and when employed, women

Figure 4.7 Daily Income (Wage/Salary) by Education for Men and Women (Urban and Rural)
Source: IHDS 2004–5 data.

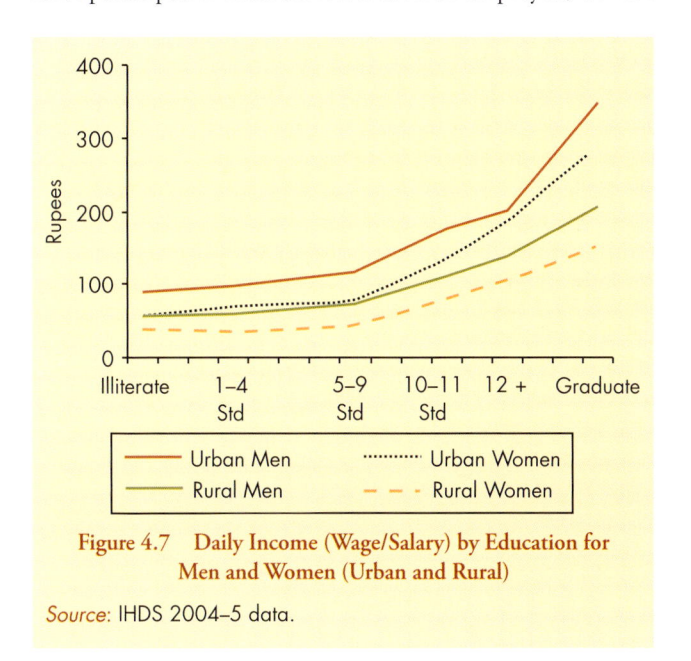

[7] Daily earnings here include monthly salaries divided by 22, and daily wages for labourers.

consistently earn less than men in both agricultural wage work and salaried employment. While male work participation rates are high, the vast majority of the men do not have year-round employment and often struggle to make ends meet by working multiple jobs, often combining agricultural and non-agricultural activities. Access to a sufficient income seems closely tied to access to government and public sector jobs, since salaried work pays considerably more than daily wage work, and public sector jobs pay far more than private sector jobs. Government and public sector jobs are particularly important to less educated workers and workers who may experience more discrimination in the private sector based on gender, caste, ethnicity, or religion.

The importance of government employment goes far beyond the income it provides. Stability of income and job security offered by government employment is unparalleled in private sector work. As noted, only one in five salaried workers in private sector see themselves as permanent workers. Job security is an important dimension of individual well-being. Moreover, social prestige associated with government work and growth in social networks has a substantial impact on the long term well-being of families, and must be recognized as an important marker of human development. Consequently, it is not surprising that access to public sector jobs has emerged as one of the key areas of contestation around which a variety of groups jockey for job quotas and reservations.

Gender differences in work and remuneration patterns deserve particular attention. While deeper probing by the IHDS on animal care and agricultural work has increased the enumeration of women's work, gender differences in the quantity and quality of work remain stark. Women are far less likely to participate in the labour force than men, with the differences being particularly stark in urban areas. When women do work, their work is largely limited to labour on family farms, the care of the animals and, to a lesser extent, daily agricultural labour. Their participation in non-farm work remains limited, especially in towns and cities. Their wage rate for agricultural labour is only 66 paise for each rupee earned by a man. In non-agricultural labour, it dips to 57 paise. Even when women are able to get a salaried job, their income remains significantly lower than men's. The only silver lining is that gender differences in salaries are lower in government jobs than in the private sector; but even here, women's salaries are only 73 per cent of men's salaries. Some of these disparities may be attributable to gender inequalities in educational attainment, which we document in Chapter 6. However, although higher education may lead to better incomes by women, their labour force participation seems to decline with education—even when income of other family members is taken into account—and this decline reverses itself only at the college graduate level.

HIGHLIGHTS

- Work participation rates for men and women rise with age and decline after age 60. However, nearly 77 per cent of rural men and 47 per cent of rural women continue to work at ages 60–4.
- While most men work, womens' labour force participation rates are considerably lower, reaching their peak around age 30–4 at about 70 per cent for rural women and 25 per cent for urban women.
- Workers who receive monthly salaries are better paid than those who work at daily wages.
- The average monthly salary is Rs 2,303 per month for casual workers in the private sector; Rs 4,640 for permanent workers in the private sector; and Rs 6,974 for government or public sector employees.
- For each rupee earned by men, rural women earn only 54 paise and urban women earn 68 paise.

Table A.4.1a Work Participation Rates for Men and Women Aged 15–59 Years

	Rural Male (per cent)	Rural Female (per cent)	Urban Male (per cent)	Urban Female (per cent)	Total Male (per cent)	Total Female (per cent)
All India	82	58	71	20	79	47
Age						
15–19	49	34	22	8	41	27
20–9	81	50	65	16	77	40
30–9	94	72	90	26	93	59
40–59	94	68	89	27	92	56
Education						
None	91	69	82	33	90	63
1–4 Std	88	59	84	27	87	51
5–9 Std	80	47	71	16	78	37
10–11 Std	76	37	66	11	72	25
12 Std/Some college	71	35	58	13	66	23
Graduate/Diploma	75	38	76	23	76	27
Place of Residence						
Metro city			71	15	71	15
Other urban			71	22	71	22
Developed village	80	54			80	54
Less developed village	84	62			84	62
Income						
Lowest Quintile	82	64	60	30	80	61
2nd Quintile	85	63	73	25	83	57
3rd Quintile	85	60	75	25	83	52
4th Quintile	81	53	73	21	78	42
Highest Quintile	78	46	70	16	74	30
Social Group						
Forward Castes	81	52	70	15	77	37
OBC	83	60	72	24	80	51
Dalit	82	59	72	25	80	51
Adivasi	87	72	72	32	85	68
Muslim	79	46	71	17	76	36
Other religion	69	39	70	18	70	30

Source: IHDS 2004–5 data.

Table A.4.1b Statewise Work Participation Rates for Men and Women Aged 15–59 Years

	Rural Male (per cent)	Rural Female (per cent)	Urban Male (per cent)	Urban Female (per cent)	Total Male (per cent)	Total Female (per cent)
All India	82	58	71	20	79	47
States						
Jammu and Kashmir	72	60	61	21	70	53
Himachal Pradesh	86	84	75	37	85	79
Uttarakhand	82	74	70	18	79	63
Punjab	71	36	63	9	68	26
Haryana	79	57	73	15	77	47
Delhi	71	29	66	11	66	11
Uttar Pradesh	87	57	74	19	84	49
Bihar	83	48	67	17	81	45
Jharkhand	80	41	65	17	77	37
Rajasthan	82	63	74	27	80	55
Chhattisgarh	92	82	75	29	88	71
Madhya Pradesh	87	72	73	24	83	59
North-East	69	43	65	25	68	39
Assam	76	39	55	12	71	33
West Bengal	83	51	72	14	80	40
Orissa	83	57	69	18	80	52
Gujarat, Daman, Dadra	88	69	74	16	83	49
Maharashtra/Goa	83	67	70	20	77	46
Andhra Pradesh	82	66	74	27	80	56
Karnataka	83	64	75	28	81	52
Kerala	68	33	66	14	68	28
Tamil Nadu/Pondicherry	73	51	73	28	73	41

Source: IHDS 2004–5 data.

Table A.4.2a: Number of Days Worked for Employed Men and Women Aged 15–59 Years

	Rural Male	Rural Female	Urban Male	Urban Female	Total Male	Total Female
All India	206	106	282	180	226	115
Age						
15–19	132	71	216	146	144	77
20–9	205	106	272	179	222	115
30–9	230	119	293	186	248	128
40–59	213	104	289	181	234	115
Education						
None	209	109	269	161	217	113
1–4 Std	207	110	269	163	218	117
5–9 Std	200	94	278	165	219	104
10–11 Std	212	99	293	192	239	118
12 Std/Some college	208	110	282	222	236	144
Graduate/Diploma	220	164	293	245	262	214
Place of Residence						
Metro city	NA	NA	299	226	299	226
Other urban	NA	NA	276	169	276	169
Developed village	219	119	NA	NA	219	119
Less developed village	195	94	NA	NA	195	94
Income						
Lowest Quintile	162	94	209	150	165	96
2nd Quintile	203	113	249	147	208	115
3rd Quintile	212	114	280	155	227	119
4th Quintile	224	111	284	184	243	123
Highest Quintile	232	96	294	211	263	127
Social Group						
Forward Castes	204	101	292	205	238	118
OBC	202	107	279	172	219	114
Dalit	214	111	273	177	227	118
Adivasi	194	129	262	170	200	131
Muslim	213	67	279	154	236	83
Other religion	236	84	303	229	265	122

Note: NA—not available due to possible measurement errors and/or small sample sizes.
Source: IHDS 2004–5 data.

Table A.4.2b: Statewise Number of Days Worked for Employed Men and Women Aged 15–59 Years

	Rural Male	Rural Female	Urban Male	Urban Female	Total Male	Total Female
All India	206	106	282	180	226	115
States						
Jammu and Kashmir	194	61	297	133	212	67
Himachal Pradesh	223	67	275	102	228	69
Uttarakhand	210	70	291	209	226	78
Punjab	282	57	309	186	292	73
Haryana	242	86	298	194	254	93
Delhi	246	29	304	222	302	204
Uttar Pradesh	172	42	268	111	191	47
Bihar	190	83	247	103	196	84
Jharkhand	191	82	266	125	201	86
Rajasthan	205	74	276	145	221	82
Chhattisgarh	185	131	260	116	198	130
Madhya Pradesh	191	128	273	180	210	133
North-East	219	110	289	231	234	129
Assam	230	81	236	216	231	91
West Bengal	216	65	277	147	232	73
Orissa	178	62	267	138	190	66
Gujarat, Daman, Dadra	210	119	282	163	233	125
Maharashtra/Goa	235	190	302	221	262	196
Andhra Pradesh	235	172	303	235	252	180
Karnataka	214	157	278	201	234	166
Kerala	227	106	256	172	235	115
Tamil Nadu/Pondicherry	216	143	277	188	242	157

Source: IHDS 2004–5 data.

Table A.4.3a: Type of Employment for Employed Men and Women Aged 15–59 Years (Urban and Rural)

	Males (Per cent)						Females (Per cent)					
	Cultivation	Livestock Rearing	Agricultural Labour	Non-Agricultural Labour	Salaried Work	Business	Cultivation	Livestock Rearing	Agricultural Labour	Non-Agricultural Labour	Salaried Work	Business
All India	34	31	23	24	22	16	38	56	27	9	9	6
Age												
15–19	33	40	23	22	10	10	32	57	25	8	4	4
20–9	33	27	22	28	20	15	37	50	26	10	10	6
30–9	32	28	24	25	24	18	38	55	30	10	10	6
40–59	35	33	23	21	26	16	40	59	26	7	8	6
Education												
None	35	36	42	34	9	9	40	58	35	10	4	4
1–4 Std	38	34	35	29	11	13	42	54	26	8	7	7
5–9 Std	37	32	20	27	18	16	38	57	17	7	8	8
10–11 Std	31	26	11	15	34	19	32	51	8	6	19	11
12 Std/Some college	31	26	7	10	36	24	23	44	7	3	34	13
Graduate/Diploma	18	16	2	4	60	22	8	17	1	1	70	11
Maximum Adult Education in the Household												
None	33	35	44	36	8	8	33	53	43	13	5	4
1–4 Std	37	36	39	32	10	11	37	54	39	12	4	4
5–9 Std	37	33	23	29	16	15	42	59	24	9	7	6
10–11 Std	33	28	13	18	28	18	41	58	16	6	8	8
12 Std/Some college	35	28	10	13	31	22	43	58	13	4	11	10
Graduate/Diploma	24	21	4	6	50	22	30	46	6	3	30	8
Place of Residence												
Metro city	1	1	2	16	61	21	2	7	1	11	63	19
Other urban	4	6	4	25	42	27	7	25	10	17	34	18
Developed village	37	32	29	22	16	14	38	54	32	7	6	6
Less developed village	51	47	30	26	11	11	46	66	28	8	3	3
Income												
Lowest Quintile	49	44	40	24	6	8	42	58	34	7	4	4
2nd Quintile	36	36	39	34	9	10	36	54	40	11	5	5
3rd Quintile	34	31	27	31	15	15	36	55	31	12	7	6
4th Quintile	28	26	16	24	27	19	35	54	20	9	11	8
Highest Quintile	25	20	4	10	46	23	34	54	6	4	21	9

(contd)

(Table A.4.3a contd)

	Males (Per cent)						Females (Per cent)					
	Cultivation	Livestock Rearing	Agricultural Labour	Non-Agricultural Labour	Salaried Work	Business	Cultivation	Livestock Rearing	Agricultural Labour	Non-Agricultural Labour	Salaried Work	Business
Social Group												
Forward Castes	36	28	10	11	32	21	42	58	13	3	13	7
OBC	38	36	22	22	21	16	43	56	26	7	8	7
Dalit	24	25	35	34	19	10	25	53	39	12	8	4
Adivasi	49	44	41	29	13	7	56	49	45	13	5	3
Muslim	26	22	15	31	20	24	24	64	9	12	8	8
Other religions	23	12	11	16	35	19	16	55	7	5	23	9

Note: Distribution of workers across categories is not exclusive to only one category. For example, a person might be engaged in cultivation as well in animal care at different times in a day, or on different days. This person would then get classified as worker in the cultivation as well as animal care category. Consequently, the row totals for both male and female categories will not add up to 100 per cent.
Source: IHDS 2004–5 data.

Table A.4.3b: Statewise Distribution of Type of Employment for Employed Men and Women Aged 15–59 Years

	Males (Per cent)						Females (Per cent)					
	Cultivation	Livestock Rearing	Agricultural Labour	Non-Agricultural Labour	Salaried Work	Business	Cultivation	Livestock Rearing	Agricultural Labour	Non-Agricultural Labour	Salaried Work	Business
All India	34	31	23	24	22	16	38	56	27	9	9	6
Jammu and Kashmir	45	30	3	17	40	11	51	78	0	3	6	2
Himachal Pradesh	58	54	12	22	31	14	69	87	1	1	4	3
Uttarakhand	38	43	7	39	20	15	61	84	4	9	6	1
Punjab	22	16	15	18	32	17	14	83	3	2	12	4
Haryana	31	28	12	17	26	14	33	81	7	5	5	3
Delhi	1	2	1	15	65	17	1	19	0	16	53	14
Uttar Pradesh	40	53	16	31	14	18	30	85	10	3	4	5
Bihar	39	40	32	21	13	21	45	59	27	4	3	7
Jharkhand	37	31	7	37	20	18	60	57	12	19	6	3
Rajasthan	44	22	7	34	19	15	45	78	6	10	5	4
Chhattisgarh	57	55	46	31	15	10	62	54	56	19	3	4
Madhya Pradesh	44	44	33	23	14	13	50	39	46	15	4	6
North-East	27	24	11	11	41	20	39	43	7	4	21	10
Assam	46	29	2	29	20	13	59	73	1	5	6	4
West Bengal	28	25	27	22	24	20	9	73	12	10	14	5
Orissa	49	40	26	26	17	17	31	70	26	7	5	5
Gujarat, Daman, Dadra	36	20	28	14	24	16	46	54	37	4	7	5
Maharashtra/Goa	32	28	22	13	30	18	52	30	40	6	12	9
Andhra Pradesh	19	15	41	19	24	11	21	23	54	11	14	8
Karnataka	37	27	30	17	20	15	42	32	41	9	9	9
Kerala	14	5	20	39	22	11	17	47	14	11	17	8
Tamil Nadu/Pondicherry	9	14	24	27	34	9	16	34	36	16	18	10

Note: As in Table A.4.3a.
Source: IHDS 2004–5 data.

Table A.4.4a: Distribution of Rural Workers between Farm and Non-farm Sector

	Males (Per cent)			Females (Per cent)		
	Farm Oriented	Combine Farm & Non-Farm	Non-Farm Work	Farm Oriented	Combine Farm & Non-Farm	Non-Farm Work
All India	51	21	28	84	7	9
Age						
15–19	66	13	21	88	4	7
20–9	49	20	31	82	7	11
30–9	46	25	29	82	9	9
40–59	52	22	26	86	7	7
Education						
None	55	24	21	85	8	6
1–4 Std	57	21	22	85	7	8
5–9 Std	51	21	28	85	5	10
10–11 Std	48	17	35	78	5	17
12 Std/Some college	46	18	36	67	7	26
Graduate/Diploma	33	22	46	42	6	52
Place of Residence						
Developed village	50	17	34	82	6	12
Less developed village	52	26	22	85	9	6
Income						
Lowest Quintile	66	20	14	88	6	6
2nd Quintile	53	25	22	82	10	8
3rd Quintile	49	22	29	82	9	10
4th Quintile	43	21	36	82	7	12
Highest Quintile	41	20	39	85	5	10
Social Group						
Forward Castes	57	17	26	88	4	7
OBC	54	21	26	86	6	8
Dalit	46	25	29	82	9	10
Adivasi	55	26	19	81	13	6
Muslim	39	21	40	82	7	12
Other religions	50	8	42	81	4	15

Source: IHDS 2004–5 data.

Table A.4.4b: Statewise Distribution of Rural Workers between Farm and Non-farm Sector

	Males (Per cent)			Females (Per cent)		
	Farm Oriented	Combine Farm & Non-Farm	Non-Farm Work	Farm Oriented	Combine Farm & Non-farm	Non-Farm Work
All India States	51	21	28	84	7	9
Jammu and Kashmir	40	27	34	93	3	4
Himachal Pradesh	38	45	18	93	4	2
Uttarakhand	36	35	29	89	9	2
Punjab	51	9	40	92	3	6
Haryana	51	13	37	91	5	4
Delhi	23	13	64	90	3	7
Uttar Pradesh	47	34	20	92	5	3
Bihar	52	26	22	87	7	6
Jharkhand	29	24	47	75	13	12
Rajasthan	41	26	33	86	9	5
Chhattisgarh	53	38	9	77	21	2
Madhya Pradesh	63	23	14	81	12	7
North-East	39	19	42	76	7	16
Assam	43	11	46	90	2	8
West Bengal	47	22	31	77	9	14
Orissa	48	28	24	86	7	7
Gujarat, Daman, Dadra	69	10	22	92	2	6
Maharashtra/Goa	64	16	21	87	6	7
Andhra Pradesh	61	12	27	77	7	17
Karnataka	69	11	20	86	4	10
Kerala	33	8	59	71	3	26
Tamil Nadu/Pondicherry	44	9	47	67	10	23

Source: IHDS 2004–5 data.

Table A.4.5a: Daily Income for Wage and Salary Workers Aged 15–59 Years

| | \multicolumn{4}{c|}{Daily Income in Rupees (Wage work or Salary)} | \multicolumn{4}{c|}{Daily Wages for Labourers (Rs)} |
| | Rural | | Urban | | Agricultural | | Non-Agricultural | |
	Male	Female	Male	Female	Male	Female	Male	Female
All India	79	42	173	118	50	33	76	43
Age								
15–19	51	38	65	59	43	33	59	36
20–9	66	40	115	105	48	33	73	43
30–9	79	42	165	113	51	33	80	42
40–59	95	46	228	141	51	34	80	47
Education								
None	57	38	91	58	48	33	68	42
1–4 Std	60	37	98	72	48	33	70	38
5–9 Std	73	43	117	78	52	34	78	43
10–11 Std	111	80	177	133	55	35	92	56
12 Std/Some college	139	104	202	184	51	44	95	58
Graduate/Diploma	206	153	347	290	48	40	102	94
Place of Residence								
Metro city			216	167	74	69	109	71
Other urban			157	104	70	33	91	47
Developed village	87	46			55	34	80	43
Less developed village	71	39			44	32	63	40
Income								
Lowest Quintile	47	33	57	39	42	29	51	32
2nd Quintile	54	35	67	41	46	31	61	36
3rd Quintile	62	39	81	48	51	35	72	41
4th Quintile	89	51	116	75	61	40	93	58
Highest Quintile	198	114	282	236	72	42	123	67
Social Group								
Forward Castes	112	56	243	192	55	34	89	49
OBC	77	40	154	93	49	33	79	44
Dalit	69	41	142	81	52	35	71	42
Adivasi	62	40	180	174	39	30	58	42
Muslim	86	45	114	76	53	32	77	39
Other religions	147	104	228	208	105	77	141	66

Source: IHDS 2004–5 data.

Table A.4.5b: Statewise Daily Income for Wage and Salary Workers Aged 15–59 Years

	Daily Income in Rupees (Wage work or Salary)				Daily Wages for Labourers (Rs)			
	Rural		Urban		Agricultural		Non-Agricultural	
	Male	Female	Male	Female	Male	Female	Male	Female
All India	79	42	173	118	50	33	76	43
States								
Jammu and Kashmir	170	112	97	188	99	0	115	62
Himachal Pradesh	135	121	251	215	78	77	85	76
Uttarakhand	92	68	176	124	81	48	80	56
Punjab	105	68	193	205	75	52	103	73
Haryana	116	72	213	272	82	63	94	71
Delhi	228	124	222	219	80	0	126	76
Uttar Pradesh	67	38	145	101	45	32	63	40
Bihar	71	48	159	156	51	41	76	53
Jharkhand	89	55	243	183	48	33	60	39
Rajasthan	81	50	147	127	60	41	72	46
Chhattisgarh	49	33	218	112	30	27	56	44
Madhya Pradesh	51	32	130	58	37	31	54	35
North-East	201	169	336	338	77	59	136	58
Assam	126	73	198	149	56	44	70	47
West Bengal	73	51	209	149	48	45	66	33
Orissa	63	36	162	134	39	29	57	35
Gujarat, Daman, Dadra	63	46	182	145	41	37	72	52
Maharashtra/Goa	74	32	180	137	48	28	79	39
Andhra Pradesh	64	38	164	70	51	34	84	43
Karnataka	69	34	168	102	47	28	92	45
Kerala	155	123	159	137	123	88	149	85
Tamil Nadu/Pondicherry	88	45	132	82	68	34	89	38

Source: IHDS 2004–5 data.

5

Household Assets and Amenities

The preceding chapters have focused on the way in which Indian households earn their livelihood and on their levels of income and poverty. In this chapter, we turn to the day to day lifestyles of these households by focusing on their consumption patterns through access to amenities such as clean water, sanitation, electricity, and a variety of other household goods. The provision of basic services such as piped water, sanitation systems, and electricity has been an important goal of Indian developmental planning. Hence, a description of these services from a household perspective provides an overview of the success of public policies as well as the challenges facing these policies.

Household assets and amenities reflect a household's quality of life. Electric lights enable more reading and education; new fuels and improved stoves provide a cleaner environment and better health; clean water and sanitation reduce the prevalence of gastrointestinal diseases; motor vehicles and mass media strengthen the household's connection to the country as a whole; access to piped water and use of kerosene or liquefied petroleum gas (LPG) for cooking reduces the time women spend in water and fuel collection, thereby reducing domestic drudgery and increasing time devoted to other activities. While these amenities improve the quality of life, they also demonstrate to family and neighbours that the household has succeeded financially. In modern life, household possessions are both the signs of social status and instruments for a better life.

Assets and amenities cost money, so their acquisition is determined primarily by household income. Household possessions reflect accumulation over many years, so they may be a better indicator of a household's long term economic standing than annual measures, such as income. Many surveys on non-economic issues actually rely on household possessions as their primary economic indicator. Fortunately, the IHDS measured income, consumption, and household possessions, so it is possible to compare household assets and amenities with other measures such as income and expenditure.

A household's assets and amenities are also determined by its economic context and the development of local infrastructure, such as roads, electricity, and water. For example, a television is not of much use if the village has no electricity. Motorcycles, scooters, or cars are not very useful without a network of roads and easy access to a petrol pump. Gas cylinders are difficult to replace if the household is many kilometres from the nearest supplier. And because these possessions are also a sign of the family's economic success, owning a television, scooter, or gas stove becomes more important when one's neighbour has one. Thus, a rich household in a rich state will have many more amenities than an equally rich household in a poor state.

This chapter addresses three major themes. First, it provides a description of households' standard of living as measured by basic assets and amenities such as access to water, sanitation, fuel, and electricity, and the possession of a variety of consumer goods. Second, it documents inequalities in the possession of these assets and amenities, with a particular focus on regional inequalities. Third, it highlights the public policy challenges of providing high quality services by documenting the reliability (and lack thereof) of electricity and water supply.

WATER AND SANITATION

Clean water and sanitation form the backbone of an effective public health system. However, the challenges of providing these services in a large and heterogeneous country can be vast. As Figure 5.1 documents, the provision of piped water in villages, at best, remains sketchy.

More than half (55 per cent) of urban households get piped water in their homes; another 19 per cent get piped water outside their homes. In villages, only 13 per cent get piped water in their homes; another 15 per cent have piped water outside their home. Hand pumps (39 per cent), open wells (18 per cent), and tube wells (13 per cent) are more common in rural areas.

Whether in villages or towns, piped water is rarely available 24 hours a day (see Table A.5.1a). Only 6 per cent of households with piped water report that water is available all day. Most (63 per cent) have water available fewer than three hours on a typical day. The inconsistent supply means that most households have to store their water in household containers, allowing the potential for contamination.

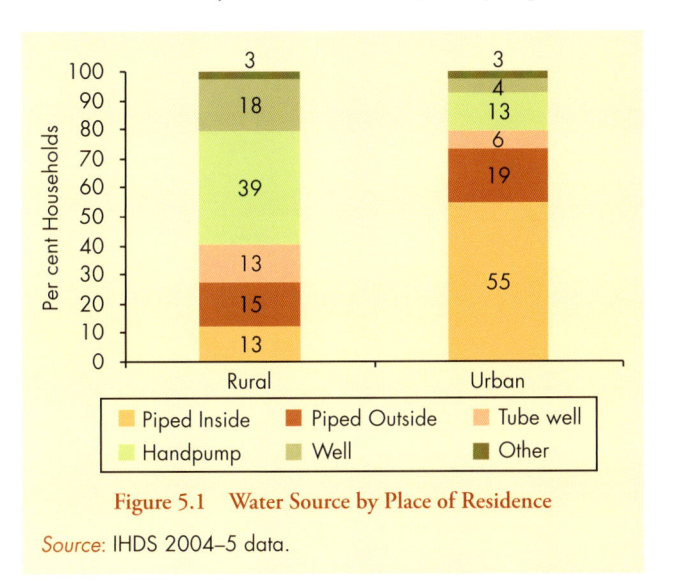

The availability of piped water largely follows state wealth (see Table A.5.1b). For instance, 59 per cent of households in Gujarat have indoor piped water, compared with only 2 per cent in Bihar. Nevertheless, the reliability of water service remains a significant problem throughout most of India. Although most households in Gujarat have piped water inside their homes, over two-thirds (68 per cent) of them get service for fewer than three hours per day.

Piped water is also more common in high income households. About one-half (52 per cent) of the most affluent households, but only 11 per cent of the poorest households, have indoor piped water. Some of the advantage for high income households is owing to the fact that they more often live in high income states and in urban areas. But even within rural and urban areas, the higher the income, the more likely the household is to have indoor piped water (Figure 5.2).

However, household income does not fully explain either the urban–rural difference, or the state differences.

For those without tap water in their households, the burden of collecting water can be time consuming. The typical[1] Indian household without indoor water spends more than one hour per day collecting water. But some households spend much more time collecting water, so the mean time spent is even higher, at 103 minutes a day. As might be expected, the time spent collecting water is substantially greater in rural areas (109 minutes a day) than in

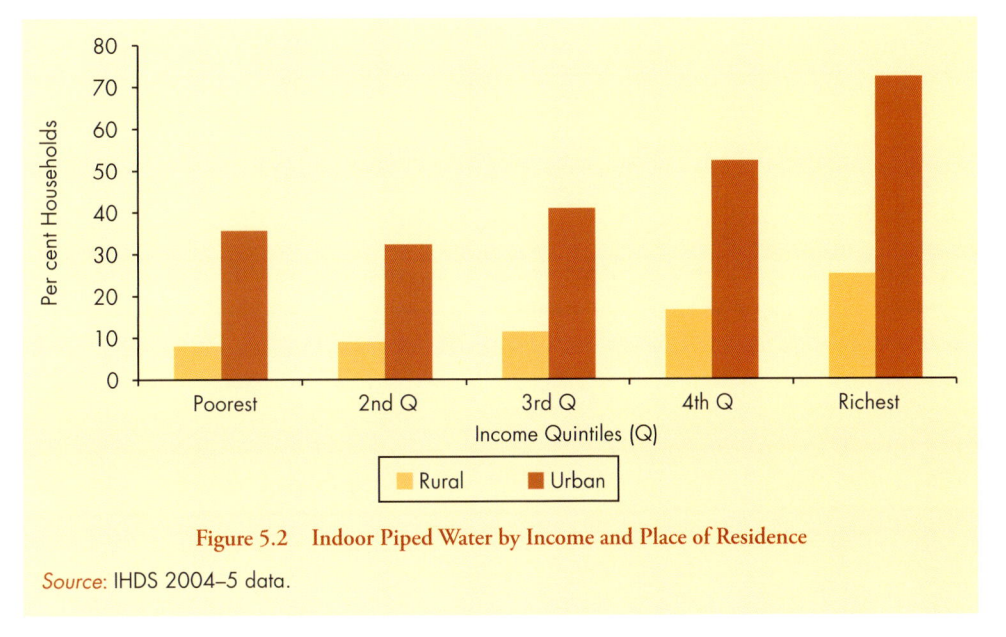

Figure 5.1 Water Source by Place of Residence
Source: IHDS 2004–5 data.

Figure 5.2 Indoor Piped Water by Income and Place of Residence
Source: IHDS 2004–5 data.

---

[1] In this context (and throughout the report), a reference to the typical household is based on the median.

urban areas (76 minutes). Thus, not only are villagers less likely to have indoor water than town and city dwellers, they have to go farther when they do not have it. When averaged over households that have piped water and those that do not, the average time spent per household fetching water is 53 minutes per day (Table A.5.1a). This is a substantial loss of time that could be used for other purposes. As Box 5.1 documents, this burden is largely borne by women.

shared toilet, a facility available to only 9 per cent of the rural households without a toilet.

Although household wealth is associated with access to piped water and sanitation, contextual factors play an even greater role. Many of these systems cannot be set up by individuals for their own use. They require a societal investment. Hence, even rich households are far less likely to be able to obtain piped water or a flush toilet if they live in villages or in poorer states (see Box 5.2).

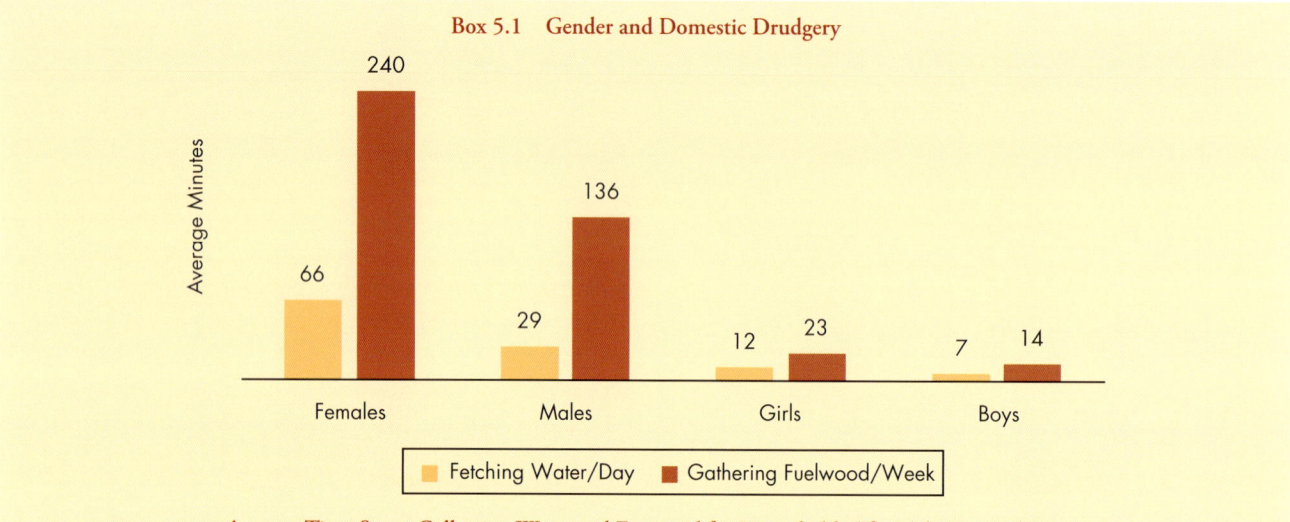

Box 5.1 Gender and Domestic Drudgery

Average Time Spent Collecting Water and Firewood for Households (if any) by Sex and Age

	Fetching Water/Day	Gathering Fuelwood/Week
Females	66	240
Males	29	136
Girls	12	23
Boys	7	14

Lack of indoor piped water and clean fuel for cooking affects females disproportionately. The graph in this box suggests that women spend nearly twice as much time gathering firewood and fetching water as men. A similar ratio exists between girls and boys in the time devoted to these activities. Households in which water is brought from outside spend an average of 103 minutes, more than 1.5 hours per day, fetching water, including the time required to wait in line. Gathering firewood is not necessarily a daily activity but requires longer trips and households spend an average of 369 minutes, or more than 6 hours, per week on this activity. A disproportionately large share of this work rests with women, and any improvement in access to water and kerosene, or LPG is likely to result in a considerable reduction in domestic drudgery for women, freeing up their time for other activities, including labour force participation.

Given past research that has documented substantial participation of young women and men in collecting firewood and water, it is somewhat surprising to see that in this 2005 data, this burden mostly rests with adults. This may be a function of rapidly growing school enrolment.

Source: IHDS 2004–5 data.

The time spent collecting water takes time away from the household's quality of life and its productivity. In addition, poor water supply has obvious health costs for both urban and rural households. Research on health outcomes suggests that both the quality and the quantity of water are important determinants of the prevalence of gastrointestinal diseases. This problem is further compounded by lack of access to sanitation. About 58 per cent of Indian households do not have a toilet, 19 per cent have a pit or some other type of latrine, and 23 per cent have a flush toilet. The absence of toilets is particularly stark in rural India, where 72 per cent of households have no toilet, compared to 27 per cent in urban areas (Figure 5.3).

Moreover, among urban households that do not have a toilet, nearly half are able to use some form of public or

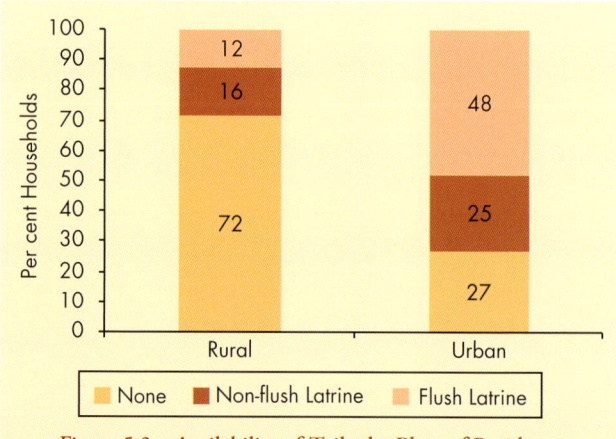

Per cent Households	Rural	Urban
Flush Latrine	12	48
Non-flush Latrine	16	25
None	72	27

Figure 5.3 Availability of Toilet by Place of Residence
Source: IHDS 2004–5 data.

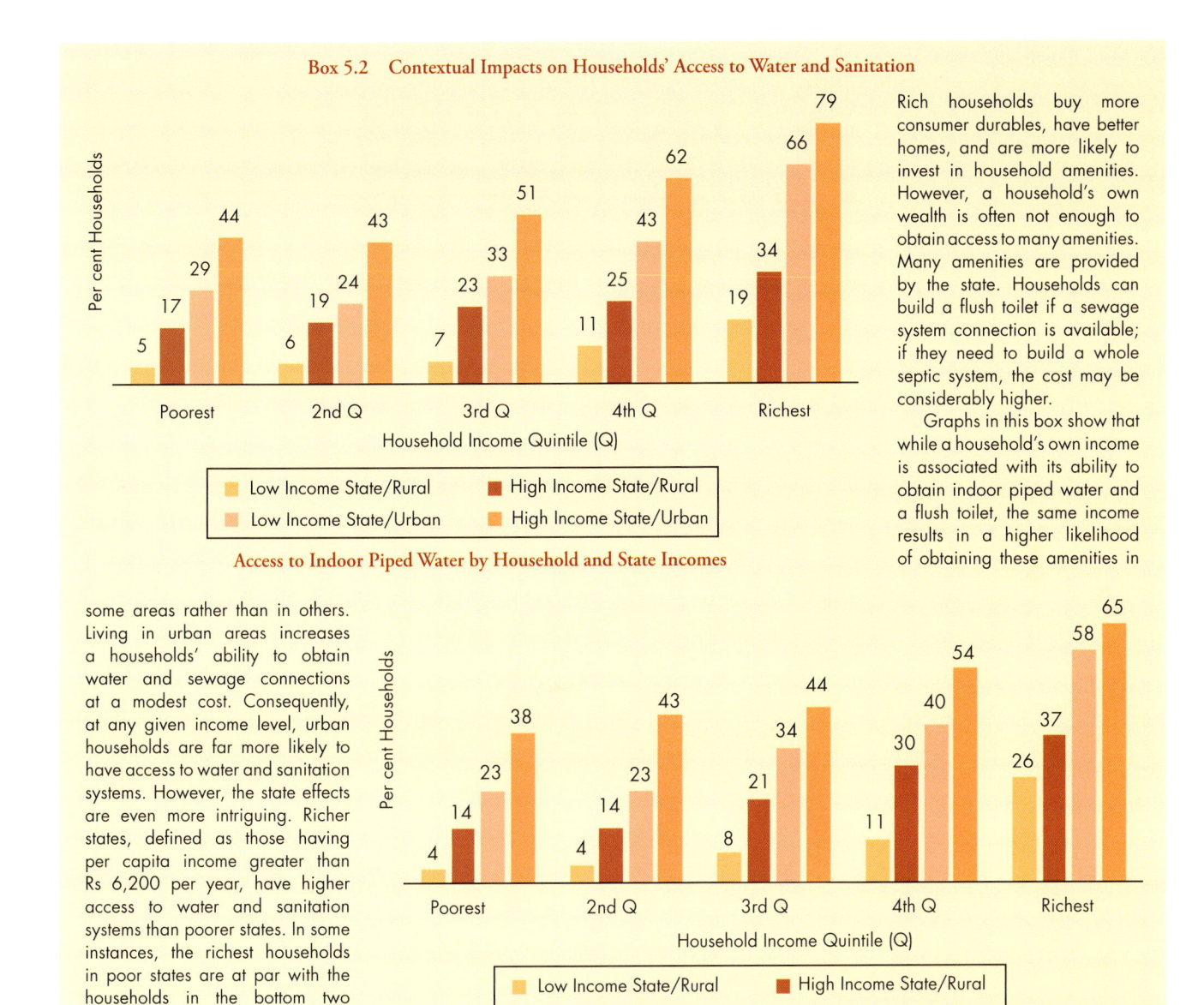

HOUSEHOLD ASSETS AND AMENITIES 63

Box 5.2 Contextual Impacts on Households' Access to Water and Sanitation

Access to Indoor Piped Water by Household and State Incomes

Household Income Quintile	Low Income State/Rural	High Income State/Rural	Low Income State/Urban	High Income State/Urban
Poorest	5	17	29	44
2nd Q	6	19	24	43
3rd Q	7	23	33	51
4th Q	11	25	43	62
Richest	19	34	66	79

Access to Flush Toilet by Household and State Incomes

Household Income Quintile	Low Income State/Rural	High Income State/Rural	Low Income State/Urban	High Income State/Urban
Poorest	4	14	23	38
2nd Q	4	14	23	43
3rd Q	8	21	34	44
4th Q	11	30	40	54
Richest	26	37	58	65

Rich households buy more consumer durables, have better homes, and are more likely to invest in household amenities. However, a household's own wealth is often not enough to obtain access to many amenities. Many amenities are provided by the state. Households can build a flush toilet if a sewage system connection is available; if they need to build a whole septic system, the cost may be considerably higher.

Graphs in this box show that while a household's own income is associated with its ability to obtain indoor piped water and a flush toilet, the same income results in a higher likelihood of obtaining these amenities in some areas rather than in others. Living in urban areas increases a households' ability to obtain water and sewage connections at a modest cost. Consequently, at any given income level, urban households are far more likely to have access to water and sanitation systems. However, the state effects are even more intriguing. Richer states, defined as those having per capita income greater than Rs 6,200 per year, have higher access to water and sanitation systems than poorer states. In some instances, the richest households in poor states are at par with the households in the bottom two quintiles in rich states.

Source: IHDS 2004–5 data.

COOKING FUELS

Cooking fuels have aroused increasing interest over the past twenty years because fuel wood harvesting has caused extensive deforestation, and because cooking with biomass fuels on open fires causes significant health problems. An estimated 1.6 million people worldwide die prematurely due to exposure to indoor air pollution. Of course, households use energy for a wide variety of activities besides cooking.

In India, the use of biomass energy in traditional stoves is still quite common, but the use of modern fuels such as LPG has increased as well. The IHDS found that Indian households use many different fuels for cooking, lighting, and heating (see Table 5.1).

Table 5.1 Household Fuel Used for Different Fuels

(in per cent)

	Firewood	Dung	Crop Residue	Kerosene	LPG	Coal
Not Used	26	59	84	19	67	95
Cooking	51	30	10	15	26	4
Lighting	0	0	0	53	0	0
Heating	2	1	1	2	0	0
Combination	21	9	4	11	7	1
Total	100	100	100	100	100	100

Source: IHDS 2004–5 data.

Almost half of all households use at least three different fuels at different times, or for different purposes. It is not uncommon, for instance, for a cook to rely primarily on firewood for cooking the main meals, to use a fuel like LPG or kerosene for quickly making tea, and to use dung cakes for the slow heat needed to simmer fodder for animals, or heat milk. The IHDS captured this variety by asking about each type of fuel use independently, thus providing a more complete picture than is possible with a single question as is common in other surveys.

As shown in Table 5.1, the most widely used fuel in India is kerosene, but most households (53 per cent) use it only for lighting. However, kerosene is a poor lighting fuel. It provides less light than a simple 40-watt light bulb and is more expensive. Households with electricity immediately switch to electric lighting and use kerosene primarily as a backup fuel when the power is unreliable.

For household cooking, the picture is quite different. The most widely used cooking fuel remains firewood, used by 72 per cent of households. Dung cakes are the second most common cooking fuel, used by 39 per cent of households. The other biomass fuel used for cooking is crop residue, that is, stalks left over after threshing and not used for animal fodder; 15 per cent of households use these for at least some of their cooking. The use of coal or charcoal is very localized and used by only 5 per cent of households, and is more important in Jharkhand and West Bengal which are closer to coal sources.

Liquid fuels must be purchased in the marketplace, but they have the advantage of being used in more efficient stoves that emit far less air pollution and reduce utensil cleaning. Kerosene is almost universally available across India, through both the open market and the Public Distribution System, and is used by 26 per cent of households for at least some cooking. The use of LPG has increased significantly as a result both of market liberalization to encourage private vendors and of the expansion of public sector outlets. About one-third of Indian households now use LPG for some or all of their cooking, and this figure has been increasing steadily.

The use of modern fuels—kerosene, LPG, or coal—is vastly greater in urban than in rural areas (Figure 5.4).

Almost all urban households (89 per cent) use some modern fuel for some of their cooking, and the majority (65 per cent) do not use biomass fuels at all. In rural areas, the reverse is true. Almost all (93 per cent) use some form of biomass fuel for cooking, and the majority (55 per cent) do not use modern fuels at all.

States also differ widely in the use of modern fuels. Over half of rural households in Jammu and Kashmir (68 per cent), Himachal Pradesh (53 per cent), Punjab

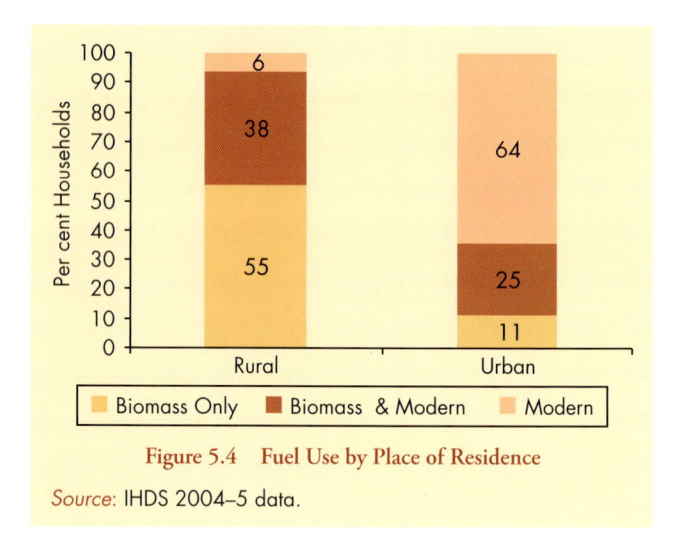

Figure 5.4 Fuel Use by Place of Residence
Source: IHDS 2004–5 data.

(61 per cent), the North-East (54 per cent), and Kerala (59 per cent), use LPG in their households. Less than one in 20 rural households in Jharkhand (3 per cent), Chhattisgarh (2 per cent), and Orissa (5 per cent) do. These differences are partly due to higher incomes in cities and in the states with greater availability of LPG. In fact, the wealthiest households in urban areas use modern fuels almost exclusively, while the poorest rural households are almost completely dependent on biomass. But as with water and sanitation systems (see Box 5.2a and Box 5.2b), household income is only part of the explanation.

Urban households use modern fuels not only because they are better off financially but also because modern fuels are easily available in towns and cities. Rural households use biomass fuels not only because they tend to be poorer but also because biomass is easily available there unlike urban areas. Income definitely matters, but fuel availability in both urban and rural markets appears to be an even more important factor in determining the fuels that households adopt for cooking (see Figure 5.5).

ELECTRICITY

The Indian government is committed to providing adequate electricity for all segments of the society. However, rapid economic growth has increased electricity demands. Government policies have emphasized rural electrification through the Rajiv Gandhi Grameen Vidyutikaran Yojna and these efforts appear to be reflected in the rapidly rising rates of electrification. Nevertheless, a significant number of rural households lack electricity and the quality of service still lags behind that of many other countries.

The IHDS found that 72 per cent of households have electricity.[2] These levels are higher than the 56 per cent reported by the Census just four years earlier. There may be

---

[2] The 61st round of the NSS and the *National Family Health Survey-III*, which were conducted around the same period as the IHDS, found electrification rates of 68 and 65 per cent, respectively (NSSO 2005b and IIPS 2007).

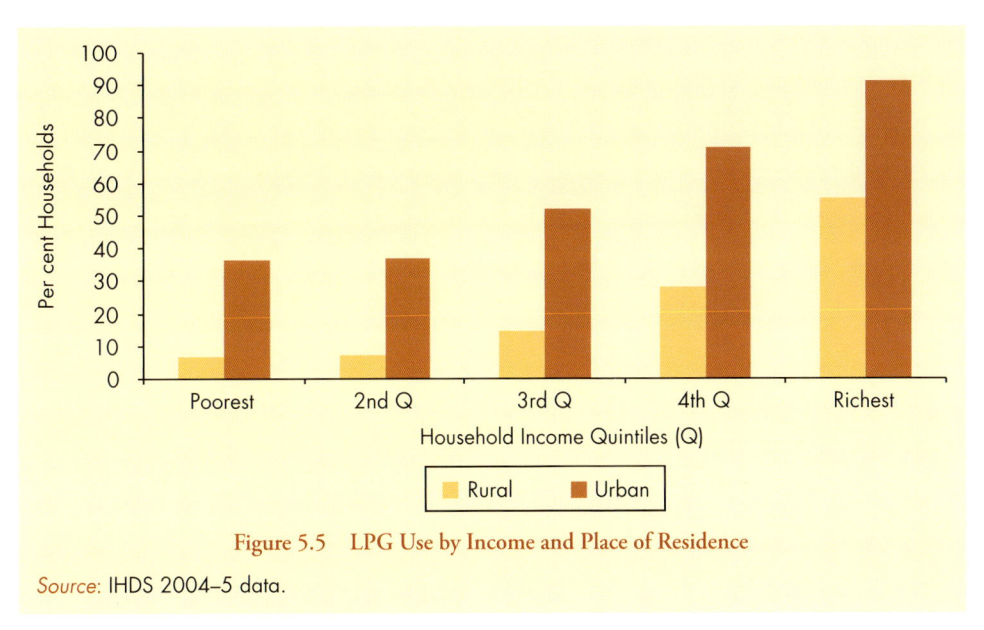

Figure 5.5 LPG Use by Income and Place of Residence
Source: IHDS 2004–5 data.

several reasons for this difference. First, the Rajiv Gandhi Grameen Vidyutikaran Yojna has made significant investments to increase rural electrification, so the electrification rate has been rising during the intervening years. Second, the IHDS includes non-standard and unofficial connections. Many of households may have illegal connections, a practice that is quite common in rural India. These households may not report their illegal connection to the Census, which is an official arm of the government. It is also likely that the electrification rate may be underreported in the IHDS, as well.

The central government has financed much of the electricity development, but the actual delivery of electricity to consumers is primarily a state responsibility. Therefore, the enormous statewise variations in electrification, especially in rural areas, are not surprising. In Himachal Pradesh, a well-managed state with extensive hydroelectricity production, virtually all households have electricity, including 98 per cent of rural households. The highly developed states of Punjab, Jammu and Kashmir, and Haryana also have achieved rural connection rates greater than 90 per cent. All states in the south have rates of rural electrification greater than 80 per cent. In contrast, the poor states have low rates of rural electrification: only 29 per cent of Bihar villagers have electricity. Orissa (36 per cent) and Uttar Pradesh (34 per cent) are only slightly better off. Even the more affluent households in these states often lack electricity. Electrification, like all household amenities, depends not only on how wealthy a household is but also on how wealthy the neighbours are.

Although most urban households (94 per cent) have electricity, for urban dwellers the problem is the poor reliability of the electricity supply. Only 25 per cent of households in urban India report a steady supply of electricity 24 hours a day, and as many as 18 per cent of urban consumers have 12 or fewer hours of electricity each day (see Figure 5.6).

Inadequate supply is an even bigger problem for rural households: only 6 per cent have a steady 24 hour supply, another 26 per cent have only twelve or fewer hours, and about 37 per cent do not have any electricity service.

It is the poor who suffer the most from the lack of access to electricity. Poverty is related to low access to electricity in two ways. First, poverty at individual as well as state level reduces access to electricity. Second, low access to electricity reduces income growth. Poor households find it difficult to pay for a connection and monthly charges. Poor states find it difficult to ensure supply to remote areas. However, the absence of electricity also affects income growth. Many home based businesses, particularly those run by women, such as tailoring or handicraft, may be more feasible if electric

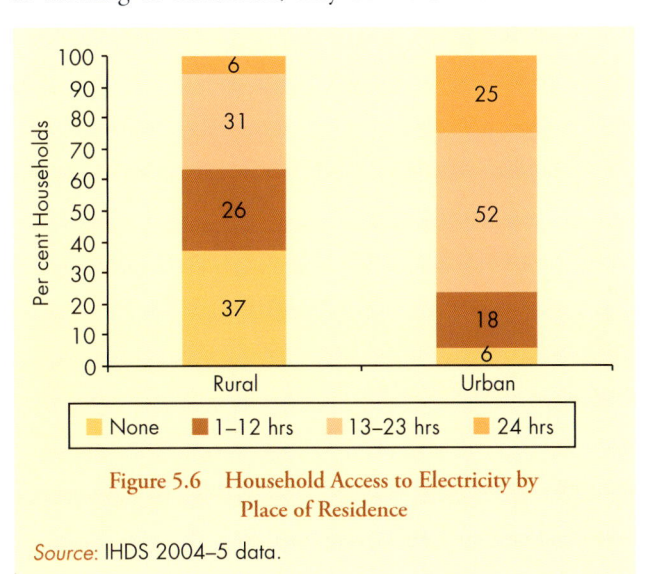

Figure 5.6 Household Access to Electricity by Place of Residence
Source: IHDS 2004–5 data.

lighting could extend the hours available to work. Similarly, states with poorly developed electric supply may experience low investment and productivity growth.

The relationship between state level conditions and household conditions in shaping access to electricity is complex. Poor households often live in poor states. So their lack of access to electricity is affected both by their own inability to pay for the connection/operating costs as well as lack of electric supply. However, IHDS finds that the poor are less likely to have electricity, no matter where they live (see Figure 5.7) suggesting a greater importance of household level factors than the state level factors.

Most poor households actually live in villages where electricity is available. Only 8 per cent of the 38 per cent of rural households without electricity live in non-electrified villages.

As noted earlier, many households have illegal connections. It is difficult to ask in a survey about illegal connections, but the IHDS inquired about the mode of payment for electric connections and the amount of payment. The results, presented in Table 5.2, indicate that 80 per cent households receive bills from the State Electricity Board, 9 per cent pay to neighbours or landlords, and 11 per cent of households with electricity do not receive a bill and do not make payment.

Among other modes of payment, households who get a bill from the State Electricity Board pay the greatest amount followed by generator users. Households who make payments to neighbours or landlords pay the least.

HOUSEHOLD POSSESSIONS

Electricity, piped water, and cooking fuels provoke extensive policy debates about the proper public role for the state. However, from a household's point of view, they are part of a family's standard of living, much like motor vehicles, refrigerators, and other household possessions, which are not the focus of such policy scrutiny. As income rises, a household is more likely to acquire a motor vehicle or refrigerator, just as it is more likely to have electricity, piped water, or modern cooking fuel.

The IHDS asked questions about 27 other household goods or housing amenities (in addition to a flush toilet, LPG,

Table 5.2 Mode of Payment for Electricity by Place of Residence (for households with electricity)

	Rural	Urban	Total
Per cent Households			
No Bill	15	5	11
State Electricity Board	77	85	80
Neighbour	4	3	3
Part of Rent	2	6	3
Generator	0	0	0
Other	3	2	2
Amount of Payment (Preceding Month)			
No Bill	0	0	0
State Electricity Board	153	272	201
Neighbour	71	172	104
Part of Rent	91	142	123
Generator	180	168	175
Other	92	136	103
All households with Electricity	138	255	185

Source: IHDS 2004–5 data.

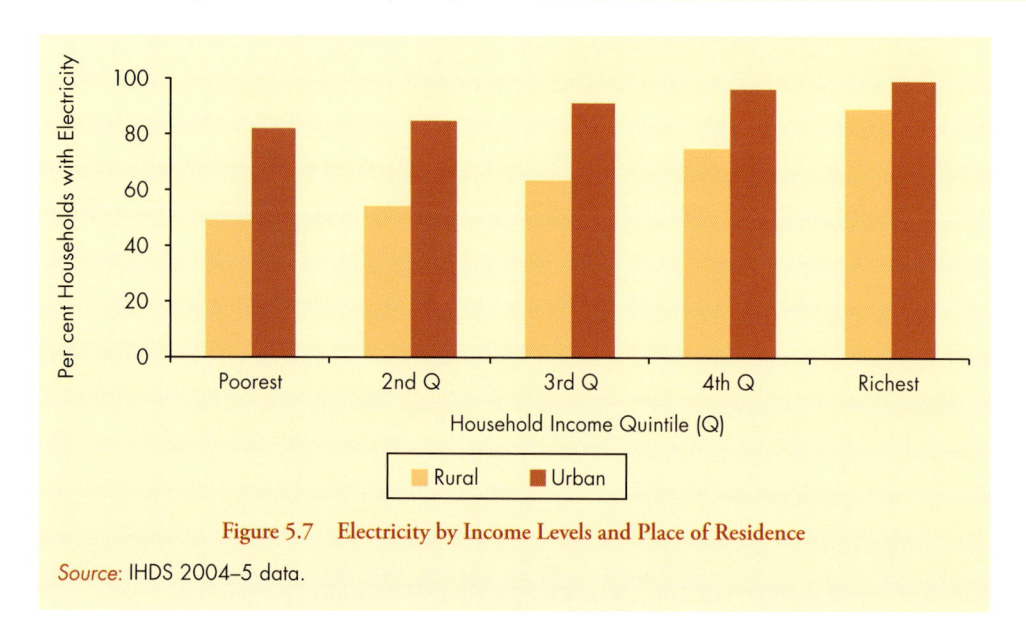

Figure 5.7 Electricity by Income Levels and Place of Residence
Source: IHDS 2004–5 data.

and electricity) that reflect a household's standard of living.[3] These items range from an electric air conditioner, owned by less than .01 per cent of Indian households, to the most commonly owned item, two sets of clothes (97 per cent, see Figure 5.8). Together, these 30 assets and amenities provide a simple measure of a household's standard of living.

Summing the number of items in each household produces an index from 0–30 that has a normal bell-shaped distribution with an average of 12.8 items per household. Ninety per cent of Indian households have at least four of these items; only 10 per cent have as many as twenty. Figure 5.9 demonstrates most clearly the difference in amenities available to urban as against rural households.

Although income differences between urban and rural households were documented in Chapter 2, when we compare their lifestyles, the divide between urban and rural India is far more clear.

Like income and consumption (discussed in Chapter 2), the asset index is a measure of a household's economic standing. A household in the lowest income quintile has, on an average, just six of these assets and amenities. A household in the highest quintile has close to eighteen. Differences among social groups, household educational levels, and states (see Tables A.5.1a and 5.1b) for the asset index are very similar to those for the income and consumption measures reported in Chapter 2. Because these assets are acquired over several years, the index reflects a household's medium- or long-term economic position, in contrast to the more volatile annual income or consumption measures. As a result, the relationships of other enduring household characteristics, such as educational level, caste, and religion, are even stronger for the asset index than for measures of annual income or consumption. But the shape of the relationships is similar. On an average, forward caste households, households with college graduates,

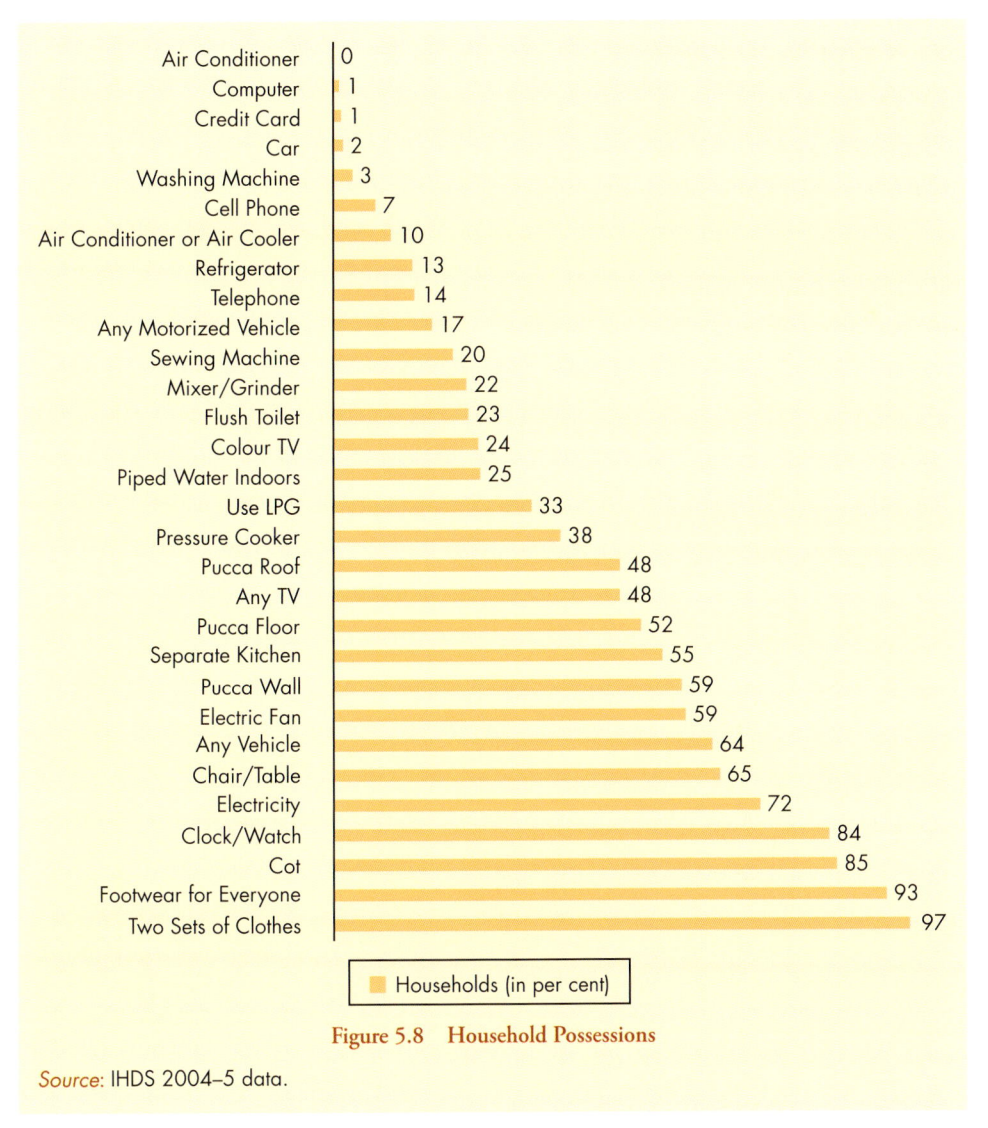

Item	Households (in per cent)
Air Conditioner	0
Computer	1
Credit Card	1
Car	2
Washing Machine	3
Cell Phone	7
Air Conditioner or Air Cooler	10
Refrigerator	13
Telephone	14
Any Motorized Vehicle	17
Sewing Machine	20
Mixer/Grinder	22
Flush Toilet	23
Colour TV	24
Piped Water Indoors	25
Use LPG	33
Pressure Cooker	38
Pucca Roof	48
Any TV	48
Pucca Floor	52
Separate Kitchen	55
Pucca Wall	59
Electric Fan	59
Any Vehicle	64
Chair/Table	65
Electricity	72
Clock/Watch	84
Cot	85
Footwear for Everyone	93
Two Sets of Clothes	97

Figure 5.8 Household Possessions

Source: IHDS 2004–5 data.

[3] In fact, the IHDS asked about several other items that were originally thought to reflect a household's standard of living (for example, a generator, the number of rooms in the house), but because they did not correlate well with other items, they were dropped from the index.

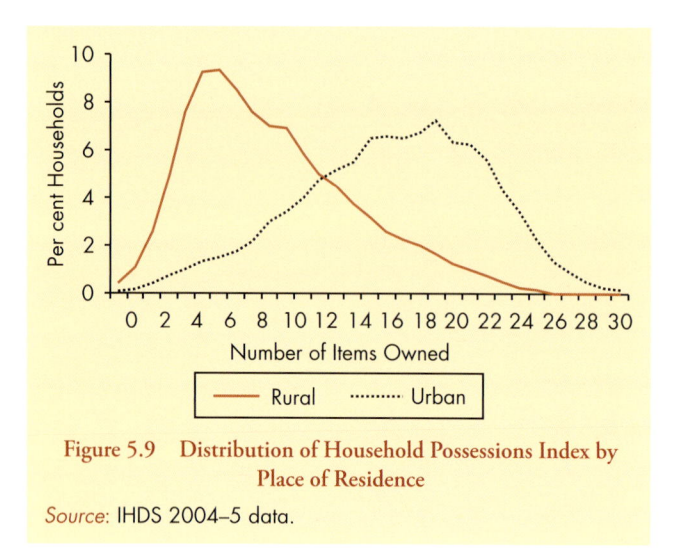

Figure 5.9 Distribution of Household Possessions Index by Place of Residence
Source: IHDS 2004–5 data.

and those living in affluent states such as Punjab or Kerala have more household assets and amenities, just as they earn higher incomes and spend more on consumption.

In Chapter 2, we remarked on the higher total incomes of households with a large number of adults. This advantage diminishes when we consider per capita income. However, large families are able to pool resources and acquire assets and amenities that are often not easy for a smaller household to acquire. For example, a four-person household spends the same amount of money acquiring a mixer or grinder that a six-person household does. These economies of scale are reflected in better access to assets and amenities in larger households, as shown in Figure 5.10.

CONCLUSION

To sum up, amenities such as access to electricity, a clean water supply, and the quality of cooking fuels are major factors in determining the quality of life for ordinary citizens. The availability of these services and the number of household assets vary considerably throughout the country. Household income is closely related to all of these services and assets, but local and statewise income levels are also important, especially for many of the public services. Wealthy households have better access to quality household fuels, reliable electricity, and tap water, in part because they more often live in wealthier states and communities.

While access to services has been expanding, with great strides made in some areas (for example, rural electrification) and slow progress in others (water supply and sanitation), quality and reliability emerge as paramount considerations in our analysis of water and electricity supply. It is not uncommon for household members to wake up in the middle of the night, during the hour in which the water supply is available, to fill water storage containers for use in the daytime. Nor is it uncommon for unexpected electricity outages to disrupt the rhythm of daily life.

DISCUSSION

Access to amenities can often affect lives in unanticipated ways. Ownership of a television provides an interesting example. Increasingly, the government tends to rely on television to communicate information about health, access to government programmes, and other relevant topics. As Box 5.3 documents, household ownership of a television gives exposure to current issues and excludes certain households from this informational network, a topic to which we return when discussing knowledge of HIV/AIDS spread in Chapter 7 on health. Similarly, electrification is associated with better education outcomes for children, a topic we will discuss in Chapter 6 on education.

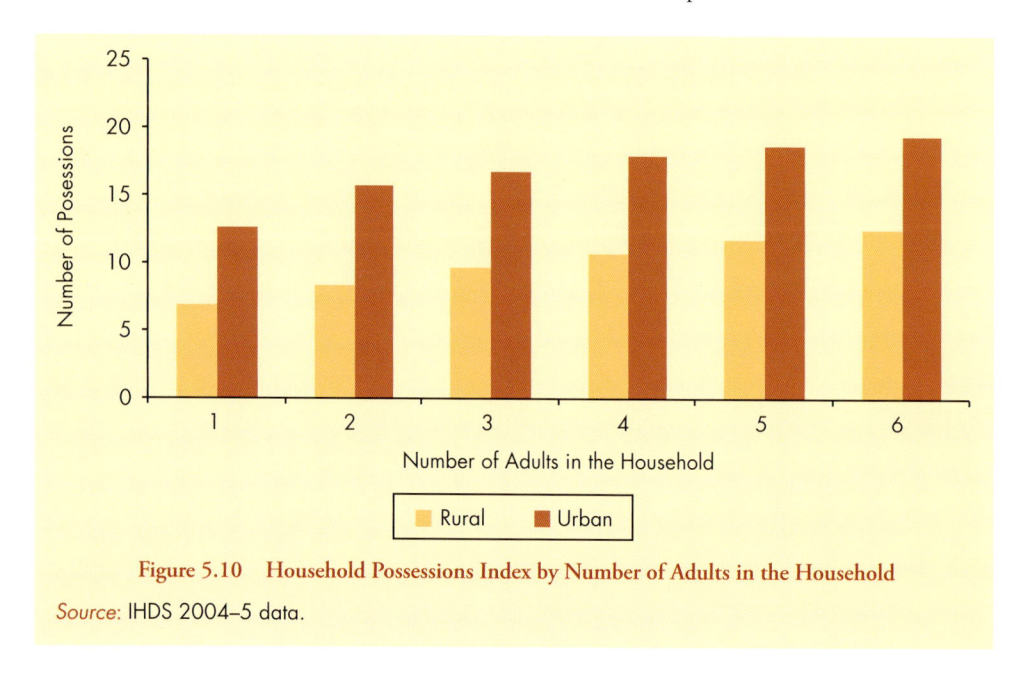

Figure 5.10 Household Possessions Index by Number of Adults in the Household
Source: IHDS 2004–5 data.

Box 5.3 Have Television, Will Watch

While it is not unusual to see Indian families watching television at a neighbour's home, owning a television makes a considerable difference in television-watching habits, particularly for women. Among the IHDS households, nearly 48 per cent own a television set. These households are far more likely to watch television and to watch it regularly than households that do not own a television set. This may limit the likelihood that informational messages, such as those about HIV/AIDS or polio vaccination, will reach their intended audience.

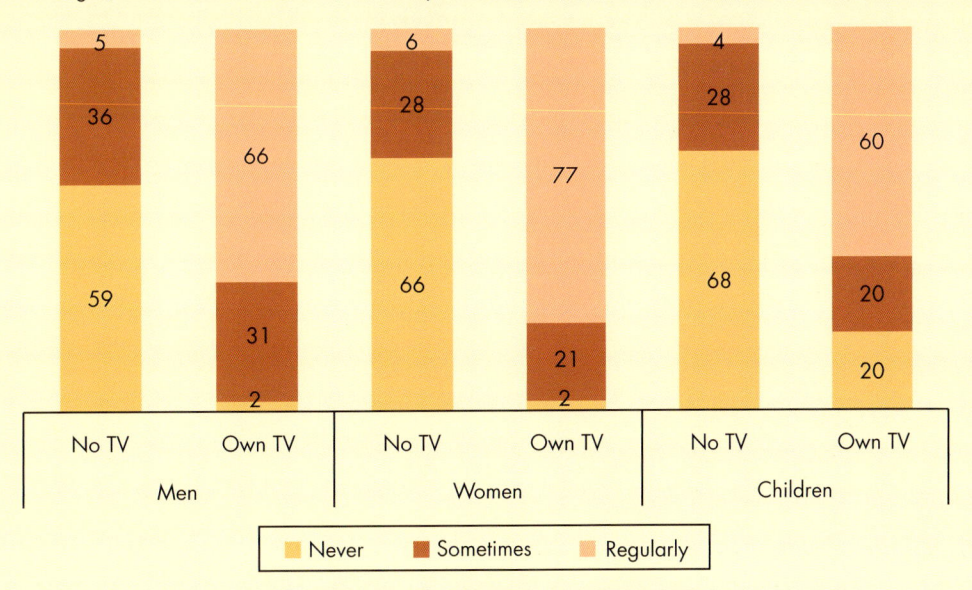

	No TV	Own TV
Men — Never / Sometimes / Regularly	59 / 36 / 5	2 / 31 / 66
Women — Never / Sometimes / Regularly	66 / 28 / 6	2 / 21 / 77
Children — Never / Sometimes / Regularly	68 / 28 / 4	20 / 20 / 60

Legend: Never, Sometimes, Regularly

TV Ownership and Frequency of TV Watching

Source: IHDS 2004–5 data.

HIGHLIGHTS

- 72 per cent of the surveyed households report having electricity. However, access to piped indoor water and a flush toilet is far more limited.
- The supply of water and electricity tends to be highly irregular: only 37 per cent of households with piped water report water availability of at least 3 hours per day, while only 57 per cent of households report that electricity is available at least 18 hours per day.
- Only 80 per cent households with electricity report getting a bill from the State Electricity Board. About 11 per cent get no bill at all.
- Access to all services: water, sanitation, and electricity differ sharply between urban and rural areas; even upper income households in villages do not have access to piped water and sanitation.
- Households' access to a variety of consumer durables and other amenities varies considerably across states.
- In spite of rapid economic growth in the 10 years preceding the survey, few households own expensive goods: 2 per cent own a car; 1 per cent a computer; 3 per cent a washing machine; and 1 per cent a credit card.

Table A.5.1a Household Access to Assets and Amenities

	Water Piped indoors (per cent)	Water At least 3 hours/day if piped (per cent)	Water Mins/day Spent Fetching	Flush/Toilet (per cent)	Fuel Any Bio-Fuel (per cent)	Fuel Min/Week Spent Collecting	Electricity Any Electricity (per cent)	Electricity At least 18 hrs/day if Any Electricity (per cent)	No. of Assets Owned
All India	25	37	53	23	77	186	72	57	11
Maximum Household Education									
None	10	29	76	6	95	275	49	41	7
1–4 Std	14	30	67	9	92	244	57	47	8
5–9 Std	21	35	58	18	83	198	72	57	10
10–11 Std	34	38	41	31	68	130	85	62	14
12 Std/Some college	37	39	35	36	64	122	88	60	15
Graduate/Diploma	50	46	19	54	41	68	94	67	18
Place of Residence									
Metro city	68	55	8	55	14	3	97	90	18
Other urban	50	40	27	46	43	33	94	69	16
Developed village	18	23	57	18	91	207	75	51	11
Less developed village	7	40	73	7	96	293	51	38	8
Household Income									
Lowest Quintile	11	24	69	8	95	243	52	45	7
2nd Quintile	13	28	68	10	93	271	59	49	8
3rd Quintile	20	32	58	19	82	194	72	55	10
4th Quintile	30	41	46	29	69	147	83	61	13
Highest Quintile	52	47	22	48	45	78	95	66	18
Social Groups									
Forward Caste Hindu	41	46	36	37	58	136	86	64	15
OBC	23	29	56	20	80	180	73	54	11
Dalit	17	33	67	14	87	229	63	55	9
Adivasi	12	31	74	7	89	375	53	47	7
Muslim	21	47	42	24	80	117	69	49	11
Other religion	37	52	15	59	63	39	95	74	18

Source: IHDS 2004–5 data.

Table A.5.1b Household Access to Assets and Amenities by State

	Water			Flush/Toilet	Fuel		Electricity		No. of Assets Owned
	Piped indoors (per cent)	At least 3 hours/day if piped (per cent)	Mins/day Spent Fetching	(per cent)	Any Bio-fuel (per cent)	Min/Week Spent Collecting	Any Electricity (per cent)	At least 18 hrs/day if Any Electricity (per cent)	
All India	25	37	53	23	77	186	72	57	11
Jammu and Kashmir	43	70	56	22	75	263	98	30	12
Himachal Pradesh	51	55	48	28	85	617	98	99	14
Uttarakhand	25	70	103	39	80	432	80	41	13
Punjab	35	89	7	43	67	49	97	26	18
Haryana	47	63	40	18	78	186	94	37	16
Delhi	70	82	6	64	10	6	99	84	19
Uttar Pradesh	8	80	53	13	88	186	45	10	10
Bihar	2	97	58	5	93	196	35	3	7
Jharkhand	9	63	65	13	76	245	61	50	9
Rajasthan	35	29	86	22	84	249	64	46	11
Chhattisgarh	13	48	41	7	88	576	68	72	8
Madhya Pradesh	18	22	92	24	86	322	76	18	9
North-East	37	54	21	20	77	112	87	54	12
Assam	8	60	8	2	81	78	70	18	10
West Bengal	15	83	20	23	79	108	53	83	10
Orissa	6	75	69	5	90	223	43	92	8
Gujarat	59	32	65	40	65	209	88	77	14
Maharashtra, Goa	48	23	40	18	60	143	87	78	13
Andhra Pradesh	27	17	82	21	77	168	89	50	12
Karnataka	37	16	87	20	77	187	91	33	11
Kerala	13	86	22	67	91	49	90	98	16
Tamil Nadu	23	22	32	38	63	92	90	94	13

Source: IHDS 2004–5 data.

Education and Health

6

Education

The chapters on income (Chapter 2) and employment (Chapter 4) clearly identified education[1] as an important determinant of the economic well-being of households. Apart from its monetary returns, as we will show in the subsequent chapters, education also appears to be linked to other dimensions of well-being, including health outcomes, investments in the next generation, social networks, and civic participation. Most importantly, ensuring equal access to education is increasingly viewed as a basic duty of a mature civil society. However, in spite of the universal agreement about the importance of education, public discourse often seems to be divorced from the realities on the ground. While this disjunction often becomes visible in demands from courts for more data when adjudicating cases regarding educational reservations, many other dimensions of the Indian educational landscape—such as the increasing privatization of education and inequalities in skills—have escaped attention, sometimes because of data limitations. This chapter seeks to fill some of these gaps and identify critical challenges facing Indian educational policy, using specially designed data collection modules from the IHDS.

This chapter highlights several themes. First, it documents the striking success of the Indian educational system in improving school entry. Among recent cohorts, 90 per cent of children enter school. This is a far cry from the 30 per cent of men and 60 per cent of women from cohorts aged 40–59 who never enrol. However, as we begin to move beyond simple access, the challenges of keeping children in school emerge as a paramount concern. The second theme in this chapter reflects a concern with educational quality. Inequality in educational quality and quantity, between different sections of society, is a third theme emerging from these analyses. Although gaps in literacy and school enrolment, between different social groups, have been declining over time, substantial gaps in educational attainment still remain between men and women, and between children from Dalit, Adivasi, Muslim communities, and other social groups. A fourth theme documents the growing privatization of education in India, as reflected in both private school enrolment and increases in private tuition. A fifth theme focuses on the readiness of the Indian labour force to meet increasing skill demands in a global world. At the lower end of the skill spectrum, these demands include basic literacy and at the higher end, they include English language and computing skills. As rewards to skilled jobs increase, it is important to identify who is ready to enter these jobs. This chapter documents the striking regional differences in English and computing skills across different parts of India, foreshadowing a growing regional cleavage.

DATA ON EDUCATION, EDUCATIONAL EXPENDITURES, AND SKILLS

Education forms an important marker of human development and is included in the widely used human development indices, such as those developed by the UNDP. These indices focus on enrolment at the primary, secondary, and tertiary

---

[1] The terms education and schooling are used differently by different disciplines. Human development literature tends to use the term schooling to distinguish between formal school-based education and individual growth and development. In contrast, in some educational literature the term schooling is used somewhat pejoratively, to reflect the hierarchical nature of schools and physical punishment. Hence, we use the simple term education.

levels. Although these are useful and handy markers of access to education, they do not capture the processes through which the observed patterns emerge, nor do they provide any guidance on the quality of education. Unfortunately, a deeper understanding of social forces shaping educational opportunities and outcomes is limited by the lack of empirical data. Surveys can document attendance or the completion of educational certification relatively easily, but they are singularly ill-equipped to assess quality or processes. These limitations are not easily overcome, a shortcoming the data presented in this chapter shares with other studies. However, the IHDS makes a modest beginning in addressing these shortcomings in two ways. First, it assesses the quality of education by measuring reading, writing, and arithmetic skills of children aged between 8–11 years. Second, it provides a description of day to day educational experiences from a household perspective by focusing on key markers such as educational expenditure, type of school attended, and hours spent in the classroom, doing homework, and in private tuition.

The IHDS collected basic information on educational attainment for all household members through questions about ever attending school, the ability to read and write a sentence, repeating or failing a class, standards completed, and fluency in English. For those household members who were enrolled in school or college at the time of the survey, further questions were asked about the type of school, the medium of instruction, hours spent in school, homework, and private tuition, as well as a variety of questions about school expenditure.

Most importantly, the IHDS incorporates the direct measurement of reading, writing, and arithmetic skills of children aged 8–11 years. The ultimate test of any educational system must lie in how well it manages to impart education to all students regardless of their background. However, evaluating the success of this mission is far more complicated than one imagines. First, the children's knowledge must be directly tested in a way that reduces test anxiety and measures basic skills. Second, tests must not rely on schools as sites for testing because it is likely to miss children who are not enrolled or who are absent from school—precisely those children who are likely to be at the lower end of the spectrum. Third, it is important to focus on skills such as reading that cannot easily be tested through a written examination. Although several institutions, such as the National Council of Education Research and Training (NCERT), have developed skills tests, these tests do not meet the criteria just highlighted. The IHDS survey development team was concerned about using tests that can be administered relatively easily and with low anxiety levels on the part of children. In order to do this, the IHDS worked with PRATHAM[2] to modify some of the tests they have used in their work over the years. These same tests are also used in PRATHAM's large survey, the *Annual Status of Education Report (ASER), 2005*.[3] These tests are simple and intuitive and were translated in 13 languages. In many ways, the IHDS results presented below compliment the data presented in the *ASER, 2005* through 2008. The ASER results are based on a larger sample of children but do not contain detailed information about their home conditions, particularly their social background and parental characteristics. The data from the IHDS survey contains a smaller sample but has information on a rich array of home and background characteristics.[4]

LITERACY LEVELS AND TRENDS

The past few decades have seen a rapid transformation of the Indian educational landscape. Figures 6.1a and 6.1b provide striking evidence.

As we compare different age cohorts, it is clear that literacy rates have risen sharply for all segments of Indian society. As of 2005, 79 per cent of males and 58 per cent of females aged seven and older could read and write a sentence.[5]

Tables A.6.1a and A.6.1b describe literacy levels in the sample of individuals aged seven and older. While presenting a familiar picture of inequalities based on sex and social class, these tables contain many surprises. They particularly highlight sharp improvements in literacy. While only 54 per cent of men and 19 per cent of women aged 60 and older are literate, among children aged 10–14 years, literacy rates are 92 per cent for males and 88 per cent for females. Even among children as young as seven to nine, 82 per cent of boys and 78 per cent of girls are literate. This improvement in literacy has also reduced the male–female gap, with girls

---

[2] PRATHAM is a non-governmental organization devoted to improving literacy.

[3] We thank Dr Rukmini Banerjee from PRATHAM and her colleagues for their collaboration and advice throughout the test development and interviewer training.

[4] These tests were administered to 12,274 children aged 8–11 from a total sample of children 17,069 in the target households. This is a rate of 72 per cent. The children who interviewers were unable to interview, were missed for various reasons, such as: they were away on vacation, they were unwilling to be interviewed, or they could not be found. Although the interviewers were asked to make as many trips as needed to contact all eligible children, logistical demands often prevented many repeat visits. This is not a totally random sample. More children from poor and disadvantaged groups were omitted than those from better off families. Thus, the reported differences in student achievement are likely to be somewhat smaller than actual differences.

[5] The IHDS literacy rate of 68 per cent for those aged seven and older is comparable to the 69 per cent observed in the *NFHS-III* and the 67 per cent in the NSS, which were fielded at about the same time as the IHDS. All are higher than the 64 per cent found in the 2001 Census, reflecting improvements in the intervening four years (NSSO 2005a and IIPS 2007).

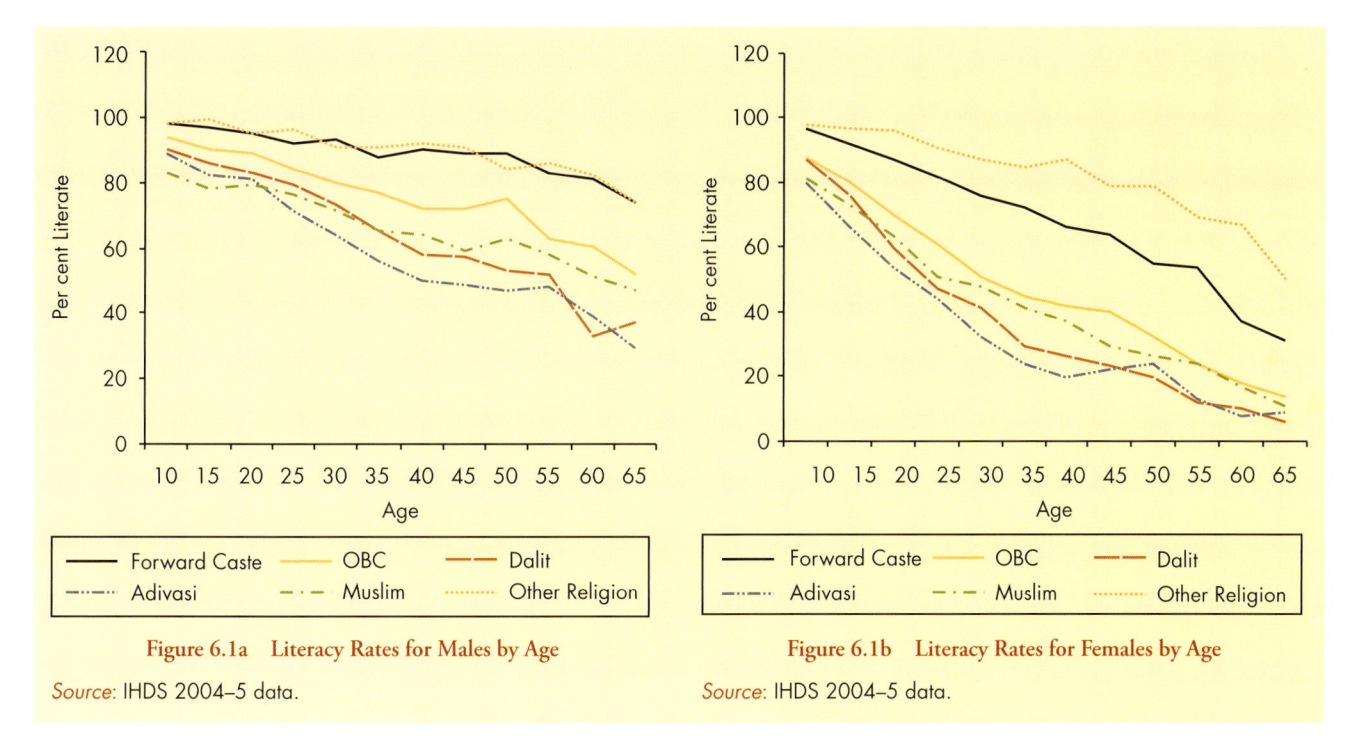

Figure 6.1a Literacy Rates for Males by Age
Source: IHDS 2004–5 data.

Figure 6.1b Literacy Rates for Females by Age
Source: IHDS 2004–5 data.

rapidly catching up with boys in recent years. This table also highlights the differences in education between different social classes and groups and shows higher levels of literacy for individuals in large metropolitan areas,[6] those in upper income groups, and forward castes, as well as Christians, Jains, and other religious minorities.

Figures 6.1a and 6.1b show the trends in literacy for males and females of different social groups by age. As one looks across different cohorts, two trends are noticeable. First, literacy rates for all social groups have steadily improved across successive age cohorts, although in each generation differences between social groups persist. In each cohort, forward castes and Christians, Jains, and other religious minorities have the highest literacy rates, followed by OBCs. Dalits, Adivasis, and Muslims have the lowest literacy rates. These differences hold true for both males and females. In fact, differences among females by social groups are even greater than those among males. Second, Table A.6.1b documents statewise differences in literacy. Literacy rates are the highest in Kerala, followed by Delhi, the North-East, and Himachal Pradesh. Some of the lowest levels are recorded in Jammu and Kashmir, Bihar, Rajasthan, and Andhra Pradesh. It is important to note that this data on literacy comes from a question about whether the individual can read and write a sentence. In the following sections we examine these educational inequalities in greater detail.

EDUCATIONAL PROGRESSION AND DROPOUT

Recent public discourse has been overwhelmed with concerns about the educational backwardness of specific communities such as Dalits, Adivasis, OBCs, and Muslims. Even after 60 years of independence and a variety of policy initiatives, the differences in educational attainment persist. However, most of the policies continue to focus on reservations in higher education without paying attention to the educational stage at which these inequalities emerge. A stagewise examination of dropouts offers an interesting insight.

Table A.6.2a shows the stages at which different individuals drop out. In calculating these discontinuation rates, at each stage, we focus only on individuals who have progressed up to that level. Among males, 20 per cent do not even enrol. Of those enrolling, 15 per cent discontinue before completing Standard 5; of those completing Standard 5, 50 per cent drop out before completing Standard 10; of those completing Standard 10, 43 per cent drop out before completing Standard 12; of those completing class 12, 44 per cent do not get a college degree or diploma. The picture for women is broadly similar with one exception. Women also face a greater hurdle in initial enrolment—40 per cent never enrol. This overall picture combines the experience of several cohorts, and can be seen in the subsequent rows in Table A.6.2a, the proportion of individuals who never enrol drops significantly across different age cohorts. Among men aged 60 and older, 46 per cent never enrol;

---

[6] Urban agglomerations include New Delhi, Mumbai, Kolkata, Bangalore, Chennai, and Hyderabad.

among those aged 10–14, only 6 per cent never enrol. For recent cohorts, it seems clear that non-enrolment is relatively low for men, and only a little higher for women.

The greatest educational hurdle appears to be between Standards 5 and 10. At an all India level, for individuals completing Standard 5, 50 per cent of males and 57 per cent of females do not complete Standard 10. Over half of these, that is, 34 out of 100 men and 29 out of 100 women stop their education between Standards 5 and 10. Hence, a focus on this level offers the greatest potential for improvement in the education level of the population.

At each educational level, the discontinuation rate among females is higher than that for males, although we see heartening evidence of a declining gender gap when we compare younger cohorts. The gender difference in enrolment is 19 percentage points at ages 20–9 but only 4 percentage points at ages 10–14. The discontinuation rates for Dalits, Adivasis, and Muslims are considerably higher than that for forward castes, with OBCs falling in between. High discontinuation rates for Dalits and Adivasis deserve particular attention in the context of reservation politics. In spite of the widespread feeling that Dalits and Adivasis take away seats from more deserving, forward caste students, the results presented in Table A.6.2a show that while 39 per cent of forward caste males who have completed Standard 12 drop out without getting a degree or a diploma, at least 53 per cent of Dalits and Adivasis do so. These results suggest that at the aggregate level, there is little evidence of a disadvantage to forward caste students as a result of reservation, although it is possible that finer attention to highly competitive colleges like the Indian Institutes of Technology or medical schools may reveal a different pattern.

This table also indicates the importance of understanding the underlying nature of educational inequalities if we want to redress social inequalities. Reservations—arguably one of the most contentious issues facing Indian civil society today—address only a minor portion of inequality. Most of the educational inequalities based on social background seem to take place in entering and completing primary school. Whereas, only 8 per cent of upper caste males do not enter school, about 26 per cent to 31per cent of Muslim, Dalit, and Adivasi males do not enrol. For women, these differences are even greater.

A deeper examination of the social inequalities in dropout rates indicates that in addition to social group, income, and urban residence are associated with school dropout rates. Causal directions are not easy to establish in a study of this type. Low income may be a cause as well as a consequence of dropping out. But the associations seem fairly clear.

Table A.6.2b records statewise differences in dropout rates at various educational stages. Many familiar regional differences again emerge, but much of the regional variation is clustered at the lower end of the educational spectrum. A great deal of the difference between low-performing Bihar and high-performing Himachal Pradesh would be eliminated if children in Bihar entered and finished primary school at the same rate as those in Himachal Pradesh. This suggests that regional inequalities will narrow considerably if we can address inequalities in primary education.

CRITICAL YEARS: SCHOOLING AT AGES SIX TO FOURTEEN

Given the importance of early schooling as discussed above, it is important to focus on the correlates of early school enrolment and achievement. This focus is particularly important at this time in Indian history because school enrolment has increased rapidly in the past decade, and new programmes such as Sarva Shiksha Abhiyan have made primary education a priority. In this section, we examine school enrolment of children aged 6–14. The results presented below reflect the recent situation in India, as compared to the statistics presented above, which reflect the cumulative experience of many cohorts.

The first column of Table A.6.3a shows the proportion of children who never enrolled in school, the second shows the proportion who enrolled but dropped out, and the third column shows the proportion who are currently in school. The all India figure shows that only 10 per cent of children fall in the never-enrolled category, about 5 per cent enrolled but dropped out, and 85 per cent were in school at the time of the interview.[7]

Social group differences in enrolment are striking. Dalit, Adivasi, and Muslim children are far less likely to enrol in school and are slightly more likely to drop out than others. Consequently, while 94 per cent of children from the forward caste and 96 per cent of other religious groups were enrolled at the time of the interview, the figures were 83 per cent for Dalit children, 77 per cent for Adivasi children, and 76 per cent for Muslim children. This disadvantage is a function of both lower initial enrolment and higher dropout rates. Other social advantages, such has having educated adults living in the household, having a higher income, and living in metropolitan areas, also translate into higher current enrolment.

Regional differences in school enrolment shown in Table A.6.3b are vast. Although they are comparable to those presented in Table A.6.2b, they reflect a recent situation and, hence, are more relevant to the policy discourse. More than

---

[7] The IHDS data show a lower percentage of children as being currently enrolled than did a survey conducted around the same time by PRATHAM, which showed that about 94 per cent of children were in school. The IHDS figures are closer to the gross enrolment ratio of 83 recorded by the Seventh Educational Survey of the NCERT.

95 per cent children aged 6–14 are in school in Himachal Pradesh, Kerala, and Tamil Nadu; only 70 per cent are enrolled in Bihar. Even when compared with relatively disadvantaged states such as Uttar Pradesh, Chhattisgarh, and Madhya Pradesh, Bihar is particularly striking in its low enrolment levels.[8] A sex-disaggregated examination suggests that while both boys and girls in Bihar are less likely to be in school, girls in Bihar are particularly disadvantaged. For example, enrolment rates among boys and girls in Madhya Pradesh are 85 per cent and 80 per cent, respectively, while rates for boys and girls in Bihar are 76 per cent and 63 per cent, respectively.

The IHDS also asked about absences from school in the month before the survey. While a day or two of absence is unlikely to have a significant effect on education, an absence of six or more days in the preceding month could be quite detrimental. The results in the fourth column of Table A.6.3a show that at an all India level, about 20 per cent of children experienced this lengthy absence. Children in villages with low infrastructure and poorer children are more likely to be absent.[9]

The IHDS survey is unusual in collecting data on whether students have ever failed or repeated a class. The IHDS data show that about 5 per cent of students in Standards 1–5 ever failed or had to repeat a class, compared to 9 per cent in Standards 6–10. While Adivasi students are somewhat more likely to fail or be held back than others (9 per cent verses 5–8 percent for all other groups), social class differences in repeating or failing a class are far smaller than state-level differences (see Table A.6.3b). Ironically, these differences do not correspond to state-level enrolment differences (noted above) and learning differences (noted in a subsequent section). Himachal Pradesh has the largest proportion of students reported being held back: 19 per cent of 6–14 year olds. At the same time, this is the state with one of the greatest enrolment rates and higher levels of educational quality compared with other states. Other states with high reported rates of being held back are Uttarakhand, the northeastern states, and Gujarat. In contrast, Uttar Pradesh, Bihar, and Rajasthan—states with a relatively poor record, otherwise—have some of the lowest rates of failure or repeating a grade.

EDUCATIONAL QUALITY

With rapidly rising school enrolment, attention must turn to educational quality. This section reports the results from skill tests described above. The goal of these tests was to measure students' performance on the three R's: reading, writing, and arithmetic. This section focuses on children aged 8–11 because all of these children should have acquired the basic reading, writing, and arithmetic skills. The reading skills are divided into five categories: cannot read at all, can read letters, can read words, can read a short paragraph, and can read a short story. The results presented in Figure 6.2a show that 11 per cent of the children surveyed cannot recognize letters, 14 per cent recognize letters but cannot read words, 21 per cent can read words but not connect them into sentences, 22 per cent can read simple two-to-three sentence paragraphs but not a one-page story, and 33 per cent can read a one-page story. Because 95 per cent of the children tested completed at least Standard 1 and 65 per cent completed Standard 2, they are generally expected to be able read at least a simple paragraph with three sentences. This is what is defined as reading ability in the subsequent discussion.

The arithmetic skills are divided into four categories: no recognition of written numbers, can read numbers, can subtract a two-digit number from another two-digit number, and can divide a three-digit number with a one-digit number. The results presented in Figure 6.2b show that among the IHDS sample of 8–11 year old children, 19 per cent cannot identify numbers between 10 and 99, 33 per cent can identify numbers only, a further 26 per cent can subtract two-digit numbers with borrowing but cannot divide numbers, and 22 per cent can divide as well as subtract. Again, two-digit subtraction is considered to be a basic numerical skill that 8–11 year olds should have. Thus, in all subsequent discussion, we focus on this skill as the basic arithmetic skill.

In terms of writing, 8–11 year olds are expected to be able to write a simple sentence—such as, 'My mother's name is Madhuben'—with two or fewer mistakes. About 67 per cent of the kids were able to do this.

Table A.6.4a shows differences in these achievement levels for children from different backgrounds. The impact of family background on children's skills acquisition is far greater than that noted above on school enrolment. Only 45 per cent of children from the lowest income quintile families are able to read a short paragraph, while 73 per cent of children from the highest quintile are able to do so. Among higher caste Hindus and other religious groups, more than 70 per cent of children are able to read a short paragraph. This figure is only 44–46 per cent for Dalit, Adivasi, and Muslim children. Urban–rural differences

---

[8] ASER 2005, conducted by PRATHAM at around the same time as the IHDS, also found that among major states, Bihar has the lowest enrolment rates (PRATHAM 2005).

[9] It is important to use caution in interpreting the data on absences. The survey was conducted over nearly one year. Although the question asked about absences in the month preceding survey or, if survey was conducted in a month with holidays, in the last regular school month, some of the state-level variations could be due to differences in survey timing.

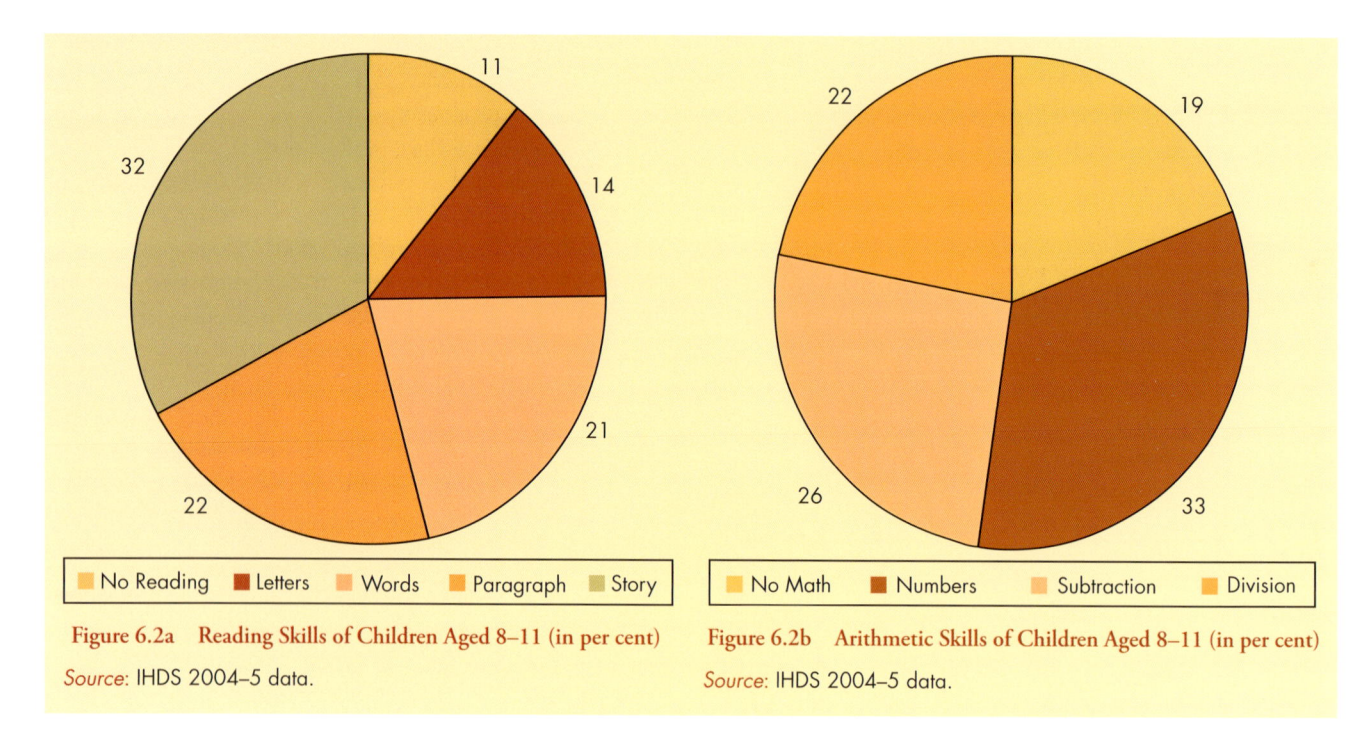

Figure 6.2a Reading Skills of Children Aged 8–11 (in per cent)
Source: IHDS 2004–5 data.

Legend: No Reading, Letters, Words, Paragraph, Story
Values: 11, 14, 21, 22, 32

Figure 6.2b Arithmetic Skills of Children Aged 8–11 (in per cent)
Source: IHDS 2004–5 data.

Legend: No Math, Numbers, Subtraction, Division
Values: 19, 33, 26, 22

are pretty large, as are those between households in which adults have had some education and those in which all adults lack literacy. Table A.6.4b documents the differences in these skills across states. These differences are also vast. More than 80 per cent of children in Himachal Pradesh and Kerala can read a short paragraph, while only 39, 40, and 44 per cent can do so in Uttar Pradesh, Jammu and Kashmir, and Bihar, respectively.

Like the ASER surveys conducted by PRATHAM, the IHDS survey found that students' achievement on arithmetic tests is lower than their achievement in reading tests. Social class differences in arithmetic skills seem to be somewhat larger than those in reading skills. In an era of increasing technical sophistication, this is a worrisome observation. Regional diversity in arithmetic skill acquisition is also striking. While Kerala leads the nation in reading and writing skills, it lags behind many states, including Himachal Pradesh, Punjab, Delhi, and the North-East, in mathematical skills.

COSTS OF EDUCATION

Educational costs in India involve a variety of expenditures, with school fees forming only a small part of those expenditures. Transportation, uniforms, and books are other major components. Moreover, with the growing importance of private tutoring, private coaching expenditures can also be substantial for students obtaining coaching.

Figure 6.3 shows the distribution of different educational expenditures by standard attended.

The annual total expenditure per child aged 6–14 ranges from Rs 933 for a child in Standard 1 to Rs 2,983 for child in Standard 10. The higher expenses for a child in kindergarten reflect the high likelihood of kindergarten enrolment in private nurseries. Not surprisingly, while the cost of fees climbs slowly at higher standards, the costs for other educational components climb sharply. These all India figures mask the high costs of private tuition because they average across all students, whether they pay tuition, or not. The cost of private tutoring ranges from Rs 630 per year in Standard 1 to nearly Rs 1,500 in Standard 10. These educational costs of Rs 933–2,983— per year, per child—should be seen in the context of the annual income of Indian families, with median income being Rs 27,857 per year (Chapter 2).

While the gender gap in school enrolment is fast closing, educational expenditures on girls are consistently lower than those for boys. As Figure 6.4 shows, these differences are approximately 10–12 per cent at most educational levels.

These differences come both from a slightly lower likelihood of girls' enrolment in private schools and private tutoring, and from policies in some states that offer education to girls at lower or no fees.

Not surprisingly, educational expenditures are higher in urban areas and among better off and more educated families. Attention to these social class differences in educational expenditures is important as we try to understand inequalities in children's educational outcomes based on parental social class. As Figure 6.5 documents, families in the top income quintiles spend about eight times the amount spent by the lowest income quintile on school fees, largely because they send children to private schools and spend five times as much on private tutoring.

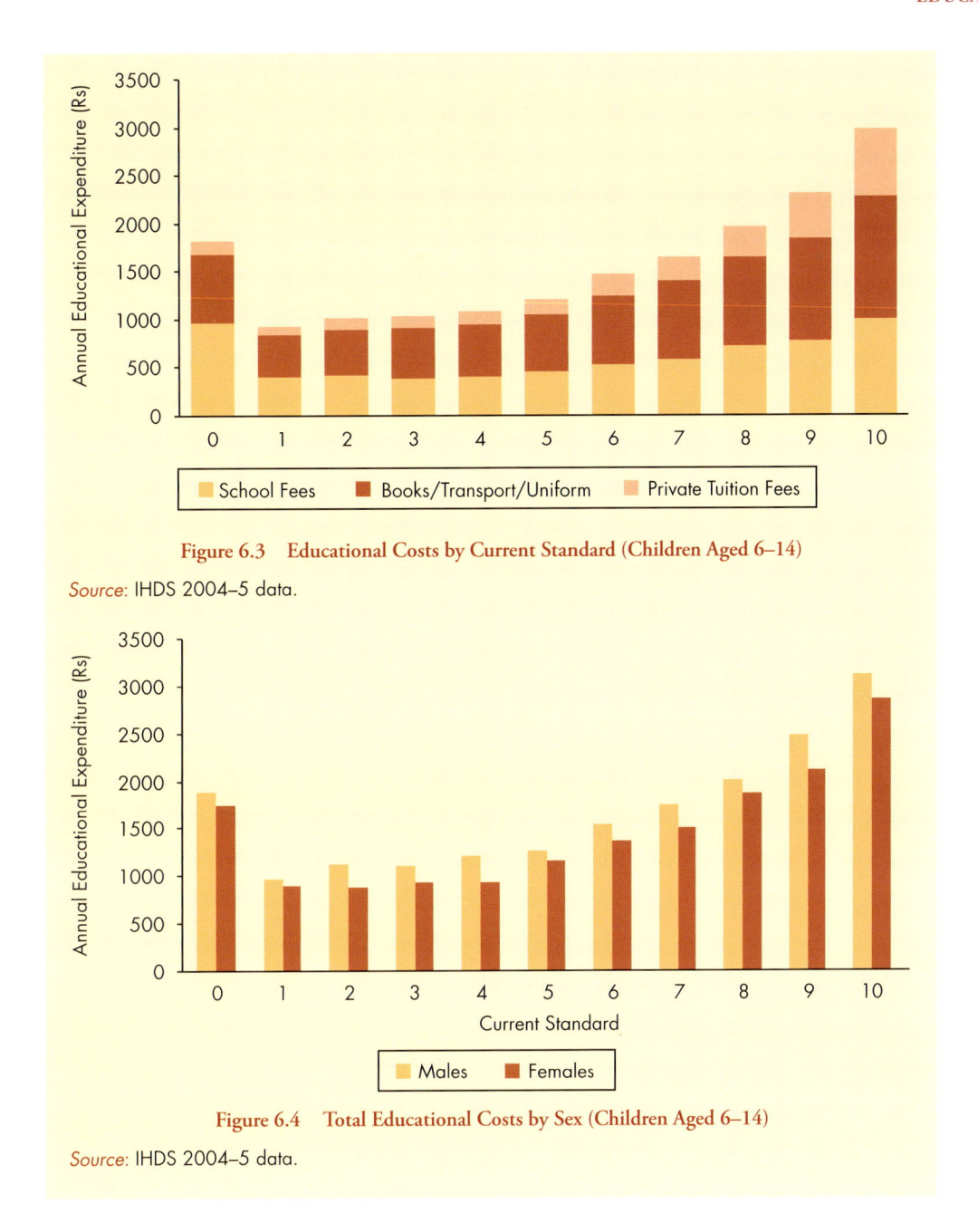

Figure 6.3 Educational Costs by Current Standard (Children Aged 6–14)
Source: IHDS 2004–5 data.

Figure 6.4 Total Educational Costs by Sex (Children Aged 6–14)
Source: IHDS 2004–5 data.

Many upper-income families are located in urban areas and have highly educated adults in the family. All of these factors combine to privilege children from upper-income households and these inequalities are reflected in the children's educational outcomes: 73 per cent of children from the top income quintile are able to read simple paragraphs as compared to 45 per cent from the bottom quintile.

GROWING ROLE OF THE PRIVATE SECTOR
The discussion of educational costs and outcomes points to the importance of the type of schooling children receive. The Indian educational sector is characterized by a complex interplay between private and public inputs. Historically, the government has played a dominant role in the provision of educational services, via the operation of government schools, largely managed by state governments and local bodies, as well as through privately managed but publicly funded schools called government-aided schools. These aided schools are operated by charitable trusts, voluntary organizations, and religious bodies but receive substantial funding from the government. Table 6.1 documents the distribution of the type of school attended by enrolled children, aged 6–14, in the IHDS. The results indicate that about 67 per cent of students attend government schools, about 5 per cent attend government-aided schools, and 24 per cent attend private schools. Convents and Madrasas account for

Figure 6.5 Per Child Educational Expenditure by Household Income Quintiles (Children Aged 6–14)

Source: IHDS 2004–5 data.

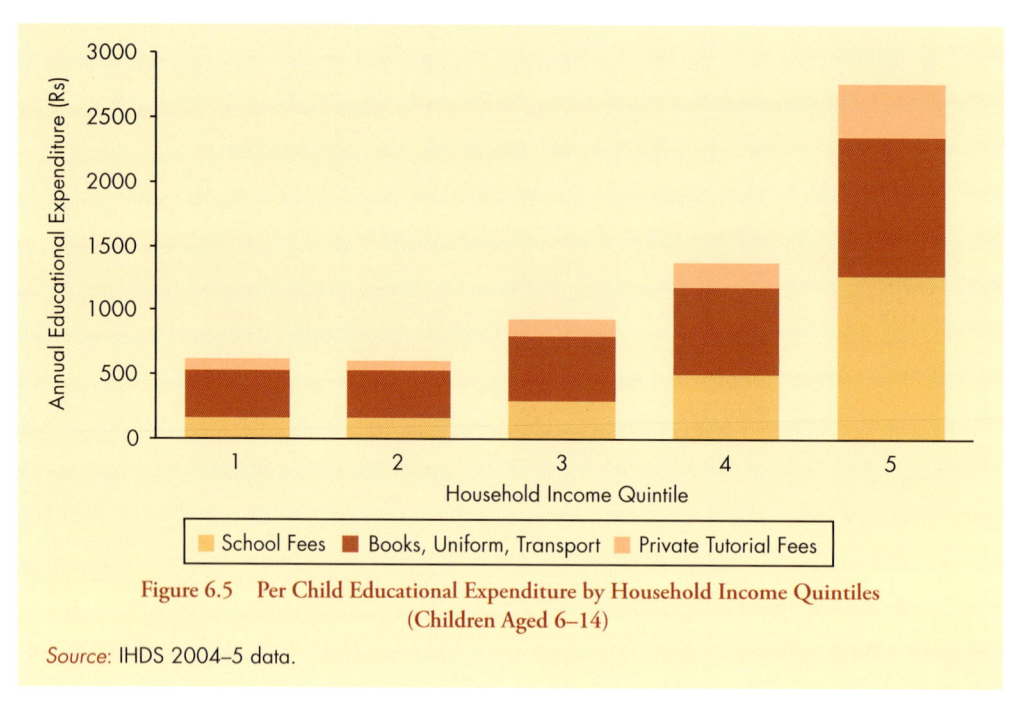

about 1–2 per cent. Note that the school categorization was obtained from households and in some cases parents may not be fully aware of the formal categorization of schools, particularly regarding whether the school is government-aided. Aided schools are schools that receive grant-in-aid from the government but are privately run and managed. In the early years, these schools were closer to private schools, but increasingly they have been brought under governmental oversight.

Arguably one of the most striking things about the educational panorama over the past decade is the explosion of the private sector in the educational field. The Fifth All India Education Survey documented a bare 2 per cent attendance in private primary schools in 1986. By 1994, the Human Development Survey documented that 10 per cent of rural children aged 6–14 were enrolled in private schools, and in 2005, the IHDS found that 21 per cent of rural and 51 per cent of urban children were enrolled in private schools. Some of this increase in private school enrolment has come about through a decline in enrolment in government-aided schools. In 1994, nearly 22 per cent of rural children were enrolled in government-aided schools. By 2005, this declined to a bare 7 per cent in rural areas and 5 per cent in urban areas. In the data presented here, government-aided schools are combined with government schools and Madrasas, and convents are included with private schools. As Table 6.1 indicates, at an all India level, 72 per cent of children are enrolled in government schools, and about 28 per cent are in private schools.

Table 6.1 Enrolment by School Type for Children Aged 6–14

	Per cent	Per cent
Public	72	
Government		67
Government Aided		5
Education Guarantee Scheme		1
Private	28	
Privately Managed		24
Convent		2
Madrasa		1
Technical/other		1

Source: IHDS 2004–5 data.

Private school enrolment, reported in Table A.6.3a, reflects well-known socioeconomic inequalities, with high income families more likely to send their children to private schools than low income families. But it also reflects hope on the part of the poor. Even among the lowest income quintile, 15 per cent of children attend private schools. Privatization of education extends beyond enrolment in private school. Dissatisfaction with formal schooling has led many parents to enrol their children in private tutoring, sometimes with teachers whose job it is to teach these children in regular schools. Twenty percent of enrolled children received some form of private tutoring in the year before the interview.[10] Thus, in the IHDS sample of

---

[10] Private tutoring is defined as spending any money for private tuition in the year before the interview, or spending at least one hour per week in private tuition in the month before the interview.

6–14 year old, about 40 per cent participated in private sector education either through enrolment in private school (20 per cent), through private tuition (13 per cent), or both (7 per cent).

Growth of private tuitions also increases the work burden on children, as documented by Box 6.1. Children who receive additional tutoring continue to spend the same or greater amount of time at school, and doing homework resulting in an additional eight to ten hours of work per week.

In general, boys are more likely (than girls) to be enrolled in private school (29 per cent versus 26 per cent) and to have private tuition (22 per cent versus 19 per cent), resulting in the gender difference in educational expenditure noted in Figure 6.4. But gender differences are smaller than social class differences in access to private schooling.

Additionally, regional differences in the prevalence of private school enrolment are noteworthy (see Table 6.3b).

The greatest prevalence of private school enrolment is in Punjab and Haryana. But lest we attribute this to state-level wealth, even in a poor state like Uttar Pradesh about 43 per cent attend private school. Assam and Orissa seem to have the lowest private school enrolment. The variation in school expenditures across different states presented in Table 6.2 is also noteworthy. While expenditure variation for children going to government schools is relatively minor (with higher expenditures, for example, in Jammu and Kashmir, Himachal Pradesh, and the North-East, where transportation costs are high), the variation in expenditures for children going to private schools is quite large, ranging from Rs 6,273 in Himachal Pradesh to Rs 1,636 in Assam.

This growing preference for private schooling and the reliance on private tutoring must be seen in the context of differences in skill acquisition of children in government and private schools. As Table A.6.4a indicates, there is a substantial difference in the skills of children who attend government schools compared to those who attend private schools. Among private school children, 69 per cent can read a simple paragraph, while only 50 per cent of those in government schools can do so. Similar differences exist in arithmetic and writing skills. Private school benefits persist in all categories of households but are greater for children from less-advantaged backgrounds. Children from less developed villages, the poorest households, and those in which parents have had the least education seem to benefit the most from attending private schools. Some of the differences between government and private schools may be attributable to the higher incomes and motivations of parents who send their children to private schools. However, even when we compare children with similar backgrounds, in terms of parental education and income, children from private schools perform somewhat better on reading and arithmetic tests than their government school counterparts. A variety of explanations

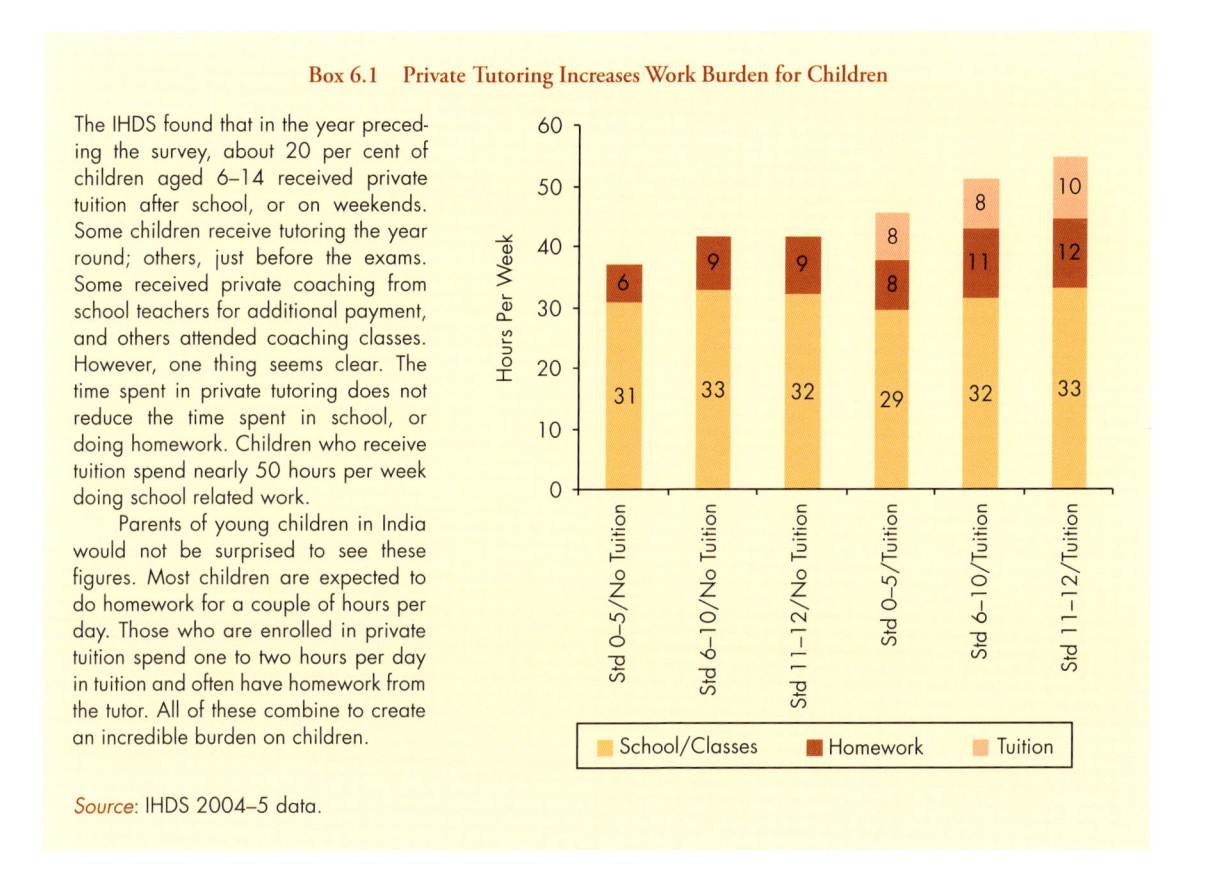

Box 6.1 Private Tutoring Increases Work Burden for Children

The IHDS found that in the year preceding the survey, about 20 per cent of children aged 6–14 received private tuition after school, or on weekends. Some children receive tutoring the year round; others, just before the exams. Some received private coaching from school teachers for additional payment, and others attended coaching classes. However, one thing seems clear. The time spent in private tutoring does not reduce the time spent in school, or doing homework. Children who receive tuition spend nearly 50 hours per week doing school related work.

Parents of young children in India would not be surprised to see these figures. Most children are expected to do homework for a couple of hours per day. Those who are enrolled in private tuition spend one to two hours per day in tuition and often have homework from the tutor. All of these combine to create an incredible burden on children.

Source: IHDS 2004–5 data.

Table 6.2   Private Schooling Costs for Children Aged 6–14 by State

	Private School Enrolment (%)	Annual Total Expenses Government	Annual Total Expenses Private
All India	28	688	2,920
Jammu and Kashmir	47	1,045	3,719
Himachal Pradesh	19	1,709	6,273
Uttarakhand	27	972	3,422
Punjab	52	1,444	5,160
Haryana	47	1,043	4,372
Delhi	28	1,044	5,390
Uttar Pradesh	43	427	1,733
Bihar	18	704	2,466
Jharkhand	32	502	2,932
Rajasthan	32	676	2,612
Chhattisgarh	15	317	2,039
Madhya Pradesh	27	333	1,935
North-East	34	1,441	4,237
Assam	6	371	1,636
West Bengal	10	1,136	5,045
Orissa	8	612	2,851
Gujarat	22	766	4,221
Maharashtra, Goa	20	599	2,370
Andhra Pradesh	31	574	3,260
Karnataka	28	638	3,848
Kerala	31	1,537	3,259
Tamil Nadu	23	606	3,811

Source: IHDS 2004–5 data.

above clearly show that children in private schools perform better than children in government schools. At the same time, parents who send their children to private schools have greater resources, both in terms of monetary resources and their own education. Hence, their departure from government school reduces the most vocal and active parents who are capable of demanding accountability from schools and able to compensate for teacher deficiencies through home teaching. The departure of these children from government schools may well diminish the pressure on government schools to be accountable and reduce the quality of the classroom learning environment. Thus, once the middle-class exodus from government schools begins, schools could easily get caught for this phenomenon have been offered in the literature. Some studies suggest that teacher absenteeism in government schools is to blame. Others suggest that teacher indifference and corporeal punishment in government schools may be implicated.[11] Box 6.2 indicates some of the differences in the characteristics and facilities of the private and government schools surveyed by the IHDS.

The differences between government and private schools in skill acquisition point to a core dilemma facing Indian educational policy. Parents choose to send their children to private schools, often at a considerable financial sacrifice, with expectations that private schools will impart a better education than government schools. The results presented

Box 6.2   Characteristics of Government and Private Elementary Schools

(in percentage)

	Government Schools	Private Schools
Teachers present in school at the time of the visit	87.6	89.4
Teachers have training	85.9	43.8
Teachers with college degree	43.7	64.4
Students present in school at the time of the visit	86.9	91.9
Some subjects taught in English+	26.8	51.1
English instruction begins in Standard 1	53.2	88.2
No. of classes meeting outside	0.7	0.3
No. of Mixed standard classrooms	0.9	0.6
Any toilet facility	60.9	78.3
Chairs/desk for all students	29.2	63.5
Blackboard in all classrooms	95.4	98.1
Computer available for student use	5.9	29.2
School has fans	28.4	63.3
Kitchen for cooked meals	41.3	10.8
Cook employed by school	74.9	11.1
Any teaching material on the wall	77.3	78.9
Children's work on the wall	67.6	73.9
No. of Schools Surveyed	2,034	1,748

Notes: IHDS selected one predominant private and one government school per village/urban block. The school sample is nationwide but not nationally representative.
+ Many schools teach some subjects in English and others in vernacular languages.
Source: IHDS 2004–5 data.

[11] See Muralidharan and Kremer (2008) and Desai et al. (2009).

in a lose–lose situation, leading to a progressive deterioration of standards. This observation is consistent with results from the United States, where the flight of the white middle class from inner-city schools led to a decline in the quality of the school system.

In urban areas with 51 per cent enrolment in private schools, the situation seems irreversible. But rural private schools offer an environment that is far from ideal, and government schools still enrol 79 per cent of the student population. Investing in the quality and accountability of rural schools may help stem the tide of private schooling in rural areas, and help reduce educational inequalities.

WORKFORCE IN A CHANGING ECONOMY

The preceding sections have focused on the state of education for children aged 6–14. The present section focuses on individuals aged 15–49. The goal of this section is to examine the extent to which the Indian labour force is likely to be competitive in an era of increasing globalization and international competition.

The IHDS shows that overall, 81 per cent of males and 60 per cent of females aged 15–49 are literate (see Table A.6.5a). This number is comparable to the 2001 Census figures of 75 per cent and 53 per cent for individuals aged 15 and older. Since we omit ages 50 and above, our literacy rates are slightly higher than those recorded by the Census. Literacy rates vary tremendously by social group, and across different states. While literacy is a basic determinant of the quality of life as well as the quality of the labour force, far more complex skills will increasingly be required as industrialization continues apace. As incomes in skilled occupations have grown, demands of these occupations have also increased, and a college degree or an advanced technical diploma is often needed for well paying jobs. Only 9 per cent of males and 5 per cent of females hold such qualifications. Moreover, these skill levels are differentially distributed across different parts of the country. As Table A.6.5b indicates, whereas, 18 per cent of males in Delhi, 17 per cent in the North-East, and 13 per cent in Kerala and Tamil Nadu have a college degree or diploma, the proportion is only 4 per cent in Madhya Pradesh. Social group differences in the attainment of a college degree or diploma are vast. Among working age men, 16–17 per cent of forward caste Hindu and other religious groups have a degree, but among Dalits, Adivasis, and Muslims, this proportion is only 4–6 per cent. About 8 per cent of OBC males have a degree or diploma. Among women, 2 per cent of Dalit, Adivasi, and Muslim women have a degree or a diploma. Gender differences in the receipt of a degree or diploma are the lowest in Kerala and Punjab, while Bihar and Jharkhand exhibit some of the greatest gender differences in this regard.

Above and beyond formal education, the new workforce will be increasingly expected to have skills in computer usage and English, the lingua franca of technology. Although the IHDS did not collect detailed information regarding computer skills, it did ask about skills in basic computer usage. The IHDS results show that about 7 per cent of males and 4 per cent of females have some computer skills. However, these skills are highly unevenly distributed across social groups and regions. Among the top income quintile, about 18 per cent of males and 10 per cent of females have computer skills. Among the lowest quintile, virtually no one claims to have computer skills. After Kerala, Delhi, and Tamil Nadu, men in the North-East, Gujarat, and Maharashtra/Goa have the highest level of computer skills, but other states are far behind. Uttar Pradesh, Bihar, Madhya Pradesh, and Orissa are particularly disadvantaged in this area.

English skills were evaluated by a simple question assessing whether individuals speak no English, speak some English, or converse fluently. Moreover, these skills for all household members were reported by the person responding to household income and employment questions. Among men, 72 per cent do not speak English, 28 per cent speak at least some English, and 5 per cent are fluent. Among women, the corresponding proportions are 83 per cent, 17 per cent, and 3 per cent. However, English skills for men are regionally concentrated, with many more individuals having some English skills in Punjab, the North-East, Himachal Pradesh, Jammu and Kashmir, and Uttarakhand, than in other regions. The North-East is particularly surprising. This is not an area known for its industrial base, and yet it boasts of a highly skilled workforce as measured by the percentage of individuals with college degrees and English skills. The prevalence of English skills in this region may be due to its high concentration of missionary led English medium schools. Similarly, the high prevalence of some English skills in Uttarakhand may be due to the high level of tourism in the region. These inequalities seem destined to continue in the next generation, given the low prevalence of English medium enrolment in central parts of India (see Box 6.3).

DISCUSSION

This chapter has identified four major challenges facing the Indian educational policy. First, educational inequalities between different social and economic strata seem pervasive, and are visible in school enrolment, type of schooling, educational expenditures, and school performance. While the educational deprivation of Dalit and Adivasi students is well recognized, we also find that Muslim students are equally deprived in spite of the fact that a greater proportion of Muslims live in urban areas. Social background is also associated with economic background and parental education, which exert an independent effect on education, but we find

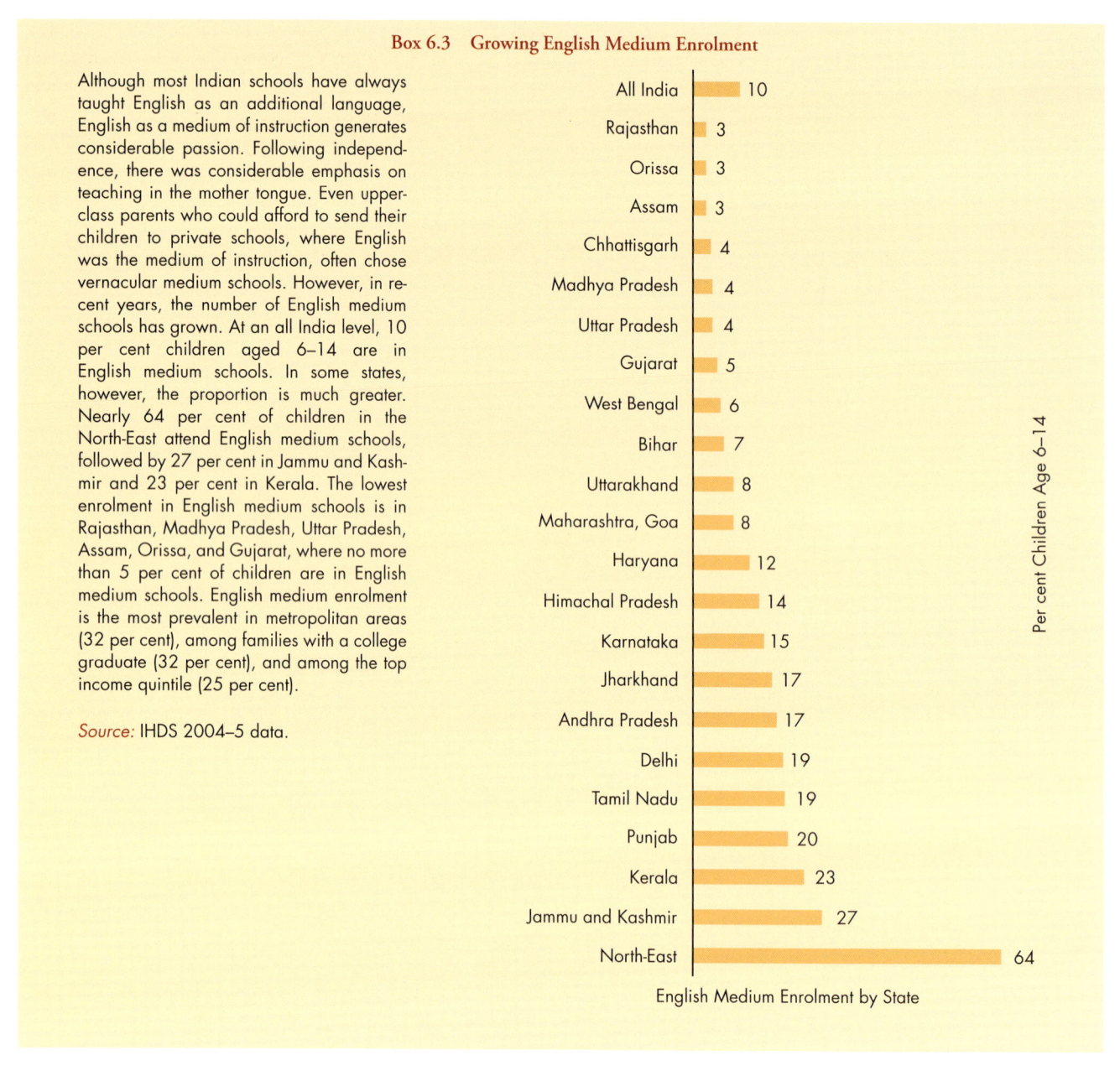

Box 6.3 Growing English Medium Enrolment

Although most Indian schools have always taught English as an additional language, English as a medium of instruction generates considerable passion. Following independence, there was considerable emphasis on teaching in the mother tongue. Even upper-class parents who could afford to send their children to private schools, where English was the medium of instruction, often chose vernacular medium schools. However, in recent years, the number of English medium schools has grown. At an all India level, 10 per cent children aged 6–14 are in English medium schools. In some states, however, the proportion is much greater. Nearly 64 per cent of children in the North-East attend English medium schools, followed by 27 per cent in Jammu and Kashmir and 23 per cent in Kerala. The lowest enrolment in English medium schools is in Rajasthan, Madhya Pradesh, Uttar Pradesh, Assam, Orissa, and Gujarat, where no more than 5 per cent of children are in English medium schools. English medium enrolment is the most prevalent in metropolitan areas (32 per cent), among families with a college graduate (32 per cent), and among the top income quintile (25 per cent).

Source: IHDS 2004–5 data.

English Medium Enrolment by State (Per cent Children Age 6–14):

State	%
All India	10
Rajasthan	3
Orissa	3
Assam	3
Chhattisgarh	4
Madhya Pradesh	4
Uttar Pradesh	4
Gujarat	5
West Bengal	6
Bihar	7
Uttarakhand	8
Maharashtra, Goa	8
Haryana	12
Himachal Pradesh	14
Karnataka	15
Jharkhand	17
Andhra Pradesh	17
Delhi	19
Tamil Nadu	19
Punjab	20
Kerala	23
Jammu and Kashmir	27
North-East	64

that not all of the effects of social background can be reduced to poverty or low parental education. Children from Dalit, Adivasi, and Muslim families, and to a lesser extent those from OBCs, face unique disadvantages. Much of the policy focus has been directed at positive discrimination via reservations in college admissions, but we find that this is too little and too late in students' educational careers. Many disadvantages begin as early as primary school.

Second, previous sections noted the rapid privatization of education, both through increased enrolment in private schools and through reliance on private tuition. Parental decisions to send children to private schools seem understandable given that even among the poorest families or those with very low education levels, children in private schools have higher reading and arithmetic skills than those in government schools. However, this rapid privatization is also associated with the flight of middle-class families from government schools, possibly leading to the further deterioration of these schools and greater inequality between government and private school students. The potential for stemming this tide in urban areas seems to be very low. In rural areas, however, private school systems are not very well developed, and increased attention to school quality in government schools may succeed in bridging an incipient divide.

Third, while school enrolment has grown rapidly and forms a cause for jubilation, the poor quality of schooling remains a major cause for concern. That 46 per cent of 8–11 year old children cannot read a simple three-sentence paragraph does not augur well for the future of the civic society. Arithmetic skills are even poorer. It is time to turn our attention from getting children into schools, to focusing on the quality of schooling to lay a strong foundation for a future labour force. Teacher absenteeism and corporeal punishment in schools remain rampant, and even private schools are not free from it. This suggests that a focus on school quality should be one of the highest priorities of the coming decade.

Fourth, regional disparities in a variety of educational indicators are striking. While states like Himachal Pradesh have made rapid strides, Bihar, Rajasthan, Chhatisgarh, and Madhya Pradesh remain far behind. These inequalities can be seen even in basic skills such as literacy, but the differences are vast when we consider advanced skills, such as knowledge of English or computer usage. Moreover, inequalities between women from different states are even greater than those between men. This digital divide may lead to widening income differences between regions in the years to come and deserves greater attention than hitherto accorded.

> **HIGHLIGHTS**
>
> - Literacy rates in India have been rising sharply for *all* social groups, leading to a reduction in disparities by gender, caste, and religion.
> - However, improving the quality of education is going to be the next major challenge. Only about 54 per cent of Indian children aged 8–11 are able to read a simple paragraph with even lower attainment for Dalit, Adivasi, and Muslim children.
> - Education is rapidly being privatized, with about 28 per cent children aged 6–14 in private schools and about 20 per cent receiving private tutoring.
> - Only 9 per cent of males and 5 per cent of females aged 15–49 have a college degree or diploma; 5 per cent males and 3 per cent females speak fluent English; and 7 per cent males and 4 per cent females have any computing skills.

Table A.6.1a Literacy Rates for Population Age 7 and Above

	Males	Females
All India	79	58
Age		
7–9	82	77
10–14	92	88
15–19	89	79
20–9	85	66
30–9	77	50
40–59	70	38
60+	54	19
Place of Residence		
Metro	93	82
Other urban	87	74
More developed village	77	56
Less developed village	73	48
Household Income		
Lowest Quintile	68	45
2nd Quintile	70	48
3rd Quintile	75	54
4th Quintile	82	63
Top Quintile	92	77
Social Groups		
High Caste Hindu	91	74
OBC	80	57
Dalit	72	50
Adivasi	66	44
Muslim	72	55
Other religion	91	84
Maximum Household Education		
None	38	25
1–4 Std	79	47
5–9 Std	85	60
10–11 Std	92	72
12 Std/Some college	94	75
Graduate/Diploma	96	85

Source: IHDS 2004–5 data.

Table A.6.1b Statewise Literacy Rates for Population Age 7 and Above

	Males (Per cent)	Females (Per cent)
All India	79	58
Jammu & Kashmir	70	51
Himachal Pradesh	89	72
Uttarakhand	85	64
Punjab	81	68
Haryana	78	56
Delhi	92	77
Uttar Pradesh	75	52
Bihar	71	42
Jharkhand	73	48
Rajasthan	71	40
Chhattisgarh	72	48
Madhya Pradesh	75	49
North-East	90	81
Assam	83	75
West Bengal	78	65
Orissa	80	57
Gujarat	85	63
Maharashtra, Goa	89	71
Andhra Pradesh	69	49
Karnataka	81	62
Kerala	96	91
Tamil Nadu	81	65

Source: IHDS 2004–5 data.

Table A.6.2a Discontinuation Rates for Men and Women by Educational Level

	Never Enrolled (age 7+)	Men 1 & 5 (age 12+)	Men 5 & 10 (age 17+)	Men 10 & 12 (age 19+)	Men 12 & Degree (age 23+)	Never Enrolled (age 7+)	Women 1 & 5 (age 12+)	Women 5 & 10 (age 17+)	Women 10 & 12 (age 19+)	Women 12 & Degree (age 23+)
All India	20	15	50	43	44	40	16	57	45	44
Age										
7–9	7					11				
10–14	6	23				10	22			
15–19	10	9	51	46		19	9	53	42	
20–9	14	9	48	38	49	33	11	52	39	46
30–9	22	12	48	40	45	49	17	60	48	46
40–59	30	18	53	50	39	61	22	66	54	40
60+	46	29	59	55	39	80	39	75	57	37
Place of Residence										
Metro	7	6	34	38	30	18	9	43	39	37
Other urban	11	9	40	36	38	25	10	46	38	39
More developed village	21	15	53	50	53	42	18	62	52	55
Less developed village	25	20	61	48	54	49	24	73	57	60
Income										
Lowest Quintile	29	24	65	50	57	52	26	73	56	58
2nd Quintile	27	22	68	54	63	49	23	73	55	71
3rd Quintile	23	17	63	53	61	43	20	69	60	58
4th Quintile	17	13	52	52	53	36	15	61	50	50
Top Quintile	7	6	30	33	35	22	8	41	37	39
Social Groups										
High Caste Hindu	8	8	37	36	39	25	11	48	40	40
OBC	18	15	52	47	47	41	16	61	50	46
Dalit	26	19	61	51	53	48	21	66	47	55
Adivasi	31	23	65	43	54	54	25	69	48	49
Muslim	26	21	59	45	47	43	23	66	51	54
Other religion	8	6	34	45	41	14	8	42	40	45

Source: IHDS 2004–5 data.

Table A.6.2b Statewise Discontinuation Rates for Men and Women by Educational Level

	Never Enrolled (age 7+)	Men Between Classes 1 & 5 (age 12+)	Men 5 & 10 (age 17+)	Men 10 & 12 (age 19+)	Men 12 & Degree (age 23+)	Never Enrolled (age 7+)	Women 1 & 5 (age 12+)	Women 5 & 10 (age 17+)	Women 10 & 12 (age 19+)	Women 12 & Degree (age 23+)
All India	20	15	50	43	44	40	16	57	45	44
Jammu and Kashmir	22	7	41	44	41	41	11	47	50	50
Himachal Pradesh	11	8	42	51	52	28	8	51	54	61
Uttarakhand	15	9	64	35	41	37	9	65	31	43
Punjab	18	6	40	53	52	31	6	45	47	42
Haryana	21	8	40	47	42	43	8	48	47	39
Delhi	8	4	32	36	32	22	6	38	31	48
Uttar Pradesh	23	15	53	39	49	47	16	62	34	42
Bihar	27	24	48	49	45	56	29	54	61	66
Jharkhand	23	15	53	38	54	46	19	63	56	58
Rajasthan	25	10	59	40	40	57	15	62	38	34
Chhattisgarh	24	19	57	33	40	48	21	67	34	30
Madhya Pradesh	22	17	64	39	45	47	21	68	39	30
North-East	9	15	48	34	36	18	17	53	38	35
Assam	15	19	55	40	63	24	21	67	48	76
West Bengal	22	24	52	36	32	35	27	63	42	35
Orissa	19	23	62	48	32	41	22	70	51	34
Gujarat	15	16	54	44	46	37	19	56	39	50
Maharashtra, Goa	10	14	45	44	48	27	17	54	48	46
Andhra Pradesh	28	13	48	44	49	48	13	62	53	40
Karnataka	19	15	43	44	49	38	14	49	49	49
Kerala	3	9	48	53	45	8	13	49	47	50
Tamil Nadu	18	7	46	50	33	33	7	56	46	41

Source: IHDS 2004–5 data.

Table A.6.3a Schooling Experiences of Children Aged 6–14

(in percentage)

	Never Enrolled	Dropped Out	Now in School	Absent 6+ days Last Month	Repeated or Failed	In Private School	In Private Tuition	Avg. Annual Expenditure on School Fees	Avg. Annual Expenditure on Books Uniform & Transport	Avg. Annual Expenditure on Private Tuition	Total Expenditure
All India	10	5	85	20	6	28	20	481	606	178	1,265
Sex											
Male	9	5	87	20	6	29	22	521	625	199	1,344
Female	12	5	83	19	6	26	19	436	584	155	1,175
Current Standard											
1–5				21	5	28	18	427	514	127	1,068
6–10				16	9	26	26	636	855	300	1,791
Place of Residence											
Metro	5	4	91	5	6	44	33	1,564	991	506	3,060
Other urban	6	5	89	13	5	52	30	1,052	923	329	2,303
More developed village	9	5	87	18	6	24	19	318	609	137	1,065
Less developed village	14	6	81	26	6	17	15	187	395	92	674
Income											
Lowest Quintile	14	6	79	24	6	15	15	162	374	78	614
2nd Quintile	14	5	81	23	7	15	14	161	373	76	610
3rd Quintile	10	6	84	21	6	22	19	295	502	128	925
4th Quintile	9	5	87	18	6	33	22	505	676	190	1,370
Top Quintile	4	2	94	11	4	52	31	1,269	1,081	414	2,764
Social Groups											
High Caste Hindu	3	3	94	15	5	40	27	904	924	346	2,174
OBC	9	4	87	21	5	26	20	398	543	149	1,090
Dalit	12	5	83	22	8	17	18	271	471	134	876
Adivasi	16	7	77	19	9	15	9	203	392	73	669
Muslim	17	8	76	21	5	33	19	428	521	130	1,079
Other religion	2	2	96	4	4	54	27	1,446	1,370	224	3,040
Maximum Household Education											
None	23	7	70	25	6	15	14	152	367	70	589
1–4 Std	11	8	81	22	9	13	19	132	379	95	607
5–9 Std	7	5	88	21	7	22	19	288	498	126	912
10–11 Std	4	2	94	15	4	39	24	662	773	228	1,663
12 Std/Some college	3	3	95	17	5	45	25	806	876	282	1,964
Graduate/Diploma	2	1	97	11	3	58	34	1,620	1,219	500	3,339

Note: Avg. refers to Average; + refers to 6 or more.
Source: IHDS 2004–5 data.

Table A.6.3b Schooling Experiences of Children Aged 6–14 by State

(in percentage)

	Never Enrolled	Dropped Out	Currently in School	Absent 6 or More Days Last Month	Repeated or Failed a Class	In Private School	In Private Tuition	Avg. Annual Expenditure on... School Fees	Books Uniform & Transport	Private Tuition	Total Expenditure
All India	10	5	85	20	6	28	20	481	606	178	1,265
Jammu and Kashmir	5	2	93	16	6	47	29	952	1,088	228	2,269
Himachal Pradesh	2	2	97	5	19	19	10	651	1,813	80	2,543
Uttarakhand	6	3	90	40	16	27	7	522	1,062	42	1,626
Punjab	6	4	91	3	5	52	24	1,441	1,623	177	3,240
Haryana	9	3	88	6	6	47	10	1,186	1,240	87	2,513
Delhi	7	3	91	4	4	28	10	1,205	819	180	2,204
Uttar Pradesh	11	5	84	32	2	43	10	396	462	118	976
Bihar	25	5	70	47	2	18	42	230	443	293	967
Jharkhand	20	6	74	13	7	32	23	509	479	193	1,181
Rajasthan	16	5	79	15	2	32	6	526	683	48	1,257
Chhattisgarh	9	6	85	20	12	15	3	263	280	29	572
Madhya Pradesh	13	5	83	28	10	27	10	341	353	55	749
North-East	5	5	91	18	16	34	52	835	980	539	2,353
Assam	13	11	76	41	8	6	14	103	205	121	428
West Bengal	10	7	83	14	11	10	58	375	538	587	1,500
Orissa	6	8	86	42	7	8	38	129	314	318	760
Gujarat	6	6	88	5	14	22	17	459	766	256	1,481
Maharashtra, Goa	4	4	92	5	6	20	15	279	463	155	897
Andhra Pradesh	5	5	90	11	2	31	20	603	658	107	1,367
Karnataka	7	5	89	10	3	28	9	608	820	50	1,477
Kerala	3	0	97	3	4	31	27	705	1,050	289	2,044
Tamil Nadu	2	3	96	3	9	23	23	672	529	109	1,310

Note: Avg. refers to Average.
Source: IHDS 2004–5 data.

Table A.6.4a Reading, Writing, and Arithmetic Skills of Children Aged 8–11 by School Type

(in percentage)

	All Children Currently Enrolled or Not			Private Schools (Only Enrolled Children)			Government Schools (Only Enrolled Children)		
	Read	Subtract	Write	Read	Subtract	Write	Read	Subtract	Write
All India	54	48	67	69	64	79	50	43	64
Sex									
Male	56	51	69	69	65	80	52	46	65
Female	52	45	65	68	63	76	49	40	62
Current Standard									
0	17	13	34	19	13	32	12	12	37
1	11	11	33	22	21	47	6	6	27
2	27	25	49	47	42	68	19	19	42
3	48	42	63	66	62	79	41	35	58
4	66	56	75	83	78	88	59	49	70
Place of Residence									
Metro	69	70	82	72	74	89	67	69	77
Other urban	67	61	76	75	70	82	62	55	73
More developed village	54	47	67	63	58	72	52	45	66
Less developed village	47	40	61	66	60	79	45	37	59
Income									
Lowest Quintile	45	38	63	60	55	77	43	37	61
2nd Quintile	45	38	60	57	50	72	45	38	59
3rd Quintile	51	45	64	62	54	74	49	43	62
4th Quintile	61	53	71	70	66	79	58	48	69
Top Quintile	73	69	80	77	75	83	68	63	76
Social Groups									
Forward Caste Hindu	71	63	79	81	78	88	65	55	75
OBC	56	49	67	69	64	80	53	45	64
Dalit	44	39	60	58	54	68	42	36	60
Adivasi	46	37	60	60	60	77	47	35	59
Muslim	45	40	60	55	49	67	41	38	58
Other Religion	79	78	89	82	81	90	76	76	88
Household Education									
None	35	30	52	48	40	62	35	30	52
1–4 Std	46	37	61	55	40	65	47	38	61
5–9 Std	55	47	67	66	58	78	52	44	64
10–11 Std	66	61	76	67	69	76	66	57	77
12 Std/Some college	72	66	82	74	73	83	71	60	82
Graduate/Diploma	80	75	87	86	82	92	72	66	80

Source: IHDS 2004–5 data.

Table A.6.4b Reading, Writing, and Arithmetic Skills of Children Aged 8–11 by School Type and State

(in percentage)

	All Children Currently Enrolled or Not			Private Schools Enrolled in Private School			Government Schools Enrolled in Govt. School		
	Read	Subtract	Write	Read	Subtract	Write	Read	Subtract	Write
All India	54	48	67	69	64	79	50	43	64
Jammu and Kashmir	40	60	74	58	75	81	26	50	67
Himachal Pradesh	83	68	79	95	93	93	81	64	77
Uttarakhand	63	47	66	84	71	73	53	35	62
Punjab	66	72	75	79	85	86	54	61	65
Haryana	65	62	68	69	68	77	63	58	61
Delhi	76	71	76	79	75	82	76	70	74
Uttar Pradesh	39	34	59	55	52	72	29	22	51
Bihar	44	46	65	77	74	80	40	43	65
Jharkhand	59	59	64	81	74	84	51	54	56
Rajasthan	55	42	57	74	60	73	50	37	53
Chhattisgarh	61	36	49	86	67	70	58	31	46
Madhya Pradesh	46	32	45	71	55	64	39	25	38
North-East	58	76	89	66	83	93	56	75	88
Assam	72	45	97	100	84	95	73	45	97
West Bengal	51	57	73	70	80	85	51	56	72
Orissa	58	50	73	81	90	95	58	48	73
Gujarat	64	44	68	84	75	84	60	36	64
Maharashtra, Goa	66	54	74	70	61	87	65	53	71
Andhra Pradesh	50	51	67	64	64	82	44	46	62
Karnataka	53	55	81	75	74	93	45	48	76
Kerala	82	60	82	86	52	78	80	64	84
Tamil Nadu	79	71	85	85	86	93	78	67	82

Source: IHDS 2004–5 data.

Table A.6.5a Skill Levels of Men and Women Aged 15–49

(in percentage)

	Males					Females				
	Literate	Degree Diploma	English Skills Any	English Skills Fluent	Any Comp. Skills	Literate	Degree Diploma	English Skills Any	English Skills Fluent	Any Comp. Skills
All India	81	9	28	5	7	60	5	17	3	4
Age										
15–19	89	2	29	3	8	80	1	25	3	6
20–9	85	12	31	6	9	66	8	22	4	5
30–9	77	11	27	5	6	50	4	13	3	2
40–59	71	8	22	5	4	42	3	9	2	1
Education										
None	4		0	0	0	1		0	0	0
1–4 Std	94		2	0	0	92		1	0	0
5–9 Std	99		14	1	1	99		12	1	1
10–11 Std	100		47	3	7	100		47	3	6
12 Std/Some college	100		69	9	17	100		70	11	17
Graduate/Diploma	100		88	35	39	100		88	34	34
Place of Residence										
Metro	93	18	48	16	19	84	12	39	11	11
Other urban	89	15	39	8	14	77	11	30	6	9
More developed village	80	7	25	3	5	57	3	15	1	2
Less developed village	74	5	19	2	2	47	1	8	1	1
Income										
Lowest Quintile	69	3	15	1	2	43	1	7	1	1
2nd Quintile	71	2	14	1	1	46	1	8	1	1
3rd Quintile	77	4	18	2	2	54	2	11	1	1
4th Quintile	85	7	28	4	6	65	4	17	2	3
Top Quintile	94	22	52	13	18	82	13	39	9	10
Social Groups										
High Caste Hindu	93	17	44	9	13	79	10	29	6	7
OBC	83	8	26	4	6	59	4	15	2	3
Dalit	75	5	20	2	3	48	2	12	1	2
Adivasi	67	4	15	3	3	42	2	10	3	1
Muslim	73	6	21	3	4	54	2	13	2	2
Other religion	94	16	55	12	18	90	15	51	12	12

Note: Comp. refers to Computer.
Source: IHDS 2004–5 data.

Table A.6.5b Statewise Skill Levels of Men and Women Aged 15–49 Years

(in percentage)

	Males					Females				
	Literate	Degree Diploma	English Skills Any	English Skills Fluent	Any Comp. Skills	Literate	Degree Diploma	English Skills Any	English Skills Fluent	Any Comp. Skills
All India	81	9	28	5	7	60	5	17	3	4
Jammu and Kashmir	75	11	49	11	5	52	4	31	5	2
Himachal Pradesh	95	10	52	8	7	81	5	34	5	3
Uttarakhand	88	8	46	5	6	70	5	29	4	3
Punjab	85	7	69	4	7	72	8	56	4	4
Haryana	83	9	30	3	6	57	6	19	3	3
Delhi	92	18	45	17	17	78	11	38	11	10
Uttar Pradesh	76	7	29	5	3	48	3	14	3	1
Bihar	71	7	24	3	2	39	1	8	0	1
Jharkhand	78	9	16	3	4	51	2	7	1	3
Rajasthan	75	7	25	3	5	38	3	13	2	2
Chhattisgarh	76	9	13	1	4	50	5	5	0	2
Madhya Pradesh	78	4	11	1	3	49	3	7	1	2
North-East	92	17	57	18	11	86	12	51	17	7
Assam	85	8	40	4	4	77	4	28	2	1
West Bengal	77	8	15	4	5	65	5	10	2	2
Orissa	81	8	14	2	3	60	4	7	1	1
Gujarat	86	8	18	3	11	63	6	10	2	6
Maharashtra, Goa	91	11	33	5	10	76	5	23	3	5
Andhra Pradesh	70	7	24	4	7	49	3	13	2	3
Karnataka	82	10	25	6	8	65	6	17	5	6
Kerala	98	13	39	8	19	97	13	37	7	14
Tamil Nadu	86	13	38	11	14	70	8	29	6	8

Note: Comp. refers to Computer.
Source: IHDS 2004–5 data.

# Health and Medical Care

Throughout the preceding chapters, this report has noted the disparities in different indicators of human development. These inequalities are arrayed against two axes: one reflects household background, such as caste, religion, education, and income, and the other reflects the characteristics of the area the respondents live in, as characterized by urban or rural residence, level of infrastructure development, and state of residence. While both sets of inequalities are reflected in most indicators of human development, their relative importance varies. As this chapter discusses a variety of health outcomes and health care, it is striking how regional inequalities dwarf inequalities in the household background. A poor, illiterate Dalit labourer in Cochi or Chennai is less likely to suffer from short- and long-term illnesses, and has greater access to medical care than a college graduate, forward caste, or large landowner in rural Uttar Pradesh. Social inequalities matter, but their importance is overwhelmed by state and rural–urban differences.

Another theme to emerge from the IHDS data is the dominant position of the private sector in medical care. In the early years following independence, discourse on health policy was dominated by three major themes: providing curative and preventive services delivered by highly trained doctors, integrating Indian systems of medicine (for example, Ayurvedic, homeopathic, *unani*) with allopathic medicine, and serving hard to reach populations through grassroots organization and use of community health care workers.[1]

This discourse implicitly and often explicitly envisioned a health care system dominated by the public sector. Public policies have tried to live up to these expectations. A vast network of Primary Health Centres (PHCs) and sub-centres, as well as larger government hospitals has been put in place, along with medical colleges to train providers. Programmes for malaria, tuberculosis control, and immunization are but a few of the vertically integrated programmes initiated by the government. A substantial investment has been made in developing community-based programmes, such as Integrated Child Development Services, and networks of village-level health workers. In spite of these efforts, growth in government services has failed to keep pace with the private sector, particularly in the past two decades.[2]

The results presented in this chapter show that Indian families, even poor families, receive most of their medical care from private practitioners. Maternity care is a partial exception here. For most other forms of care, however, the public sector is dwarfed by the reliance on the private sector, even though the quality of private sector providers and services remains highly variable.

MEASURING HEALTH OUTCOMES AND EXPENDITURES

This chapter reviews health outcomes and expenditures in four main sections:

---

[1] These themes were emphasized in reports from three major committees around independence: the *Bhore Committee Report* of 1946, the *Chopra Committee Report* of 1946, and the *Sokhey Committee Report* of 1948.
[2] For a description of Indian health services and debates surrounding the role of government, see Gangolli et al. (2005).

1. Prevalence of various types of illnesses, days lost from work or other usual activity, disabilities, pregnancy problems, and self-reported health
2. Medical care for illnesses and maternity
3. Expenditures for medical care
4. Health beliefs and knowledge

Information for many of these topics is collected in other surveys, such as the *National Family Health Surveys* (*NFHS*) and NSS. Each of these surveys occupies a unique niche. The *NFHS* tends to focus on child health and circumstances surrounding delivery, and the NSS focuses on the prevalence of ailments and the cost of treatment, particularly hospitalization. The IHDS was developed using a combination of these two approaches and collected some additional information for assessing health status, including data on the ability to perform activities of daily living for all household members. The questions were asked separately for short- and long-term illnesses. The reference period for short-term illnesses such as cough, cold, fever, diarrhoea was 30 days, and that for long-term illnesses such as diabetes, heart disease, and accidents was one year. The questions for maternal care focused on all births in the preceding five years. For all illnesses, information on the source of treatment/advice and the cost of treatment was collected.

ILLNESS

The IHDS inquired about four types of medical issues:

1. Short-term morbidity from coughs, fevers, and diarrhoea
2. Long-term morbidity from chronic diseases ranging from asthma to cancer
3. Disabilities that prevent normal daily functioning, and,
4. Maternal medical care as well as self-reported overall health for women.

Survey responses can assess some of these issues better than others. For example, self-reports of fevers during the past month are undoubtedly more accurate than survey assessments of diabetes and other long-term illnesses. In other countries, economic development was associated with a health transition toward the more chronic but less easily assessed diseases. Thus, it seems likely that long-term illnesses will become an increasingly important topic—but also more challenging to measure—in future surveys in India. For the moment, there is much to be learned about household responses to all medical problems. The IHDS investigation of chronic illnesses was limited to what had been diagnosed by a doctor. Of course, getting a physician's diagnosis is itself economically and socially structured, so the responses reported here should not be interpreted as a proxy measure of the prevalence of chronic illnesses. Since diagnosis for some of the ailments such as coughs and diarrhoea, and blindness and immobility is easier, there can be more confidence in studying both the household responses and the rates at which they vary across different segments of the society.[3]

It is important to note that at the start of health transition, much progress can be made by addressing communicable diseases. However, as easy gains to the eradication of communicable diseases are achieved, attention must shift to the role of unhealthy lifestyles in causing illness (see Box 7.1). In this chapter, we discuss both communicable and endogenous illnesses but do not focus on lifestyles.

Short-Term Morbidity

As Table 7.1 indicates, about 124 of every 1,000 individuals reported having a fever (107), cough (86), or diarrhoea (41) in the past month.[4] Almost half (45 per cent) of all Indian households had someone who suffered from one of these minor illnesses.

Short-term morbidity accounts for substantial lost time from usual activities. The typical sick person was sick for seven days in the previous month and was incapacitated, or unable to perform his or her usual activities for four-and-a-half of those days. Based on the illness prevalence rate and days incapacitated, if sick, the average person was sick almost ten days per year with fever, cough, or diarrhoea, of which seven days were spent out of school, work, or other usual routine. Although these illnesses are more common for children, days lost per illness increases with age, somewhat counterbalancing the lower prevalence at younger ages. The result is that working age adults (that is, those aged 15–59) lose about 5.5 days per year because of fevers, coughs, and diarrhoea, school-age children lose 7; and the elderly lose 10 days per year respectively.

As Figure 7.1 indicates, fevers, coughs, and diarrhoea are especially young children's illnesses. They peak in the first two years of life and steadily decline until adolescence. Their reported incidence increases again in old age. Gender

---

[3] However, both short- and long-term illness are reported more for household members who were physically present at the interview than for household members who were not present. Because the health questions were usually asked of a married woman in the household, the reporting bias affects age and sex relationships, and caution should be exercised in interpreting these relationships.

[4] While strictly comparable data for morbidity prevalence are not available from other sources, the *NFHS-III* figures for children under five provide a reasonable comparison (IIPS 2007). *National Family Health Survey-III* was conducted with a reference period of 15 days, whereas the IHDS reference period is 30 days. The *NFHS-III* reported prevalence rates of 149, 58, and 98, respectively, for fever, cough/cold, and diarrhoea for the preceding 15 days for children under five. The IHDS-reported prevalence rates for a 30 day period for children under five are 245 for fever, 214 for cough/cold, and 94 for diarrhoea.

Box 7.1 Alcohol and Tobacco Use

The IHDS asked households about the use, and frequency of use, of alcohol and tobacco by household members. Because this involved reports by one member of the household for others, the figures reported in this survey are likely to be underestimates of actual tobacco and alcohol use. Even so, the figures are startling. Among males aged 25–59, 6 per cent smoke occasionally and 27 per cent smoke daily. A substantial proportion also chew tobacco; 24 per cent chew tobacco daily, and 4 per cent do so occasionally. Alcohol is consumed daily by 6 per cent of the male population and occasionally by 13 per cent.

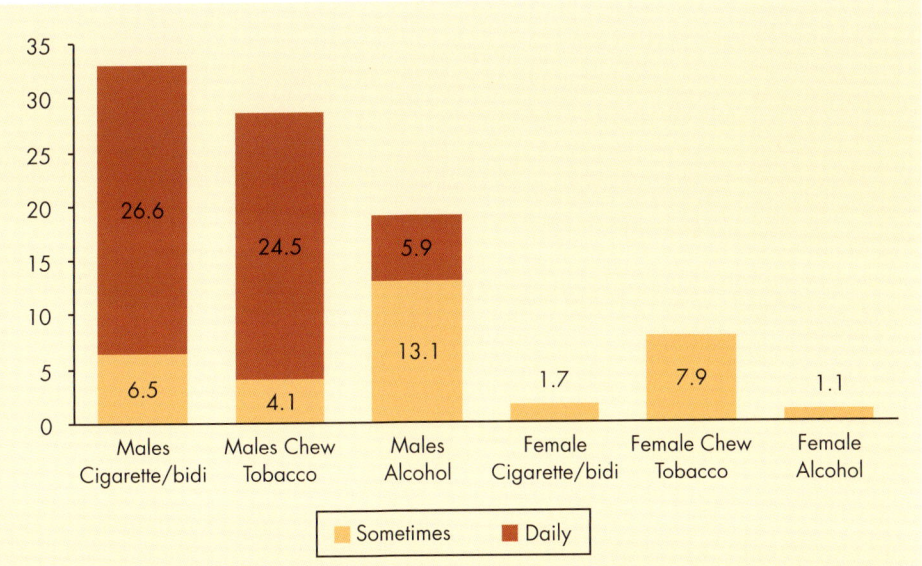

Tobacco and Alcohol Use by Males and Females Aged 25–9 Years

Category	Sometimes	Daily
Males Cigarette/bidi	6.5	26.6
Males Chew Tobacco	4.1	24.5
Males Alcohol	13.1	5.9
Female Cigarette/bidi	1.7	
Female Chew Tobacco	7.9	
Female Alcohol	1.1	

Note: Sometimes and daily combined for women.

Source: IHDS 2004–5 data.

---

differences in reported illness are quite small. Among infants under one, boys (357) reported sick more often than girls (319), but this trend reverses for adults.

Economic and social disadvantages bring with them health disadvantages as well (see Table A.7.1a). Dalits are somewhat more likely to experience short-term illnesses (139) than forward caste Hindus (116). Individuals living in households in the highest income quintile are less likely to be ill with short-term maladies (91) than those in lowest income quintile (159), and respondent's high educational attainment is strongly associated with lower morbidity (52 for college graduates versus, 171 for uneducated individuals). In results not shown here, we find that children, however, do not benefit this much from educational levels of parents. It is the working age adults and, especially, the elderly whose morbidity rates decline with household education.

Part of the income effect is due to home characteristics and amenities. The use of biomass fuels (discussed in Chapter 5) spreads particulates and carbon monoxide, thus, increasing morbidity (133) among households using these fuels relative to households using only clean fuels (88). Morbidity is lower in homes with piped indoor water (92)

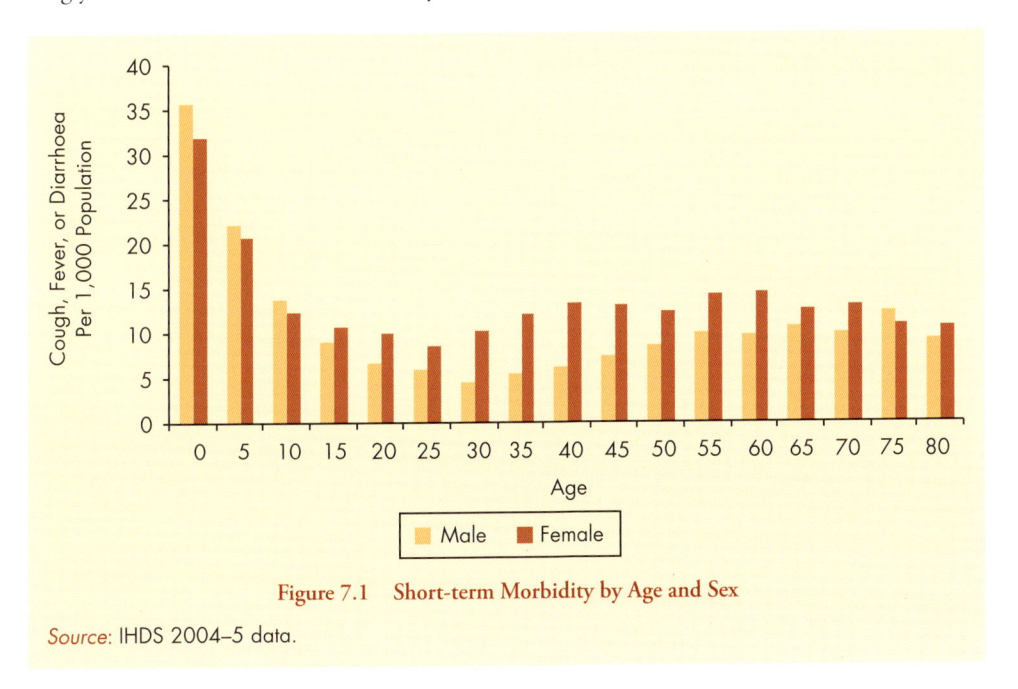

Figure 7.1 Short-term Morbidity by Age and Sex

Source: IHDS 2004–5 data.

Table 7.1 Illness Types and Source of Treatment

	Prevalence			Treatment			
	Morbidity per 1000	Days Unable To Do Usual Activity (if sick)*	Days Lost Per Year Entire Population+	In Hospital (Per cent)	Treated in Government Centre (Per cent)	Treated Outside Local Area (Per cent)	Medical Expenses If Sick (Rs)
Any Short-term Illness	124	4.7	7.0	3	17	42	120
Fever	107	4.9	6.2	3	18	44	130
Cough	86	4.6	4.8	3	17	43	120
Diarrhoea	41	5.3	2.6	5	13	46	150
Any Long-term Illness	64	58.8	3.8	25	23	62	1,900
Cataract	6	58.5	0.4	35	29	61	1,000
Tuberculosis	4	72.8	0.3	24	26	69	2,450
High BP	14	50.1	0.7	14	24	51	1,500
Heart Diseases	5	56.2	0.3	35	24	65	3,100
Diabetes	8	48.4	0.4	21	27	54	2,400
Leprosy	1	80.2	0.1	17	20	73	1,250
Cancer	1	93.9	0.1	36	27	79	3,800
Asthama	7	68.5	0.5	21	26	65	2,000
Polio	1	77.8	0.1	18	13	44	500
Paralysis	2	148.0	0.3	38	20	61	3,600
Epilepsy	1	84.2	0.1	27	17	71	1,800
Mental Illness	2	101.1	0.2	22	20	62	2,000
STD/AIDS	1	127.5	0.1	18	28	66	1,750
Others	23	54.6	1.3	32	20	69	2,200

Notes: *Reference period is one month for short-term illness, one year for long-term illness.
+ Calculated from prevalence and days sick. Henceforth, STD refers to Sexually Transmitted Diseases and AIDS is Acquired Immune Deficiency Syndrome.
Source: IHDS 2004–5 data.

than in homes without it (134). Flush toilets are also associated with reduced illness (100) compared with households without toilets (131). Unfortunately, the majority of Indian homes (62 per cent) have none of these amenities, and only 7 per cent have all three. These amenities are not just proxies for overall household wealth, they have their own direct health advantages.

Regional differences in reported short-term morbidity are striking (see Table A.7.1b). These regional differences should be treated with caution because interviews were conducted in different seasons across different parts of the country, and short-term morbidity is very sensitive to seasonality. Bihar has especially high morbidity (209); the next highest rate is West Bengal, at 173. The state with lowest reported short-term morbidity is Karnataka (73), but most states are in the range of 80 to 140. The prevalence of short-term morbidity in metro cities is low, at about 81. Other urban areas have morbidity rates that are higher (110), and villages have highest morbidity (131–3). Much of this difference is probably attributable to the greater prevalence of clean fuels, indoor piped water, and flush toilets in towns and cities. Some of the differences may also be due to differential climate patterns as well as the season during which the interviews were conducted.

Strong regional clustering of illnesses is likely to be associated with two factors. First, illnesses like diarrhoea and cough are often caused by environmental conditions such as the severity of rainfall and moisture in the air, risks shared by all residents of an area regardless of the their wealth or education. Second, many of these illnesses are spread through contact, and once some individuals get sick, the sickness can easily spread.

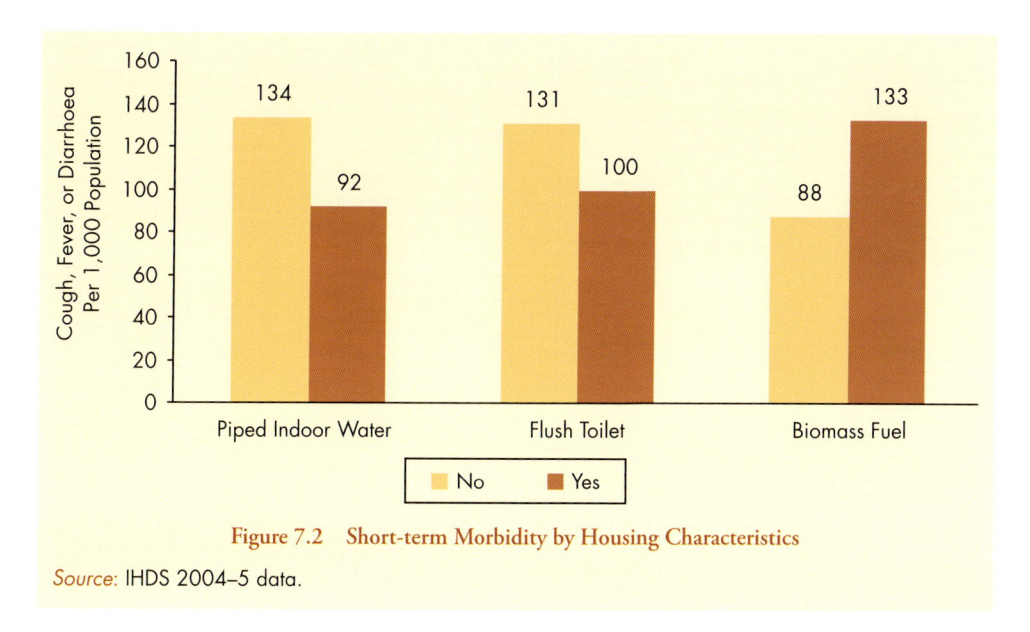

Figure 7.2 Short-term Morbidity by Housing Characteristics
Source: IHDS 2004–5 data.

Long-term Morbidity

The survey also asked whether anybody in the household had ever been diagnosed by a physician for any of the 14 long-term illnesses. A small fraction reported that they had once had some long-term illness but had been cured (see Figure 7.3).

The only noticeable cure rates were reported for cataracts (25 per cent) and tuberculosis (21 per cent). These cured cases are included with the positive reports in this chapter.

As shown in Table 7.1, the most frequently reported long-term illness was the last, unspecified 'other' category (23 per 1,000). Retrospective inquiries revealed that most of

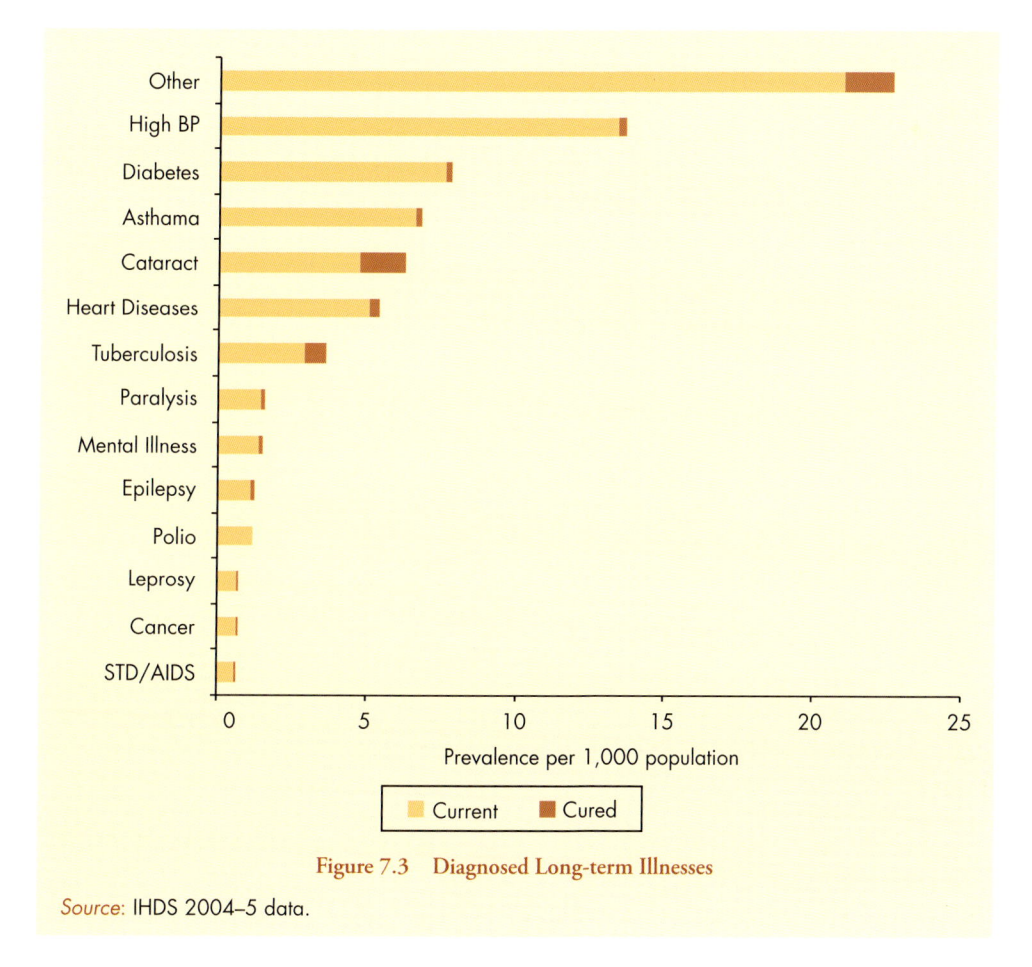

Figure 7.3 Diagnosed Long-term Illnesses
Source: IHDS 2004–5 data.

these people had been accident victims. Hypertension (14) was the next most widely reported disease. Cataracts (6), tuberculosis (4), heart disease (5), diabetes (8), and asthma (7), also were widely reported. Less often noted were the remaining seven categories: leprosy, cancer, polio, paralysis, epilepsy, mental illness, and STDs/AIDS, each reported for about 1or 2 persons per 1,000.

A total of 6 per cent of all individuals in the survey were reported to suffer from at least one of these illnesses. Of these, few (14 per cent) reported more than one illness. Slightly over a quarter of all households (27 per cent) had a member who had been diagnosed with one of these illnesses. These rates are, of course, lower bounds of true prevalence rates in the population. Prevalence estimates of these diseases would require more sophisticated testing than the IHDS could attempt. But analyses of how households used the medical care system to respond to these diseases depend on first identifying who was aware that they suffered from them.

The risk of being diagnosed with one of these illnesses increases dramatically with age. About 21 per cent of the elderly (aged 60 or older) have one of these illnesses. Only 6 per cent of the working age population and only 1 per cent of children have a diagnosed long-term illness (see Figure 7.4 for gender disaggregated figures). Of course, the elderly are only a small part of the Indian population, so most people (64 per cent) who report one of these diseases are between 15 and 59 years.

Although long-term illnesses are less prevalent, such an illness is more likely to incapacitate a person for many more days than does a short-term illness. A person who was ill with a long-term disease was, on an average, unable to perform his or her normal activities for almost 60 days during the previous year. The elderly were more affected than others. They lost 71 days of normal activity if sick with one of these diseases (see Table A.7.1a). Across the entire population, long-term illnesses accounted for about four days of lost activity, compared with seven days for short-term illnesses. This difference is due to the lower prevalence of long-term than short-term morbidity. Among the elderly, the consequences were worse (15.2 days incapacitated for long-term illnesses versus 10.1 days for short-term illnesses).

The requirement of a physician's diagnosis limited these assessments to small fractions of the population and tilted reporting to those who had the best access to diagnostic medical care. For example, urban residents are more likely to report higher long-term morbidity than rural residents, and those in the south have higher reported morbidity than those in the central plains. This is quite different from the reporting pattern for short-term morbidity.

Disability

Being blind, deaf, or unable to walk imposes enormous burdens on some individuals. How widespread are these disabilities? The survey asked if any household member, eight years old or older, had to cope with any of seven problems (for example, walking one kilometre) that created difficulty for daily activity. If there was some difficulty with a particular activity, respondents were asked whether the person was unable to do that activity or whether the person could do it with some difficulty. As shown in Figure 7.5, total disabilities were recorded around 3–4 per cent for each of the activity of daily living.

Activities that could be done only with some difficulty varied more, so overall disability/difficulty ranged between 7 persons per 1,000 (for example, speaking) to 15 persons per 1,000 (seeing from far distances).

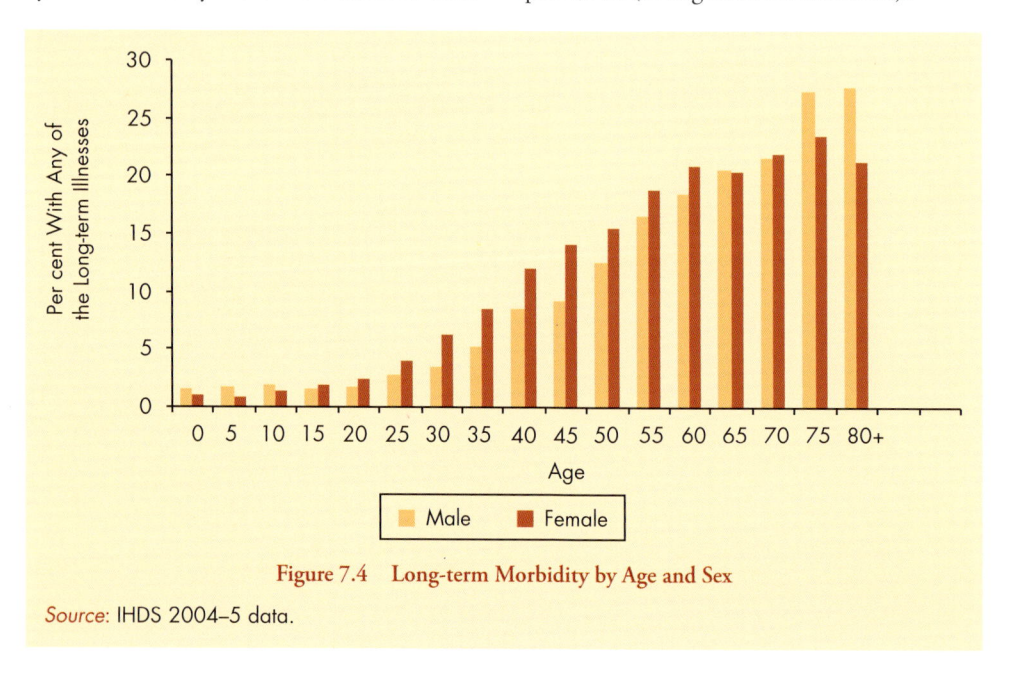

Figure 7.4 Long-term Morbidity by Age and Sex

Source: IHDS 2004–5 data.

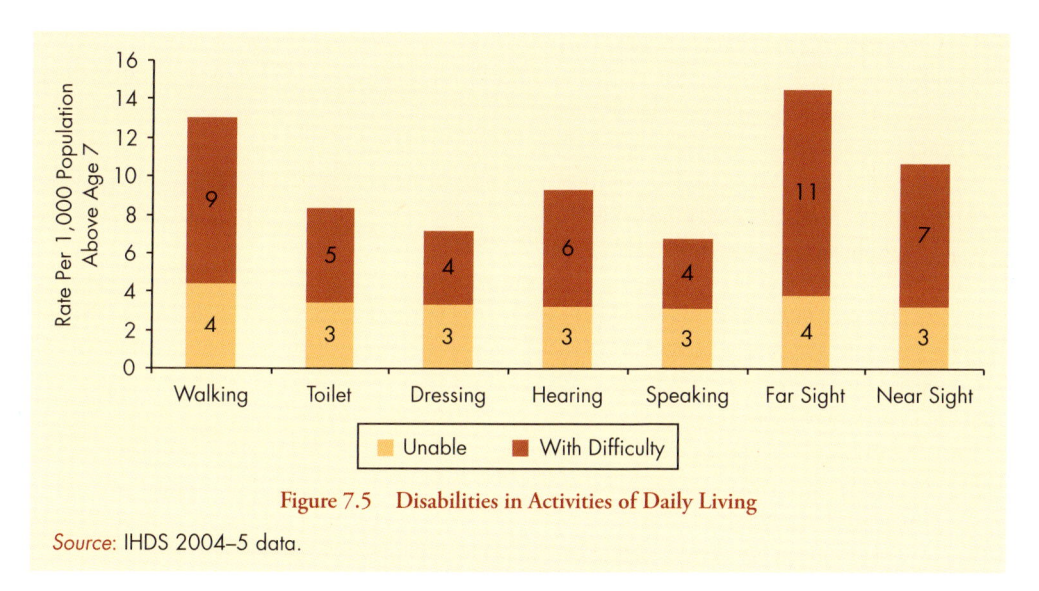

Figure 7.5 Disabilities in Activities of Daily Living
Source: IHDS 2004–5 data.

When all activities are considered together, about 24 people per 1,000 have difficulty doing at least one of these activities. Of these, nine have total disability. Four percent of households have a totally disabled person. Ten per cent have a person who has difficulty doing one of these seven activities. Disabilities increase with age (Figure 7.6).

Of a thousand elderly, 39 have complete disability in one of the seven activities of daily living. This is more than six times the rate for working-age adults (six), or for children between ages 8–14 (four). Nevertheless, because the elderly are now such a small proportion of the Indian population, the majority of Indians with a disability (58 per cent) are below the age of 60.

Disabilities are quite equally distributed across class and caste (see Table A.7.1a). The disabled are slightly more concentrated among the poor and less educated, but the differences are small. There are also few differences across caste and religion. State differences again exceed social inequalities (see Table A.7.1b). The high disability rates in Kerala and Tamil Nadu are the result of their older age structure, an ironic consequence of the generally better health and medical care in the South. Among 15–59 year olds, Bihar's disability rate (15 per 1,000) is more than twice the national rate (six) and well above Kerala and Tamil Nadu's (eight).

Maternal Health

Maternal mortality rates have been declining, but complications before and after birth are common. The IHDS asked about whether recent mothers had experienced any of the

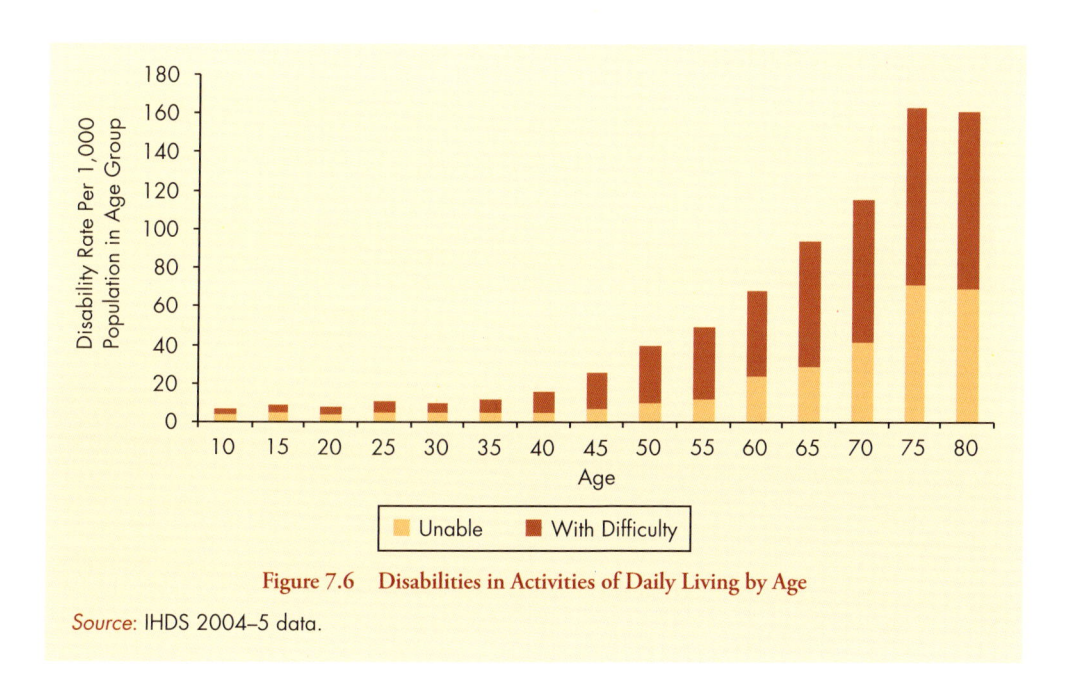

Figure 7.6 Disabilities in Activities of Daily Living by Age
Source: IHDS 2004–5 data.

eight medical problems during, or shortly after their pregnancies as listed in Figure 7.7.

Fatigue during pregnancy was most common (36 per cent), but more serious medical risks were also apparent. Eighteen per cent of recent mothers reported they had been anaemic, and 14 per cent had had convulsions. Excluding fatigue, 40 per cent of recent Indian mothers reported having at least one of the more serious maternity problems.

Poor and illiterate mothers are more likely to have a serious maternal medical problem, but the important variation is again more geographic than social (see Table A.7.1a). Rural women—particularly those living in the least developed villages—reported a problem more often (45 per cent) than those in metro cities (30 per cent), and the statewise differences are enormous. About four out of five women in Jammu and Kashmir and in Assam reported a medical problem surrounding their last pregnancy. Less than one out of six suffered any of these problems in Tamil Nadu (see Table A.7.1b).

Self-reported Health

Surveys around the world have shown that a simple question, asking respondents for their own evaluation of their health, is a good indicator of overall health status and a good predictor of future outcomes. The IHDS asked one ever-married woman between ages 15–49 in each household to rate her own health. The majority reported either very good (15 per cent) or good (50 per cent) health, but that leaves a substantial minority who reported their health as only okay (*thik-thak,* 30 per cent) or poor (5 per cent).

Throughout this report, we have noted disparities in various indicators of human development by income and health indicators are no exception. The affluent and the educated not only enjoy more extrinsic rewards, but their self-reports of health were also higher: 77 per cent of college or secondary school graduates reported good health and only 59 per cent of illiterate women managed that (see Table A.7.1a).

Self-reported good health also declines with age and frequently seems to be associated with childbearing. The more children a woman has had, the worse her self-reported health (see Figure 7.8).

A health decline is modest up to three births, but becomes more dramatic after that. This strong relationship is partly explained by the lower education and greater poverty of women with high fertility.

As with many aspects of health in India, social class and age are less important than geographical location (Tables A.7.1a and 7.1b). Urban women reported that they are healthier (71 per cent) than rural women (62 per cent). The south has especially good self reported health: women in Karnataka (96 per cent) and Tamil Nadu (88 per cent) were most likely to say that their health is good or very good; at the opposite extreme, less than half of women in Jammu and Kashmir (36 per cent), Jharkhand (39 per cent), and Assam (37 per cent) reported good health. However, it is important to exercise caution in interpreting these responses because of cultural and linguistic variation in the propensity of individuals to respond that their health is good. For example, many fewer women in Punjab reported good health

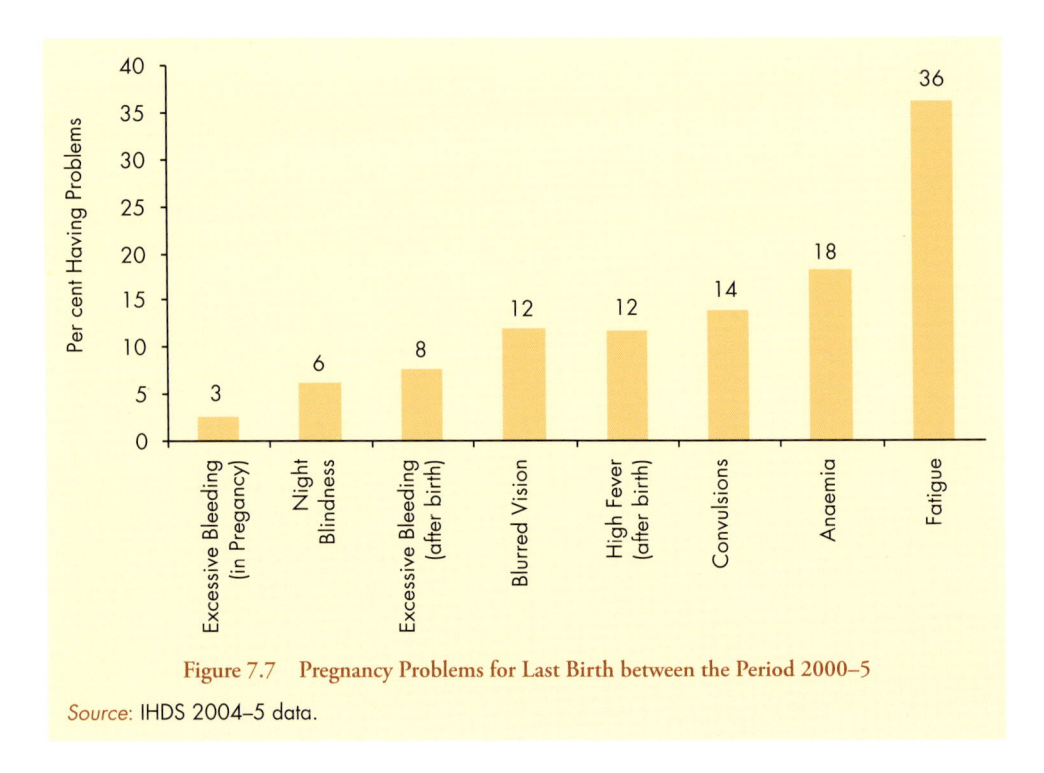

Figure 7.7 Pregnancy Problems for Last Birth between the Period 2000–5

Source: IHDS 2004–5 data.

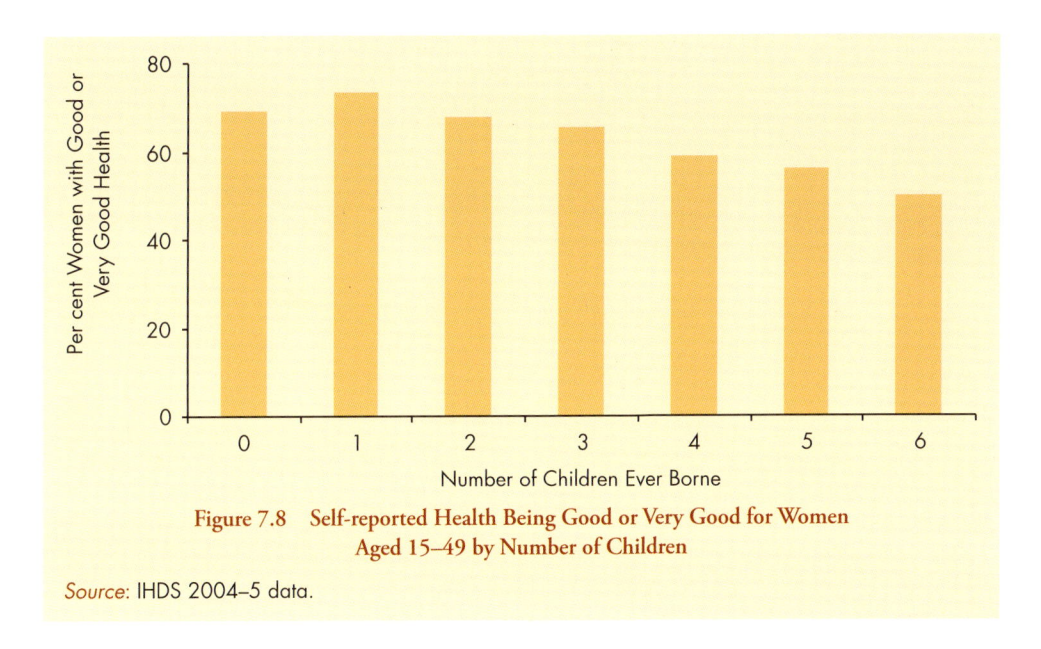

Figure 7.8 Self-reported Health Being Good or Very Good for Women Aged 15–49 by Number of Children
Source: IHDS 2004–5 data.

(48 per cent) than in Orissa (72 per cent). That Orissa is one of the poorest states in India and documented higher self-reported short-term illnesses than Punjab (137 versus 117 per 1,000) suggests the need for caution in interpreting these reports.

In summary, looking across various dimensions of self-reported health status discussed in this section, poor health is a consequence of biology, behaviour, and aging, but those outcomes also appear to be socially structured. While education and income play some role in the prevalence of illnesses, rural–urban and state differences are particularly important. Although not all health problems show the same statewise patterns, the south is noticeably healthier along several dimensions, while the poorer Hindi heartland (that is, Uttar Pradesh, Bihar, and Madhya Pradesh) reports more illness and disability. In Chapter 8, we note similar differences in infant and child mortality, with Kerala's infant mortality at nine per 1,000 births (rivalling that of developed countries) and infant mortality for Uttar Pradesh at 80 per 1,000. This suggests that the regional differences in morbidity are not simply due to differences in reporting.

Next, we will see that similar geographic differences are found for medical care. Unfortunately, the areas with the most need because of the high prevalence of illnesses are the areas with the worst medical care.

MEDICAL CARE

A massive expansion of government health facilities occurred under the 6th and 7th Five Year Plans in the 1980s with a goal of providing one health sub-centre per 5,000 population and a PHC per 30,000 population. In 2005, access to some sort of government medical facilities was almost universal in urban areas. Even for the rural population, a substantial proportion lived in villages with at least a sub-centre, and a vast majority had a sub-centre in a neighbouring village. The IHDS documents that about 86 per cent of the households at least have a government sub-centre within three kilometres. However, most individuals seem to seek medical care from private providers. This is true for both short-term and long-term illnesses, although slightly less so for long-term illness. Maternity care is the one exception. More women rely on government doctors and midwives for pregnancy and births than go to private clinics (although the majority still have births at home). The poor, the elderly, and women make somewhat more use of the government services, in general, but the majority of all groups use private sector care for most illnesses. Government-provided medical care is more common in some parts of India, but only in a few areas is it the most common choice for medical care.

It is important to keep in mind the diversity of medical facilities in India. Government facilities range from places like the All India Institute of Medical Sciences, capable of performing complex surgeries, to poorly equipped village sub-centres. The private sector is even more diverse. It consists of facilities ranging from dispensaries run by untrained and unlicensed individuals to high technology, for-profit hospitals catering to medical tourists from abroad. The IHDS surveyed one predominant private facility and one government medical facility in each village/urban block. This is a nationwide sample, but should not be seen as being representative of health facilities in India because the sampling frame did not consist of all possible facilities. Nonetheless, the results presented in Box 7.2 provide an interesting snapshot of the private and public health facilities in India and are important in informing the results on the source and cost of medical care discussed below.

Box 7.2 Government and Private Health Facilities

The IHDS documents that households rely overwhelmingly on private providers. The IHDS visited one private and one government health facility for each sample village/urban block. In each sample area, facilities that were the most frequently used by residents for treatment of minor illnesses were selected. The resulting sample of 3,777 facilities is nationwide but not nationally representative; thus, results should be treated with caution.

These data present a mixed picture. Government facilities are far better equipped than private facilities, with better-trained doctors and greater availability of medicines, greater ability to conduct routine blood and urine tests, and advanced equipment. However, they also seem to suffer from neglect. Walls and floors are more often unclean, and the facilities are open slightly fewer hours than the private ones. Most importantly, only 76 per cent of the doctors/directors were present at the time of a visit, compared with 87 per cent in private facilities.

	Government	Private
	(in percentage)	
Type of Practice (not mutually exclusive)		
Allopathic	96	89
Ayurvedic	12	31
Homeopathy	4	10
Unani	1	2
Other	2	1
Hours open weekly	62	66
Infrastructure		
Electricity	83	90
Toilet	80	46
Examination table	85	81
Floors not clean	15	8
Walls not clean	18	9
Medical Facilities		
Any antibiotics available	95	35
Stethoscope	95	98
Sterilization equipment/Autoclave	81	54
Thermometer	97	97
Haemoglobin test done (internally or externally)	61	29
Routine urinalysis done (internally or externally)	52	26
Doctor/Director		
Has MBBS	86	60
Has ayurvedic degree/diploma	3	16
No medical training	11	24
Present at the time of the interviewer visit	76	87

Notes: IHDS selected one predominant private and one government health facility typically used for treating minor illnesses in the village/urban block. The provider sample is nationwide but not nationally representative.

Source: IHDS 2004–5 data.

Medical Care for Short-term Illnesses

The survey households reported that they almost always (94 per cent of the time) sought medical treatment when someone became sick with a cough, fever, or diarrhoea. This high rate suggests that most respondents equated illness with medical treatment. If they didn't seek some help, then they assumed they weren't really sick.

When sick, only 17 per cent of the time did respondents go to a government dispensary. Most often (71 per cent) people went to a doctor, nurse, or untrained practitioner in private practice. Of these visits, sometimes (5 per cent) it was to a government doctor or nurse who was practising part-time in private practice. Another 8 per cent of the sick went to the local pharmacist (chemist) for treatment, and 2 per cent went to someone else, such as a traditional healer. Note that the distinction between private doctors and traditional healers is somewhat fuzzy, and most patients do not really know the qualifications of their service providers. Thus, while there is strong credential control for government service providers, that for private providers is quite weak. Quality of treatment in government health centres can also be variable. Government doctors and nurses often engage in private practice during their free time. Ostensibly, this is done to allow patients who prefer to pay for individualized care or greater flexibility of timing to do so. However, in practice, it results in a conflict of interest, encouraging providers to remain absent or unavailable during official working hours and to provide poor quality care in order to build up a private practice. On the other hand, the ability to engage in private practice supplements their government incomes and increases service availability in hard-to-reach areas.

The local availability of government services affects where the sick go for treatment. While urban residents generally have a choice of public or private providers, rural residents face far fewer choices. The IHDS finds that 57 per cent of villages do not have a government health centre. Of the 43 per cent that do have a government centre, 28 per cent have only a health sub-centre, and only 15 per cent have a full PHC or Community Health Centre (CHC). Usually villages without any government health facility are smaller and often have access to a sub-centre in easy reach.

About 80 per cent of the rural IHDS households live within three kilometres of a sub-centre. However, access to a sub-centre is not enough to encourage the use of a government facility for short-term care, particularly if a private facility is also present. When the village does not have a health centre, about 16 per cent go outside the village (see Figure 7.9) to get public health care and 69 per cent go outside the village for private health care.

If only a sub-centre is present without any private facility, about 30 per cent use public facilities. However, if both private facility and sub-centre are present, only 13 per cent use the public facility. When a PHC or CHC is present in the village, more people are likely to go there for treatment, but still about 63 per cent of the villagers go to a private clinic in these villages.

The availability of private services in the village also affects how the sick choose treatment. Forty six per cent of rural residents live in a village without any private practitioner. They are more likely to go to a government centre, especially if one is in the village. But even in villages with a PHC or CHC and no private alternative, only 35 per cent of the sick go to the public dispensaries or hospitals and 53 per cent leave the village for private treatment (Figure 7.9).

One would generally expect the use of private health care to be concentrated among privileged groups, the rich, the educated, and working age men. However, these

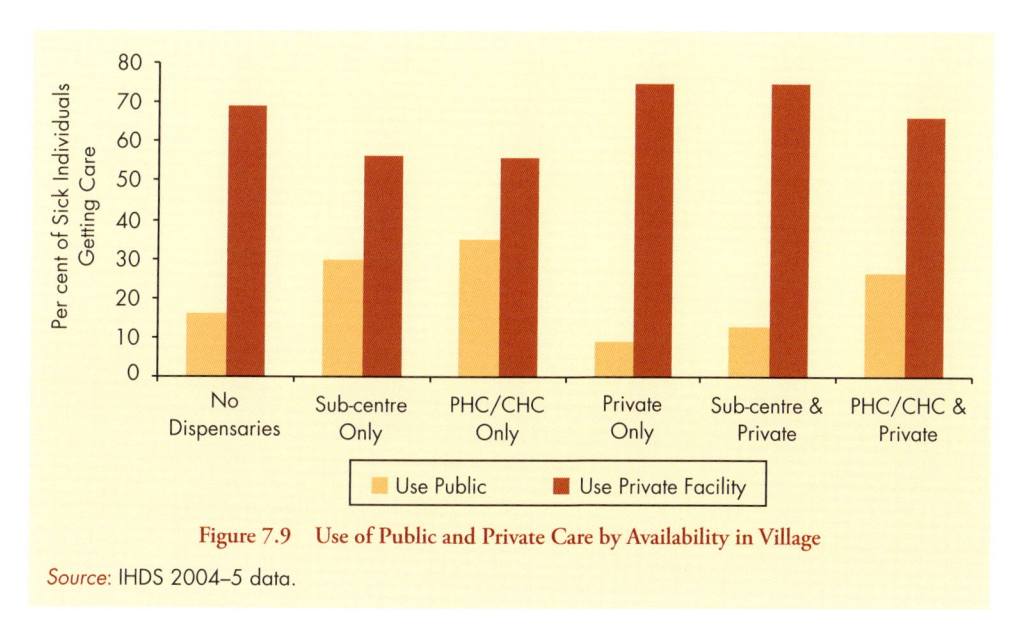

Figure 7.9 Use of Public and Private Care by Availability in Village

Source: IHDS 2004–5 data.

relationships do not appear to be strong in the IHDS data. When any short-term care is obtained, we see virtually no difference in the use of public versus private care between men and women, elderly, adults, and children, and educated and uneducated families (see Table A.7.2a). Arguably, the most surprising absence of difference exists between the rich and the poor. When seeking care for short-term maladies, about 18 per cent of the individuals from the highest income quintile use public care, and 17 per cent of those from the lowest income quintile do so. This small income difference becomes less surprising when we consider that treatment costs don't differ very much between public and private services—a topic addressed in greater detail in the following section. Among social groups, Adivasis and Christians use government services more often than other groups (24 and 29 per cent, respectively), probably because of their concentration in Kerala and the North-East, where government services are widely used.

The state differences in the use of government services are large. In Himachal Pradesh, government services are preferred over private practitioners (56 per cent), as they are in Jammu and Kashmir (49 per cent) and the North-East (43 per cent). However, almost nobody goes to a government facility in Bihar (2 per cent), Uttar Pradesh (7 per cent), or Punjab (8 per cent). These state differences are not associated with state wealth or development because both rich and poor states have low usage of government services. Himachal, Kashmir, and the North-East have a high usage of public services because about one-third of their villages have a PHC or CHC, not just a health sub-centre (Figure 7.10).

In the south, Kerala, Tamil Nadu, and Karnataka also have many PHCs but somewhat lower rates of public usage because there are also many private clinics there, unlike in the hill states.[5]

Surprisingly, urban and rural areas have similar rates of usage of public health centres (Table A.7.2a). However, rural residents in less developed villages are more than three times as likely (53 per cent) to leave their villages for treatment as metro city dwellers are to leave their neighbourhoods (13 per cent). Where treatment happens is important because the cost of treatment in one's own village or neighbourhood is typically half that of outside treatment (a median of Rs 100 versus Rs 200). Rural residents' greater need to leave their home areas for medical care is almost entirely a result of the lack of adequate local medical facilities, especially private practitioners. In a village that has a private medical practice, a pharmacy, and a PHC, a sick person is no more likely to leave the village for treatment than urban residents are to leave their neighbourhood for medical care.

Only 3 per cent of patients with short-term illnesses were hospitalized, and only 1 per cent were hospitalized for more than a week. Hospitalization was highest among the elderly, followed by working age adults. Hospitalization was very low among children aged 6–14. Males of all age groups were hospitalized slightly more than females.

Medical Care for Long-term Illnesses

Of the 6 per cent of individuals diagnosed with a major long-term illness, private medical care was again the preferred method of treatment, as it was for short-term morbidity.

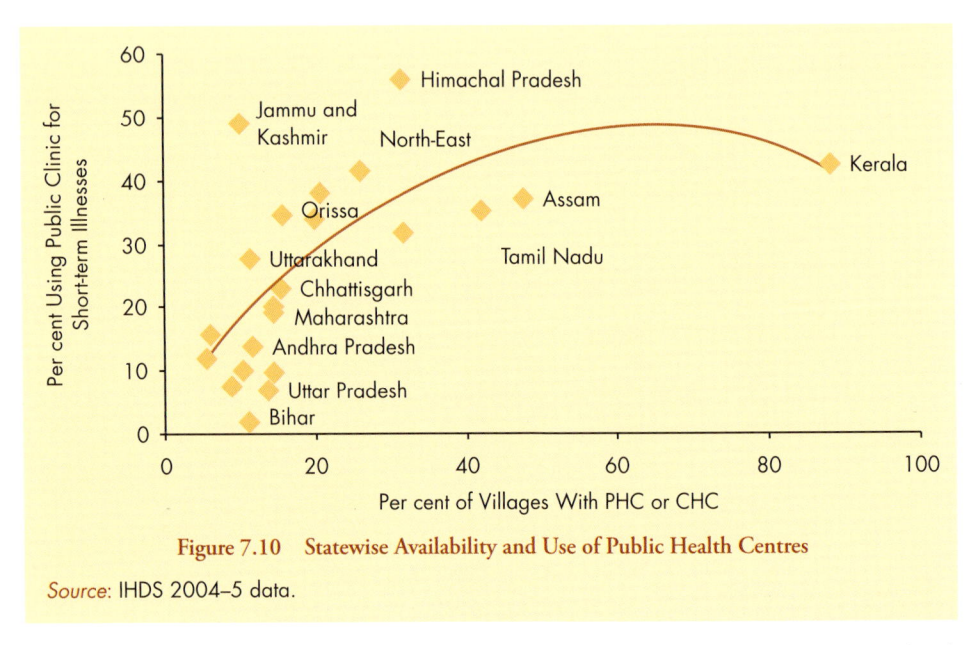

Figure 7.10 Statewise Availability and Use of Public Health Centres
Source: IHDS 2004–5 data.

---

[5] While the IHDS surveyed a large number of households, it surveyed 1,503 villages. Data for village infrastructure is based on a small number of villages per state, ranging from seventeen in Uttarakhand to 134 in Uttar Pradesh. Thus, data for villages is subject to greater sampling error than data for households and should be treated with caution.

Sixty nine per cent of the long-term ill went to private practitioners (similar to the 71 per cent of the short-term ill), 23 per cent went to government facilities (somewhat higher than the 17 per cent of the short-term ill), only 5 per cent went to pharmacists or some other medical care (only half of the 10 per cent for those with a short-term illness), and 9 per cent reported not seeking any medical treatment. The proportion seeking no treatment in the past year may be an underestimate resulting from our focus on diagnosed illnesses. Polio (58 per cent), mental illness (76 per cent), and cataracts (79 per cent) have especially low rates of medical treatment.

The pattern of private and public service usage for long-term illnesses is much the same as that discussed above for short-term illnesses. There are only small differences between men and women, and between the elderly and the working age population (see Table A.7.2a). Educational and social group differences in treatment options are also minor.

Again, the major determinants of public and private medical care are regional. More than half the long-term patients were treated at public health facilities in Himachal Pradesh and Delhi (see Table A.7.2b). On the other hand, the same states with low rates of public medical service usage for coughs, fevers, and diarrhoea, also have low usage of public services for more serious diseases. Bihar, at 4 per cent, is again the lowest. Metropolitan cities show the greatest usage of government services (27 per cent), while less developed villages document the lowest usage (20 per cent), reflecting the greater availability of high quality training hospitals in metropolitan areas.

Treatments occur outside the village or neighbourhood more often for major illnesses (62 per cent) than for minor illnesses (42 per cent). Among major illnesses, chronic conditions like hypertension (51 per cent) and diabetes (54 per cent) are less often treated outside the area than other major illnesses (see Table 7.1).

The young, although less likely to suffer from a major illness, travel farther for treatment (Table A.7.2a). But genders, income levels, and social groups differ little in where they are treated. Residential location is the primary determinant of local treatment of long-term illnesses, as it is for short-term illnesses. The sick in metropolitan cities are far more likely to be treated locally (71 per cent) than are those in the least developed villages (25 per cent). States also differ in how often long-term illnesses are treated locally; travelling for treatment of major illnesses is much more likely in Himachal Pradesh (81 per cent), Uttar Pradesh (77 per cent), or Bihar (77 per cent), than in West Bengal (44 per cent) or Kerala (52 per cent).

Patients with major illnesses were hospitalized more often (25 per cent) and for longer periods than were those with short-term illnesses (3 per cent). The average hospital stay was seven days, although 10 per cent of the patients stayed for a month or more. Hospitalization stays were the shortest for cataracts, with a median of four days, but were typically 7–12 days for each of the other diseases. Because of the 'Others' (Table 7.1) category's high prevalence, about half of the hospital days are accounted for by the 'Others' category, which is composed primarily of accidents.

Hospitalization rates vary little by income, education, or social group (Table A.7.2a). However, states differ substantially in their hospitalization rates (Table A.7.2b). Himachal, Haryana, Gujarat, and Maharashtra had high rates of hospitalization. Punjab, Delhi, West Bengal, and Orissa had low rates, as did Andhra Pradesh and Chhattisgarh.

Maternal Medical Care

About half of all recent births were attended by trained medical personnel. As shown in Figure 7.11, 43 per cent of babies were delivered by a physician. Another 11 per cent were delivered by a nurse or other trained medical personnel.

Major social, geographic, and demographic differences, separate the half of babies delivered by medical personnel from the other half who were attended only by traditional midwives, family, or friends. Poor, illiterate mothers having their sixth child in rural Bihar are almost never attended by medical personnel. Affluent, college educated mothers having their first child in Chennai almost always are.

Deliveries are the most visible part of a larger system of maternal care, whose parts are closely related. Prenatal checkups, blood and urine tests, sonograms, tetanus injections, iron supplements, and postnatal checkups have widely varying levels of acceptance across India (Figure 7.11), but a mother who has any one of these is more likely to have the others as well. For example, 82 per cent of mothers who had a physician-assisted birth had had a prenatal blood test. Only 34 per cent of other mothers had that test. Moreover, the personal, social, and geographic factors, that affect any one of these, are the same as the factors that affect the others. To avoid repetition, this report will concentrate on physician assisted deliveries, but the reader should realize that what is found for deliveries applies as well to the other elements of the maternal health complex.

The mother's education and her household's income are strong determinants of what kind of medical care she receives during delivery (Table A.7.2a). Ninety-one per cent of college graduated women delivered their babies with a physician attending. Only 24 per cent of uneducated women received that level of attention. Similarly, only 27 per cent of women in the poorest income quintile had a physician attended delivery, compared to 69 per cent of women in the most affluent quintile. This suggests that delivery care for women is far more dependent on the household socioeconomic status than is care for illnesses that afflict both men and women.

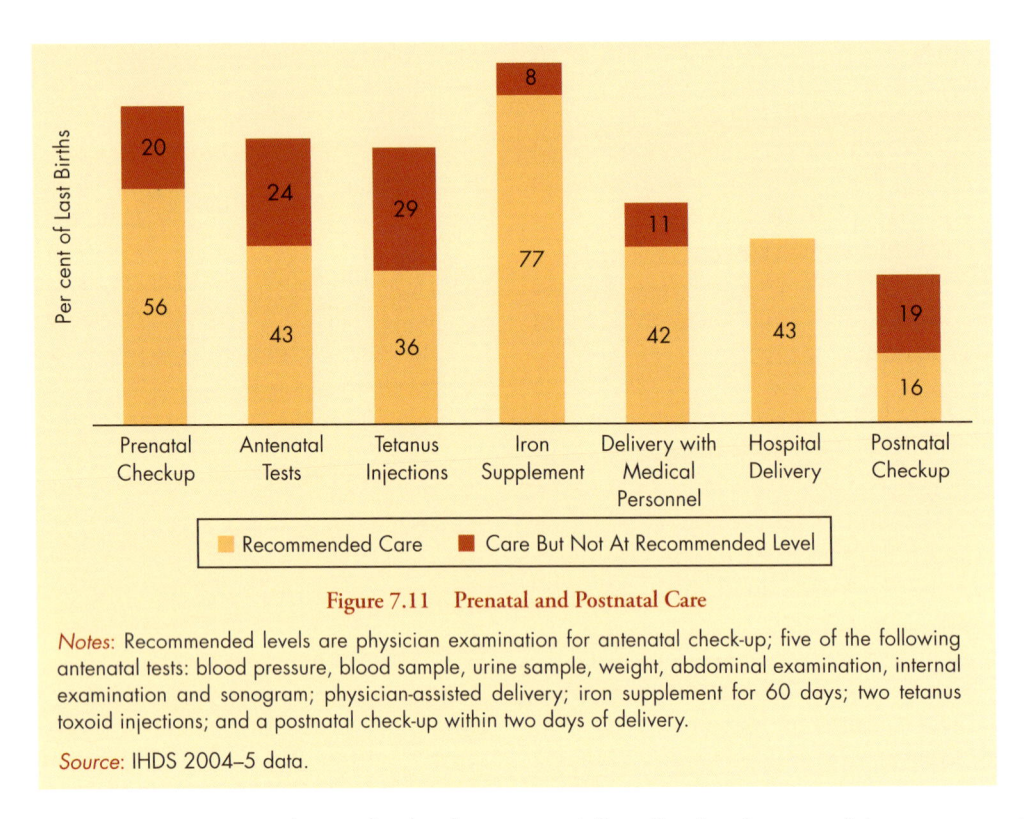

Figure 7.11 Prenatal and Postnatal Care

Notes: Recommended levels are physician examination for antenatal check-up; five of the following antenatal tests: blood pressure, blood sample, urine sample, weight, abdominal examination, internal examination and sonogram; physician-assisted delivery; iron supplement for 60 days; two tetanus toxoid injections; and a postnatal check-up within two days of delivery.

Source: IHDS 2004–5 data.

Medical care varies across a woman's own fertility history, regardless of the education and wealth she begins with. The majority (59 per cent) of first births are attended by a physician. A small minority (14 per cent) of births, after the fifth birth, have a physician attending (Figure 7.12).

This relationship is partly due to the relationship between birth order and mother's education and income. Poor, less educated women are more likely to have a larger number of children and poverty may also lead to lack of attendance at delivery. But regardless of mother's characteristics such as age, education, and income later births are less likely to be attended by a physician. The birth order effect has been partially offset by the general increase over time in medical assistance for deliveries. The *NFHS* reports an increase from 26 per cent of institutional deliveries in their first wave (1992–3) to 41 per cent in 2005–6. Thus, women who have had two recent births benefit from the general trend towards more medical care (of the 64 per cent of women without physician care in their next to last birth, 6 per cent improved to physician care in their most recent birth) but are deterred by the birth order effect (of the 36 per cent of women who did use medical care on the next to last birth, 8 per cent dropped physician care in their next birth). Because the birth order decline is slightly greater than the over the time

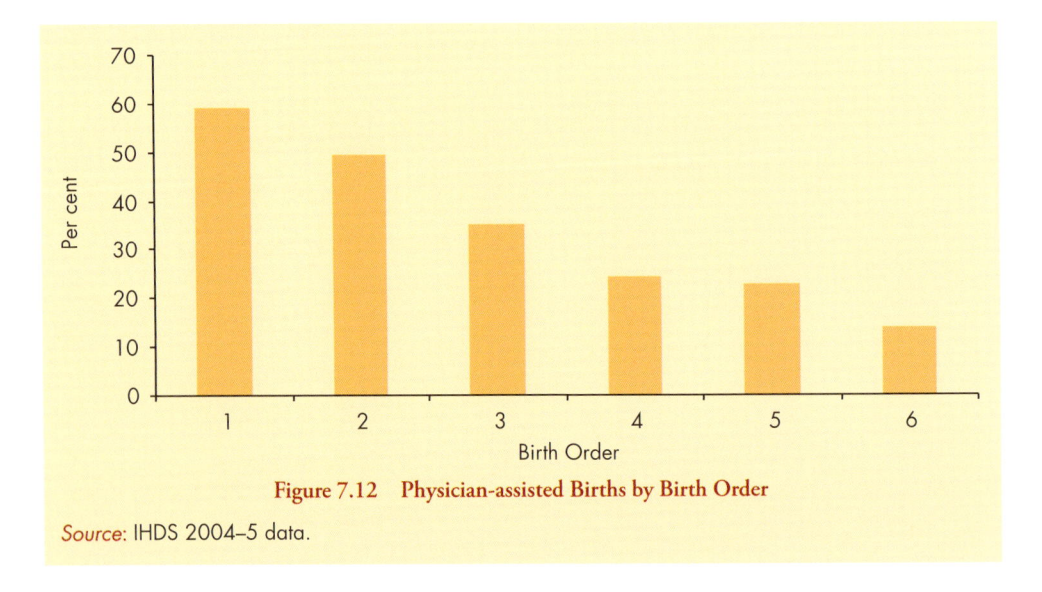

Figure 7.12 Physician-assisted Births by Birth Order

Source: IHDS 2004–5 data.

increase in medical care, mothers are less likely to receive physician assistance as they have more children.

In addition to these strong class and birth order effects, geography is again associated with much of a mother's medical care during delivery (Table A.7.2b). Almost all births (98 per cent) in Kerala are physician attended. The rest of the South also has high rates of physician assistance. Andhra Pradesh (82 per cent) and Tamil Nadu (79 per cent) are notably high. Even Karnataka, at 57 per cent and the lowest in the south, is still well above the national average. At the opposite extreme, only 15 per cent of births in Uttar Pradesh and only 16 per cent in Madhya Pradesh are assisted by physicians. Mothers in the Hindi belt appear to inhabit a different medical world than mothers in the south. Even within the states, where people live makes a major difference in medical care. The majority (75 per cent) of metropolitan area births are assisted by physicians. Rural mothers in less developed villages enjoy only one-third that rate (25 per cent).

Finally, government services play a somewhat greater role in maternal medical care than they do for minor or major illnesses. For both long- and short-term illnesses, among individuals who receive any care, only one in four gets it from public providers, with the other three are using private care. In contrast, for deliveries, about half occur at home, and the remaining are evenly split, at about 22 per cent each, between public and private maternity homes. Government services also play an important role in antenatal care, with 39 per cent women receiving care in government health centres and another 11 per cent being visited by a public health worker. Most importantly, public hospitals provide delivery to the most vulnerable sections of the population, the poor, the less educated, Dalits, Adivasis, and Muslims (Table A.7.2a).

EXPENDITURES ON MEDICAL CARE

Indian households spend a surprisingly large proportion of their incomes on medical care. Medical expenses are an important reason why households fall into the debt trap, with nearly 16 per cent of households reporting that their largest loan in the preceding five years was taken for medical expenses. The typical minor illnesses (cough, fever, and diarrhoea) cost Rs 120, although 10 per cent of these illnesses cost more than Rs 500. Because of this skewed distribution, the mean expense was Rs 294, more than twice the expense for the typical household with an illness. There was little difference in expenditures among the three minor illnesses (see Table 7.1 and Figure 7.13).

Major illnesses were considerably more costly. A major illness cost the average sick person Rs 1,900 during the year, although 10 per cent spent Rs 11,000 or more. Mean expenditures for persons with a major illness were Rs 5,053. Cancer treatments were especially expensive (Rs 3,800), while cataracts were treated for Rs 1,000.

When we combine expenditures on all household members, on an average, each Indian household spent Rs 190 on minor illnesses during the year (even though three-quarters spent nothing) and even more, Rs 1,680, on major illnesses during the year. The relationship between household income and illness expenditures presented in Figure 7.14 is interesting.

For minor illnesses, the expenditures do not vary by household income. For major illnesses, the expenditures vary substantially by household income, with a range of Rs 1,274 in the lowest income quintile to Rs 2,571 in the highest income quintile, and a sharp increase between the fourth and fifth quintile. This is not surprising. For minor illnesses, the costs are mostly medicine related and are

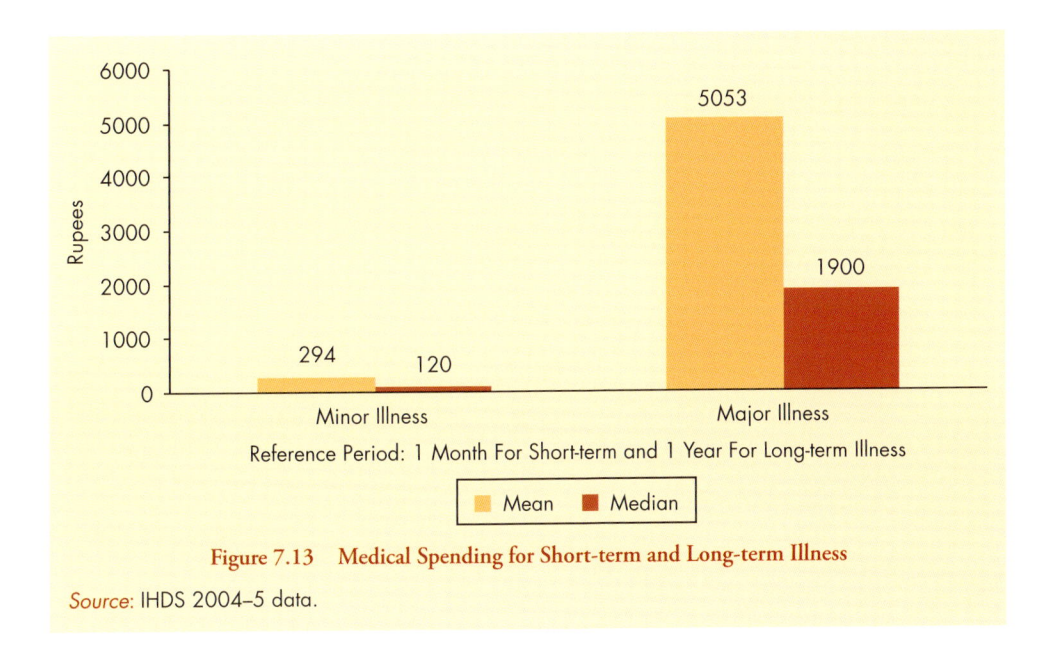

Figure 7.13 Medical Spending for Short-term and Long-term Illness
Source: IHDS 2004–5 data.

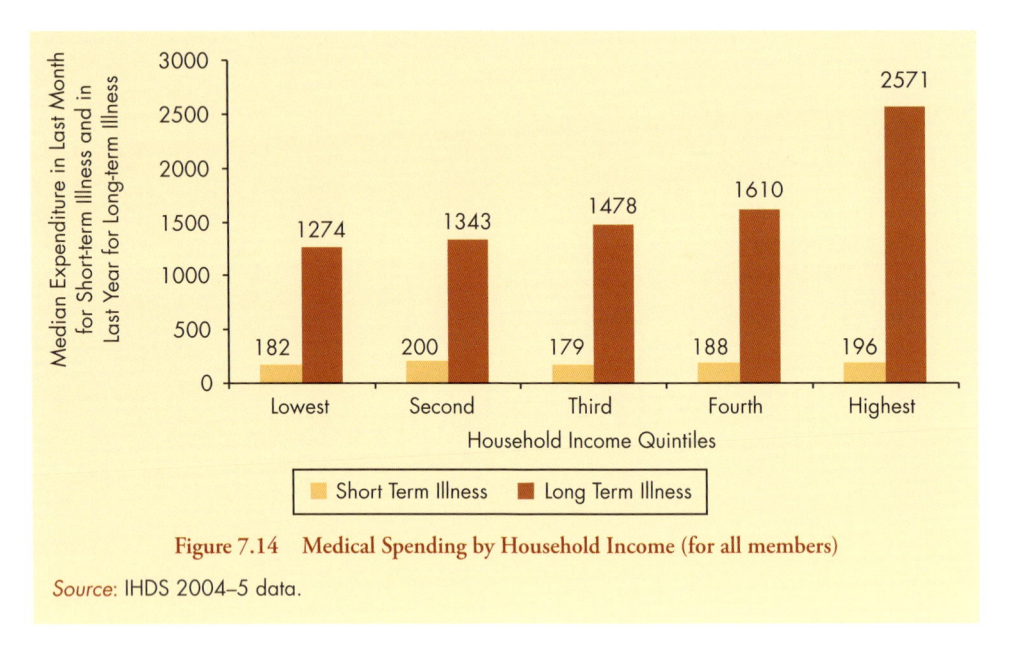

Figure 7.14 Medical Spending by Household Income (for all members)
Source: IHDS 2004–5 data.

unlikely to vary by household income. However, major illnesses require more expensive tests and treatment options, which physicians may hesitate to recommend to poor patients, and poor households may be less likely to undertake, even if recommended.

Despite these striking income differences, relative to urban households, rural households spend more on minor illnesses and almost as much for major illnesses (Table A.7.2a). Medical care is least expensive in the major metropolitan areas despite the higher concentration of affluent households there. Part of the reason for their higher expenses is that villagers, more often, have to leave their local areas for treatment and are slightly more likely to be hospitalized (Table A.7.2a), both of which raise costs. Leaving the village or neighbourhood raises the median expense from Rs 95 to Rs 200 for minor illnesses and from Rs 650 to Rs 2,700 for major illnesses. Hospitalization, of course, results in major expenses. The rare cough, fever, or diarrhoea that requires hospitalization, typically costs Rs 1,000 compared to Rs 110 for outpatient costs. Major illnesses cost Rs 5,400 with hospitalization and only Rs 1,200 without hospitalization.

Overall, going to a public provider costs less than going to a private provider, but these savings are frequently small. For minor illnesses, going to a public health centre results in a median expenditure of Rs 100 as compared with Rs 150 for the private healthcare provider, but going to a pharmacist costs only Rs 50 (Figure 7.15).

For major illnesses, the median public provider expense is Rs 1,970, which is Rs 580 less than the median private care expense (Figure 7.16).

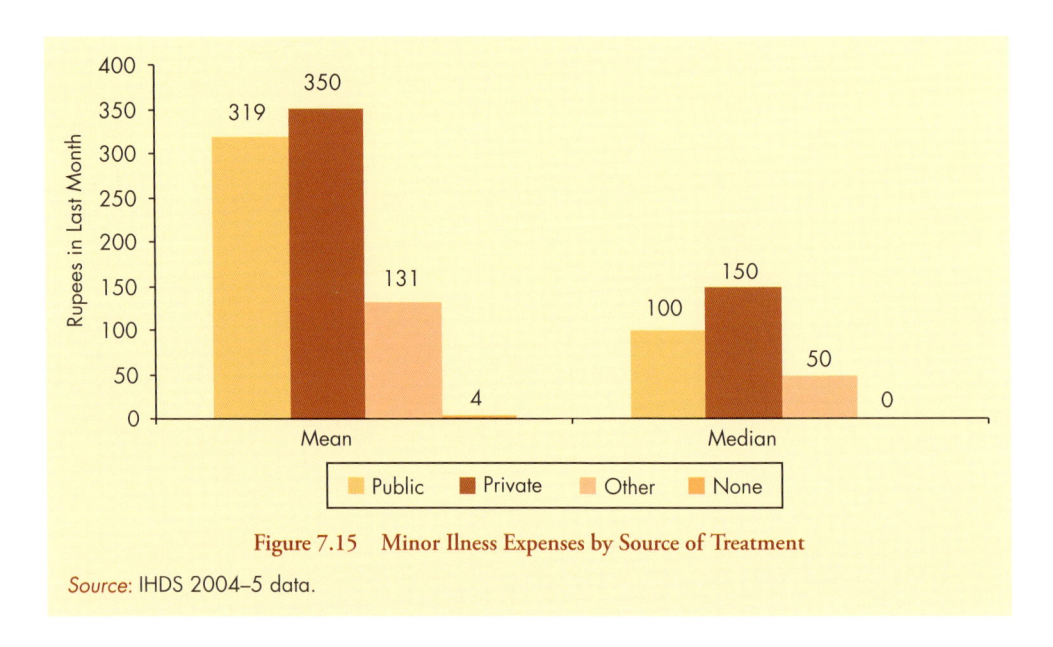

Figure 7.15 Minor Illness Expenses by Source of Treatment
Source: IHDS 2004–5 data.

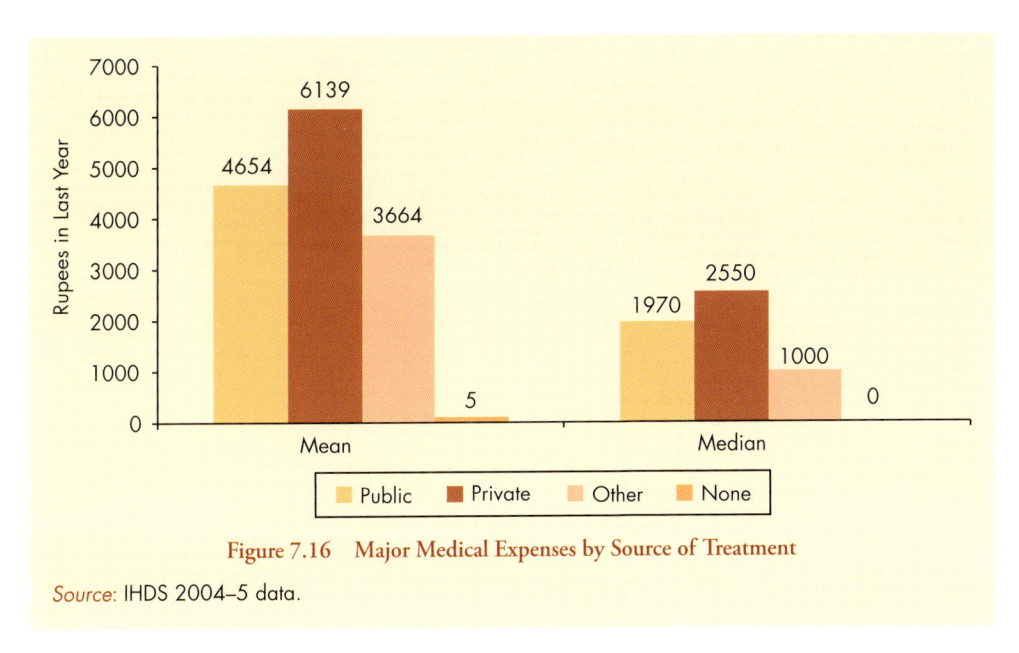

Figure 7.16 Major Medical Expenses by Source of Treatment
Source: IHDS 2004–5 data.

The difference in mean expenses is higher because of some extreme values, but the comparison is not much different, Rs 6,139 versus Rs 4,654. The real cost savings are realized by going to some other provider, such as a pharmacist, for which the median expense is only Rs 1,000.

This small difference in cost between public and private healthcare in short-term morbidity is surprising.[6] Healthcare costs include a variety of expenditures. doctor or nurse's fees, medicines, costs of diagnostic tests, travel and lodging, and gratuity or tips. Public healthcare providers charge minimal fees, but the costs of medicine, transportation, and lodging remain large, and tips may be even more prevalent in public health centres. Of these, doctor's fees in public centres are free or minimal, and diagnostic costs could be small. However, for short-term illnesses, the main expenses appear to be medicines and other treatments (Figure 7.17), which are higher, rather than lower, for patients visiting government providers (Rs 112 versus Rs 87). Indirect expenses, such as tips, transportation, and lodging are also higher when using public facilities (Rs 33 versus Rs 19). This balances out the benefit of lower doctor's fees (Rs 21 versus Rs 28).

The finding of a minor difference between government and private healthcare is partly due to our lack of distinction between various sources of private healthcare. As mentioned earlier, the Indian medical sector is extremely heterogeneous. For minor illnesses, it is not at all unusual to go to local *vaid*, with somewhat ambiguous training, who prescribes relatively cheap ayurvedic or homeopathic medicines. However, when it comes to major illnesses, the difference in doctors' costs between public and private providers is greater, possibly because this is where patients visit more qualified and expensive private doctors.

HEALTH KNOWLEDGE AND BEHAVIOUR

General Health Awareness

Households with more-educated persons tend to have fewer illnesses, perhaps because they know more about good health

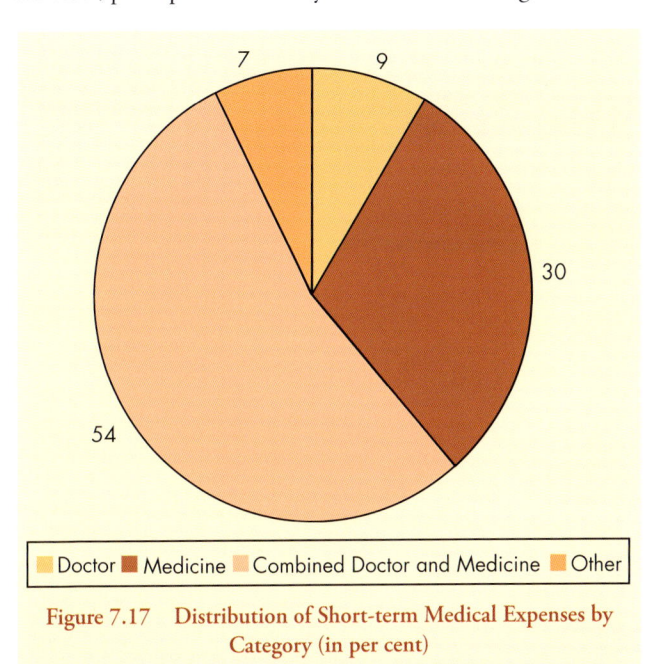

Figure 7.17 Distribution of Short-term Medical Expenses by Category (in per cent)
Source: IHDS 2004–5 data.

---

[6] This a major point of difference between medical expenditure data collected by the NSS 60th Round and IHDS. NSS finds that for non-hospitalized treatments, when healthcare if obtained from the government sources, the expenditure is negligible (NSSO 2004).

practices. The IHDS asked women aged 15–49 in each household about five common health beliefs (Figure 7.18).

Most women were able to identify that *chulha* smoke is bad for health (79 per cent), that it's not harmful to drink milk during pregnancy (77 per cent), and that the colostrum from the mother's breast is good for the newborn baby (74 per cent). However, only 59 per cent were aware that children should be given more to drink when they have diarrhoea, and surprisingly, only 41 per cent denied that sterilization weakens men for a long while.

These five items are combined to form a scale that ranges from 0 to 100, where 0 means that the respondent was unable to answer any of the five items correctly and 100 means that all five items were answered correctly. The average score from these five items was 62 per cent. Forty percent of the women reported correct answers on at least four of the questions. Only 11 per cent responded correctly on all five. Not surprisingly, these scores were closely related to woman's education. College graduates averaged 78 per cent, whereas, women without any education scored only a 57 per cent (Table A.7.3). Women in states with widespread education also did well (that is, 82 per cent in Kerala) compared with those in states with less education (that is, 51 per cent in Bihar), and even uneducated women from states with higher levels of education were better informed than those in states with lower levels of education. More unexpectedly, young women, especially those under 20, although better educated than their elders, scored lower on this health knowledge scale. And within each educational level, scores improved regularly with age. Apparently, women learn about health from experience as well as from schools.

HIV/AIDS Awareness

Only 55 per cent of ever-married women aged 15–49 had heard about AIDS. Those women who reported they had heard about AIDS were asked about five possible ways that the disease might spread. Three of these were correct ways (via sex, infected needles, and transfusions), and two were incorrect (via mosquito bites and sharing food). Many women simply agreed that all five vectors were ways in which AIDS spreads, so the two incorrect methods were the principal items that tested true AIDS knowledge. Of the respondents who had heard of AIDS, 94 per cent identified sex with an infected person as a way of becoming infected. Transmission through infected needles was recognized by 92 per cent, and through blood transfusion by 91 per cent. However, 24 per cent of the women believed incorrectly that AIDS could be spread by sharing food with an infected person, and another 12 per cent were unsure. Even more, 41 per cent believed that it could spread by being bitten by an infected mosquito, and 12 per cent were unsure.

Like the health beliefs scale, a woman's education is the main determinant of whether she has heard of AIDS, and how much she knows about how it is spread (Table A.7.3a). The educational level of the state again matters. Kerala and Tamil Nadu show widespread AIDS awareness. Most women in Uttar Pradesh, Bihar, and Assam have not heard of AIDS, and if they have, they don't have a good understanding of how it is spread.

DISCUSSION

Regional inequalities in reported morbidity and medical care may be even greater than regional inequalities in wealth and

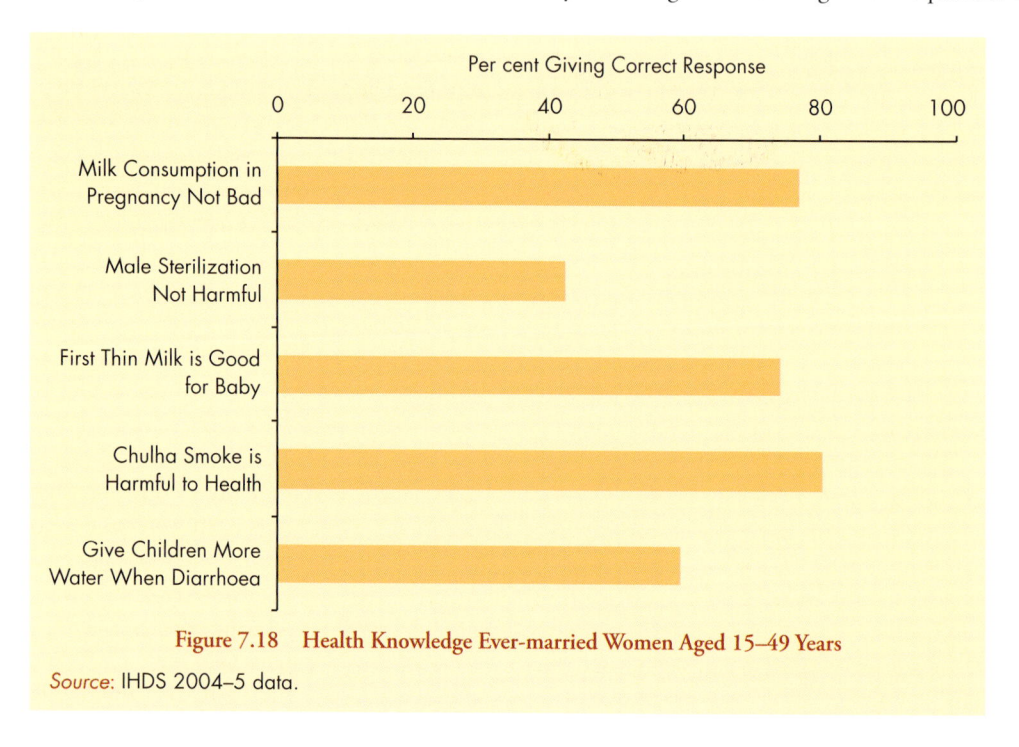

Figure 7.18 Health Knowledge Ever-married Women Aged 15–49 Years
Source: IHDS 2004–5 data.

> **Box 7.3 Television and HIV/AIDS Education**
>
> Television (TV) has played an important role in disseminating information about HIV/AIDS. The *NFHS* found that nearly 80 per cent of the individuals who have heard of AIDS have done so through television. This is not surprising, given that television has emerged as one of the most powerful forces for the transmission of information in the modern world. The proportion of women with any awareness of AIDS is barely 28 per cent among those who rarely or never watch TV, and 76 per cent among those who regularly watch TV.
>
> Thus, the data support the notion that television programming is an important cornerstone of the AIDS prevention strategy. However, there are two major problems on relying solely on TV to obtain information about HIV/AIDS. Although television appears to be a fine medium for providing basic information, its educational value remains unknown. For example, with urban residence, state of residence, education, and household consumption held constant, women who watch TV are 2.5 times more likely to know that that HIV/AIDS is spread through sexual contact. On the other hand, there is little difference between TV watchers and non-watchers regarding beliefs that AIDS is spread through mosquito bites, or by sharing food and utensils with an infected person. Thus, it appears that while sound bites focusing on warnings about sexual contact or blood transfusions are easily conveyed, the more complex understanding needed to prevent the stigmatization of an HIV-infected individual is difficult to convey through TV programmes.
>
> Another problem in relying largely on TV is that TV watching for women is more common in some parts of the country than in others, and among some social groups compared to others. Only about 45 per cent women in Bihar, Uttar Pradesh, Jharkhand, and Rajasthan watch TV, even occasionally, compared with 75–80 per cent in Maharashtra, Kerala, Tamil Nadu, and Punjab. Similarly, only 60 per cent of Dalit women and 42 per cent of Adivasi women watch TV, compared to more than 80 per cent of forward caste women. Not surprisingly, these figures regarding differences in TV watching are reflected in AIDS awareness. Only 30–45 per cent women in Bihar, Uttar Pradesh, Jharkhand, and Rajasthan have AIDS awareness, compared with 80–95 per cent for Maharashtra, Kerala, and Tamil Nadu. Similarly, while 77 per cent of the forward caste women have heard of AIDS, only 31 per cent of Adivasi women know anything about it.
>
> These statistics strongly suggest that television programming for increasing AIDS awareness was an effective strategy in the early stages of AIDS prevention, but that the strategy now needs to be broadened. Education must be increased both among individuals who have never heard of HIV/AIDS, and among men and women who have some awareness. Developing these strategies will require strengthening the community based initiatives being organized by the National AIDS Control Organization and greater involvement of health services personnel than has been the case so far. Although TV will continue to play a role in AIDS education, it is clear that the easy fruit has already been plucked and that much hard work remains to be done.
>
> *Source:* IHDS 2004–5 data.

education. The south consistently leads the country in reporting low levels of short-term morbidity and higher levels of health care. More southerners report themselves to be in good or very good health, fewer report short-term illnesses, and expectant mothers there report fewer medical problems than elsewhere in the country. Disabilities don't show the same southern advantage, but these are themselves the result of better health and longer life expectancy in the south. Better health means older people and, thus, more disabilities and greater mortality risks. Higher long-term morbidity rates in the south also result from this older age structure (and from the IHDS' emphasis on physician diagnoses as evidence of long-term morbidity). Chapter 8 carries this theme further. Southern states have lower infant and child mortality, and greater levels of vaccination than the central plains. Better medical care undoubtedly contributes to the south's health advantage. The south outperforms the rest of the country on every indicator of maternal medical care. More physician assisted deliveries in recognized medical facilities, more complete antenatal testing, and more common ante and postnatal physician examinations. All of these may also combine to reduce infant and child mortality.

The consistent urban bias in Indian health also deserves closer attention. City- and town-dwellers more often perceive themselves to be healthy, less often report suffering from minor illnesses, and are incapacitated for shorter periods when sick. Medical care is more accessible to them when they get sick and, perhaps more surprisingly, they spend somewhat less money on a typical minor illness than a villager. Urban mothers have fewer pregnancy problems and get much better antenatal, delivery, and postnatal care. The urban–rural differences are not as great as the state differences, but the consistency of the urban advantage across so many indicators testifies to the pervasive inequality rural residents suffer.

Only a small part of these regional inequalities result from differences in population composition. To some extent, individuals in the south and cities report lower morbidity and have better medical care because the people living there are better educated and have higher incomes. But most of the regional inequalities would remain even if we looked only at equivalent people, for instance, at primary school graduates in households with median incomes. Most of the regional differences are contextual. Everybody benefits from living in Kerala, regardless of his or her social position. Nevertheless, social inequalities matter. The poor, the illiterate, and the socially discriminated are disadvantaged in health and medical care, as they are in all aspects of life. The differences are smaller than the regional differences, but they are real.

Finally, the survey results also confirm the obvious fact that aging brings more health problems. Coughs, fevers, and diarrhoea may be especially common among children, but even short-term morbidity increases after middle age. Because of India's current youthful age structure, most illnesses and disabilities occur among the non-elderly, so the strong relationships with age may not be as obvious to the casual observer (or the policy maker) as they are in more developed countries. However, as India develops, its population will age, so many of the health problems analysed here may actually increase despite improved medical care, more education, cleaner cooking fuels, and better sanitation.

However, the greatest challenges to health policy are posed by high levels of household health expenditures combined with high use of private health care. While some private providers may be highly qualified, the data presented in Box 7.2 suggest considerable heterogeneity in private health care. Although the medical facility data in the IHDS are not nationally representative, they highlight the differences in qualification between government and private doctors. Whereas 86 per cent of government doctors had an MBBS (Bachelor of Medicine and Bachelor of Surgery) only 60 per cent of the private doctors are so qualified. Similarly, on an average, government facilities are better equipped and more likely to offer diagnostic testing. Why do most people rely on private health care providers? We have no definitive answer to this question, but a comparison of private and public facilities provides some clues. In spite of better equipment and training of providers, government facilities show signs of neglect and dereliction. The IHDS interviewers found that 15–18 per cent of government facilities had dirty walls or floors, compared with 5–8 per cent for the private facilities. Most importantly, nearly 24 per cent of the government doctors were not present at the time of this visit, compared to 13 per cent doctors in private facilities. These subtle differences may be amplified in direct experiences of patients, resulting in a preference for private providers.

Maternal care is one area in which government continues to play an important role. Fifty-one perce nt of hospital deliveries take place in government hospitals. Moreover, maternal care seems highly sensitive to household income. The importance of the public sector in providing maternal health care has been recognised in recent years, and programmes such as Janani Suraksha Yojana have been put in place to encourage greater maternal care. This is a promising beginning, and the coming decade may see substantial improvement in maternal health care.

HIGHLIGHTS

- There are substantial urban-rural and regional differences in morbidity. Reported short-term morbidity follows an expected pattern of lower morbidity in south than in the east and central plains.
- About four out of five individuals reported using a private health care provider for both short- and long-term illnesses; maternity care is a partial exception.
- Only 42 per cent women deliver in a hospital, and barely 35 per cent get a post-natal checkup.
- Household expenditures on long-term illnesses vary considerably by household economic status but there is little social class variation for expenditures on short-term illnesses.

Table A.7.1a Prevalence Rates and Days Lost Due to Different Types of Illnesses

	Cough, Fever, Diarrhoea			Long-term Illness			Disability		Maternity	Per cent of
	Morbidity Per 1,000	Days Incapacitated in Last Month (if sick)	Days Lost Per Year for Whole Population	Morbidity per 1,000	Days Incapacitated in Last Year (if sick)	Days Lost Per Year for Whole Population	Difficulty Per 1,000	Inability Per 1,000	Problems Last Birth (in Last 5 Years) Per cent	Self-reported Health Good or Very Good
All India	124	4.7	7.0	64	59	3.8	24	9	40	65
Sex										
Male	113	4.7	6.4	58	62	3.6	23	9	0	
Female	136	4.6	7.5	70	56	3.9	25	9	40	65
Age										
0–5	286	3.6	12.4	13	50	0.6				
6–14	136	4.1	6.7	17	53	0.9	8	4		
15–59	89	5.2	5.5	69	55	3.8	17	6	40	65
60+	118	7.1	10.1	215	71	15.2	106	39		
Own Education										
None	171	4.8	9.8	74	68	5.0	37	17	41	59
1–4 Std	130	4.8	7.5	46	59	2.7	21	6	41	65
5–9 Std	91	4.7	5.1	61	56	3.4	18	5	41	67
10–11 Std	75	4.1	3.7	65	43	2.8	18	4	38	72
12 Std/Some college	66	4.2	3.4	45	33	1.5	12	2	35	77
Graduate/Diploma	52	3.1	1.9	70	31	2.2	16	5	31	78
Place of Residence										
Metro	81	3.5	3.4	69	42	2.9	16	3	30	78
Other urban	110	3.9	5.1	70	51	3.6	24	8	33	69
More developed village	131	4.8	7.6	72	65	4.7	31	11	40	66
Less developed village	133	5.0	8.0	52	60	3.1	20	8	45	58
Income										
Lowest Quintile	159	5.4	10.3	70	66	4.6	33	14	42	61
2nd Quintile	143	4.8	8.3	60	69	4.2	23	9	42	62
3rd Quintile	128	4.7	7.3	60	58	3.5	21	8	40	63
4th Quintile	111	4.2	5.6	61	53	3.2	22	8	37	66
Top Quintile	91	3.9	4.3	65	49	3.2	22	6	38	70
Social Groups										
High Caste Hindu	116	4.2	5.8	72	58	4.2	26	8	39	66
OBC	125	4.9	7.3	68	59	4.0	24	10	38	68
Dalit	139	4.8	8.0	59	68	4.0	21	9	39	63
Adivasi	107	4.7	6.1	35	48	1.7	19	8	34	62
Muslim	123	4.7	7.0	55	51	2.8	21	7	51	56
Other religion	113	4.2	5.7	109	52	5.7	68	11	36	71

Source: IHDS 2004–5 data.

Table A.7.1b Statewise Prevalence Rates and Days Lost Due to Different Types of Ilnesses

| | Cough, Fever, Diarrhoea ||| Long-term Illness ||| Disability || Maternity | Per cent of |
	Morbidity Per 1,000	Days Incapacitated in Last Month (if sick)	Days lost Per Year for Whole Population	Morbidity Per 1,000	Days Incapacitated in Last Year (if sick)	Days lost Per Year for Whole Population	Difficulty Per 1,000	Inability Per 1,000	Problems Last Birth (in Last 5 Years) Per cent	Self-reported Health Good or Very Good
All India	124	4.7	7.0	64	59	3.8	24	9	40	65
Jammu and Kashmir	123	6.0	8.8	80	35	2.8	42	6	79	36
Himachal Pradesh	145	2.8	4.8	54	37	2.0	35	7	37	56
Uttarakhand	158	3.4	6.5	33	24	0.8	10	3	58	62
Punjab	119	4.4	6.2	66	93	6.1	24	7	49	48
Haryana	104	3.7	4.6	26	119	3.1	15	6	21	52
Delhi	83	2.9	2.9	43	52	2.2	3	0	54	60
Uttar Pradesh	139	4.9	8.2	50	72	3.6	10	6	49	48
Bihar	209	5.8	14.6	92	55	5.1	18	14	45	69
Jharkhand	108	3.7	4.8	44	20	0.9	12	4	58	39
Rajasthan	90	4.5	4.9	43	33	1.4	28	9	31	61
Chhattisgarh	148	5.7	10.1	51	61	3.1	41	12	24	60
Madhya Pradesh	134	3.8	6.1	46	44	2.0	23	13	27	70
North-East	107	4.5	5.7	19	44	0.8	6	1	24	43
Assam	76	2.9	2.6	20	49	1.0	2	2	76	37
West Bengal	173	3.8	7.9	85	38	3.2	39	11	44	53
Orissa	137	6.0	9.9	54	32	1.7	6	5	48	72
Gujarat	86	4.1	4.2	70	47	3.3	29	13	30	85
Maharashtra, Goa	107	4.4	5.7	54	78	4.2	31	8	36	76
Andhra Pradesh	108	6.1	7.9	85	120	10.2	7	5	33	59
Karnataka	73	4.5	3.9	57	65	3.7	23	10	31	96
Kerala	119	4.5	6.4	120	44	5.3	114	16	41	78
Tamil Nadu	97	3.9	4.5	106	31	3.2	29	16	15	88

Source: IHDS 2004–5 data.

Table A.7.2a Utilization of Medical Care and Expenditure for Illnesses and Delivery

	Cough, Fever, Diarrhoea			Long-term Illness				Maternity		
	Treated in Government Centre (per cent)	Treated Outside Local Area (per cent)	Median Expenses If Sick (Rs)	No Treatment (per cent)	Hospitalized (per cent)	Treated in Government Facility (per cent)	Treated Outside Local Area (per cent)	Median Expenses If Sick (Rs)	Doctor Delivery (per cent)	Per cent in Public Hospital if Hospital Delivery
All India	17	42	120	9	25	23	62	1,900	42	51
Sex										
Male	17	44	126	10	27	25	63	2,100		
Female	18	41	105	8	24	22	62	1,700	42	51
Age										
0–6	15	44	115	9	33	19	75	2,030		
6–14	17	40	100	21	26	15	59	1,250		
15–59	19	42	140	8	24	23	64	2,000	42	51
60+	22	47	140	8	27	26	59	2,000		
Education										
None	16	45	120	10	26	24	66	1,700	24	61
1–4 Std	18	41	100	7	25	23	66	1,800	37	65
5–9 Std	20	40	110	10	27	24	58	2,000	52	57
10–11 Std	22	35	150	5	24	19	60	2,200	68	42
12 Std/Some college	21	37	150	5	25	23	59	2,050	78	36
Graduate/Diploma	15	32	120	4	20	20	51	2,550	91	25
Place of Residence										
Metro	15	13	100	3	21	27	29	1,710	75	51
Other urban	18	27	110	6	25	23	46	2,000	66	46
More developed village	21	41	130	9	27	25	67	2,000	43	50
Less developed village	15	53	110	12	25	20	75	1,632	25	61
Income										
Lowest Quintile	17	48	100	12	23	22	69	1,460	27	60
2nd Quintile	18	44	110	14	27	22	66	1,500	28	63
3rd Quintile	17	42	116	10	26	23	64	1,750	41	59
4th Quintile	18	38	120	6	28	27	59	2,000	51	51
Top Quintile	18	39	130	5	23	23	56	2,450	69	36
Social Groups										
High Caste Hindu	16	39	115	6	23	20	58	2,250	58	44
OBC	17	46	150	9	26	21	65	1,800	44	47
Dalit	17	39	100	11	26	27	63	1,500	35	65
Adivasi	24	50	80	20	32	28	64	600	18	68
Muslim	17	40	120	7	24	27	64	2,025	36	60
Other religion	22	37	150	5	24	22	58	2,400	84	24

Source: IHDS 2004–5 data.

Table A.7.2b Statewise Utilization of Medical Care and Expenditure for Ilnesses and Delivery

	Cough, Fever, Diarrhoea			Long Term Illness					Maternity	
	Treated in Government Centre (per cent)	Treated Outside Local Area (per cent)	Median Expenses If Sick (Rs)	No Treatment (per cent)	Hospitalized (per cent)	Treated in Government Facility (per cent)	Treated Outside Local Area (per cent)	Median Expenses If Sick (Rs)	Doctor Delivery (per cent)	Pe cent in Public Hospital if Hospital Delivery
All India	17	42	120	9	25	23	62	1,900	42	51
Jammu and Kashmir	49	55	282	6	20	49	73	2,500	66	89
Himachal Pradesh	56	61	131	5	38	65	81	3,700	37	82
Uttarakhand	28	43	100	NA	NA	NA	NA	NA	20	NA
Punjab	8	29	100	2	17	19	61	2,900	47	19
Haryana	20	49	160	4	37	34	76	5,200	36	47
Delhi	34	11	100	3	12	76	23	510	62	67
Uttar Pradesh	7	43	100	8	29	20	77	3,000	15	49
Bihar	2	44	170	8	22	4	77	1,360	29	25
Jharkhand	10	47	100	27	20	9	60	700	33	37
Rajasthan	38	51	130	11	26	44	61	3,000	25	72
Chhattisgarh	23	39	80	21	18	22	62	850	21	NA
Madhya Pradesh	12	49	120	11	31	16	69	2,200	16	75
North-East	42	36	112	NA	NA	NA	NA	NA	66	76
Assam	37	32	40	NA	NA	NA	NA	NA	24	NA
West Bengal	10	27	50	12	15	20	44	900	40	81
Orissa	35	50	100	18	16	44	56	700	36	88
Gujarat	16	50	100	17	34	19	65	1,800	57	40
Maharashtra, Goa	19	37	100	3	37	20	56	1,500	68	45
Andhra Pradesh	14	42	250	5	17	13	58	2,200	82	39
Karnataka	32	60	200	8	31	25	68	3,080	57	53
Kerala	43	36	150	6	24	33	52	2,050	98	41
Tamil Nadu	35	54	157	7	33	37	58	1,700	79	49

Note: NA—not available due to small sample sizes.
Source: IHDS 2004–5 data.

Table A.7.3a Health Knowledge: Ever-married Women Aged 15–49 Years

(in percentage)

	Health Knowledge	AIDS Awareness	AIDS Spread Knowledge
All India	62	55	76
Age			
15–19	57	47	73
20–9	62	59	77
30–9	63	55	77
40–9	63	47	75
Education			
None	57	30	67
1–4 Std	61	51	70
5–9 Std	65	74	76
10–11 Std	70	93	83
12 Std/Some college	75	96	87
Graduate/Diploma	78	99	90
Place of Residence			
Metro	74	87	86
Other urban	65	78	79
More developed village	62	56	74
Less developed village	60	35	72
Income			
Lowest Quintile	58	36	71
2nd Quintile	58	42	70
3rd Quintile	61	49	73
4th Quintile	64	61	77
Top Quintile	69	78	82
Social Groups			
High Caste Hindu	68	73	81
OBC	62	54	76
Dalit	60	48	71
Adivasi	58	33	68
Muslim	59	44	75
Other religion	75	87	85

Source: IHDS 2004–5 data.

Table A.7.3b Health Knowledge: Ever-married Women Aged 15–49 Years by State

(in percentage)

	Health Knowledge	AIDS Awareness	AIDS Spread Knowledge
All India	62	55	76
Jammu and Kashmir	67	37	76
Himachal Pradesh	73	84	76
Uttarakhand	63	61	75
Punjab	69	60	77
Haryana	71	59	79
Delhi	74	80	78
Uttar Pradesh	66	31	76
Bihar	51	25	73
Jharkhand	60	48	62
Rajasthan	69	37	69
Chhattisgarh	68	35	73
Madhya Pradesh	64	44	76
North-East	61	81	79
Assam	26	32	62
West Bengal	64	44	72
Orissa	69	61	72
Gujarat	69	55	82
Maharashtra, Goa	62	78	80
Andhra Pradesh	50	72	74
Karnataka	57	53	84
Kerala	82	98	87
Tamil Nadu	61	93	73

Source: IHDS 2004–5 data.

Vulnerable Population

8

Child Well-being

The well-being of children is one of the most important markers of development for any nation and has formed an integral part of all discussions about human development. As India experiences record economic growth rates, it is fair to ask whether the advantages of economic growth reach this vulnerable section of society. Children face different risks at different ages. Young children need a chance to grow up healthy and strong through the risky years of infancy and early childhood. Children who survive these risks past age five need an opportunity to feed their minds in a nurturing educational environment and teenagers need an opportunity to prepare themselves for adult roles, without being thrust into premature responsibilities. This chapter assesses how well India has done by her most vulnerable citizens in providing these opportunities. Although education and health have received considerable attention in Chapters 6 and 7, respectively, this chapter attempts to place some of these discussions in the context of broader societal patterns by focusing on two dimensions of child well-being, child health and survival, and labour force participation.

INFANT AND CHILD SURVIVAL

While sweeping epidemics and widespread famines seem to be a thing of the past, young children still face substantial risks in the first five years of life. Many sources of data, including the Sample Registration System as well as the three waves of the *NFHS*, document substantial declines in infant and child mortality. For example, the *NFHS* recorded a decline in the infant mortality rate (that is, the number of children dying before completing the first year of life) from 79 per 1,000 births in 1992–3 to 57 per 1,000 births in 2005–6. In spite of this impressive decline, the *NFHS* recorded that one out of 14 children die before reaching age five, and the IHDS records an infant mortality rate of 52 per 1,000 births.

Although levels of infant and child mortality are important, as we think about policies to address this, it is the age pattern of mortality that deserves the greatest attention. Death in the first month of life, called neonatal mortality, is frequently associated with gestational and delivery problems, genetic factors, premature birth, or a complicated delivery. Post-neonatal deaths (that is, death in the second through twelfth months of life) may be somewhat influenced by low birth weight or delivery related factors, but the role of environmental factors in post-neonatal deaths becomes far more important. Infant deaths in this age range are often due to respiratory illnesses as well as poor nutrition. Among children who survive to be one-year old, between age one and five, most of the deaths are due to environmental causes, which include diarrhoea and other gastrointestinal diseases, respiratory illness and other contagious diseases, and accidents.

Figure 8.1 indicates the distribution of deaths among children under five in the IHDS.

In calculating these figures, we focused on all live births occurring in the ten-year period preceding the survey.[1] Figure 8.1 indicates that a majority of deaths occur to newborn

---

[1] In surveys with larger samples, such as the *NFHS*, it is common to focus on births in the preceding three years. Given the sample size limitations in the IHDS, however, we focused on births in the preceding ten years. While the number of births covered by IHDS is quite large, 38,259 births in the preceding ten years, the number of deaths is much smaller at 2,373 reducing the precision of the estimate. Hence, results presented here should be treated with caution.

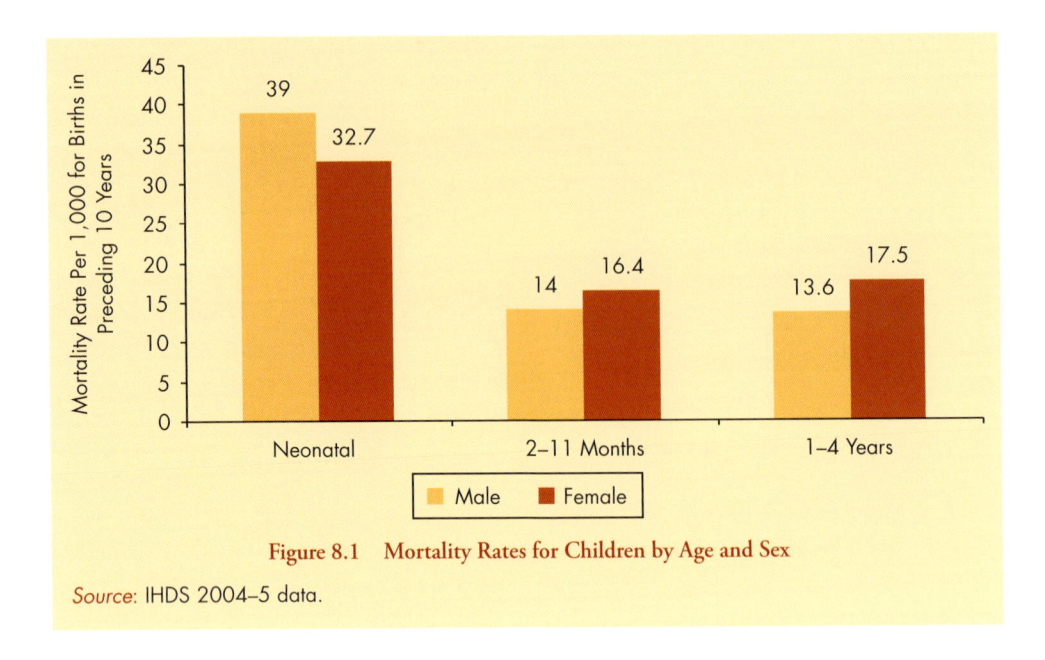

Figure 8.1 Mortality Rates for Children by Age and Sex

Source: IHDS 2004–5 data.

Neonatal: Male 39, Female 32.7
2–11 Months: Male 14, Female 16.4
1–4 Years: Male 13.6, Female 17.5

infants and that the risk of death declines with age. The IHDS documents that averaging over births occurring in the prior ten years, about 52 out of 1,000 infants die before reaching the one-year mark; of these, nearly 36 deaths occur in the first month of life. That most of these deaths are associated with gestational factors and delivery complications highlights the importance of providing adequate care to pregnant women and providing emergency care for women with difficult births. Survival past this dangerous period reduces the chances of death. Another 16 out of 1,000 children die before reaching age one, and an additional 16 die before turning five.

A comparison of infant and child mortality across different parts of the country and different social groups presented in Tables A.8.1a and A.8.1b highlights the inequalities in infant and child survival. Much of the neonatal mortality is concentrated among families living in villages, with poorly developed infrastructure, as well as among those in the lowest income quintile. It has been argued in the literature that delivery related complications often cannot be anticipated. Hence, when a woman experiences pregnancy related complications, emergency assistance is necessary. As documented in Chapter 7, women in higher income households are more likely than those in lower income households to have a hospital delivery, where emergency assistance is constantly available. Moreover, women in metropolitan cities can be easily rushed to a hospital in case of emergency. However, in remote villages it may be difficult to get women to hospital in time to save the mother and/or child.

Social group differences in neonatal mortality are also quite large. Dalit children have a considerably higher likelihood of death in the first month than children from other households, as also Adivasis, who generally suffer from similar, if not greater disadvantages. High neonatal mortality among Dalits has been documented in the IHDS as well as the *NFHS-III* and deserves particular attention because it represents a cascading of inequality that we have documented in other chapters, with Dalits having lower educational attainment and incomes. However, these inequalities are shared by Dalits and Adivasis. What makes Dalit children particularly vulnerable in the first month of life? This vulnerability may reflect a greater inability of Dalit and Adivasi families to obtain emergency obstetric care since, for the post-neonatal period, they exhibit a similar pattern of mortality. Although it is not possible for us to draw any conclusions regarding the role of social exclusion in this context, we believe that this is an area of concern that requires particular attention and future research.

Regional and state differences in neonatal mortality are also striking. All the hill states—Jammu and Kashmir, Himachal Pradesh, and Uttarakhand—document relatively high neonatal mortality although, with the exception of Uttarakhand, their post-neonatal mortality and child mortality are not particularly high. It seems highly likely that the high neonatal mortality in these states is associated with the difficulties in obtaining emergency obstetric care due to vast distances and difficulties in transportation across mountainous roads. However, it is important to exercise caution in interpreting these results. These results are based on a substantial number of births—with minimum sample of about 550 births in a state. However, given the rarity of deaths, number of deaths being quite small, and omission of a few dead children from maternal reports can substantially change the results.

When we look at overall child mortality, that is, mortality rates for children under five, we see stark differences between privileged and vulnerable sections of the society. Dalit and Adivasi children have higher mortality rates than other social groups with Dalit children being particularly vulnerable. Educational and income differences are important, as well as those between less developed villages and metropolitan cities. Gender differences are also important and discussed in greater detail in the following section. Figure 8.2 provides an interesting snapshot of infant and child mortality by birth order.

While children of mothers at higher parities are generally disadvantaged, when it comes to neonatal mortality, the first-born children face higher risks than those born to women who already have one child. First births are usually more risky than second births, but most of these risks are related to delivery complications and mostly affect neonatal mortality rates. However, children at parity 4 and at parity 5 and beyond face substantially higher mortality risks. These higher risks are undoubtedly partly attributable to the lower education and income of parents who have large families, but a higher birth order also poses some risks.

IMMUNIZATION

In spite of the emphasis on immunization for vaccine-preventable diseases—polio, diphtheria, whooping cough, tetanus, measles, and tuberculosis—universal immunization remains far from reality. The World Health Organization recommends three doses of polio vaccine, three doses of DPT (diphtheria-pertussis-tetanus), one dose of BCG (Bacillus Calmette-Guérin) against tuberculosis, and one dose of measles vaccine before 12 months. Only about 48 per cent of children under five in the IHDS sample received full vaccination (see Table A.8.2a). About 7 per cent received no vaccine, and the remaining 45 per cent received an incomplete series of vaccinations. These figures are comparable to those from the *NFHS-III*, which found that only 44 per cent of those aged 12–23 three months received all basic vaccinations.

Given the tremendous fanfare with which Pulse Polio campaigns are being conducted, this low level of vaccine coverage might seem surprising. However, an examination of trends in vaccination in the three waves of *NFHS* surveys documents that although polio coverage increased sharply from 54 per cent in 1992–3 to 63 per cent in 1998–9 and to 78 per cent in 2005–6, improvement in the full series of DPT vaccinations was far more limited, 52 per cent in 1992–3, 55.1 per cent in 1998–9, and 55.3 per cent in 2005–6. The stagnation in DPT coverage between 1998–9 and 2005–6 is in striking contrast to the growth in the rate of polio vaccinations. In many ways it points to the limits of campaigns for providing basic health services. The Pulse Polio campaigns have focused on vaccinating as many children as possible on specified days, with vaccination booths being set up at train stations, on street corners, and in schools. This has clearly borne fruit with rapid increase in polio immunization. However, it may well have diverted attention from regular immunization services, causing the proportion of children receiving full vaccinations to lag behind the proportion of children receiving polio vaccinations. The results from the IHDS indicate that while 71per cent of children received three or more doses of polio, only 55 per cent received three doses of DPT (see Table A.8.2a).

Vaccination is an area in which family education plays a particularly important role. While inequalities in income and residence are reflected in vaccination status, the difference, between families in which no one has attended school and those in which even one adult has completed

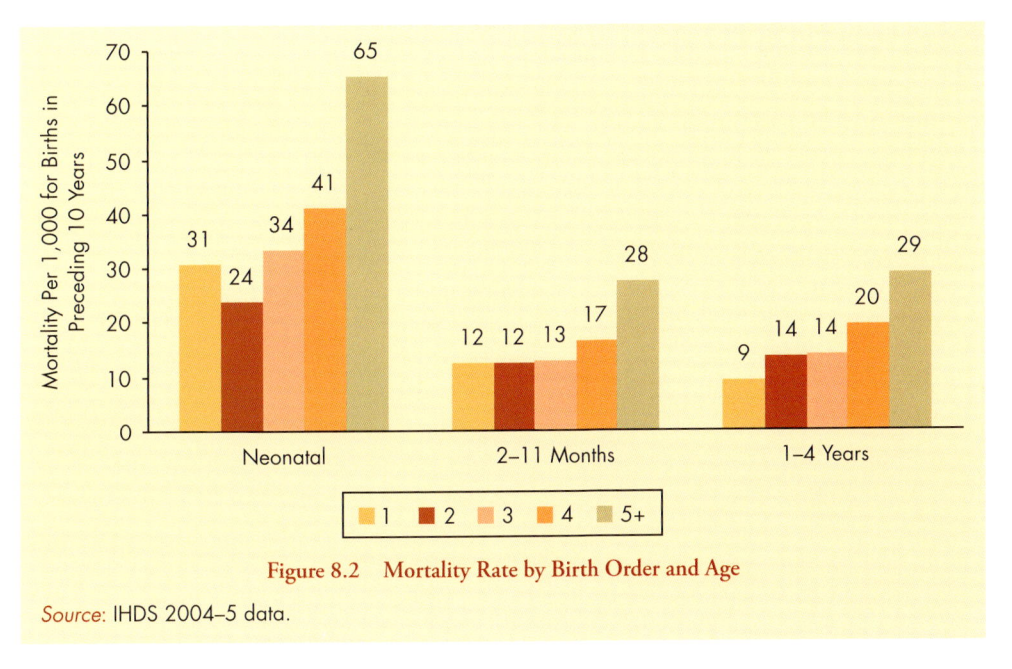

Figure 8.2 Mortality Rate by Birth Order and Age

Source: IHDS 2004–5 data.

primary school, is quite striking. Households in which an adult has a college degree is associated with a fairly high rate of vaccination coverage, although even in these households, only 67 per cent children get all recommended vaccines.

Regional differences in vaccination coverage are vast. Only 32 per cent of children in Rajasthan receive a full battery of immunizations, compared with more than 80 per cent for children in Tamil Nadu. Note that our statewise figures are affected by smaller sample sizes. For example, the figures in Bihar are based on only 655 children aged 12–59 months. Full vaccination coverage seems particularly less likely in villages with poorly developed infrastructure. Home visits by a health worker during pregnancy seem to increase the likelihood of completing a full series of vaccinations, and this improvement is particularly noticeable in villages. As Figure 8.3 indicates, relatively few women in urban areas receive home visits, and they are able to find vaccination services for their children regardless of the home visit.

In contrast, it appears that home visits during pregnancy (and presumably following delivery) form a major source of vaccinations for children in rural areas.

GENDER AND CHILD HEALTH AND SURVIVAL

It is difficult to talk about child health without recognizing that child well-being in India is highly gendered. In spite of the euphemism about a daughter being the image of Goddess Laxmi, daughters are welcomed with far less enthusiasm than sons. Declining juvenile sex ratios have drawn our attention sharply to this phenomenon. Around the world, in the absence of deliberate selection the sex ratio at birth is 105 boys to 100 girls, about 51 per cent of births are boys and 49 per cent are girls (that is, a sex ratio of 98 female births to 100 male births). But in many parts of India, the sex ratio at birth is far more masculine oriented, with only 85–90 female births per 100 male births, suggesting prevalence of female foeticide (Figure 8.4).

The IHDS documents that, on an average, 52 per cent of the births are boys while only 48 per cent are girls. This overall statistic understates the extent of sex selection in some states. Punjab is most striking, with only about 85 female births per 100 male births. In contrast, the North-East, Chhattisgarh and Jharkhand show little evidence of female disadvantage at birth. Perhaps the greatest evidence of sex selection comes from comparing families with and without a prior male birth at parities 2 and 3. As Figure 8.5 documents, at parities 2, 3, and 4 or greater, when a household does not have any sons, the likelihood of the birth of a boy exceeds the likelihood of the birth of a girl substantially.

After a son has been born, however, the sex ratio at birth becomes more favourable to girls. This suggests that sex-selective abortion may have something to do with skewing the sex ratio at birth in families with no sons.

How is this possible given the legislation against sex determination? According to the 2001 legislation titled Pre-Conception and Pre-Natal Diagnostics Test Act, although a physician may perform amniocentesis or a sonogram to determine a child's health risks, he or she is not allowed to tell the parents the sex of the child. However, our results suggest that this law is honoured in the breach. First, results presented in Figure 8.6 for births occurring in the five years

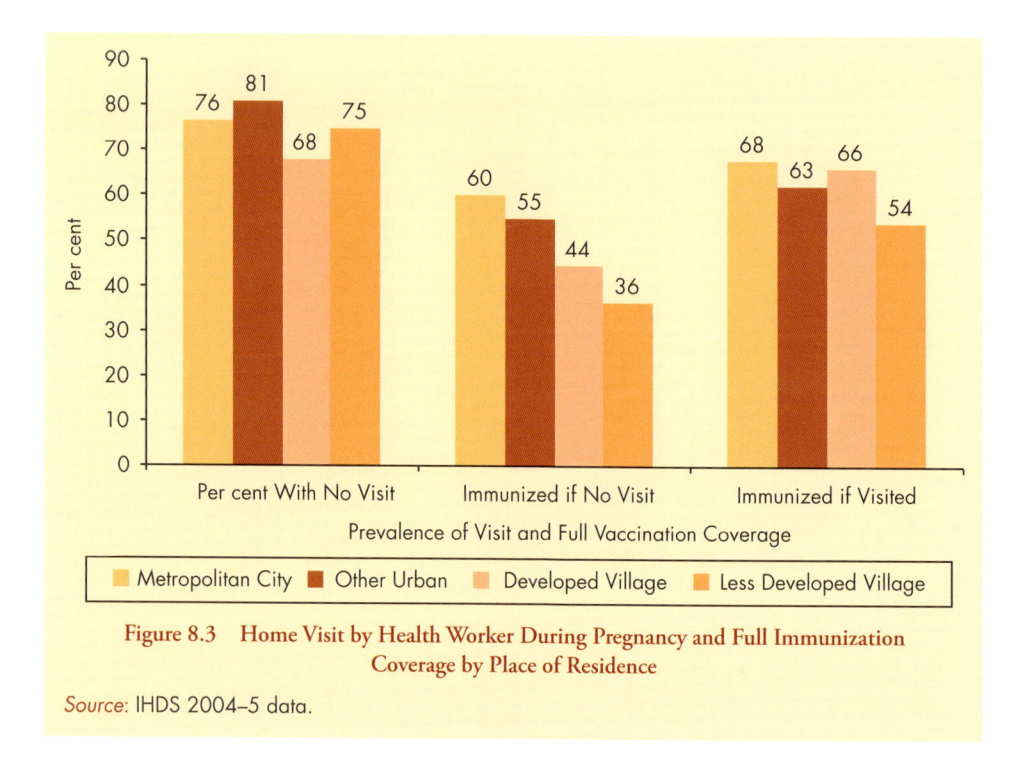

Figure 8.3 Home Visit by Health Worker During Pregnancy and Full Immunization Coverage by Place of Residence

Source: IHDS 2004–5 data.

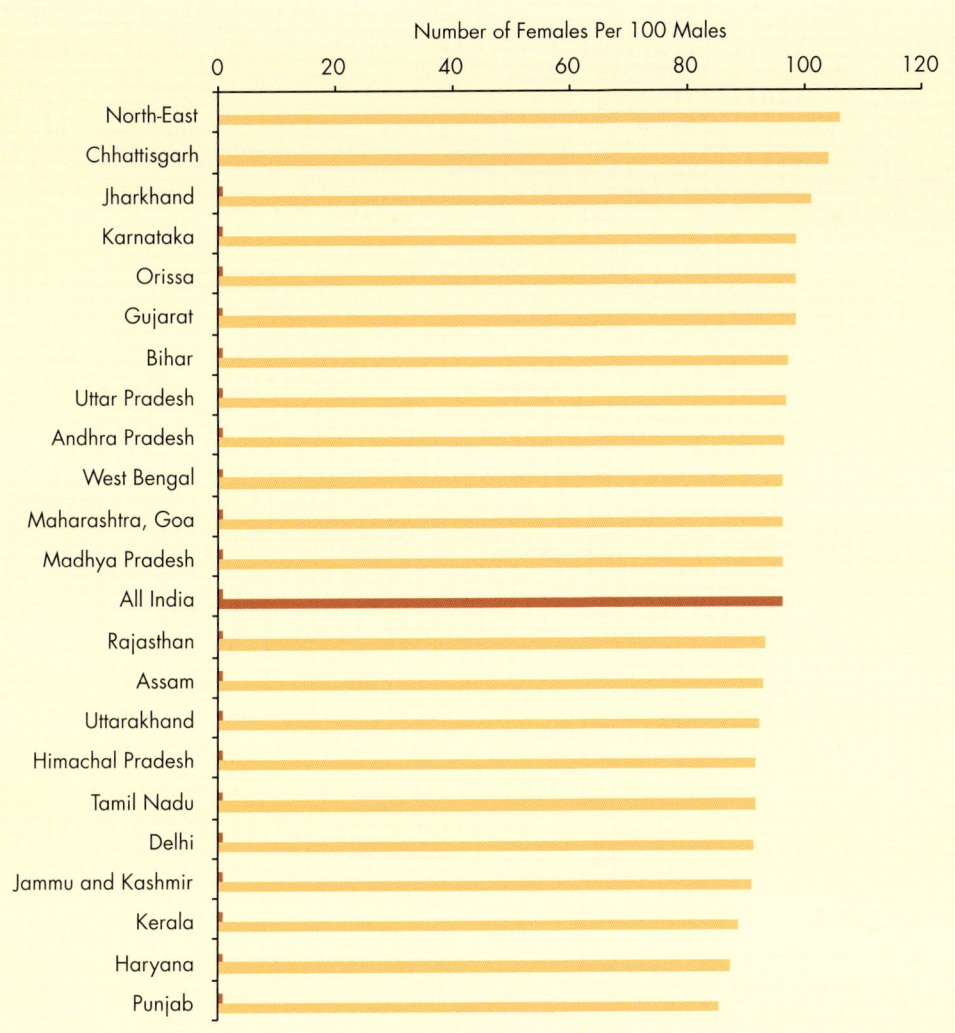

Figure 8.4 Sex Ratio at Birth

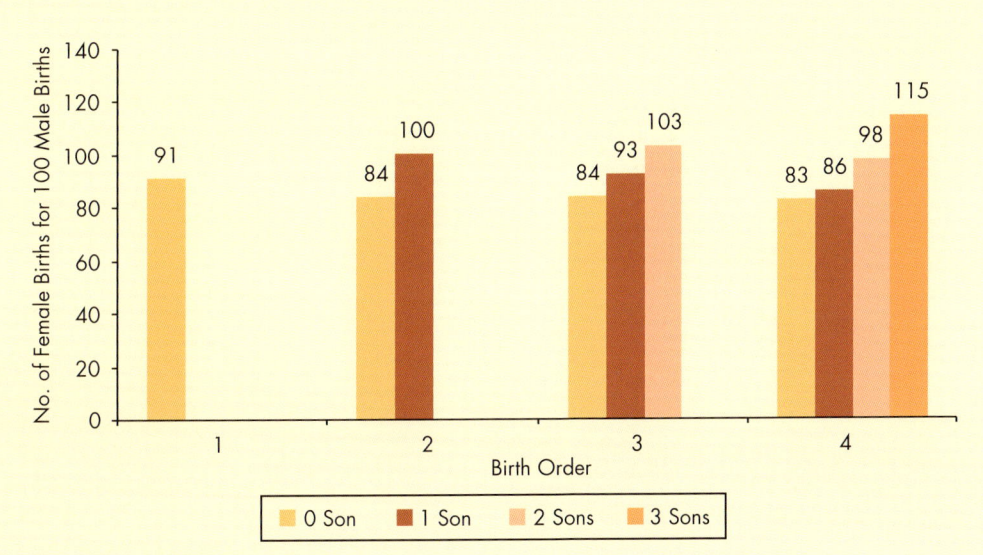

Source: IHDS 2004–5 data.

Figure 8.5 Sex Ratio at Birth by Birth Order and Number of Children

Source: IHDS 2004–5 data.

Figure 8.6 Percentage of Women Getting Ultrasound/Amniocentesis by Birth Order and Number of Sons

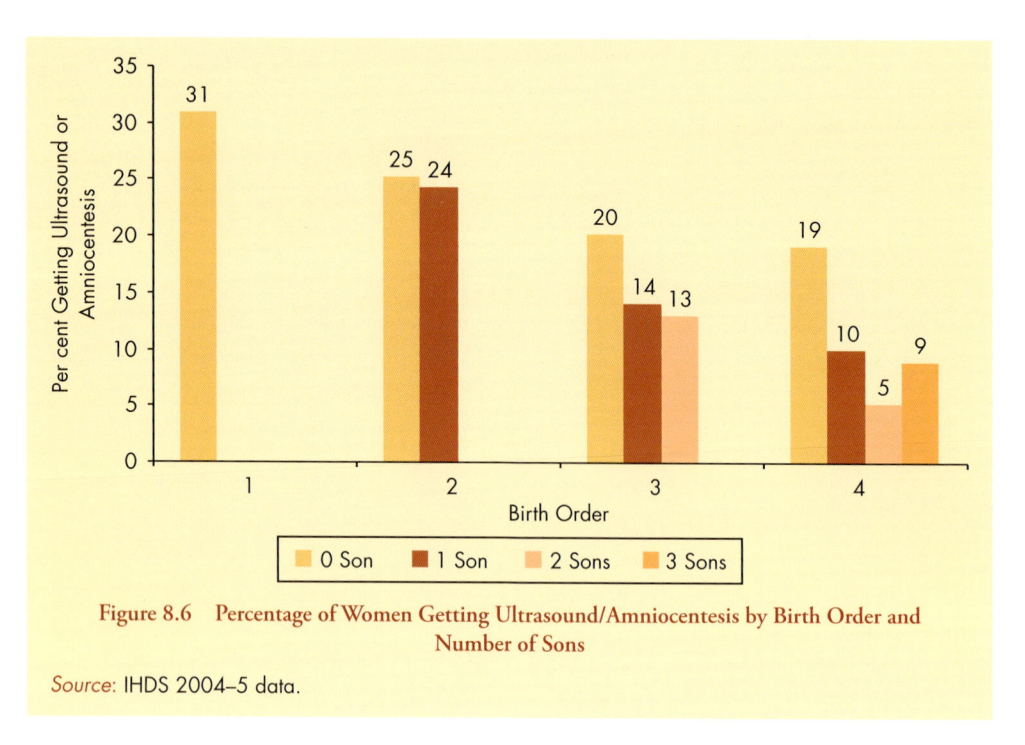

Source: IHDS 2004–5 data.

preceding the survey show that at each parity the proportion of women who have undergone a sonogram is higher for women who have no sons, than for those who already have a son.

This difference is particularly large for third and later births. Second, the IHDS asked women who had undergone a sonogram or amniocentesis whether they knew the sex of the child. Nearly 34 per cent said they were aware of the sex of the child. This suggests that the role of sex determination in shaping the sex ratio at birth cannot be ignored.

While sex-selective abortion results in a lower likelihood of female birth than might be biologically expected, the neglect of girls leads to their higher mortality. Figure 8.1 had shown the likelihood of death during the first month, 2–11 months, and one to four years, for boys and girls. As discussed earlier, neonatal deaths are often due to pregnancy and delivery related factors, but subsequent deaths are more environment-driven. Research also indicates that in the absence of preferential treatment of boys, boys have higher mortality at all ages than girls, until girls reach reproductive

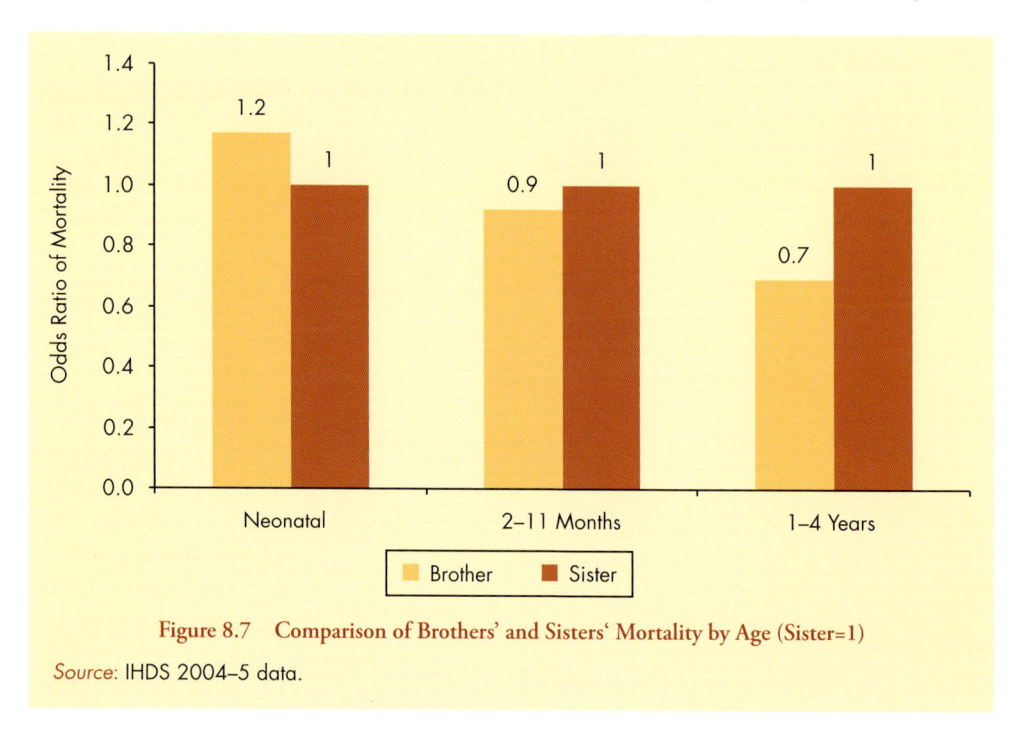

Figure 8.7 Comparison of Brothers' and Sisters' Mortality by Age (Sister=1)

Source: IHDS 2004–5 data.

age. Our results confirm this for the neonatal period, when boys suffer from higher mortality than girls. However, after the first month of life, the mortality rate is higher for girls than for boys.

The clearest evidence of the higher mortality of girls comes from comparing mortality rates of brothers and sisters. When we compare siblings, we hold family income, education, place of residence, and neighbourhood infrastructure constant and allow only the sex of the child to vary. As Figure 8.7 indicates, within the same family, boys are 1.4 times as likely as girls to die in the first month of life, but their relative mortality rate falls to barely 66 per cent of that of their sisters at ages one to four years.

CHILD LABOUR AND SCHOOL ENROLMENT

As one travels through India and is served by young boys in corner tea shops or sees young children driving animals on rural roads, it is natural to worry about children's exploitation by employers and the impact of a heavy work burden leading to school dropout. However, most studies of child labour in India have documented that although there are pockets of industries in which children may be employed, in general, relatively few Indian children are employed. The IHDS is no exception. As Figure 8.8 indicates, only about 11 per cent of children aged 10–14 are employed, even when we use a fairly generous definition of labour force, including work on the family farm, care for animals, work for a family business, and wage work.

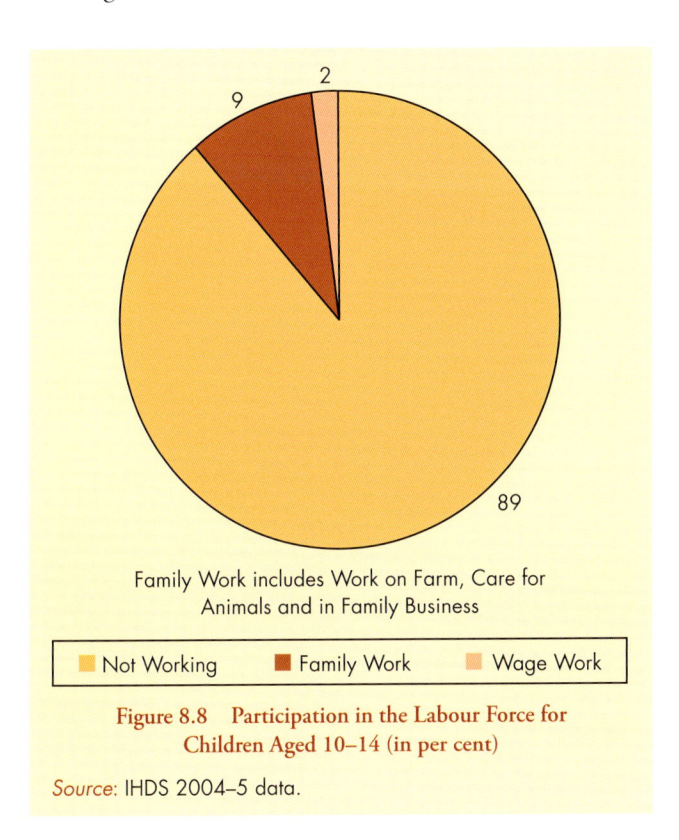

Of these 11 per cent, 9 per cent mostly participate in family-based work; 8 per cent care for animals; 7 per cent work on the family farm, 1 per cent work in family business, and several do more than one activity. Most of the children who work on the family farm do so during harvesting or other high demand period, with 50 per cent working sixty or fewer days in farm work during the preceding year. Most of this work is limited to a few hours per day; the median number of hours worked per day is two for teenagers (as compared with six for adults). This suggests that most of the work by children takes the form of helping in family-based work rather than labouring in sweatshops.

Tables A.8.3a and A.8.3b examine this issue in greater depth. The results indicate that 77 per cent of children are in school and do not participate in the labour force as defined above. A further 11 per cent are neither working nor enrolled in school. Among the 14 per cent that are employed, 8 per cent seem to combine this work with being in school and only 3 per cent are in the labour force and have dropped out. The proportion of children out of school and in the labour force increases with age and is greater among poorer households.

However, two very striking things emerge from this table. First, an overwhelming majority of Indian children are enrolled in school and do not participate in the labour force. Second, the next biggest group consists of children who are neither employed, nor in school. Thus, if one is concerned about school enrolment, it is this group that deserves greater attention. Some of these children may have dropped out to care for younger siblings, others may have dropped out because school was uninteresting or oppressive, and still others may see little benefit in formal education. As we think about improving school enrolment, focusing on this group may give the greatest payoff. In Chapter 6, we noted that young children often face poor quality instruction and physical punishment in schools, with nearly 25 per cent parents of children aged 8–11 indicating that their children had been beaten or pinched in the preceding month. Improvements in school conditions to keep these children in school may be more important for increasing educational attainment than focusing on controlling or eliminating child labour.

DISCUSSION

The data presented in this chapter points to family and public policy as two distinct but interrelated forces shaping child well-being. Families influence children's well-being by valuing and investing in each child differently. They also serve as the intermediaries through which public services are delivered to children. Hence, when families are unwilling or unable to mobilize these services on behalf of their children, children are often marginalized from public institutions. While the data we presented on parental preference for

Figure 8.8 Participation in the Labour Force for Children Aged 10–14 (in per cent)

Source: IHDS 2004–5 data.

boys over girls is most clearly seen in gender differences in child mortality and prenatal sex selection, almost all the data presented in this chapter as well as in Chapters 6 and 7 document girls' disadvantage in education and health care. Immunization data presented in this chapter indicates that 46 per cent of girls are fully vaccinated, compared with 49 per cent of boys. When their children were sick with minor illnesses like a cough, cold, or fever, parents spent about Rs 126 on treatment and doctors for boys in the preceding month, compared to Rs 105 for girls. These are all small differences but may accumulate to create disadvantages for girls. However, we see little of this gender difference in polio immunizations, for which government campaigns do not rely on parental cooperation. This suggests that public policies must be devised in a way that takes into account a parental preference for boys.

The results also suggest that children of poor and less educated parents are most likely to be left out of the medical system and experience higher rates of mortality and lower levels of vaccination. This points towards another reason why government outreach programmes for children must be strengthened to cover all children and programmes must rely less on parents and focus more on the delivery of universal services.

Public policies have also sometimes relied on assumed parental indifference or poverty when explaining the poor educational performance of schools. For example, child labour is frequently blamed for poor school performance and dropout. Although child labour is present in Indian society and may well be responsible for some proportion of school dropout, the fact that a large proportion of children are neither in school nor working suggests that making schools more welcoming and interesting to these students may have a greater payoff in terms of increasing school enrolment than a focus on child labour elimination.

HIGHLIGHTS

- Infant mortality is largely concentrated in the first month of life.
- Infant and child mortality rates vary dramatically by place of residence. Metropolitan cities have an infant mortality rate of 18 per 1,000, compared with 60 per 1,000 for less developed villages.
- Although girls have a biological advantage in survival in the first month of life, they experience higher mortality after the first month and into early childhood.
- Even within the same family, once past the first month, girls are less likely than their brothers to survive childhood.
- At an all India level, 77 per cent of children aged 10–14 are in school and do not engage in any remunerative work. Only 2 per cent of children aged 10–14 are involved in wage work; 9 per cent work on farms or family businesses.
- However, 11 per cent are neither employed nor in school.

Table A.8.1a Infant and Child Mortality Rate (Per 1,000 Births) for Births in Preceding 10 Years

	Mortality Rate		
	In Month 1	In Year 1	Under Age 5
All India	36	52	69
Sex of Child			
Male	39	53	67
Female	33	50	70
Place of Residence			
Metro area	14	18	31
Other urban	33	47	56
More developed village	34	49	64
Less developed village	41	60	82
Income			
Lowest Quintile	48	68	78
2nd Quintile	39	59	85
3rd Quintile	35	50	68
4th Quintile	35	46	63
Top Quintile	20	29	37
Social Groups			
Forward Caste Hindu	31	42	50
OBC	33	46	63
Dalit	45	67	94
Adivasi	35	57	76
Muslim	37	51	63
Other religion	16	21	32
Maximum Household Education			
None	45	69	92
1–4 Std	41	62	75
5–9 Std	38	52	70
10–11 Std	28	33	45
12 Std/Some college	26	35	38
Graduate/Diploma	17	30	37

Source: IHDS 2004–5 data.

Table A.8.1b Statewise Infant and Child Mortality Rate (Per 1,000 Births) for Births in Preceding 10 Years

	Mortality Rate		
	In Month 1	In Year 1	Under Age 5
All India	36	52	69
Jammu and Kashmir	43	47	58
Himachal Pradesh	36	41	49
Uttarakhand	54	60	81
Punjab	31	44	60
Haryana	31	41	39
Delhi	3	5	10
Uttar Pradesh	53	80	116
Bihar	25	43	69
Jharkhand	38	60	63
Rajasthan	47	63	89
Chhattisgarh	36	52	85
Madhya Pradesh	33	54	58
North-East	21	38	48
Assam	24	33	28
West Bengal	31	51	59
Orissa	59	69	86
Gujarat	24	38	52
Maharashtra, Goa	26	37	42
Andhra Pradesh	27	34	46
Karnataka	38	46	62
Kerala	6	9	11
Tamil Nadu	34	40	57

Note: Statewise differences in mortality should be interpreted cautiously due to small samples.
Source: IHDS 2004–5 data.

Table A.8.2a Vaccination Rate for Children Aged 12–59 Months

(in percentage)

	Number of Vaccination	All Basic Vaccines	No Vaccines	3 Polio Doses	3 DPT Doses
All India	5.83	48	7	71	55
Sex of Child					
Male	5.91	49	6	72	57
Female	5.74	46	7	71	53
Place of Residence					
Metro area	6.91	62	1	84	69
Other urban	6.37	56	5	75	63
More developed village	5.94	51	6	73	58
Less developed village	5.37	40	9	67	48
Income					
Lowest Quintile	5.44	42	8	66	48
2nd Quintile	5.43	43	10	69	51
3rd Quintile	5.79	45	7	71	53
4th Quintile	6.02	50	5	72	59
Top Quintile	6.75	63	3	80	69
Social Groups					
Forward Caste Hindu	6.66	60	2	79	67
OBC	5.87	48	5	73	57
Dalit	5.76	47	7	71	53
Adivasi	5.64	40	11	65	51
Muslim	4.87	34	14	60	41
Other religion	7.39	76	0	86	89
Maximum Household Education					
None	4.71	31	11	62	37
1–4 Std	5.37	43	10	65	50
5–9 Std	5.93	48	6	72	56
10–11 Std	6.24	54	4	74	64
12 Std/Some college	6.59	60	5	79	65
Graduate/Diploma	7.03	67	2	83	76

Source: IHDS 2004–5 data.

Table A.8.2b Statewise Vaccination Rate for Children Aged 12–59 Months

(in percentage)

	Number of Vaccination	All Basic Vaccines	No Vaccines	3 Polio Doses	3 DPT Doses
All India	5.83	48	7	71	55
Jammu and Kashmir	6.48	47	4	71	68
Himachal Pradesh	7.48	80	3	91	88
Uttarakhand	6.86	68	5	86	74
Punjab	6.89	62	3	82	73
Haryana	6.63	57	7	75	67
Delhi	6.70	52	3	82	58
Uttar Pradesh	4.88	31	8	72	37
Bihar	3.11	13	8	46	18
Jharkhand	5.15	38	20	50	47
Rajasthan	4.89	32	15	53	44
Chhattisgarh	6.40	52	6	85	67
Madhya Pradesh	6.11	46	7	67	49
North-East	5.50	32	6	52	47
Assam	2.63	3	22	19	9
West Bengal	6.54	68	10	74	71
Orissa	6.80	55	5	77	68
Gujarat	6.47	55	4	79	64
Maharashtra, Goa	7.18	66	1	83	71
Andhra Pradesh	7.01	67	2	85	74
Karnataka	7.24	67	1	84	83
Kerala	7.20	70	2	82	85
Tamil Nadu	7.56	84	1	90	87

Source: IHDS 2004–5 data.

Table A.8.3a School Enrolment and Work for Children Aged 10–14 Years

	In School			Not in School				Total
	Not Working	Family Work	Wage Labour	Family Work	Wage Labour	Family & Wage	Not Working	
All India	77	7	1	2	1	0	11	100
Sex of Child								
Male	79	8	1	2	1	0	9	100
Female	75	6	0	3	1	1	14	100
Child's Age								
10	87	5	0	1	0	0	8	100
11	85	5	0	1	0	0	8	100
12	78	8	0	2	1	0	11	100
13	73	8	1	3	2	1	13	100
14	64	9	1	5	3	1	17	100
Place of Residence								
Metro city	90	1	0	0	1	0	8	100
Other urban	86	2	0	1	1	0	11	100
More developed village	79	7	0	2	1	0	10	100
Less developed village	70	10	1	3	2	1	13	100
Income								
Lowest Quintile	69	9	0	3	1	1	17	100
2nd Quintile	73	8	1	3	2	1	14	100
3rd Quintile	75	8	1	3	1	1	12	100
4th Quintile	80	5	0	2	1	0	11	100
Top Quintile	90	4	0	1	1	0	5	100
Social Groups								
Forward Caste Hindu	87	7	0	1	1	0	4	100
OBC	79	8	0	3	1	0	10	100
Dalit	74	7	1	2	2	0	13	100
Adivasi	67	8	1	4	2	3	16	100
Muslim	68	6	0	3	2	0	21	100
Other religion	95	1	0	1	0	0	4	100
Maximum Household Education								
None	60	8	1	4	3	1	23	100
1–4 Std	71	9	0	3	1	1	15	100
5–9 Std	81	8	0	2	1	0	8	100
10–11 Std	89	6	0	1	0	0	4	100
12 Std/Some college	90	5	0	1	0	1	3	100
Graduate/Diploma	94	4	0	0	0	0	2	100

Source: IHDS 2004–5 data.

Table A.8.3b Statewise School Enrolment and Work for Children Aged 10–14 Years

	In School			Not in School				Total
	Not Working	Family Work	Wage Labour	Family Work	Wage Labour	Family & Wage	Not Working	
All India	77	7	1	2	1	0	11	100
Jammu and Kashmir	86	5	0	3	0	0	6	100
Himachal Pradesh	73	23	0	2	0	0	2	100
Uttarakhand	84	8	0	1	0	0	7	100
Punjab	87	3	0	1	1	0	9	100
Haryana	80	9	0	1	0	0	10	100
Delhi	91	2	0	0	0	0	7	100
Uttar Pradesh	67	16	1	4	1	0	12	100
Bihar	62	11	1	5	1	0	20	100
Jharkhand	69	6	0	1	0	0	23	100
Rajasthan	73	6	0	4	1	0	17	100
Chhattisgarh	79	6	1	2	2	3	8	100
Madhya Pradesh	78	5	1	2	2	1	11	100
North-East	85	6	0	3	0	0	6	100
Assam	62	15	0	5	1	0	18	100
West Bengal	71	8	0	3	3	1	15	100
Orissa	78	2	0	3	1	1	15	100
Gujarat	82	2	1	1	2	1	10	100
Maharashtra, Goa	89	3	0	1	1	0	7	100
Andhra Pradesh	84	2	1	1	4	0	8	100
Karnataka	85	3	1	2	2	1	7	100
Kerala	100	0	0	0	0	0	0	100
Tamil Nadu	92	3	0	0	1	0	5	100

Source: IHDS 2004–5 data.

9

Well-being of the Older Population

Throughout this report we have focused on different dimensions of human development and, in each context, highlighted vulnerabilities faced by specific populations. The present chapter focuses on the well-being of the older population and is different in that it addresses an area of concern that has received little attention in the past, but seems likely to pose substantial challenges as India moves along the path of demographic transition. Consequently, the goal of this chapter is to draw attention to three issues. First, while the Indian population structure is now dominated by a preponderance of young people, as fertility and mortality decline, the proportion of population aged 60 and above will rise. Second, till date, much of the care and support of the elderly seem to come from the family rather than the state, or personal savings. How well these social support networks will survive the coming economic transformations remains open to question. Third, aging in India has a unique gender dimension. In most countries women tend to outlive men and, hence, the older population tends to be highly feminine. While the unfavourable sex ratio (discussed in Chapter 8) does not allow that phenomenon in India, most elderly men are part of a couple and receive emotional and physical support from their wives. In contrast, a vast proportion of older women are widowed. Since few women have independent sources of income, or hold title to their homes (as documented in Chapter 10), this leads to a tremendous vulnerability for women.

Rapid declines in fertility and longer life expectancy have made the older population a growing, although still small, segment of the population. But even as their numbers grow, the traditional support systems of joint families and landownership are threatened by increasing urbanization and economic growth. Migration to urban areas by the younger generation in search of jobs has led to the perception that older people may be left to fend for themselves in rural areas. New institutions have already sprung up to respond to these new insecurities, but as the IHDS results show, their impact is still quite marginal in most parts of the country.

In this chapter, we examine the size of the older population, the work they do, the economic support they receive from the state, and support from the family. The profile that emerges shows that the welfare of the elderly still depends primarily on their family situation and age. As the preceding chapters have documented, education, income, and social group help determine how well the family lives and, thereby, influences the lifestyle of the elderly. In addition, gender emerges as a special concern. Regional and urban–rural variations shape all these factors, so the elderly fare much better in some places than in others.

The common demographic definition in India classifies people aged 60 and older as the elderly. The IHDS collected data on various factors related to their well-being, including their education, living arrangements, participation in productive work (whether paid or unpaid), and their participation in government sponsored pension programmes.[1] About 17,900 people in this age category lived in the households that were surveyed.[2]

---

[1] When the elderly were not available for direct interview, proxy reports were collected, potentially resulting in some underestimation.
[2] Morbidity and access to health care play an important role in shaping the well-being of the older population, but this has been discussed in Chapter 7.

A GROWING POPULATION

According to the Census, the proportion of the population that is elderly rose from about 5.6 per cent in 1961 to 7.4 per cent in 2001. The 61st round of the NSS reported that the elderly constitute about 7.2 per cent of the total population, and the IHDS data, collected in 2005, found a slightly higher percentage of elderly persons (8 per cent). Most of the states fall within a narrow range of 7 to 10 per cent elderly. Only Kerala, at 13 per cent, is distinctive at the high end. Delhi (4 per cent), Jharkhand (5 per cent), and Assam (5 per cent) are especially low (see Figure 9.1).

Early fertility decline is one of the major reasons for the high proportion of elderly persons in Kerala. Other factors that influence their relative percentage in the population relate to the degree of urbanization and the degree of migration of the working age population. For instance, Delhi attracts a large working age migrant population, and because of the high cost of living there, many Delhites may return to their ancestral homes as they age. On the other hand, Kerala not only benefits from lower fertility and increased life expectancy but also has a substantial out-migration of its working age population for employment.

In most parts of the world, women have a relative advantage in terms of greater life expectancy than men, which results in an elderly population that is disproportionately female. But in India, the situation is more complicated and, overall, the feminization of the elderly is yet to happen. In regions of the north, that are known for discrimination

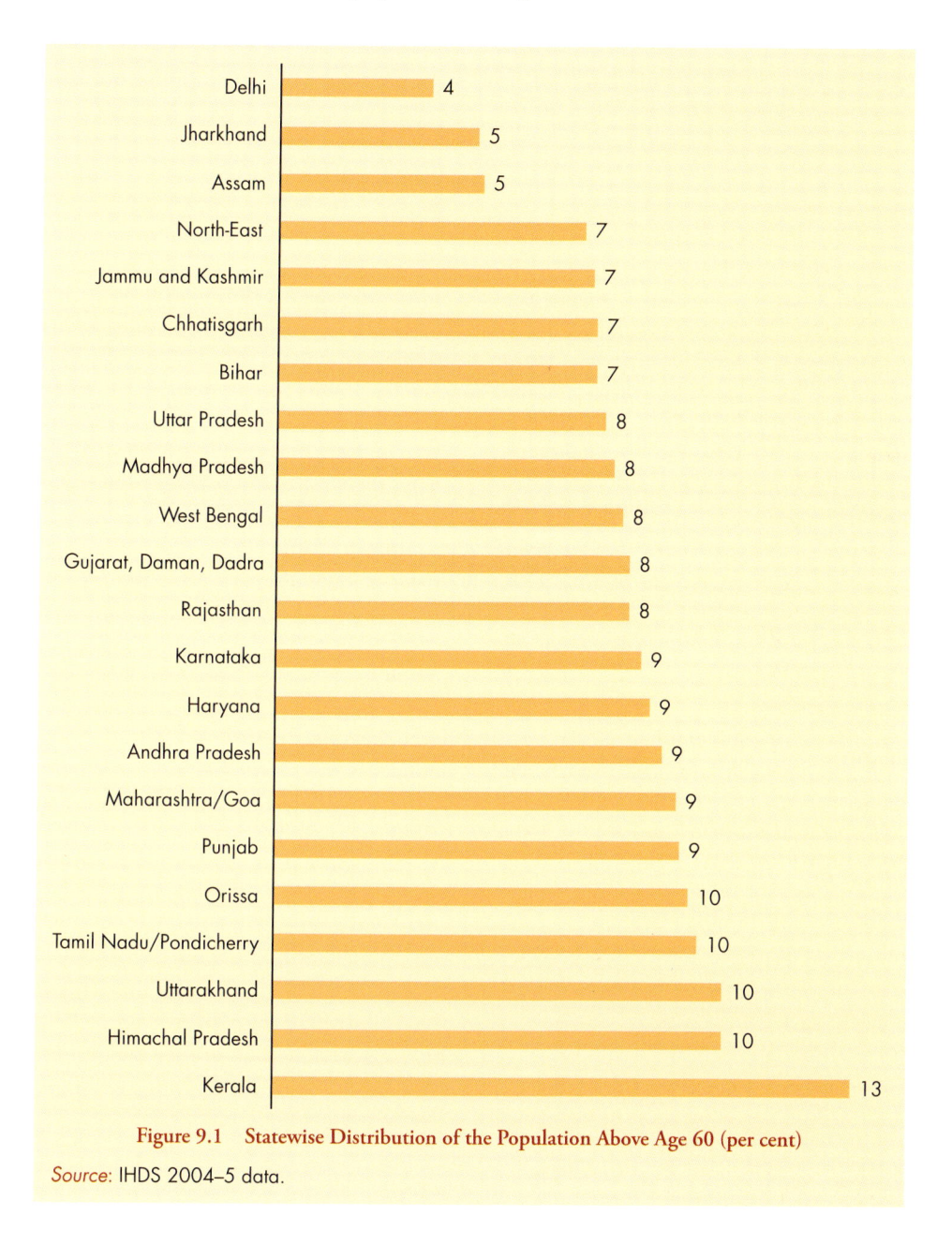

State	Per cent
Delhi	4
Jharkhand	5
Assam	5
North-East	7
Jammu and Kashmir	7
Chhatisgarh	7
Bihar	7
Uttar Pradesh	8
Madhya Pradesh	8
West Bengal	8
Gujarat, Daman, Dadra	8
Rajasthan	8
Karnataka	9
Haryana	9
Andhra Pradesh	9
Maharashtra/Goa	9
Punjab	9
Orissa	10
Tamil Nadu/Pondicherry	10
Uttarakhand	10
Himachal Pradesh	10
Kerala	13

Figure 9.1 Statewise Distribution of the Population Above Age 60 (per cent)
Source: IHDS 2004–5 data.

against females (for example, in the states of Bihar, Uttar Pradesh, or Punjab), the low sex ratio contributes to an elderly population that is more masculine than should be expected.

While the distribution of the elderly between socioeconomic groups, based on income and education, mirrors the distribution of the general population, the relative rates of fertility and age distribution has resulted in some social groups having a slightly larger percentage of elderly persons than other social groups. So, the percentage of elderly is higher among Christians, Sikhs, and Jains (12.7 per cent) and forward Hindu castes (10 per cent) than among Dalits (7.2 per cent), Adivasis (6.6 per cent), and Muslims (6.3 per cent; see Table A.9.1a). As we document in Chapter 10, fertility is somewhat lower among religious minorities and upper caste Hindus, and has been for some time, resulting in a greater proportion that is elderly. This challenge arising from the success of family planning will only magnify in the years to come and spread to all socioeconomic groups.

WORKING INTO OLD AGE

For people holding formal sector jobs in India, retirement age typically lies between the ages 58 and 62, although in some cases, such as for university professors, it stretches to 65. In all jobs in the government sector and in most jobs in large private sector companies, retirement is compulsory. However, a focus on formal sector work masks the labour force participation of the elderly. Table 9.1 documents workforce participation of individuals aged 60 and older in various types of activities.

More than 72 per cent of rural men aged 60–9 are in the labour force, as are about 40 per cent of rural women aged 60–9. The corresponding figures for urban areas are 43 per cent for men and 13 per cent for women. Although labour force participation declines with age, a substantial decline occurs only after individuals reach the age of 80.

However, the nature of work is strongly age dependent. Formal sector work imposes much greater entry and exit regulations than work that is family based, such as work on family farms and in family businesses. In rural areas, salaried work among elderly men and women is almost negligible, although 38 per cent of men and 14 per cent of women aged between 60–9 work on family farms. In urban areas, the elderly men are predominantly concentrated in family businesses (about 16 per cent). From a public policy perspective, it is interesting to speculate whether many of

Table 9.1 Labour Force Participation and Type of Work Among Older Men and Women

	Within the Preceding Year, Per cent Engaged in:						Per cent Doing Any Other Work
	Salaried	Business	Cultivation	Farm Labour	Non-Farm Labour	Animal Care	
Rural Males							
60–9 Years	3.7	7.7	38.5	15.9	8	41.1	72.3
70–9 Years	2.8	5.3	24.6	5.6	3.1	30.9	49.6
80+ Years	0.7	2.3	10.5	2.8	1.3	14.4	25.1
Rural Females							
60–9 Years	1.1	1.7	14.5	7.9	1.4	26.4	39.8
70–9 Years	0.1	1.1	4.1	2.9	1	12.6	19.1
80+ Years	0.2	1.1	1.7	0.2	0.5	6.1	8.5
Urban Males							
60–9 Years	10.4	16.5	3.9	3.8	8.5	4.8	43.4
70–9 Years	8	11	3.2	2	4.6	5.6	30.7
80+ Years	2.9	4.8	0.6	1.5	1.3	1	10.9
Urban Females							
60–9 Years	3	2.2	1.1	1.7	2.3	3.8	13
70–9 Years	1.9	1.9	0.4	0.5	1.6	2.4	7.8
80+ Years	1.7	1	0	0	0.2	0.9	3.4

Note: Multiple activities counted separately so the total may exceed 100 per cent.
Source: IHDS 2004–5 data.

these elderly persons would choose to work if they were not faced with mandatory retirement. While this question is difficult to answer definitively, a comparison of employment rates in various sectors between those aged 60–9 and 15–59 provides a clue. As shown in Chapter 4 (Figure 4.2), among urban men, 47.2 per cent of men aged between 15–59 are involved in salaried work. Only 10 per cent of urban men aged 60–9 have salaried work. Contrasting this sharp decline with a modest decline for employment in own business—from 25 per cent for those aged 15–59 to 16 per cent for those aged 60–9–suggests that there might be greater demand for employment among the elderly, if work was available. The compulsory retirement age for government and public sector employees has been slowly inching up through various state and central government decisions, but the pressure applied by ever larger incoming cohorts for jobs has made substantial changes difficult to achieve.

At the same time, workers in the formal sector have access to pensions. Workers who are self-employed in family businesses, farming, or in manual labour at daily wages, do not have this benefit, and their continued employment may be driven by both lack of mandatory retirement and lack of alternative income in the form of pensions. Table A.9.1a documents that labour force participation among the elderly is the highest in households in the lowest income quintile (46 per cent) and lowest in those in the highest quintile (33 per cent). Part of the reason for decline in salaried jobs but not self- employment may be that the formal sector work requires a full time work schedule, whereas, self-employment may often require that the elderly work for a few hours every day, or engage in overall supervision of the business while leaving younger family members to deal with more physically demanding activities.

FINANCIAL WELL-BEING OF THE ELDERLY

If the elderly do not work, do they have other sources of income? Three sources of income deserve particular attention:

(1) Private savings, including investments, pensions, and rents,
(2) Government benefits, and,
(3) Support from other family members.

Some elderly own property or have investments that may provide income, and others rely on pensions from their job. Since it is often difficult to differentiate between the property owned by the elderly and that owned by other household members, the IHDS did not determine the ownership of property. Hence, we can examine all income from property or pension only for the household. Nonetheless, this examination provides interesting insights into the sources of income for households in which the elderly live.

Table 9.2 shows that about 26 per cent of the elderly live in households in which pensions, interest income, or rents are received.

This includes rent or crops received for leasing out farmland. Although only 16 per cent households in the general population receive this type of income, the elderly appear to be more likely to receive pensions or rent from leasing out property. These households are largely located in better off segments of society: the educated, higher income households, and urban residents. Less than 20 per cent of the elderly in households in the bottom three income quintiles are likely to receive any income from interest, rent, or pensions. This figure is 45 per cent for those in the top quintile. Elderly households that receive income from interest, rent, or pensions received are substantial amounts, about Rs 27,300 in the year preceding the survey. However, given the low rate of receipt, at an all India level, the income from pensions, rent, and interest is only about Rs 6,700. About 7 per cent of all elderly households receive remittances from family members living elsewhere and 17 per cent receive some form of government benefits, such as income from the National Old Age Pension Scheme (NOAPS) or the Widow Pension Scheme. When remittances are received, they average almost Rs 20,000. In contrast, government benefits are very small (only about Rs 1,800 for households receiving any benefits), averaging Rs 303 per household, having an elderly member. Table 9.2 also documents the earned income from wage and salary, business, and farming for the household. Compared to the average earned income of about Rs 45,700 per year, the government benefits of Rs 303 suggest that much of the support of the elderly in India comes from current earnings of the elderly and other family members.

The importance of three sources of support—private savings, family transfers, and government benefits—varies across different segments of society. Income from private savings (that is, rent, interest income, and pensions) provides the most income and is concentrated in the privileged sections of society, including urban residents, the more educated, and forward castes/minority religions. In contrast, income from remittances and government benefits is concentrated in the more vulnerable sections of society, rural residents, the less educated, and Dalits and Adivasis. Because income from property and pensions is far greater than remittances or government benefits, access to pensions may well be one of the factors resulting in higher standards of living for the privileged elderly.

In 1995, the central government, with the assistance of the state governments, sponsored the NOAPS and Widow Pension Scheme to provide some relief to the elderly and widows, who are economically destitute. In the IHDS

Table 9.2 Sources of Income Among Households with Elderly

	Per cent Households with Any Income From				Mean Rs Per Year if Any Received				Mean Rs Per Year for Whole Population			
	Agr./ Bus. Wage	Property Pensions	Remitt-ances	Govern-ment Benefits	Agr./ Bus. Wage	Property Pensions	Remitt-ances	Govern-ment Benefits	Agr./ Bus. Wage	Property Pensions	Remitt-ances	Govern-ment Benefits
All India	89	26	7	17	51,323	27,320	19,899	1,771	45,717	6,713	1387	303
Gender												
Male	90	27	7	15	51,435	28,981	19,543	1,795	46,059	7,581	1324	264
Female	89	24	7	20	51,207	25,399	20,244	1,752	45,366	5,823	1451	343
Age												
60–9	90	26	7	16	50,028	28,326	18,538	1,726	45,107	6,896	1,231	273
70–9	88	25	8	19	53,289	27,021	19,155	1,719	46,854	6,371	1,447	331
80+	86	30	7	19	54,142	22,803	29,493	2,143	46,337	6,523	2,181	411
Education												
None	91	19	7	21	38,703	17,719	17,960	1,687	34,962	2,877	1,201	359
1–4 Std	91	23	8	15	50,051	19,618	17,535	1,968	45,436	4,246	1,405	302
5–9 Std	89	34	8	9	72,421	26,684	25,427	1,634	64,066	8,927	2,046	141
10–11 Std	85	57	7	8	95,239	37,516	21,319	2,591	80,486	21,339	1,379	209
12 Std/Some college	78	70	9	6	1,01,345	51,674	32,048	3,474	78,992	35,966	2,907	202
Graduate/Diploma	68	76	7	4	1,56,468	66,752	25,083	6,972	1,06,207	50,849	1,729	267
Family Type												
Single	45	35	15	30	8,833	10,445	10,607	1,799	3,948	3,589	1,638	532
Couple	58	40	10	15	30,066	32,376	14,209	2,252	17,200	12,974	1,429	347
Nuclear	90	27	6	10	39,036	30,489	17,830	1,795	35,046	8,091	1,025	170
Joint	95	24	7	18	55,260	26,505	21,990	1,715	52,189	5,819	1,425	309
Place of Residence												
Metro city	87	39	2	6	1,03,036	50,994	20,862	5,356	89,768	19,881	461	311
Other urban	87	35	5	10	75,425	37,843	23,809	2,367	65,351	13,341	1,270	245
Developed village	90	25	8	17	49,273	22,106	19,392	1,827	43,874	5,038	1,563	316
Less developed village	91	21	7	22	34,853	18,485	19,027	1,446	31,533	3,292	1,392	316
Income												
Lowest Quintile	82	19	7	24	8,252	4,493	5,047	1,512	6,617	535	365	366
2nd Quintile	93	15	7	20	16,722	9,476	8,406	1,250	15,556	1,062	558	254
3rd Quintile	92	19	7	17	25,050	13,964	16,153	1,538	23,085	2,359	1,151	267
4th Quintile	94	28	7	16	42,918	22,505	20,620	2,444	40,115	5,910	1,425	392
Highest Quintile	95	45	8	10	1,33,169	46,233	40,835	2,639	1,25,906	20,558	3,101	264
Social Group												
Forward Castes	87	40	7	10	71,985	34,413	20,215	2,353	62,311	13,291	1,498	243
OBC	89	25	7	17	41,561	22,247	18,794	1,800	36,744	5,057	1,228	313
Dalit	93	16	7	27	32,977	19,194	15,993	1,614	30,719	2,855	1,122	440
Adivasi	94	14	3	25	28,505	23,623	12,108	1,306	26,763	2,900	340	329
Muslim	88	21	9	12	52,616	22,784	22,940	1,361	46,373	4,538	2,026	162
Other religion	86	30	10	8	1,55,046	41,066	36066	2,965	1,32,938	11,810	3,635	225

Notes: Calculated for the whole household, not just the elderly. Table only includes households with at least one elderly. Agr. refers to Agricultural and Bus. refers to Business.

Source: IHDS 2004–5 data.

data, less than 8 per cent of those aged 60 and older receive pension from the NOAPS, and less than 3 per cent of widows receive the widow pensions. While these are the two most widespread programmes, the older population is eligible for a wide range of programmes, including pensions given to Freedom Fighters and their widows and widowers, as well as the Annapurna Scheme, which provides free grains. When all sources of government assistance are combined, 17 per cent of the elderly live in households that receive some kind of assistance. However, government assistance appears to be targeted towards the more vulnerable sections of society. Rural residents, the less educated, and Dalits and Adivasis are more likely to receive government assistance than are the more privileged elderly. This is largely because most benefits are targeted at the poor. The only exception is assistance given to individuals who participated in the Indian freedom movement, and their spouses. Freedom Fighters who can provide documentation of their participation in the freedom movement receive substantial assistance. Because the last major movement took place in 1942, relatively few Freedom Fighters are alive today to use these benefits. But in as much as they, or their spouses, are able to obtain these pensions, many are located in the more privileged sections of society.

FAMILY AS SOURCE OF SUPPORT FOR THE ELDERLY

Traditionally, the elderly have been seen as integral to a family structure that is based on intergenerational reciprocity. A shared sense of rights and obligations binds the generations in a joint family, economically, socially, and emotionally. However, with the slow erosion of employment in the traditional sectors of the economy, like farming, and a preponderance of new jobs emerging in urban areas, it is often argued that the multigenerational family system is undergoing increasing stress.

The IHDS indicates that in spite of this potential for disintegration, most elderly persons continue to live with their children and other family members (see Figures 9.2a and 9.2b).

About 13 per cent men and 11 per cent women live alone, or with their spouse. Of the remaining some live with their married or unmarried children, and many live in extended families, with their brothers and nephews. Nearly 77 per cent of the elderly live with a married son/brother/nephew or other relative. About 11 per cent of the elderly in India reside with their unmarried children, or what is more commonly termed nuclear families. Such elderly are likely to make a living as small farmers, subsist on pensions, or engage in some kind of petty trade. About 16 per cent of elderly men reside in nuclear families, compared with 6 per cent of elderly women. Close to 10 per cent of the elderly live with only their spouses. Here again, 12 per cent of elderly men live with their spouses, as compared with 7 per cent of elderly women. The elderly who live with their spouses are mostly retired, or live in households engaged in small farming. Finally, about 2.5 per cent of the elderly live alone.

Overall, however, residence of the elderly in three-generational joint families is widely practised in India, regardless of region (Table A.9.1b) or socio-religious affiliation (see Table A.9.1a). Joint residence is slightly less likely in households that belong to the poorest quintile, and those in which the educational level is nominal. However, it remains

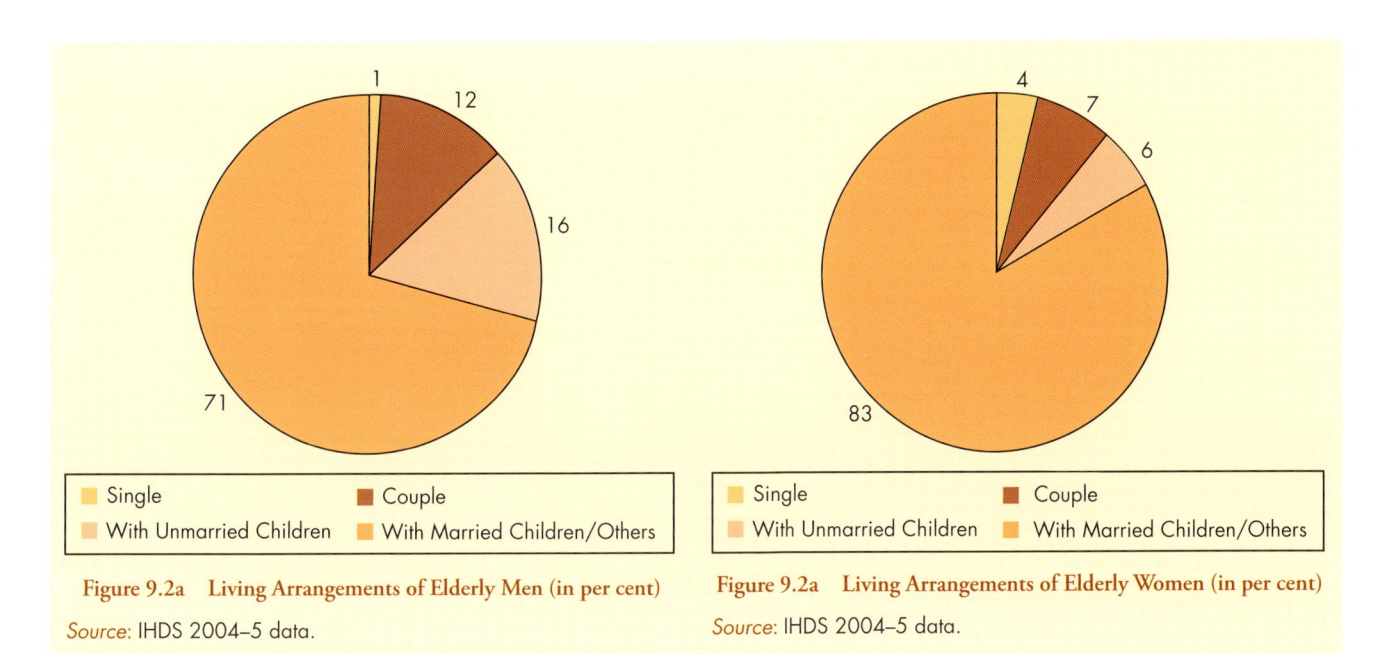

Figure 9.2a Living Arrangements of Elderly Men (in per cent)
Source: IHDS 2004–5 data.

Figure 9.2a Living Arrangements of Elderly Women (in per cent)
Source: IHDS 2004–5 data.

the type of family in which the majority of the elderly are found.

Table A.9.1a displays the characteristics of the households of the elderly in various living situations. It is important to be cautious about drawing any generalizations from this table because living situations are fluid and are often determined by income, health, marital status, and other factors. It is well recognized in many countries that poverty is associated with a variety of family-coping strategies, in which individuals move in with relatives to pool their resources and make ends meet. Hence, the elderly, who are able to live in homes that they head, may well be the fortunate ones. Similarly, remittances seem more likely for couples or single individuals whose children live elsewhere. When the elderly live with family members, they receive help via co-residence and do not receive monetary transfers.

Ownership of land is strongly associated with extended family residence (Figure 9.3).

In rural areas, only 62 per cent of elderly men in households which are landless live in joint families as compared to 84 per cent of those in households with five or more acres of land. The same relationship holds for women, but the strength of the relationship is greater for men. Farm households require more labour, increasing the likelihood that the families will stay together. Even more importantly, expectations of inheriting land may keep families from splintering, at least until the death of the patriarch.

GENDER AND AGING

Aging is a distinctly gendered phenomenon. As stated earlier, in most countries, elderly women substantially outnumber elderly men. This is a phenomenon that is not yet seen in India, largely because the Indian population has been dominated by a female shortage for several decades (as discussed at greater length in Chapter 8). However, Indian men and women experience aging differently. Most elderly men are married and have wives who are able to provide companionship as well as domestic support. In contrast, most elderly women are widows who lose companions as well as social status and become financially dependent on their children.

The longer life expectancy of women, on an average, and the normative age gap between husband and wife make widowhood more likely for women than for men. Thus, among the elderly, while 56 per cent of women are widows, only 18 per cent of men are widowers (see Table A.9.1a). Among the oldest (age 70+), 75 per cent of women are widowed, while only 28 per cent of men are (see Figure 9.4).

In a small part, this is compounded by cultural practices which dictate that it is acceptable for men to remarry after losing a wife, but not for women who are widowed. Through their life course, most women are dependent on men—first their father, then their husband, and finally their son. A woman's well-being upon widowhood greatly depends on whether her children (or, other relatives in rare cases) provide adequate support.

There is also a gender differentiation in the relative status of the elderly within a household. More elderly men occupy positions of power in a household than women (Figure 9.5).

The majority of elderly men (81 per cent) are accorded the status of head of household, whereas elderly women are more commonly found as either mothers of the head (44 per cent), or the wife of the head (35 per cent). To the extent that status within a family implies control over resources and comes with a certain degree of influence and obligation, being referred to as a parent may have implications for general well-being and access to care. When women are heads of households, it is often because they are destitute

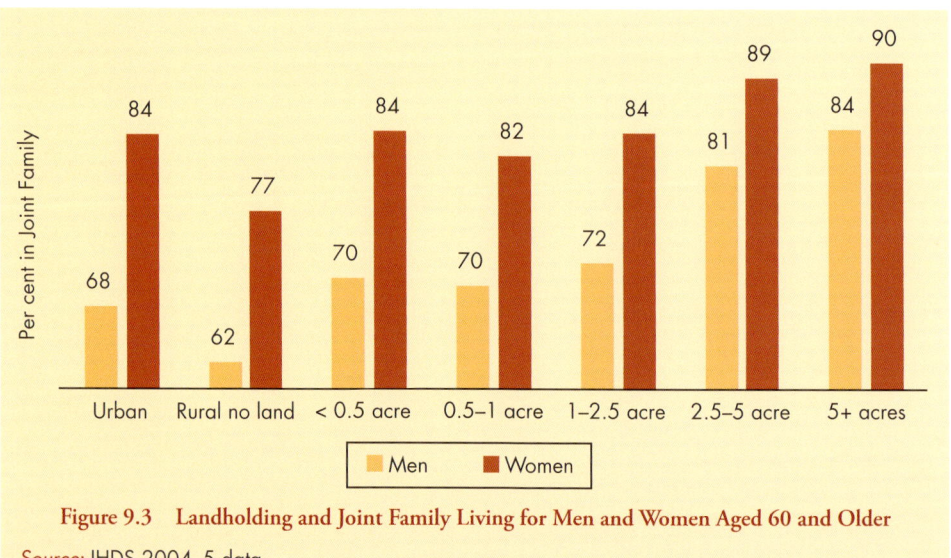

Figure 9.3 Landholding and Joint Family Living for Men and Women Aged 60 and Older
Source: IHDS 2004–5 data.

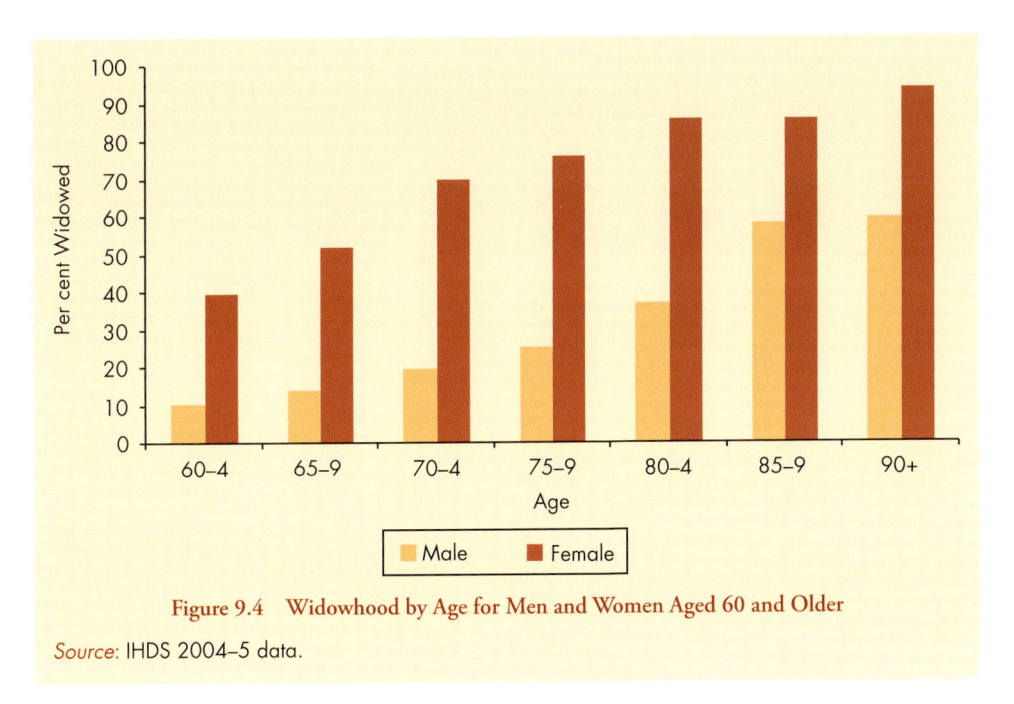

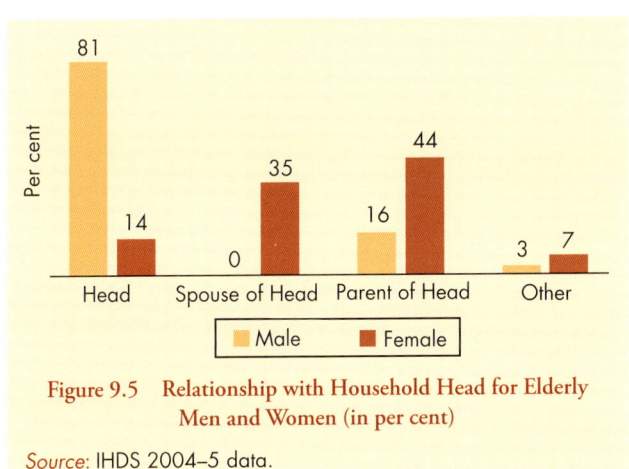

Figure 9.4 Widowhood by Age for Men and Women Aged 60 and Older
Source: IHDS 2004–5 data.

Figure 9.5 Relationship with Household Head for Elderly Men and Women (in per cent)
Source: IHDS 2004–5 data.

widows with young children, or living alone. Data from both the India Census 2001 and the *NFHS-II* reveal that more elderly women live alone than do elderly men in India.

DISCUSSION

As we noted at the beginning of this chapter, population aging has not been of great concern in India because a sustained rate of population growth has ensured that each successive cohort is larger and, hence, the population is dominated by young people. However, as fertility falls and mortality among the older population continues to decline, aging will become a larger challenge. Further, because of declining fertility, at least some elderly persons may not have a son to care for them in the old age. Given the reluctance to accept help from daughters (which we document in Chapter 10), population aging could increase the vulnerability of the elderly without sons.

Financial and social support of the elderly remain, almost entirely, located within the family, although many elderly persons work. They also live with sons/brothers/nephews and other family members, who provide financial and emotional support. While in most areas, co-residence with daughters is rare, it is often found in the North-East. Co-residence is particularly common for the oldest (age 70+) or people who own a considerable amount of land. As fertility declines and urbanization increases, extended families may come under duress, and other sources of support for the elderly may need to be developed.

HIGHLIGHTS

- With 13 per cent elderly, Kerala has the highest proportion of elderly persons.
- Labour force participation among men aged 60–9 is 72 per cent in rural areas and 43 per cent in urban areas.
- Most elderly persons subsist on earnings from their own work or that of other family members. Only 17 per cent of Indian elderly households receive government benefits of any type.
- Extended family living is the norm with about 77 per cent of the elderly living with married children or other family members.

Table A.9.1a Distribution of Elderly Population and Selected Characteristics

	Elderly As Per cent of Total Population	Per cent Distrib. in Category	Per cent Female	Per cent Widowed	Mean Household Income	Median Household Income	Per cent Poor	Per cent Working	Per cent in Joint family	Adults Aged 15–59 (per cent)
All India	8.3	100.0	49.4	36.9	56,377	30,640	22.2	41	77	2.9
Gender										
Male	8.3	50.6	NA	18	57,504	32,131	20.7	55	71	2.9
Female	8.3	49.4	NA	56.3	55,222	29,825	23.8	26	83	2.8
Age										
60–9	NA	62.1	49.8	28.2	55,705	30,460	22.6	49	73	2.8
70–9	NA	27.8	49.4	46.2	57,387	31,020	22.4	31	81	2.9
80+	NA	10.1	46.8	64.9	57,731	33,600	19.9	15	88	3.0
Education										
None	13.1	63.0	62.2	44	41,788	25,000	27.2	40	79	2.8
1–4 Std	5.6	11.2	31.5	27.1	53,183	33,750	20	49	77	2.9
5–9 Std	4.8	16.2	28.5	23.5	77,365	44,000	15.3	45	75	3.0
10–11 Std	5.4	5.3	16.4	16.5	1,05,804	74,400	4.7	43	67	3.0
12 Std/Some college	2.9	1.7	14.7	15.8	1,20,397	86,500	2.9	42	59	2.7
Graduate/Diploma	5.2	2.6	15.8	11.7	1,60,324	1,10,200	0.5	25	57	2.5
Family Type										
Single	49.9	2.5	77.1	91.9	10,048	5,500	15.1	42	0	0.0
Couple	34.7	9.8	36.9	0.1	32,359	13,200	12.3	50	0	0.3
With unmarried children	2	10.8	26.1	16.1	46,096	29,248	13.8	60	0	2.3
Joint	12	76.9	53.4	42.8	62,366	35,512	24.9	37	100	3.4
Place of Residence										
Metro city	6.8	5.4	48.4	35.7	1,10,508	84,800	12.1	17	71	2.7
Other urban	7.5	18.3	51	39.2	80,874	52,500	25.4	26	77	2.9
Developed village	9.5	39.3	49.4	36.9	53,495	28,300	18.5	42	76	2.8
Less developed village	7.9	37.0	48.6	36	39,422	23,093	26.1	51	78	2.9
Income										
Lowest Quintile	9.8	19.3	50.8	37.7	8,159	8,377	29.6	46	55	1.6
2nd Quintile	7	15.6	51.7	41.9	18,202	18,062	33.1	44	78	2.5
3rd Quintile	7.4	17.8	50.9	40.6	28,930	28,778	27.2	41	81	2.8
4th Quintile	7.9	20.3	46.6	35.7	50,717	49,700	19.3	42	84	3.3
Highest Quintile	8.9	23.7	47.8	31.4	1,54,806	1,09,000	8.8	33	87	3.8
Social Group										
Forward Castes	10	24.3	49.6	34.5	80,292	49,400	11.4	37	79	2.9
OBC	8.7	37.3	48.9	36.9	45,783	27,610	21.1	44	77	2.8
Dalit	7.2	19.0	50.3	41.2	36,825	24,000	31.1	43	76	2.8
Adivasi	6.6	6.0	50.3	40.6	32,009	19,900	44.6	51	74	2.7
Muslim	6.3	9.7	46.7	33.6	54,456	33,000	25.2	38	76	3.3
Other religion	12.7	3.7	53.1	33.8	1,50,685	59,622	15.6	24	75	2.5

Notes: Distrib. refers to Distribution.
Source: IHDS 2004–5 data.

Table A.9.1b Statewise Distribution of Elderly Population and Selected Characteristics

	Elderly As Per cent of Total Population	Characteristics Per cent Distrib. in Category	Per cent Female	Per cent Widowed	Mean Household Income	Median Household Income	Per cent Poor	Per cent Working	Per cent in Joint Family	Adults Aged 15–59 (per cent)
All India	8.3	100.0	49.4	36.9	56,377	30,640	22.2	41	77	2.9
Jammu and Kashmir	7.3	1.1	44	34.3	1,08,852	70,569	2.6	46	86	4.2
Himachal Pradesh	10.4	0.8	52.1	37.7	74,055	52,992	3.3	61	79	2.9
Uttarakhand	10.4	2.2	57.2	44.2	56,287	31,065	35.8	48	81	2.8
Punjab	9.4	2.8	48.3	33.4	87,743	60,000	3.7	32	83	3.1
Haryana	8.7	2.0	51	34	82,742	50,600	11.3	32	83	3.0
Delhi	3.5	0.6	45.2	26.1	1,09,302	93,850	11.9	19	76	3.0
Uttar Pradesh	7.6	13.4	46.8	35.2	51,722	28,180	25.5	53	80	3.1
Bihar	7.4	6.4	43.7	33	36,936	22,350	13.8	50	81	3.0
Jharkhand	4.6	2.1	37.6	23.6	56,461	31,952	41.2	42	85	4.0
Rajasthan	8.2	5.4	54	34	57,757	35,682	24	37	81	2.9
Chhatisgarh	7.4	2.5	53.6	41.1	42,053	24,503	59.1	45	76	2.6
Madhya Pradesh	7.8	5.1	50.3	36.8	44,034	22,890	39.5	44	79	3.0
North-East	7.1	1.0	45.8	34.9	88,845	66,018	10	46	65	3.1
Assam	4.7	1.3	32.7	23	45,141	27,000	23.4	46	47	3.3
West Bengal	8	7.1	49.3	39.5	58546	38,600	20	32	72	2.9
Orissa	9.6	4.6	49.6	35.7	32,473	18,252	32.8	48	78	2.8
Gujarat, Daman, Dadra	8.2	5.0	53.1	37.4	58,279	32,407	10.6	38	76	2.7
Maharashtra/Goa	9.3	11.3	52	38.1	62,974	38,300	26	40	82	2.9
Andhra Pradesh	9	7.9	50.6	39	37506	24,722	7.1	35	73	2.4
Karnataka	8.5	5.1	50.5	39.1	62,469	27,300	16.5	41	78	3.0
Kerala	13.4	5.0	54.6	37	1,02,970	45,000	26.9	23	77	2.5
Tamil Nadu/Pondicherry	9.8	7.3	46.5	44.3	44,517	26,649	20.1	35	61	2.2

Note: Distrib. refers to Distribution.
Source: IHDS 2004–5 data.

10

Gender and Family Dynamics

Many chapters in this volume have highlighted gender disparities in various markers of well-being. These disparities are receding in some areas, such as education (Chapter 6), but remain large in others, such as employment and wages (Chapter 4), and are even widening in others such as sex ratio at birth (Chapter 8). As discussed in other chapters, many of these inequalities are rooted in institutional structures—such as labour markets—which provide unequal access to men and women. In this chapter, we focus on cultural norms and their operation within households. Anyone who has seen *burqa*-clad girls zooming around on two wheelers in Ahmedabad, or women in *ghunghat* working on construction sites knows that tradition is not destiny. However, it is also important to note that gender inequality emerges within a context of cultural norms. Marriage and kinship patterns provide a background against which parents are faced with heart wrenching choices between sons and daughters, resulting in the preferential treatment of boys. This chapter provides empirical information regarding the behaviours and norms that shape the narrative of women's lives.

TRADITION AND CONTOURS OF WOMEN'S LIVES

Marriage and kinship patterns affect both men's and women's lives. As a vast number of sociological and anthropological studies attest, marriage and kinship practices in India vary tremendously between regions, social classes, and communities. But these myriad variations notwithstanding, some broad patterns shape women's lives. These patterns are identified below.

Early and Arranged Marriage

In spite of rising levels of education and images of growing westernization in India, love marriages remain a rarity, even among urban educated elite. India is unusual, even among developing countries, in that marriage in India is almost universal and most men and women marry at a relatively young age.[1] As Table A.10.1a indicates, even though the legal minimum age at marriage for women is 18, 60 per cent are married before that age. The average age at marriage ranges between 16 and 23 years among ever-married women 25 years and older in the IHDS sample.[2] Women in poor and less educated households often marry around the age of 16, but even women from better off and more educated households marry around age 19–20. The average age at marriage is 19.3 years in metropolitan cities and is considerably lower in less developed villages. Regional differences in age at marriage are striking, with an average age at marriage of 15–17 years in central states like Bihar and Madhya Pradesh, and a higher average age at marriage in Punjab and Himachal Pradesh, as well as in the southern states (see Table A.10.1b).

---

[1] For data on age at marriage in other developing countries, see Mensch, Singh, and Casterline (2005).
[2] We exclude ever-married women under age 25 from this calculation. If we were to include younger cohorts, then women who marry at young ages would be included and those who delay marriage would not. Thus, including younger cohorts would bias the sample towards women who marry at young ages, such as those in rural areas and those with low levels of education.

Not surprisingly, many of the young brides have not attained puberty at the time of marriage. In Bihar and Rajasthan, the states with the earliest age at marriage, around 25 per cent of the girls had not attained puberty at the time of marriage. At the same time, a focus on the formal age at marriage may well be mistaken in a context in which early marriage is not synonymous with an early age at entry into a sexual union.

As documented by many anthropologists, early marriage is often associated with a delay in consummation in which the bride remains with her parents until a formal *gauna* or *bidai* ceremony occurs. States with a very early age at formal marriage also follow the custom of a gap of a year or more between marriage *and gauna*. Tables A.10.1a and A.10.1b show the waiting period of at least six months following the wedding before cohabitation. About 75 per cent of women in Bihar and 88 per cent of women in Rajasthan waited six months or more to begin living with their husbands. As Figure 10.1 shows, this waiting period is often associated with the relative youth and immaturity of the bride, and tends to decline as the age at marriage increases.

Regardless of the age at which formal marriage occurs, however, the average age at which cohabitation, or effective marriage, begins is about 18–19 years in most states, and is even younger in some. Table A.10.1a also suggests a very small increase in age at marriage. The average age at marriage has changed only marginally across cohorts, although the proportion of women marrying before puberty has decreased.

Most marriages are arranged. Less than 5 per cent of women in the IHDS sample said they chose their husbands independent of their parents. The rest reported a variety of arrangements through which their families made marriage decisions. Most reported very limited contact with their husbands before marriage. Sixty nine per cent met their husbands on the day of the wedding or shortly before, and an additional 9 per cent knew their husbands for a month before the wedding. Only 23 per cent knew their husbands for more than a month when they married. Although educated women are more likely to have a longer acquaintance with their husbands, a long period of acquaintance is not normative, even among these women as Figure 10.2 indicates.[3]

Yet, in spite of the popular stereotype of women being coerced into arranged marriages, about 62 per cent felt that their wishes were considered in the selection of their partners. Not surprisingly, women from educated families and urban women are given more of a say. Women in Bihar and Rajasthan, states with the lowest age at marriage, are the least likely to report having a say in the selection of their husbands. Women who have some say in choosing the groom are also likely to have a longer acquaintance with their prospective partners. Among women who reported not having a say in the choice of spouse, only 10 per cent met their husbands at least a month before the wedding. Among women who had a say, about 30 per cent claimed such an acquaintance.

Centrality of Childbearing in Women's Lives

Fertility in India has been declining steadily. As measured by the *NFHS*, the total fertility rate dropped from 3.7 in 1992–3 to 2.7 in 2005–6. Still, childbearing remains central to women's lives: as measured by IHDS, 97 per cent women aged 25 and older had at least one child. Tables A.10.1a and A.10.1b also document differences in fertility across different social groups and across states. In these tables, we focus on women aged 40–9 who have largely completed childbearing.

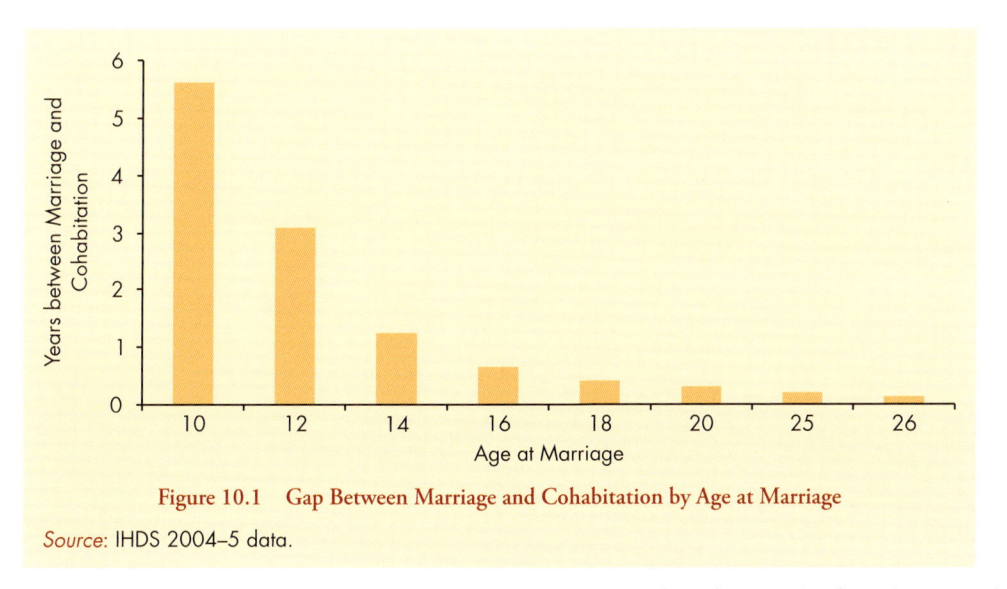

Figure 10.1 Gap Between Marriage and Cohabitation by Age at Marriage
Source: IHDS 2004–5 data.

---

[3] It is important to note that because our data was collected from women only, much of this discussion has focused on women's choices, and lack thereof. However, much of this discussion also applies to males who have little opportunity to get to know their wives.

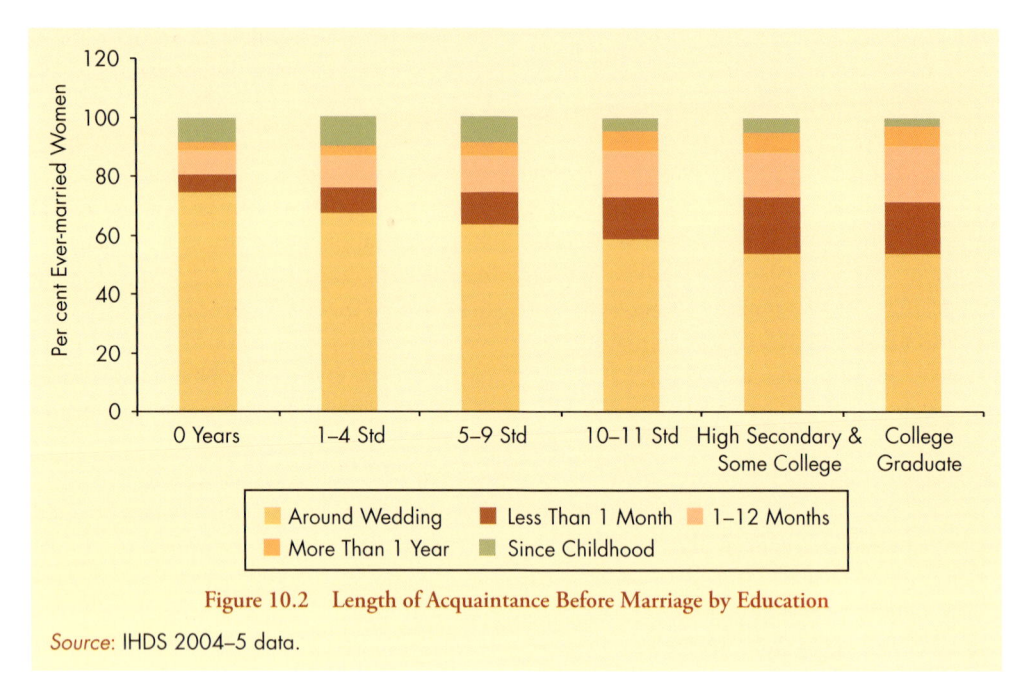

Figure 10.2 Length of Acquaintance Before Marriage by Education
Source: IHDS 2004–5 data.

On an average, women in this age group had 3.85 children in their reproductive years.[4] Educated women and women in urban areas have fewer children than women with lesser education and those in rural areas. Interestingly, although fertility is lower in richer families than poorer ones, this difference is far smaller than that associated with women's education. Women in Kerala and Tamil Nadu have the smallest family size, and those in Uttar Pradesh, Bihar, and Rajasthan have the largest.

Table A.10.1a also documents that the mean age at first birth for women aged 25 years and older is 20.6 years. The median age at first birth is slightly lower, at 20.08. A comparison of age at marriage and age at first birth presents an interesting paradox. The variation in age at marriage is not consistently reflected in age at first birth.[5] There is considerable variation in the mean age at first marriage between different states and different social groups. The difference in mean age at marriage between Bihar (15.2) and Kerala (20.9) is more than four years. Yet, the difference in age at first birth is much smaller: 20.7 for Bihar and 22.7 for Kerala. Similarly, although the difference between uneducated and college educated women is about 6.5 years for age at marriage, it is only 4.5 years for age at first birth. A variety of factors play a role in the smaller difference by education for age at first birth, including the low fecundity of adolescent girls. However, perhaps the most important factor is one we noted earlier. Marriage is not synonymous with entry into sexual union, and young brides are much more likely to delay cohabitation than older brides, reducing the risk of pregnancy. This delay also poses an interesting policy dilemma. The prevention of child marriage is important for the well-being of adolescent girls and may lead to increased education, but its fertility impact may be small until a substantial delay in age at marriage is attained.

Women's Natal Family Ties and Social Support Networks

Although emotional bonds between parents and daughters endure over time and space, wedding rituals like bidai and crossing over the threshold reflect realities of most women's lives. Marriage is a transition point at which women are expected to leave the familiar environment and the traditions of their parents' homes and assimilate into a new family, often with a relatively abrupt break.

We asked women about their immediate post-marriage residence, and an overwhelming majority (more than 90 per cent) reported that they lived with their parents-in-law. The north Indian custom of village exogamy ensures that women marry outside their own village because all men from their own village, or even a set of closely related villages, are considered close kin. Even urban families may be reluctant to marry their daughters into families originating from villages close to their native place. Consequently, as Table A.10.2b indicates, in states like Haryana and Uttar Pradesh, less than 10 per cent of women marry within their own towns or villages. While marrying within the natal village is permitted in south India and marriage with a close cousin or uncle is often preferred, the number of suitable matches

---
[4] The *NFHS-III* documents 4.0 children for women of this age group (IIPS 2007).
[5] This paradox was first noted by Basu (1993).

within a close community is limited. Consequently, even in south India, the majority of women marry outside their own village and circle of close relatives.

Within-family marriages are particularly prevalent among Muslims. About 24 per cent of the Muslim women marry within the family, compared with less than 12 per cent among the other social groups. Unlike many other aspects of social life, marriage traditions have little relationship with the socioeconomic standing of the family, and regional differences predominate. In Haryana, Uttar Pradesh, Rajasthan, and Madhya Pradesh, around 10 per cent of women marry within their own village or town, and a negligible percentage marry their uncles or cousins. In contrast, in Kerala and Tamil Nadu, more than 25 per cent marry within their own village or town, and 23–30 per cent of women in Maharashtra, Andhra Pradesh, Karnataka, and Tamil Nadu marry a cousin or an uncle.

Exogamy is associated with an abrupt transition in women's lives. Once married, many women find themselves cut off from the social support networks offered by their natal families. Although tradition dictates that a daughter visit her parents or brothers for certain festivals such as Raksha Bandhan, Makar Sankranti, or Durga Puja, many women are unable to visit regularly. Many reasons prevent these visits. For example, sometimes the natal family is far away and women are not allowed to travel unaccompanied. Sometimes women are needed to cook and care for the elderly, sometimes demands of child care and children's education restricts their travel, and a minority of women have no close family left. But regardless of the reason, when a woman barely manages to visit her family once a year or even less, she is cut off from a potential source of social support. Table A.10.2b indicates that women's visits with their families are most restricted in areas like Delhi, Uttar Pradesh, Bihar, and Jharkhand. Additionally, women in many states are married at such a distance from their natal families that many cannot visit their families and return in a day. Poor transportation networks may also play a role in women's isolation.

The location of the most recent childbirth provides an interesting marker of women's contact with their natal families. In some communities, women return to their natal family for the delivery. In others, delivery occurs in the husband's home. Over all, about 20 per cent of all recent births took place in the natal home. On the whole, returning to the natal family for delivery seems more common among upper income groups and more educated families (see Table A.10.2a). Regional differences are also important. Since 68 per cent of women delivering at the natal home either deliver in a hospital, or are attended to by a trained doctor or nurse as compared to 53 per cent for births in the marital home, delivery at the natal home is an important marker of women's well-being. It is also important to remember this dislocation when designing prenatal care systems.

THE BELOVED BURDEN: A PARENTAL DILEMMA

In previous chapters, we noted that the discrimination against daughters results in higher mortality of girls and lower educational expenditures for daughters. We would be remiss if we did not point out some of the factors motivating parents into these grievous choices. In a primarily patriarchal society, a variety of factors combine to increase the financial burdens of raising a daughter and reduce the daughter's ability to provide financial and physical support to their parents.

Dowry and Wedding Expenses

Activist groups often implicate dowry demands in increased domestic violence and the oppression of women. It has also been reported that dowry inflation belies progress on many other fronts, such as improvements in women's education. Wedding expenses and dowries are also associated with long-term debt for households. The IHDS found that more than 15 per cent of the loans that households acquired are directly related to marriage expenses. Nationwide data on dowries or wedding expenses are notoriously difficult to collect, particularly in view of the Dowry Prohibition Act. In large-scale surveys, most respondents tend to be hesitant about reporting illegal activities within their own family, but are comfortable enough to provide general information about the practices within their community, or for families with similar social and economic standing within their *jati*. While we realize that this general information can be somewhat inflated, it provides an interesting marker of differences in expectations across social and economic groups. We focus on the following dimensions of marriage-related expenses:

(1) wedding expenses for the bride's and the groom's families,
(2) types of gifts given to a daughter at the wedding, and,
(3) cash gifts, or what is commonly referred to as dowry.

The results in Table A.10.3a are interesting. While wedding expenses for bride's family are uniformly higher than those for the groom's family (on average, about 50 per cent higher), the expenses for the groom's family are not trivial. The IHDS shows a nationwide average wedding expenditure of about Rs 60,000 for the groom's family and about Rs 90,000 for the bride's family. Even among households in the lowest income quintile, the expenditure for the groom's family is about Rs 43,000, while that for the bride's family is about Rs 64,000. Among better off households, a girl's wedding can cost upwards of Rs 1,50,000. In addition to wedding expenses, gifts of large consumer durables in dowry seem to be quite prevalent. When respondents were asked whether a family with a similar socioeconomic standing as them would frequently give any of four items—a car, motorcycle, refrigerator, or TV—about 24 per cent responded in the affirmative. An additional 43 per cent reported that these gifts are sometimes given. Even among households in the lowest income quintile, nearly 16 per cent reported that these items are frequently given. The comparable figure is about 39 per cent for the top quintile.

Both wedding gifts and wedding expenses are the lowest among Adivasi households, and among this group, there is surprisingly little difference in wedding expenses for boys and girls. Given that Adivasis seem to have the most favourable sex ratio at birth, as recorded in Chapter 8, gender parity in wedding expenses is an interesting observation. Dowry and wedding expenses appear to be one area in which education, upper caste status, and upper income are associated with less favourable gender outcomes. In the IHDS, cash gifts to daughters—pure dowry, by many definitions—seem to be relatively small compared with other expenses. The average amount of cash gift is about Rs 22,000, compared with the average wedding expense of Rs 92,000 for a daughter.

Regional differences in wedding expenses and gifts reported in Table A.10.3b are striking. On the whole, the richer states of Punjab and Haryana as well as Karnataka and Kerala have higher wedding expenses than the poorer states like Madhya Pradesh and Chhattisgarh, but gifts of large consumer durables seem to be far more a northern than a southern phenomenon. In contrast, cash dowries seem to be the highest in Kerala.

Sons as a Source of Old-age Support

In addition to higher wedding costs for daughters and higher dowries, low expectations of financial support from daughters are one of the most important reasons for son preference in India. The IHDS asked women about their expectations for old-age support. First they were asked, 'Who do you expect to live with in your old age?' Those who indicated that they expected to live with their sons were further asked, 'If your son does not want to, or is unable to live with you, would you consider living with a daughter?' Similar questions were asked about financial support in old age. The results, shown in Table A.10.4a, suggest that an overwhelming majority expect to be supported by sons. Eighty five per cent expect to live with sons in old age, and 86 per cent expect financial support. Only 9 per cent expect to live with daughters, and 11 per cent expect financial support from daughters. It is even more interesting to look at expectations in the event that sons are not able or willing to care for them. The proportion of women who do not expect or are unwilling to accept any support from their daughters is striking. Only 24 per cent would be willing to live with their daughters, and 30 per cent are willing to accept financial support from them.

Responses to these questions must be placed in the cultural context, where traditions dictate that parents give to a daughter and not take from her. In some areas, even today, parents are not expected to eat or drink at their daughter's home. Moreover, as we have shown in Table A.10.2a, only 14 per cent of women marry within their village or town and, hence, most are not easily available to provide support to their parents. All of these considerations are factored into the responses of the sample women who do not see receiving support from their daughters as realistic or socially acceptable. Educated women are marginally more willing to accept support from their daughters, but on the whole there is little social class or group variation in this respect.

However, there is substantial regional variation in parental willingness to rely on daughters, as shown in Table A.10.4b. This variation is consistent with other dimensions of gender inequality we noted above. Parents in Haryana, Rajasthan, Chhattisgarh, and Madhya Pradesh are far less willing to rely on daughters for any help than are those in the south. Women in the North-East and Kerala, two regions with a long matrilineal tradition, were most likely to mention daughters as a potential source of financial and residential support. The expectation that sons will support parents in old age seems consistent with our results in Chapter 9, where we showed that an overwhelming proportion of the elderly live with their children (mainly sons) and seem to have few other sources of income.

FAMILIES DIVIDED: POWER IN THE HOUSEHOLD

While rocking the cradle may well give women a way of ruling the world, ruling the household seems to be a different matter. The Indian women's movement and scholarly research have consistently documented unequal access to household resources by women and have argued that public policies need to recognize these inequalities for the provision of services as well as ownership of resources allocated via public programmes. We focus on two dimensions of household dynamics below: women's access to and control over household resources, and women's control over their own physical space and mobility.

Access to and Control over Resources

One of the most striking features of rural bazaars—particularly in north India—is that they are predominated by male shoppers. In many families, women rely on men to purchase day-to-day necessities, as well as medicines and other necessary items. This should reduce the likelihood that women have cash in hand for such purchases. The IHDS asked ever-married women aged 15–49 whether they had cash on hand at the time of interview. The results are shown in Table A.10.5a. About 83 per cent responded affirmatively—a very high proportion, in some ways reflecting the increasing monetization of the economy. Women were also asked whether they had any say in buying an expensive item for household use. Again about 70 per cent replied affirmatively.

While this data reflect positively on women's participation in day-to-day decision making, when it comes to having control over these decisions or having control over larger family finances, the story is quite different. Only 11 per cent women are primarily responsible for making decisions regarding large household purchases such as TVs or refrigerators. In households that have a bank account, only 18 per cent of women have their names on the account; among households that have rental or homeownership papers, only 15 per cent of women have their names on the documents. These latter two facets of the household economy, in particular, reflect women's vulnerability in the event of domestic discord or the husband's death. The likelihood of the woman being one of the owners (or the sole owner) of a bank account is greater for households with higher incomes, higher education, and urban residence. But this increased likelihood with income, education, and urban residence is far less marked in women's ownership of, or title to the residential property.

Women's access to and control over resources differ substantially across states (see Table A.10.5b) with greater variation across states than between different social and economic categories. Gujarat and Uttarakhand rank the highest in women's title to property, followed by Karnataka, Delhi, and the North-East.

Control over Physical Mobility

One of the biggest challenges Indian women face in controlling their own lives is a lack of physical mobility and access to public space, which is caused by several factors. Cultural norms surrounding female seclusion and the practice of purdah or ghunghat, familial control over women's physical movement, reluctance of women as well as families to allow them to venture alone into public spaces, and sexual harassment in public places. The IHDS asked women whether they practice purdah or ghunghat, whether they need permission to go to a health centre, and whether they could go alone to a health centre. For some women, such as those in Haryana or eastern Uttar Pradesh, ghunghat may cover the face fully. For others, such as those in Gujarat, partial covering of the face is more a nod to propriety than a large impediment. In the all India sample, 73 per cent need permission from other household members to go to a health centre, and 34 per cent can't or won't go alone to the health centre. Education and urban residence seem to increase women's control over their physical mobility and reduce seclusion. But even among college graduates, nearly 60 per cent need permission to go to a health centre and 17 per cent cannot or will not go alone (see Table A.10.5a).

Regional differences in women's physical mobility are vast (see Table A.10.5b). Purdah/ghunghat prevalence is extremely low (10–12 per cent) in Tamil Nadu, Andhra Pradesh, and Karnataka. It is very high in Uttar Pradesh, Bihar, Madhya Pradesh, and Rajasthan, with more than 85 per cent of women practising purdah or ghunghat. In some states, 40–60 per cent of women cannot go to a health centre alone (see Box 10.1).

It is important to note that this is a complex issue. When women respond to questions about their physical mobility, they are not reflecting dissatisfaction with the status quo, but rather are stating the realities of their lives in the context of cultural norms governing appropriate behaviour. From a policy perspective, however, it is important to note women's exclusion from public spaces. For example, any restructuring of maternal and child health services must consider that areas where women are more constrained have a far greater need of domiciliary services. In areas where women are freer to travel, it may be possible to concentrate on clinic-based services.

WOMEN'S STRENGTHS AND VULNERABILITIES

Data on different markers of women's lives for diverse socio-economic groups and across regional divides are difficult to come by. While a large-scale survey like the IHDS has many shortcomings and is often unable to probe to uncover hidden dimensions of gendered experiences, the kinds of questions the IHDS addresses are quite unique and provide an interesting snapshot of different dimensions of gender inequality in India. Documenting these inequalities does not mean that all Indian women are downtrodden or lack agency. In fact, we are surprised by the candour and confidence with which most women responded to the questions. The IHDS asked interviewers to rate different dimensions of their interactions with the respondents and found that a vast majority of women were able to interact very well with the interviewers. Eighty one per cent had no difficulty understanding the questions, 16 per cent had some difficulty, and 3 per cent had a lot of difficulty. Regarding knowledge of household expenditures—the most difficult set of questions for women to answer, given their lack of control over resources—only a small minority had very little knowledge (9 per cent), and the rest had either fairly good knowledge (41 per cent), or excellent knowledge (51 per cent).

These strengths are reflected in increasing levels of women's participation in a variety of government and non-government activities as well as a growing desire among women to educate their daughters as much as their sons. Among the IHDS respondents, 85 per cent would like to educate their sons and daughters equally, and 3 per cent would like to give more education to their daughters than to their sons.

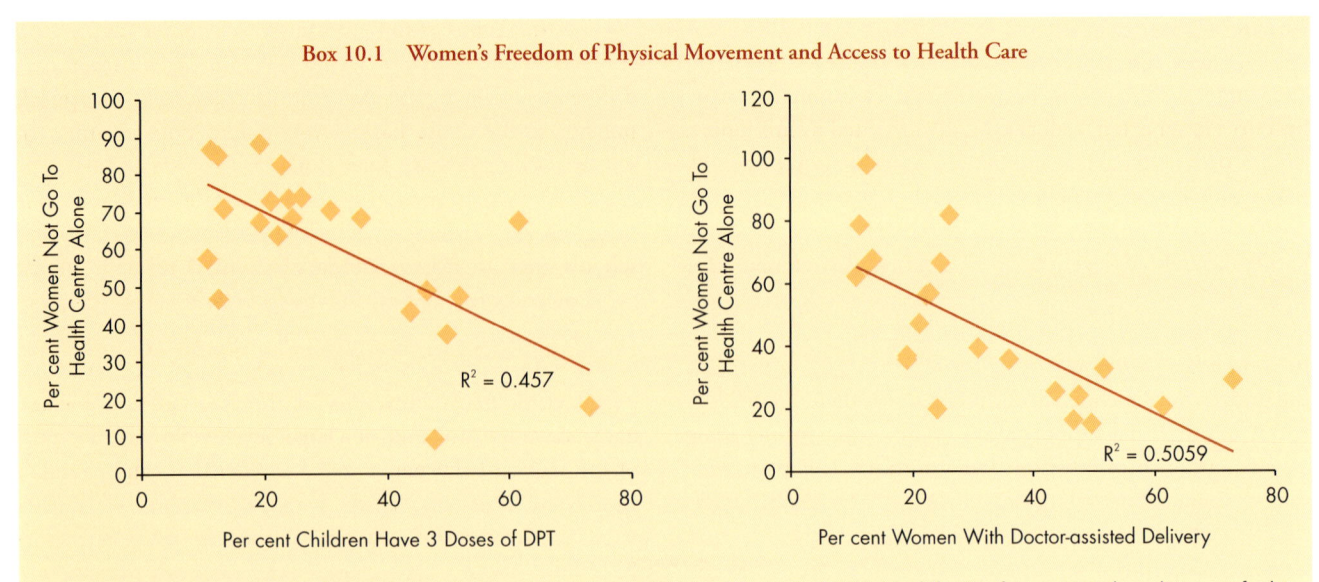

Box 10.1 Women's Freedom of Physical Movement and Access to Health Care

The absence of women from public spaces is striking in many parts of India. Women's physical mobility is often restricted, and women find it difficult to go alone to places like health centres. Several factors contribute to these limitations: fear of social sanctions, concerns about physical safety, or discomfort about venturing into unfamiliar terrain. Regardless of the causes of these limitations, they have serious consequences for women's ability to obtain government services. If they must wait for permission or need to be accompanied, they may be less likely to visit health centres than if they are able to venture out alone.

About 34 per cent of IHDS sample women claim that they cannot go alone to a health centre. The proportion varies considerably across states, with 50 per cent or more of women in Uttar Pradesh, Bihar, and Jharkhand stating that they cannot go alone to the health centre, compared with less than 15 per cent in Maharashtra, Kerala, and Tamil Nadu. The two graphs presented here correlate state-level averages for women who cannot go to a health centre alone with the completion of three DPT vaccinations for children (from Chapter 8) and doctor-assisted deliveries (from Chapter 7). These graphs show strong inverse correlations between constrained physical movement and the utilization of health services. States in which women are able to go to a health centre freely have children with higher levels of vaccination as well as a higher likelihood of a physician-assisted delivery.

Source: IHDS 2004–5 data.

However, in spite of these many strengths of individual women, their vulnerabilities are also striking. Due to ethical concerns associated with the fear of endangering respondents, the IHDS did not directly ask about women's experience of domestic violence. But to get their sense of general prevalence of domestic violence in their community, the IHDS asked whether, under a series of conditions, women in their communities are usually likely to be beaten by their husbands. These hypothetical conditions were, going out without permission, family not giving expected money (that is, dowry), neglecting the house or children, and not cooking properly.

The responses, presented in Table A.10.6a, show a striking pattern of vulnerability. Nearly 30–40 per cent of the respondents said that women are usually beaten up for going out without asking permission, not bringing the expected dowry, neglecting the house or children, and not cooking properly. Only 50 per cent do not believe that women in their communities are beaten for any of these reasons.

Special care is needed in interpreting these results. The IHDS did not ask about women's own experiences but rather those of other women in their communities. Interestingly, education and economic status seem to play an important role in these expectations. Educated women and women from upper income groups indicate a lower prevalence of violence in their communities than women from the more disadvantaged communities. It is not clear whether this is because there is actually less violence in communities where women have a higher education or because educated women are less likely to report pervasive violence. But in any case, even among the most educated group 30 per cent of women indicate that women in their communities are likely to be beaten for one of the four reasons listed above.

Given low levels of contact with natal families, it seems highly likely that many women, subject to violence or in other difficult circumstances, may find it difficult to get help from their families. Moreover, low levels of wage employment and lack of control over housing titles increase the obstacles to their building an independent life. Regional differences in expectation of domestic violence are large (Table A.10.6b) with about 70 per cent of the respondents in Assam and the North-East considering it unlikely that women are beaten for any reason, while the corresponding percentage is only about 20 per cent in Bihar and Jharkhand.

DISCUSSION

In this chapter, we attempted to provide a context for the gender differences in health, labour force participation, and (to a lesser extent) education, documented in this report. Several insights from these results are noteworthy, particularly as we consider public policy implications.

First, while many gendered outcomes are documented at the household level, such as a parental preference for investing in boys' education, it is important to look beyond the household for the sources of such behaviour. Most parents love their daughters as well as sons, but as documented in Chapter 9, the dependence of the elderly on their children for social and financial support makes a preference for investing in sons rather than daughters seem rational. This preference is strengthened by a cultural context in which daughters are married outside the village with limited contact with their natal families after marriage, and where they have few financial resources and independent decision-making powers to help their parents.

Second, while education and economic growth have changed many facets of human development in India, gender inequality in many areas seems impervious to this change. Higher income households are more gender unequal in some cases, such as with regard to dowries. Not even high levels of education empower women in all spheres. Thus, we need to think of alternative strategies for women's empowerment.

Third, regional differences in gender roles and norms are enormous, and seem to swamp other social and economic differences. These pose interesting challenges for public policy. At the most basic level, public policies must be mindful of these traditions while shaping service delivery. Health services may need to be delivered into the home in areas where women's physical mobility is curtailed. Girls' schools may increase secondary school enrolment in the cultural context emphasizing male–female separation, but may not be necessary in other areas. Policies regarding home registration and preferential banking schemes could be expanded to increase women's control over family home and bank accounts. However, at a larger level, regional differences offer a vision of alternative social realities that can be used to spur public discourse. While the Kerala story has often been told, it is interesting to note that the northeastern states fare very well on many markers of gender roles described in this chapter. These are also the states where the gender gap in literacy is very low and the sex ratio is more balanced. A focus on different cultural traditions, with some more favourable to overall social development than others, makes it possible to think of indigenous models of women's empowerment that do not rely on global norms but that are consistent with the best of Indian traditions.

HIGHLIGHTS

- The mean age at marriage for women is 17.4 years, with about 60 per cent marrying before the legal age of 18.
- Women in north India tend to marry outside of their natal village and consequently have less access to social support networks than their sisters in the south.
- Arranged marriage remains the norm, with less than 5 per cent women selecting their husbands without input from other family members.
- About 85 per cent women expect to live with their sons in old age; about 9 per cent, with daughters. A similar small proportion expects financial help from daughters.
- Many women practice ghunghat or purdah, particularly in central India, and 73 per cent need permission to go to a health centre.
- Wife beating and domestic violence remain pervasive, with about 50 per cent respondents claiming that women in their community are often beaten for minor transgressions like going out without permission.

Table A.10.1a Marriage and Family Patterns

	Per cent Married Before Age 18*	Mean Age at Marriage*	Per cent Not Cohabiting Immediately*	Mean Age at Cohabiting*	Per cent Marrying Before Puberty*	Per cent With Any Say in Marriage*	Per cent Knew Husband Before Marriage*	Children Ever Borne Women 40-9	Age at First Birth*
All India	60	17.4	51	18.0	16	62	23	3.85	20.6
Woman's Age									
25-9	57	17.6	48	18.1	13	64	24		20.0
30-9	61	17.4	50	18.0	15	62	22		20.5
40-9	60	17.3	53	18.0	18	59	23	3.85	21.3
Woman's Education									
Illiterate	75	16.1	64	17.0	20	50	20	4.38	20.1
1-4 Std	65	17.1	45	17.5	14	65	24	3.58	20.0
5-9 Std	53	17.9	40	18.3	11	68	26	3.35	20.6
10-11 Std	32	19.5	33	19.8	6	81	27	2.66	21.8
12 Std Some college	21	20.7	31	20.9	7	84	26	2.43	22.8
College graduate	7	22.6	24	22.8	5	89	29	2.13	24.6
Place of Residence									
Metro cities	38	19.3	31	19.5	5	82	26	2.73	21.5
Other urban area	47	18.5	44	19.0	11	71	27	3.46	21.2
More developed village	63	17.2	54	17.8	15	64	25	3.80	20.4
Less developed village	70	16.5	56	17.3	22	49	17	4.42	20.3
Income									
Lowest Quintile	70	16.5	56	17.3	19	55	20	4.16	20.4
2nd Quintile	68	16.7	55	17.4	18	58	23	4.07	20.3
3rd Quintile	66	17.0	54	17.7	16	58	22	4.13	20.4
4th Quintile	57	17.6	48	18.2	14	65	24	3.85	20.5
Highest Quintile	42	19.0	40	19.4	10	73	25	3.26	21.5
Social Groups									
High Caste Hindu	49	18.4	41	18.9	10	68	20	3.18	21.2
OBC	63	17.2	55	18.0	18	58	23	3.76	20.7
Dalit	71	16.5	55	17.2	17	59	19	4.20	20.0
Adivasi	64	17.1	54	17.7	18	63	29	4.01	20.8
Muslim	61	17.2	50	17.7	16	60	30	5.07	20.1
Other religion	18	20.8	30	21.1	5	84	25	2.77	22.8

Note: *Only calculated for women aged 25 years and above to reduce selectivity due to inclusion of women marrying at very young ages.
Source: IHDS 2004-5 data.

Table A.10.1b Marriage and Family Patterns by State

	Per cent Married Before Age 18*	Mean Age at Marriage*	Per cent not Cohabiting Immediately*	Mean Age at Cohabiting*	Per cent Marrying Before Puberty*	Per cent With Any Say in Marriage*	Per cent knew Husband Before Marriage*	Children Ever Borne Women 40–9	Age at First Birth*
All India	60	17.4	51	18.0	16	62	23	3.85	20.6
Jammu and Kashmir	41	18.9	57	19.3	7	43	32	4.63	21.5
Himachal Pradesh	43	18.6	28	18.9	12	64	32	3.61	21.0
Uttarakhand	55	17.6	27	17.8	16	42	13	4.49	21.1
Punjab	28	19.7	37	19.9	2	63	9	3.56	21.7
Haryana	56	17.4	74	18.3	13	65	4	3.59	20.9
Delhi	32	19.2	45	19.6	5	64	28	2.96	21.4
Uttar Pradesh	76	16.1	72	17.5	22	31	9	5.23	20.8
Bihar	86	15.2	75	16.6	26	20	6	4.92	20.7
Jharkhand	64	17.4	54	17.9	13	36	14	4.47	20.2
Rajasthan	79	15.8	88	17.4	25	21	7	4.91	20.2
Chhattisgarh	75	16.0	87	17.1	29	60	17	3.87	20.9
Madhya Pradesh	76	16.0	59	17.0	20	49	6	4.02	20.2
North-East	31	20.6	37	20.8	5	80	59	3.64	22.3
Assam	35	19.5	31	19.6	37	94	26	3.25	21.2
West Bengal	61	17.5	16	17.6	9	76	13	3.36	20.0
Orissa	53	17.9	13	18.0	3	40	19	4.15	20.4
Gujarat	48	18.2	69	18.9	29	93	17	3.31	20.9
Maharashtra, Goa	53	18.1	20	18.2	8	70	17	3.55	20.8
Andhra Pradesh	77	15.9	71	16.5	13	80	49	3.36	19.3
Karnataka	54	17.7	66	18.2	6	90	61	3.42	20.4
Kerala	19	20.9	21	21.0	1	99	40	2.45	22.7
Tamil Nadu	47	18.8	36	19.0	16	87	46	2.90	20.9

Note: *Only calculated for women aged 25 years and above to reduce selectivity due to inclusion of women marrying at very young ages.
Source: IHDS 2004–5 data.

Table A.10.2a Women's Social Support Networks

(per cent)

	Per cent Marrying in Same Village/Town	Per cent Marrying Cousins/ Relatives	Natal Family Lives Near by	Visit Natal Family 2+ times a Year	Last Delivery at Natal Home
All India	14	12	57	68	21
Woman's Age					
15–19	NA	NA	60	81	39
20–4	NA	NA	58	77	27
25–9	14	12	56	73	22
30–9	13	11	56	66	14
40–9	15	12	56	61	9
Woman's Education					
Illiterate	13	13	52	63	16
1–4 Std	16	15	61	68	24
5–9 Std	15	12	61	72	24
10–11 Std	15	9	60	76	27
12 Std Some college	14	7	61	75	34
College graduate	15	6	61	75	30
Place of Residence					
Metro cities	17	11	53	62	31
Other urban area	17	13	60	71	24
More developed village	14	15	60	72	21
Less developed village	11	8	52	64	18
Income					
Lowest Quintile	12	12	56	66	19
2nd Quintile	14	13	57	68	18
3rd Quintile	16	12	57	69	20
4th Quintile	14	12	56	68	21
Highest Quintile	13	9	57	69	27
Social Groups					
High Caste Hindu	10	8	50	66	23
OBC	12	11	57	68	21
Dalit	14	12	56	66	20
Adivasi	17	8	56	67	15
Muslim	24	24	64	70	23
Other religion	15	4	72	83	24

Note: Ever-married women age 15–49; NA—not calculated for women under 25 to avoid selectivity bias due to early marriage; and + refers to 2 or more.

Source: IHDS 2004–5 data.

Table A.10.2b Women's Social Support Networks by State

(per cent)

	Per cent Marrying in Same Villiage/Town	Per cent Marrying Cousins/ Relatives	Natal Family Lives Near by	Visit Natal Family 2+ times a Year	Last Delivery at Natal Home
All India	14	12	57	68	21
Jammu and Kashmir	23	21	55	88	31
Himachal Pradesh	11	0	61	77	7
Uttarakhand	8	1	57	51	1
Punjab	5	1	58	83	24
Haryana	3	2	39	84	13
Delhi	19	2	39	42	21
Uttar Pradesh	5	5	55	50	9
Bihar	6	6	24	50	16
Jharkhand	8	6	43	38	24
Rajasthan	11	2	53	71	18
Chhattisgarh	7	1	41	65	10
Madhya Pradesh	10	4	42	78	14
North-East	42	3	71	70	8
Assam	27	1	81	75	2
West Bengal	20	4	56	66	26
Orissa	17	9	65	52	11
Gujarat	8	3	75	85	33
Maharashtra, Goa	12	26	61	66	35
Andhra Pradesh	17	29	38	79	20
Karnataka	12	23	71	85	47
Kerala	28	3	84	90	23
Tamil Nadu	27	30	86	80	44

Note: Ever-married women aged 15–49 years; and + refers to 2 or more.
Source: IHDS 2004–5 data.

Table A.10.3a Average Expected Marriage Expenses and Dowry**

	Average Wedding Expenses Males	Average Wedding Expenses Females	Per cent Usually Giving Large Items in Dowry*	Average Cash Dowry
All India	59,879	92,853	24	22,421
Woman's Age				
15–19	41,941	63,143	15	15,534
20–4	52,065	80,698	21	19,181
25–9	58,818	90,936	25	22,823
30–9	59,903	93,620	24	22,880
40–9	67,344	1,03,741	25	24,138
Woman's Education				
Illiterate	46,045	66,766	19	15,298
1–4 Std	48,618	77,610	16	20,468
5–9 Std	64,054	1,02,405	26	24,896
10–11 Std	81,922	1,36,240	32	37,875
12 Std Some college	94,609	1,56,358	39	38,996
College graduate	1,27,966	2,05,526	43	44,488
Place of Residence				
Metro cities	86,743	1,27,151	27	34,205
Other urban area	79,931	1,22,822	32	26,999
More developed village	56,680	93,492	23	24,055
Less developed village	45,734	67,942	19	15,902
Income				
Lowest Quintile	43,426	64,553	16	17,175
2nd Quintile	41,680	63,782	16	14,959
3rd Quintile	51,105	78,422	20	19,240
4th Quintile	62,406	99,688	26	23,596
Highest Quintile	99,011	1,54,066	39	36,500
Social Groups				
High Caste Hindu	89,394	1,35,470	36	34,345
OBC	58,466	90,468	23	22,989
Dalit	43,275	66,107	20	14,373
Adivasi	30,685	37,974	6	6,352
Muslim	55,913	91,744	22	21,634
Other religion	91,231	1,83,352	34	39,972

Notes: *Large items include TV, refrigerator, car, and motorcycles.
**Refers to practise in community and not women's own experiences.
Source: IHDS 2004–5 data.

Table A.10.3b Average Expected Marriage Expenses and Dowry Across States**

	Average Wedding Expenses Males	Average Wedding Expenses Females	Per cent Usually Giving Large Items in Dowry*	Average Cash Dowry
All India	59,879	92,853	24	22,421
Jammu and Kashmir	1,53,027	2,10,342	38	18,233
Himachal Pradesh	94,237	1,14,839	72	6,555
Uttarakhand	61,216	80,619	52	9,441
Punjab	1,05,421	1,57,250	61	6,603
Haryana	1,12,527	1,58,056	65	3,709
Delhi	1,24,476	1,90,929	86	24,648
Uttar Pradesh	71,876	98,748	46	21,134
Bihar	50,801	77,798	19	28,971
Jharkhand	50,304	85,400	26	33,606
Rajasthan	88,607	1,14,649	35	8,328
Chhattisgarh	38,996	47,289	10	272
Madhya Pradesh	43,937	57,950	33	4,523
North-East	54,312	67,648	37	9,535
Assam	24,916	34,947	6	1,828
West Bengal	40,121	71,543	7	24,549
Orissa	53,619	88,745	29	25,496
Gujarat	77,586	92,331	7	2,743
Maharashtra, Goa	58,704	76,861	9	20,980
Andhra Pradesh	38,178	71,350	21	50,048
Karnataka	59,731	1,04,430	5	37,731
Kerala	49,709	1,93,112	10	72,954
Tamil Nadu	55,657	1,02,953	13	9,572

Notes: *Large items include TV, refrigerator, car, and motorcycles.
**Refers to practise in the community and not women's own experiences.
Source: IHDS 2004–5 data.

Table A.10.4a Exepctation of Old Age Support from Sons and Daughters

	Per cent Expecting to Live With...			Per cent Expecting Financial Help From...		
	Sons	Daughters	Daughters If Son Unable	Sons	Daughters	Daughters If Son Unable
All India	85	9	24	86	11	30
Woman's Age						
15–19	70	9	21	70	10	27
20–4	78	9	23	79	11	30
25–9	85	11	26	85	12	32
30–9	87	10	24	87	11	30
40–9	89	8	23	89	11	29
Woman's Education						
Illiterate	89	7	22	90	9	27
1–4 Std	86	10	24	85	13	35
5–9 Std	83	10	24	84	12	32
10–11 Std	82	13	26	82	16	33
12 Std Some college	76	17	30	76	20	36
College graduate	71	18	31	70	19	33
Place of Residence						
Metro cities	77	12	22	76	12	28
Other urban area	82	11	26	82	13	29
More developed village	87	10	25	87	13	33
Less developed village	88	7	22	88	9	29
Income						
Lowest Quintile	86	10	25	85	12	32
2nd Quintile	86	9	24	87	10	30
3rd Quintile	86	8	21	87	11	29
4th Quintile	86	10	24	86	12	30
Highest Quintile	84	11	24	84	13	29
Social Groups						
High Caste Hindu	84	9	22	84	12	28
OBC	87	9	24	87	11	30
Dalit	85	10	25	86	10	31
Adivasi	82	11	27	82	13	34
Muslim	87	8	22	87	10	30
Other religion	79	20	29	79	23	34

Source: IHDS 2004–5 data.

Table A.10.4b Statewise Expectation of Old Age Support from Sons and Daughters

	\multicolumn{3}{c}{Per cent Expecting to Live With...}	\multicolumn{3}{c}{Per cent Expecting Financial Help From...}
	Sons	Daughters	Daughters after Probing	Sons	Daughters	Daughters after Probing
All India	85	9	24	86	11	30
Jammu and Kashmir	96	6	26	93	10	34
Himachal Pradesh	78	10	31	80	9	25
Uttarakhand	77	6	29	78	6	31
Punjab	93	0	3	93	1	6
Haryana	95	3	8	95	3	12
Delhi	84	3	12	80	2	19
Uttar Pradesh	93	9	27	93	9	25
Bihar	98	3	15	98	4	16
Jharkhand	90	7	30	90	7	30
Rajasthan	95	1	17	95	1	19
Chhattisgarh	83	5	10	83	6	9
Madhya Pradesh	93	4	7	93	4	7
North-East	73	31	40	79	40	51
Assam	80	9	17	82	15	54
West Bengal	71	13	23	73	14	34
Orissa	88	7	26	88	12	35
Gujarat	83	9	31	83	14	28
Maharashtra, Goa	86	5	13	85	8	30
Andhra Pradesh	86	16	42	85	20	60
Karnataka	83	14	30	82	19	36
Kerala	75	36	45	75	43	56
Tamil Nadu	71	13	29	73	11	30

Source: IHDS 2004–5 data.

Table A.10.5a Women's Control Over Resources and Physical Mobility

(in percentage)

	Has Any Cash on Hand	Purchasing Large Items... Any Say	Purchasing Large Items... Primary Decision	Name on...* Bank Account	Name on...* Home Papers	Per cent of Women Who... Practice Purdah or Ghunghat	Per cent of Women Who... Need Permission to Go to A Health Center	Cannot Go to Health Center Alone
All India	83	71	11	18	15	55	73	34
Woman's Age								
15–19	62	52	4	5	4	70	86	66
20–4	77	62	5	10	7	61	85	50
25–9	83	66	8	16	11	56	78	39
30–9	85	74	12	19	16	53	71	27
40–9	86	76	17	22	22	52	65	27
Woman's Education								
Illiterate	82	70	12	10	14	63	77	40
1–4 Std	80	70	11	13	15	53	72	31
5–9 Std	83	70	10	18	14	52	72	30
10–11 Std	84	72	9	32	16	42	68	26
12 Std Some college	89	76	9	39	18	36	66	23
College graduate	91	79	13	58	25	28	58	17
Place of Residence								
Metro cities	92	84	12	33	18	36	56	16
Other urban area	88	73	13	25	17	44	67	23
More developed village	81	69	11	15	15	52	74	32
Less developed village	80	68	10	12	13	68	79	45
Income								
Lowest Quintile	82	72	15	10	14	61	73	38
2nd Quintile	80	69	12	9	12	59	76	38
3rd Quintile	81	69	10	12	14	56	76	35
4th Quintile	83	72	11	19	14	52	73	31
Highest Quintile	88	71	9	37	20	48	68	27
Social Groups								
High Caste Hindu	87	72	9	29	18	51	70	30
OBC	85	72	11	16	15	52	74	33
Dalit	82	72	14	13	14	55	74	33
Adivasi	78	62	10	10	13	47	76	38
Muslim	76	64	11	13	11	84	77	44
Other religion	77	80	11	33	16	15	63	15

Note: *Only for households with bank account or home ownership/rental papers.
Source: IHDS 2004–5 data.

Table A.10.5b Statewise Women's Control Over Resources and Physical Mobility

(in percentage)

	Has Any Cash on Hand	Purchasing Large Items... Any Say	Purchasing Large Items... Primary Decision	Name on...* Bank Account	Name on...* Home Papers	Per cent of Women Who... Practice Purdah or Ghunghat	Per cent of Women Who... Need Permission to Go to A Health Center	Cannot Go to Health Center Alone
All India	83	71	11	18	15	55	73	34
Jammu and Kashmir	72	50	13	25	11	76	89	25
Himachal Pradesh	91	54	12	32	19	45	81	19
Uttarakhand	91	83	12	31	34	45	68	24
Punjab	89	84	8	24	6	32	82	21
Haryana	92	86	7	12	8	81	66	19
Delhi	96	94	9	40	25	43	58	11
Uttar Pradesh	86	78	9	18	14	87	77	50
Bihar	89	71	5	27	14	88	93	73
Jharkhand	88	52	15	26	9	59	68	52
Rajasthan	81	55	6	12	8	94	79	44
Chhattisgarh	79	50	6	7	3	58	90	62
Madhya Pradesh	74	68	7	7	16	93	91	47
North-East	76	75	38	26	20	28	67	13
Assam	69	47	18	6	6	68	64	48
West Bengal	60	74	15	16	8	70	72	31
Orissa	77	57	8	6	4	64	80	36
Gujarat	93	86	5	20	49	76	78	23
Maharashtra, Goa	88	66	8	23	11	38	56	14
Andhra Pradesh	96	66	10	14	13	12	83	26
Karnataka	83	80	12	15	29	12	89	23
Kerala	43	62	7	23	20	15	52	13
Tamil Nadu	94	86	31	11	13	10	42	12

Note: *Only for households with bank account or ownership/rental papers.
Source: IHDS 2004–5 data.

Table A.10.6a Common Perception of Domestic Violence in the Community

(in percentage)

	In Respondent's Community It is Common to Beat a Women if She....				No Wife Beating Under Any of These Conditions
	Goes Out Without Permission	Family Does Not Give Expected Money	Neglects House	Does Not Cook Properly	
All India	39	29	35	29	50
Woman's Age					
15–19	48	33	40	35	43
20–4	42	31	35	29	46
25–9	41	30	35	29	48
30–9	38	29	35	30	50
40–9	35	26	32	28	53
Woman's Education					
Illiterate	45	33	38	33	43
1–4 Std	40	32	39	31	47
5–9 Std	36	27	32	27	53
10–11 Std	30	24	31	23	57
12 Std Some college	24	19	25	20	62
College graduate	18	15	20	15	70
Place of Residence					
Metro cities	29	21	22	18	63
Other urban area	29	24	31	24	57
More developed village	41	31	39	32	46
Less developed village	44	31	36	32	46
Income					
Lowest Quintile	47	35	41	36	41
2nd Quintile	42	32	38	32	46
3rd Quintile	40	30	35	30	48
4th Quintile	35	27	34	28	52
Highest Quintile	30	22	26	21	60
Social Groups					
High Caste Hindu	33	25	29	23	57
OBC	40	31	37	31	48
Dalit	43	32	37	31	46
Adivasi	40	23	35	30	49
Muslim	42	30	36	31	47
Other religion	16	20	26	21	65

Source: IHDS 2004–5 data.

Table A.10.6b Statewise Common Perception of Domestic Violence in the Community

(in percentage)

	In Respondent's Community It is Common to Beat a Women if She....				No Wife Beating Under Any of These Conditions
	Goes Out Without Permission	Family Does Not Give Expected Money	Neglects House	Does Not Cook Properly	
All India	39	29	35	29	50
Jammu and Kashmir	58	26	60	41	25
Himachal Pradesh	25	7	16	11	71
Uttarakhand	42	16	14	12	56
Punjab	12	9	7	7	86
Haryana	22	8	18	21	67
Delhi	16	21	12	7	70
Uttar Pradesh	40	25	23	19	50
Bihar	66	57	69	69	21
Jharkhand	58	55	54	46	22
Rajasthan	39	20	27	30	49
Chhattisgarh	22	9	13	15	73
Madhya Pradesh	48	23	37	29	48
North-East	10	10	23	8	73
Assam	8	10	11	8	84
West Bengal	30	28	28	24	65
Orissa	39	27	24	20	55
Gujarat	54	25	44	34	39
Maharashtra, Goa	61	41	56	44	25
Andhra Pradesh	20	29	23	17	63
Karnataka	56	50	52	46	39
Kerala	15	24	29	21	58
Tamil Nadu	20	16	37	28	56

Source: IHDS 2004–5 data.

Social Changes

11

Social Integration and Exclusion

The human development discourse, which began with attention to such basic needs as health, education, and employment, has now expanded to include social integration and exclusion.[1] Households are not isolated units but are connected to others in patterns that create the fabric of social life. In recent years, more research has focused on these personal interconnections among households. Social scientists have explored how social networks channel information, norms, and even diseases across populations. Political scientists have emphasized how institutions—formal patterns of interconnections—can tell us more about development than the simple sum of population characteristics. Economists have incorporated these interpersonal connections into their work by redefining them as the social capital that people invest in, and later draw from when needed.

By nature, sample surveys select households as independent cases and so have had some difficulty incorporating these social connections into their research agenda. The IHDS is fortunate to have inquired into a rich variety of interpersonal connections that link households to their wider social context. The IHDS is the first national survey with such a range of questions. The survey presents a unique opportunity for understanding how social integration is related to human development in India.

The four sections of this chapter report results from each type of social integration investigated in the IHDS:

(1) Membership in nine types of organizations,
(2) Reports of conflicts in the local neighbourhood,
(3) Crime victimization, and,
(4) Network contacts with formal institutions, such as schools, the medical system, and the government.

These are not the only dimensions of inclusion/exclusion that are relevant to the human development discourse, but they are somewhat easier to measure in a large sample survey than others, such as cultural identity. It is also important to note that although this chapter focuses on some very specific aspects of social integration and exclusion, social exclusion is not limited to the topics discussed here. Other chapters have also documented different dimensions of exclusion, such as women's limited access to the public space (Chapter 10) and the exclusion of Muslims from formal sector jobs (Chapter 4).

Discourse on social exclusion has emerged from the literature on ethnic and cultural minorities and, hence, tends to focus on characteristics of individuals and households, such as religion or caste, in identifying social exclusion. While these factors are important, we find that for some indicators of interest, regional and community contexts play a far more important role than social or cultural background.

Network connections are the one exception in which household characteristics combine with local context to determine the extent of social relationships. For organizational memberships, village or neighbourhood conflict, and crime, what matters is the local context. Are there organizations locally available to join? Do local and state institutions function well? Is the village full of conflict? Is crime widespread in

[1] UNDP (2004).

the state? State level variations on these issues are especially striking—more so than for the development and family issues reviewed thus far. Further, there is no simple pattern to these state variations. Each type of social integration reveals its own ranking across states, and none of these are tightly connected to state patterns of wealth, education, or gender and family norms. Emerging from this review is an even richer appreciation of the extraordinary institutional diversity across India.

ORGANIZATIONAL MEMBERSHIPS

While informal social networks are important pathways of influence and advancement, the growth of civil society depends also on the spread of formal organizations. Non-government Organizations (NGOs), self-help groups, caste associations, and the like provide an institutional basis for bringing people together consistently over time to work for common goals. They can be the foundation of a healthy social and political order.

The IHDS asked households whether they were members of any of the nine types of formal organizations. Somewhat over a third (36 per cent) of Indian households reported being a member of at least one of these groups (see Table A.11.1a). The organizations vary widely in their reach. Caste associations and groups with a social, religious, or festival focus enlist about 14 per cent of Indian households, NGOs and development groups, only about 2 per cent (see Figure 11.1).

There is a moderate tendency for a household that is a member of one type of organization to have also joined others. A count of the number of types of organizations joined reveals that 18 per cent of households are members of just one type of organization. Another 11 per cent are members of two types, and another 7 per cent have joined three or more types of organizations. This count provides a useful index for the extent of civic associations across India.

It is interesting to note that the membership of caste associations and religious and festival societies tops the list of organizational memberships. The survey items did not distinguish between different types of organizations within these broad categories. However, it would not come as surprise to people familiar with Indian society that social and religious institutions form an important avenue through which Indian households relate to the world around them.

Organizational density is strongly patterned along state boundaries. Membership is widespread in Assam and the North-East, and in the south, especially in Kerala, where more than 70 per cent of households are members of at least one organization (see Figure 11.2).

In contrast, only 6 per cent of Punjab households and 9 per cent of Uttar Pradesh households belong to any of the named organizations.

This statewise variation overwhelms variation by social position within states. As would be expected, richer and more educated households are more likely to be members of an organization, but the differences are quite small (for example, 40 per cent of households with a college graduate are organization members, while 29 per cent of households without any schooling are members).

Differences among castes and religions are negligible, and whatever differences exist are almost wholly attributable to geography. For instance, the higher membership rate of Adivasis is due to their concentration in the north-eastern states, where there is a high associational membership. Rural–urban differences are also minor compared with the state differences. A rural household is slightly more likely to be an organizational member (38 per cent) than an urban household (31 per cent), despite the lower levels of education and wealth in rural areas. Only a few types of organizations

Organization	Per cent
Caste Association	14
Religious/Social Organization	14
Self-help Groups	9
Credit/Savings Group	7
Mahila Mandal	7
Union/Business Group	5
Youth/Sports/Reading Room	4
Any Co-operative	4
Development/NGO	2

Figure 11.1 Membership in Different Organizations (in per cent)
Source: IHDS 2004–5 data.

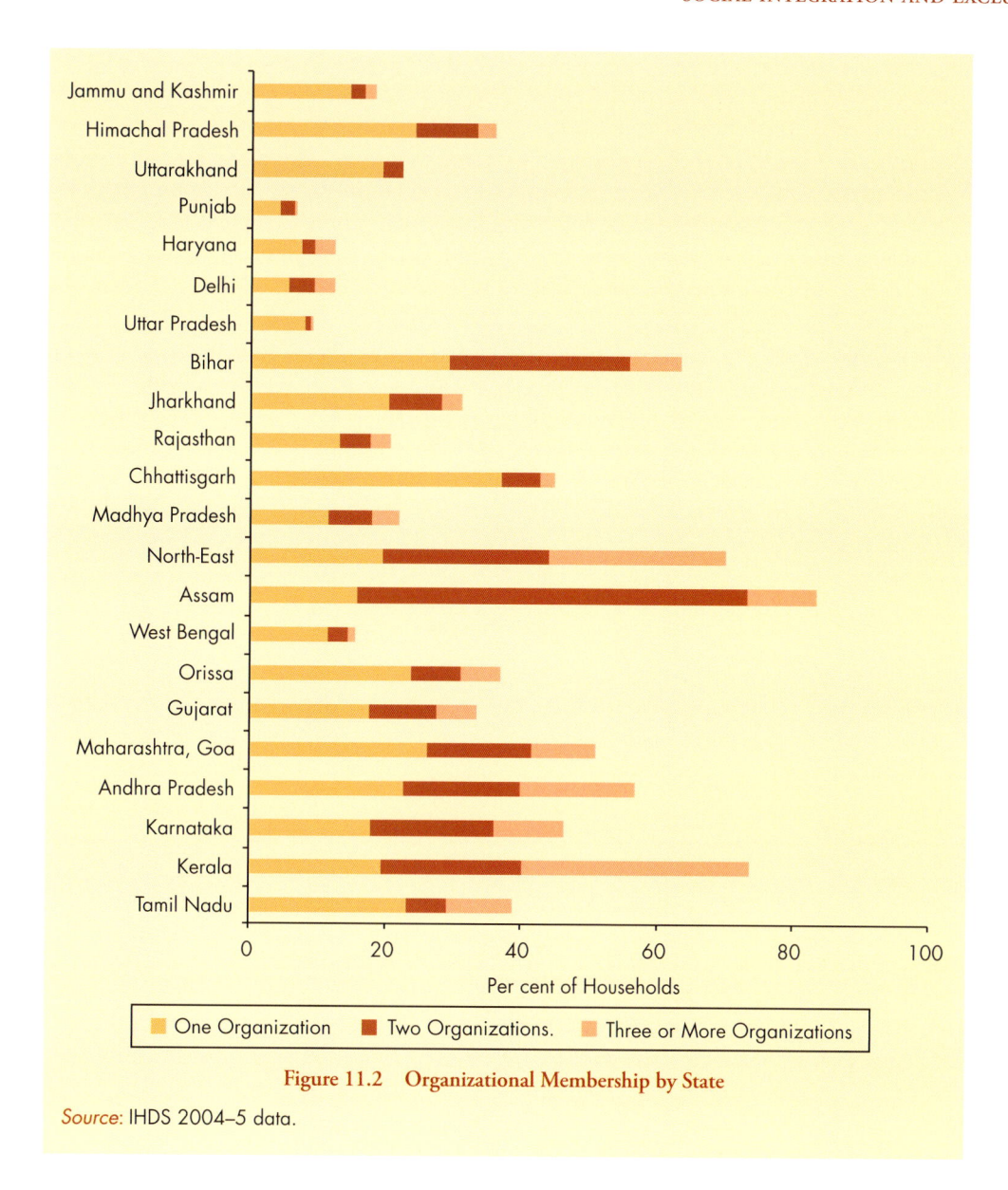

Figure 11.2 Organizational Membership by State

Source: IHDS 2004–5 data.

are more common in towns and cities—unions and business organizations, for instance.

State differences are particularly important for organizational memberships, although as we later show, they are somewhat less important for informal networks. Organizational memberships are most prevalent in Assam (83 per cent), Kerala (73 per cent), the north-eastern states (70 per cent), and Bihar (63 per cent). This greater importance of state location and lesser importance of social position for formal organizations should not be surprising. A household can usually join a formal organization only if that organization exists nearby, whereas, virtually all households throughout India have at least some potential access to a teacher, a health practitioner, or a government official, who form their informal networks. The geographic basis of most formal organizations produces the large state differences observed. The importance of caste associations strengthens state-based patterns because some castes have widespread caste associations and others do not, and different castes are located in different areas.

VILLAGE AND NEIGHBOURHOOD CONFLICT

Organizational memberships represent the positive side of social connections. But social relationships can have a negative side as well. The survey asked about two of these negative aspects: The presence of conflict within the village or urban neighbourhood, and levels of crime victimization. Both are again largely patterned by state differences; social position plays a negligible role. But the state patterns are not simply the opposite of the previously analysed positive aspects of social connections. Instead, local conflict and crime define their own patterns of state differences.

Almost half of Indian households (48 per cent) report that their village or neighbourhood has some or a great deal of conflict (see Table A.11.1a).[2] This varies from the 8 per cent reported in Andhra Pradesh to the 79 per cent reported in Uttar Pradesh (see Figure 11.3).

There is no obvious pattern to these state differences. Both poor (for example, Uttar Pradesh) and affluent (for example, Gujarat) states have high levels of conflict. States from the north, south, east, and west are found in both the high conflict and low conflict groups. Urban and rural parts of a state tend to have similar levels of conflict. Across India, there is almost no urban–rural difference in the reported levels of local conflict. However, state levels of conflict are somewhat correlated with the extent of organizational memberships. States with a rich array of formal organizations tend to be states with less conflict. Causality probably works in both directions here. Conflict impedes the creation and success of formal organizations, but working together in formal institutional settings can also help reduce conflicts.

After these state differences are accounted for, few differences are found across social groups in their reports of local conflict. Christians, Sikhs, and Jains report slightly lower levels of local conflict (38 per cent) than forward caste Hindus (49 per cent), but all religious and caste differences virtually disappear when we look at differences within states. Differences across education, income, and occupation groups are even smaller.

The survey also asked whether there was much conflict among the communities and jatis living in the local area.[3] Compared to generalized village/neighbourhood conflicts,

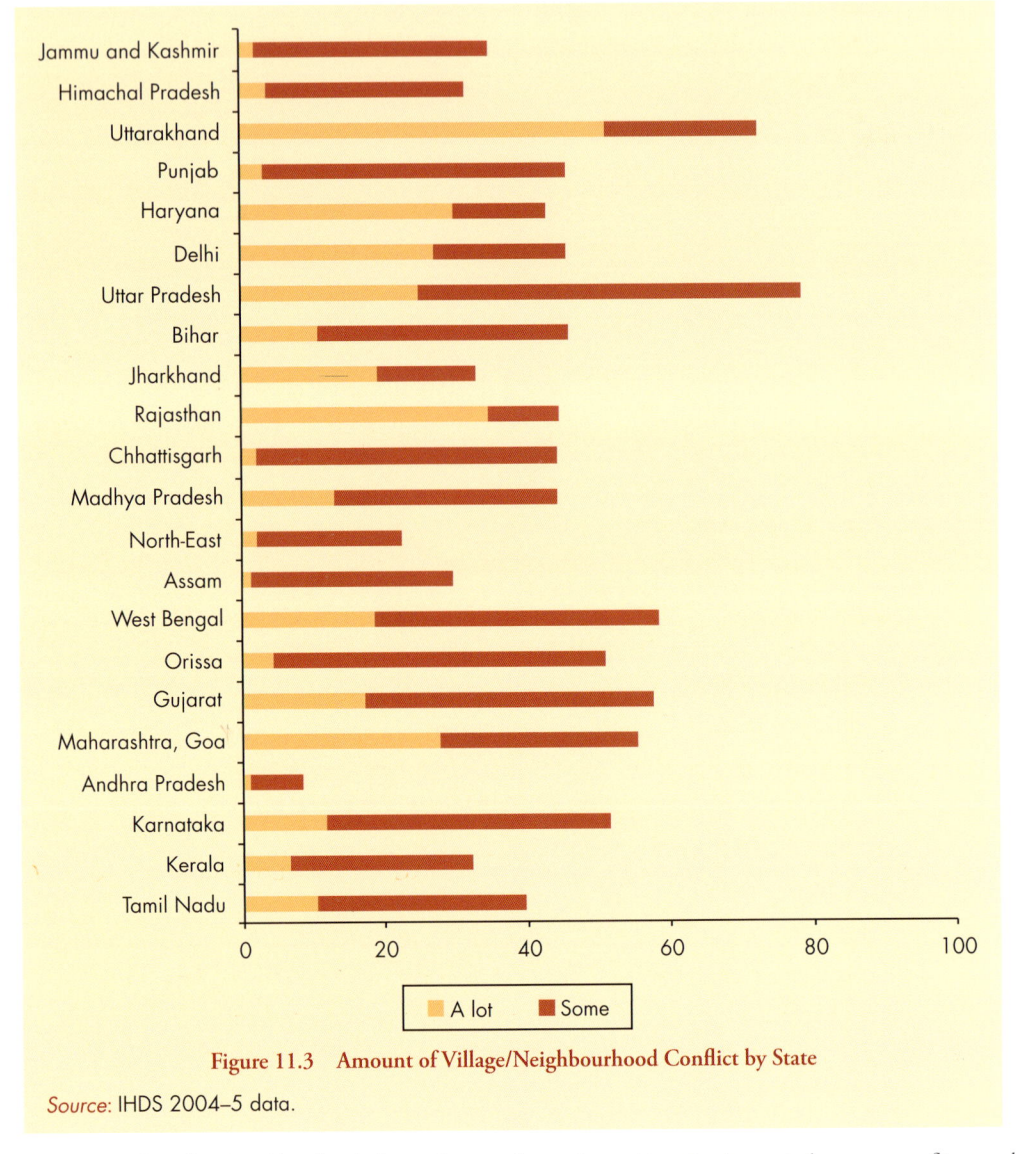

Figure 11.3 Amount of Village/Neighbourhood Conflict by State
Source: IHDS 2004–5 data.

[2] The English text was, 'In this village/neighbourhood, do people generally get along with each other, or is there some conflict, or a lot of conflict?'
[3] The English text was, 'In this village/neighbourhood, how much conflict would you say there is among the communities/jatis that live here? Lot of conflict? Some conflict? Not much conflict?'

fewer households (30 per cent) reported this specific type of conflict. Even among households reporting a lot of conflict within the village or neighbourhood, most (70 per cent) reported no community or jati conflict. Thus, while caste and religious conflicts contribute to local tensions, they are not the only or even the major source of local conflict.

CRIME VICTIMIZATION

Sample surveys of crime victimization have transformed the study of crime. Freed from the limitations of police reports, victim accounts are believed to provide a more complete picture of the level and spread of crime throughout a country. Some preliminary efforts at victimization studies have been undertaken in India, but the IHDS is the first national study with standard victimization questions on theft, burglary, and assault.[4] About 4.6 per cent of Indian households reported a theft in the last year; 1.2 per cent reported a burglary; and 2.7 per cent reported an assault. Altogether, 6.7 per cent of households reported at least one of these crimes (Table A.11.1a). Given a lack of comparable benchmarks, IHDS results should be seen as being indicative but not definitive and be treated with caution.

These crime rates vary dramatically across the country. Bihar (24 per cent) and West Bengal (16.7 per cent) report far higher levels of crime than the rest of the country (Figure 11.4). At the opposite extreme, Andhra Pradesh (1 per cent), Gujarat (1.6 per cent), and Haryana, Maharashtra, and Uttarakhand (2.2 per cent) have the lowest crime rates.

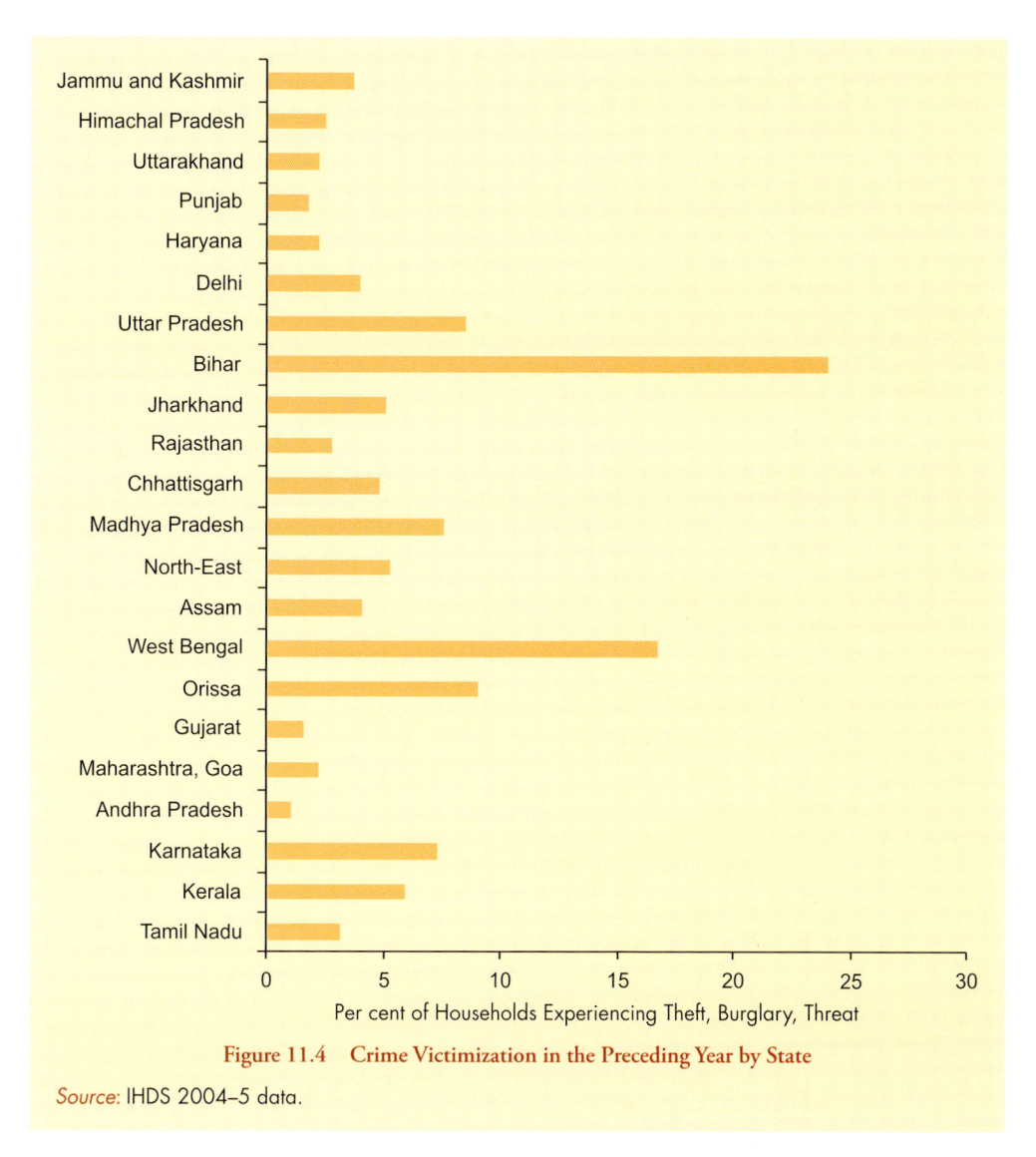

Figure 11.4 Crime Victimization in the Preceding Year by State

Source: IHDS 2004–5 data.

---

[4] The English texts were as follows:
'During the last twelve months, was anything stolen that belonged to you or to somebody in your household?'
'During the last twelve months, did anyone break into your home or illegally get into your home?'
'During the last twelve months, did anyone attack or threaten you, or someone in your household?'

While these victimization rates reveal much higher levels of crime than found in the official police statistics (as is typical of victimization studies), they also suggest a very different geographic distribution of crime. The official statistics, for instance, rank Bihar and West Bengal as relatively low in crime. Besides the concentration of crime in the eastern part of India, crime rates tend to be higher in poorer states.

Consistent with the association of crime with state poverty, crime rates are higher in rural areas (7.3 per cent) than in urban areas (4.8 per cent). Some of this difference is a consequence of higher crime rates in the more rural states (for example, Bihar and Orissa). The higher crime rates are in the less developed villages (8.2 per cent) than in more developed villages (6.3 per cent), this is entirely a function of state variation. More of the less developed villages are in the high crime eastern states and the moderately high crime central states of Uttar Pradesh and Madhya Pradesh.

In contrast to the dramatic state differences, victimization is remarkably uniform across types of households within the states. While there is some difference by household income, with the poorest households reporting higher rates of victimization than the wealthiest households (7.5 per cent versus 4.6 per cent), this difference reverses when we look at crime rates within states. In any case, these income differences are smaller than what we would expect by chance. Similarly, Dalits report being crime victims slightly more often (8.8 per cent) than forward caste Hindus (5.5 per cent), but this difference reduces to 1.7 percentage points within states. The slightly higher victimization rate among Dalits results mostly from the higher concentration of Dalits in Bihar, West Bengal, and Orissa, where all castes and communities report higher crime.

SOCIAL NETWORKS

Who people know and—perhaps more importantly—who knows them is an invaluable resource for any household. Good social networks are not only instrumental for getting ahead but are an end in themselves. One's own status in any community is defined by knowing and being known by other high status people. The survey asked households about their ties to three major institutions. Whether they had acquaintances or relatives who worked in education, the government, and medicine.[5] Across India, 38 per cent of households have ties to schools, 32 per cent have ties to the government, and 31 per cent have ties to some medical institution (Figure 11.5).

A household with ties to any one of these institutions is more likely to have ties to the others, so it is useful to

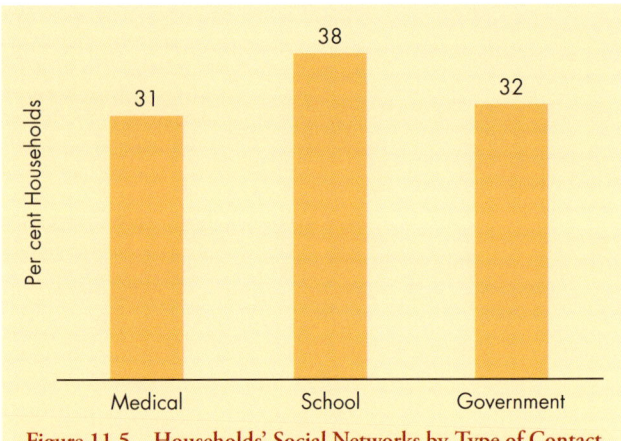

Figure 11.5 Households' Social Networks by Type of Contact
Source: IHDS 2004–5 data.

construct a scale from 0 to 3 measuring the extent of the household's social network. Forty seven per cent of households have none of the three network ties, 21 per cent have one, 16 per cent have two, and another 16 per cent have all three types of network ties.

The statewise variation in network ties is substantial (Figure 11.6).

In Himachal Pradesh, more than three-quarters of the households have ties to at least one of these institutions, and the average number of ties is greater than two. On the other hand, in Orissa and Rajasthan, only about a third of households have any ties at all, and the average number of ties is just above 0.5. This fourfold difference is only slightly related to state wealth. While the fairly affluent states of Himachal and Punjab have high network densities, Bihar, which is among the poorest of states, also has high network density. And in relatively affluent Gujarat and Haryana, approximately half of the households have no network ties.

Network ties are almost as extensive in rural villages as in towns and cities. Urban households have, on an average, 1.2 network ties, only slightly above the 0.9 network ties of rural households (see Table A.11.1a). All this difference is due to the higher education and economic status of urban households. A rural household of the same educational and economic level as an urban household is likely to have even more network ties than its similar urban counterpart.

There are sharp differences among social groups (Figure 11.7) that follow the expected status hierarchy.

Forward castes have more contacts than OBCs, who have more contacts than Dalits, who have more than Adivasis. Most of these differences are attributable to the educational

---

[5] This type of social network question is known as a 'position generator' inquiry. The English text was, 'Among your acquaintances and relatives, are there any who … are doctors, or nurses, or who work in hospitals and clinics? … are teachers, school officials, or anybody who works in a school? … are in government service?' (other than doctors, teachers, above).

Figure 11.6 Social Networks by State

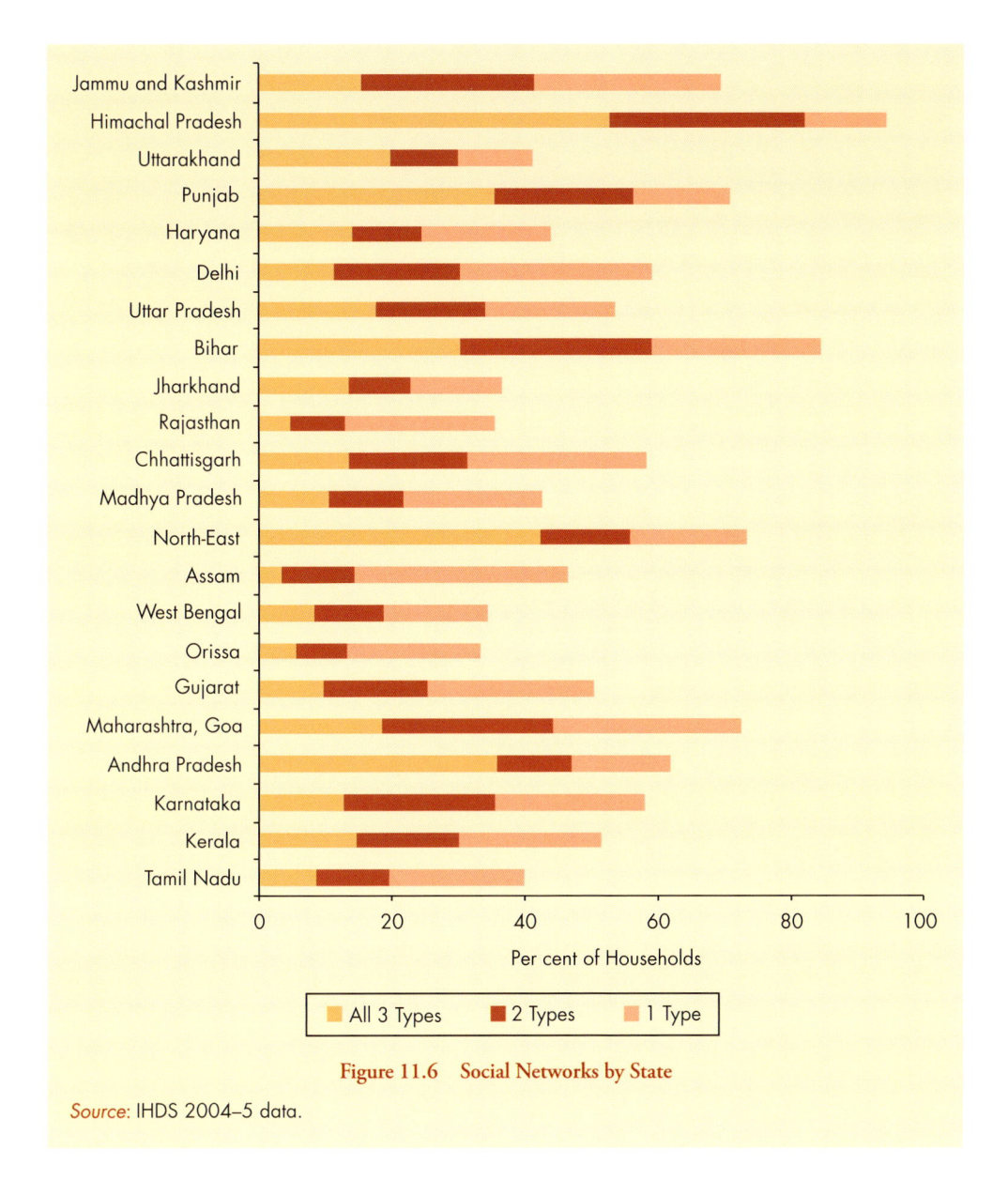

Source: IHDS 2004–5 data.

and economic differences among the groups; the exception are Adivasis, who have few contacts even when compared with educationally and economically equivalent forward caste Hindus. Muslims also have few contacts, not much different from Dalits—a low standing that remains low when compared with Hindus of equivalent education and economic position. However, minority religions other than Muslims are as well connected as forward caste Hindus.

Education, occupation, and income all have the expected relationships with social networks (see Table A.11.1a). Higher levels of status are consistently associated with more social contacts. Causality probably works in both directions here. More education and income enable a person to have more elite contacts, but better social networks also are an asset for getting into schools, finding better jobs, and earning more money.

While there are some similarities in the state patterns of informal networks and formal organizational memberships, there are also noticeable differences. Bihar and the North-East are high on both measures and West Bengal and Rajasthan low on both. But Punjab is high on informal social networks and low on formal organizations while Assam is the reverse. Neither state pattern is highly correlated with state differences in education, wealth, or family patterns. Differences in organizational densities probably follow the particular state histories of political and social mobilization that are at best loosely determined by the underlying social structure.

DISCUSSION

How do these indicators of social integration and exclusion fit into an analysis of human development? Some of these measures are important indicators of well-being in themselves.

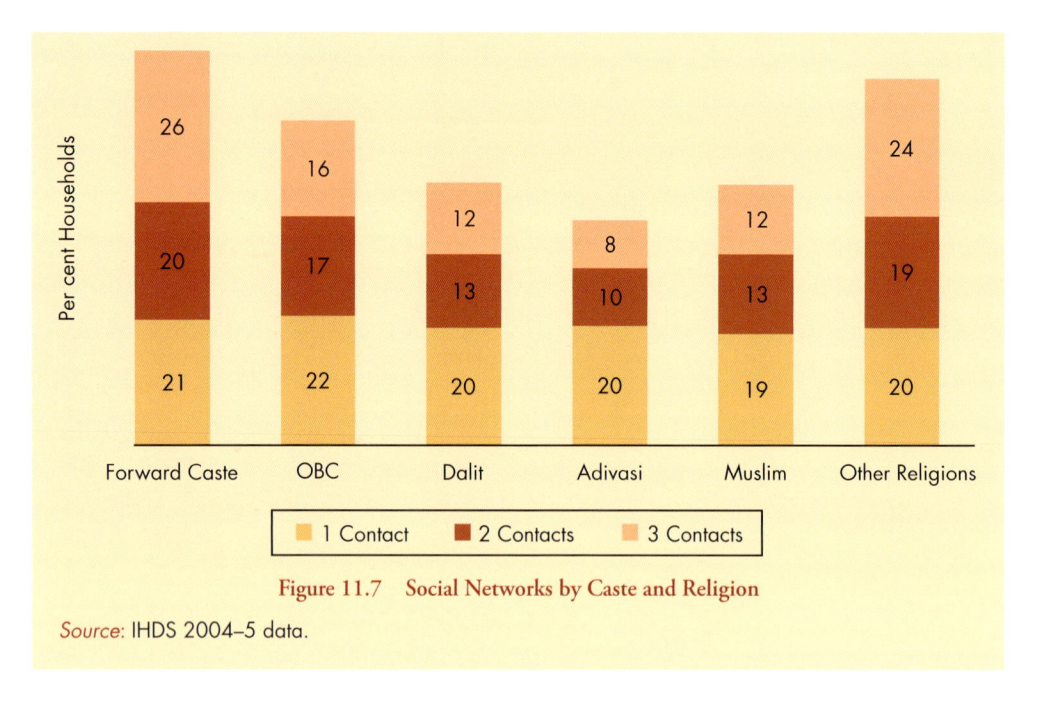

Figure 11.7 Social Networks by Caste and Religion

Source: IHDS 2004–5 data.

Experiencing theft, burglary, and threats increase vulnerability and reduce a sense of security. Other indicators—such as social networks—are associated with an ability to access formal institutions such as schools, hospitals, or government services. Still others, like organizational membership, reflect the functioning of the civil society and the participation of households in the broader social structure.

Social exclusion plays an independent role in reducing access to services and negatively impacts individual outcomes. When a child from a well-connected household is sick, parents know how to find transportation, which doctor to see, and how to talk to the doctor. If they are themselves poorly equipped, either because of poverty or low education, they know whom to ask for help. This is reflected in health outcomes for their children. Children from households with connections to all three institutions—schools, medical systems, and government—have about 13 per cent lower mortality in the first year of life than households with no connections. This relationship is independent of caste and religion, household income, education, and place of residence.[6] Similarly, when they must borrow, well connected households are about 24 per cent less likely to borrow from moneylenders (who generally lend at much higher interest rates than banks). Organizational membership is associated with a higher likelihood of obtaining a government loan for constructing a home, latrine, or improved stove. Households that are members of at least two organizations are 30 per cent more likely to receive such loans than those that are not members of any organization. Membership in three or more organizations boosts this difference to 68 per cent.

At the same time, the data presented in this chapter suggests that social context is far more important in patterning social exclusion than individuals' own characteristics, with social networks being a partial exception. For all indicators discussed above, place of residence and state play an important role in shaping social exclusion. For social networks, individual characteristics such as caste and religion also play a role. History, politics, and social structure all combine to create a climate in which civic organizations grow. A better understanding of why some areas are more hospitable to civic engagement than others will be extremely useful as more and more responsibilities devolve on local governments with an increasing focus on local control.

---

[6] All results in this paragraph are based on logistic regressions controlling for income, social group, household education, urban/rural residence, and state of residence.

Box 11.1 Trust and Confidence in Institutions

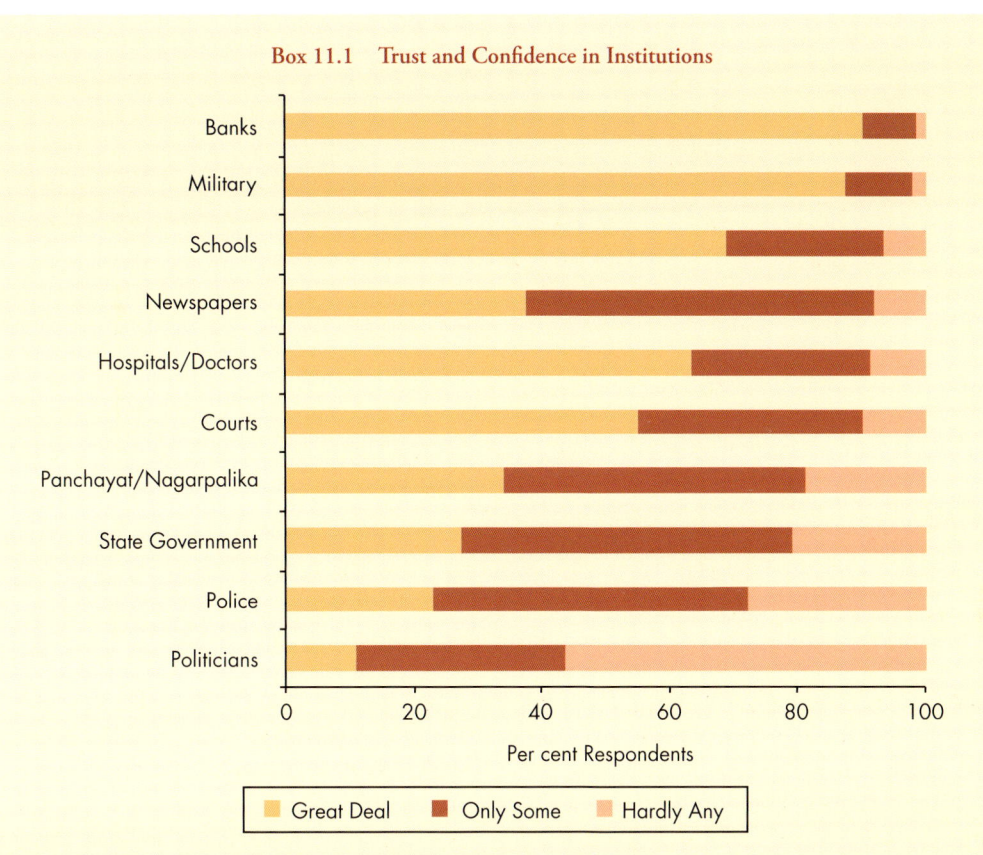

[Horizontal stacked bar chart showing Per cent Respondents for: Banks, Military, Schools, Newspapers, Hospitals/Doctors, Courts, Panchayat/Nagarpalika, State Government, Police, Politicians. Legend: Great Deal, Only Some, Hardly Any]

Studies of social capital have emphasized the subjective beliefs necessary to support strong networks of social ties and organizational memberships. Higher levels of confidence in the system's institutions and trust in one's fellow citizens facilitate the social interactions that build a strong civil society. The IHDS asked respondents how much confidence they had in 10 important institutions in Indian society ('a great deal of confidence', 'only some confidence', or 'hardly any confidence at all'). The analysis revealed that the principal division was between households that responded that they had 'a great deal of confidence' and households that responded otherwise.

The most confidence was reported for banks (90 per cent) and the military (87 per cent), followed by schools (69 per cent), hospitals/doctors (63 per cent), courts (55 per cent), newspapers (38 per cent), panchayats (34 per cent), the state government (27 per cent), police (23 per cent), and politicians (11 per cent).

Source: IHDS 2004–5 data.

HIGHLIGHTS

- Caste associations and social organizations dominate the list of association memberships.
- About 7 per cent of households reported experiencing theft, burglary, or harassment in the year preceding the survey.
- About 31–8 per cent households reported knowing someone working in a school, a medical centre, or government. These social networks are the largest among families living in Himachal Pradesh, Bihar, and the North-East.
- Social networks for Adivasi households are considerably more limited than those for other social groups.
- Households report the greatest confidence in banks and the military and the least confidence in police and politicians.

Table A.11.1a Social Integration, Social Networks, and Crime Victimization

| | Percent of Households Reporting ||| Mean Number of Social Network Connections |
	Membership in Any Organization	Village/ Neighbourhood Having Some Conflict	Victim of Crime/ Threat Last Year	
All India	36	48	6.7	1.0
Maximum Household Education				
None	29	48	7.8	0.6
1–4 Std	37	50	8.2	0.7
5–9 Std	37	47	6.6	0.9
10–11 Std	39	46	5.4	1.2
12 Std/Some college	42	48	5.8	1.4
Graduate/Diploma	40	48	5.8	1.8
Place of Residence				
Metro city	24	52	4.9	1.3
Other urban	34	45	5.1	1.2
Developed village	42	45	6.3	1.0
Less developed village	35	51	8.2	0.9
Household Income				
Lowest Quintile	32	51	7.5	0.7
2nd Quintile	36	49	8.2	0.8
3rd Quintile	35	46	6.9	0.9
4th Quintile	38	45	6.1	1.1
Highest Quintile	40	47	4.6	1.7
Social Groups				
Forward Caste Hindu	33	49	5.5	1.4
OBC	39	46	6.3	1.1
Dalit	35	51	8.8	0.8
Adivasi	42	43	5.3	0.6
Muslim	30	48	7	0.8
Other religion	45	38	5	1.3

Source: IHDS 2004–5 data.

Table A.11.1b Social Integration, Social Networks, and Crime Victimization by State

	Percent of Households Reporting			Mean Number of Social Network Connections
	Membership in Any Organization	Village/ Neighbourhood Having Some Conflict	Victim of Crime/ Threat Last Year	
All India	36	48	6.7	1.0
Jammu and Kashmir	18	35	3.6	1.3
Himachal Pradesh	36	31	2.4	2.3
Uttarakhand	22	72	2.2	0.9
Punjab	6	46	1.8	1.6
Haryana	12	43	2.2	0.8
Delhi	12	46	3.9	1.0
Uttar Pradesh	9	79	8.4	1.1
Bihar	63	46	24	1.7
Jharkhand	31	33	5	0.7
Rajasthan	20	45	2.8	0.5
Chhattisgarh	44	44	4.8	1.0
Madhya Pradesh	22	44	7.5	0.7
North-East	70	22	5.2	1.7
Assam	83	30	4.1	0.6
West Bengal	15	58	16.7	0.6
Orissa	37	51	9	0.5
Gujarat	33	58	1.6	0.8
Maharashtra, Goa	51	55	2.2	1.3
Andhra Pradesh	56	8	1	1.4
Karnataka	46	51	7.2	1.1
Kerala	73	32	5.9	1.0
Tamil Nadu	39	40	3.1	0.7

Source: IHDS 2004–5 data.

12

Villages in a Global World

Throughout this report, we have documented tremendous differences in the lives of individuals and households based on their geographic location, with rural residents having poorer health, education, incomes, and employment opportunities. However, it is also important to note the diversity among rural residents. Many rural areas have seen rapid integration into the global economy while others seem to have been forgotten. This chapter explores the regional variation in the connectedness of the villages to the larger world and finds the differences quite remarkable.

Despite rapid urbanization and migration to urban areas in search of employment, according to the 2001 Census, 72.2 per cent of Indians continue to reside in villages. As we documented earlier, characteristics of communities greatly influence the success of the men, women, and children who live in them and this has important consequences for human development. For example, access to roads is important for the movement of goods and people and for the diffusion of ideas. Electricity access not only helps agricultural productivity but also increases the efficiency with which people can accomplish tasks like fetching water, reading, working in the evening after sun down, and enjoy some leisure through access to television. Similarly, access to schools and health facilities ensures an educated and healthy population.

The IHDS collected information on 1,454 villages nationwide through interviews with key informants in each village.[1] These key informants were usually village officials, but the information collected from them was often supplemented with interviews with other individuals. The survey focuses on a variety of dimensions of village life and access to infrastructure, allowing us to ground the household-based information described in earlier chapters in a contextual perspective. While interpreting these results, caution in making interstate comparisons must be exercised because the sample of villages is far more restricted than the sample of households. Moreover, large and small villages are weighted equally in the results presented here.

This chapter focuses on the following:
(1) Village connectivity via road, rail, telephone, and availability of electricity and water; (2) The availability of public services such as schools and health care, and, (3) The presence of NGOs and development programmes.

VILLAGE CONNECTIVITY

As inclusive growth emerges as the theme for Indian economic development, it is important to recognize that this inclusion depends on how well connected the communities are to the wider economy. At its most basic level, this connectivity takes a physical form: access to electricity, post office, and telephone. Other measures include access to public transportation and banks. Paved roads are also important for connectivity, and our village level data indicates that one of the most important results of Indian growth seems to be the development of an extensive network of roads. With the exception of Uttarakhand, most villages in the IHDS sample seem to have a paved road in, or near the village. However, the geography of the state influences the distance from the nearest town and from the district headquarters. While the

[1] The IHDS surveyed 1,503 villages, but several village questionnaires were incomplete, resulting in 1,454 completed village questionnaires.

mean distance to the nearest town can be as little as 9 km, as it is in Kerala, it can be as much as 20–5 km, as it is in Uttarakhand, Jharkhand, and the North-East.

As Table 12.1 indicates, access to electricity varies by region.

While the states in the north (for example, Himachal Pradesh, Punjab, and Haryana) and in the south (for example, Andhra Pradesh and Karnataka) can boast of near complete penetration of electricity in rural areas, other states like Bihar, Assam, Jharkhand, and Orissa have a long way to go. Furthermore, penetration rates mean little if the reliability of access is poor. States that have the highest rates of penetration do not necessarily provide the most reliable services. For example, on an average, villages in Punjab and Haryana receive only 9–11 hours of electricity per day. On the other hand, states that have poor penetration rates, like Bihar or Assam, also have the fewest hours of access (four and eight hours, respectively) to the service. In comparison, the rural areas of Kerala and Tamil Nadu not only have relatively high rates of penetration in rural areas but also enjoy more than 20 hours of electricity supply per day.

Comparison of household and village access to electricity points to an interesting lacuna of public policy interest. Although a large proportion of the villages in the IHDS sample boast of electricity connection, the same cannot be said of the households. For example, while 88 per cent of the sample villages in Gujarat, Dadra and Nagar Haveli, and Daman and Diu, have electric connections, only 29 per cent of the households in the rural sample do. This suggests that

Table 12.1 Village Infrastructure by State

	Number of Completed Village Schedules	Mean Distance from Nearest Town	Mean Distance from District Town	Per cent Villages with Paved Road	Distance from Road if No Road	Per cent Villages with Electricity	Per cent Homes with Electricity in Villages	Mean Hours of Electricity Per Day
All India*	1,495	14.29	44.51	92	1.6	91	68	13.11
Jammu and Kashmir	20	9.55	33.10	90	1.8	100	81	11
Himachal Pradesh	52	19.90	47.42	85	2.4	100	98	14
Punjab/Chandigarh	61	11.10	32.72	100	0.1	100	96	11
Haryana	79	10.28	27.56	100	0.0	100	90	9
Uttar Pradesh	138	12.69	34.36	92	0.9	89	42	8
Uttarkhand	20	21.83	43.44	50	1.6	90	85	15
Bihar	61	12.80	28.70	95	2.7	62	23	4
Jharkhand	26	24.31	38.65	96	1.9	77	46	12
Rajasthan	88	12.63	53.63	93	0.4	91	56	8
Madhya Pradesh	129	17.45	47.34	90	3.6	95	78	6
Chhatishgarh	49	12.09	53.98	94	5.3	92	63	17
West Bengal	66	12.02	46.63	86	1.4	86	39	19
Orissa	84	16.84	50.51	85	2.1	76	29	19
Assam	38	13.53	42.67	87	5.9	58	27	8
North-East	33	20.91	38.30	97	3.5	94	71	17
Gujarat, Daman, Dadra	76	13.79	43.71	91	0.6	92	89	18
Maharashtra/Goa	121	12.34	51.61	98	0.4	98	79	17
Andhra Pradesh	94	17.62	65.41	89	1.5	100	85	16
Karnataka	142	16.52	51.49	99	1.1	100	82	11
Kerala	61	8.88	28.40	82	0.8	80	77	23
Tamil Nadu/Pondicherry	65	10.12	40.44	89	2.0	91	90	22

Note: *Tables present unweighted summary from village questionnaires. These data are from nationwide but not nationally representative.
Source: IHDS 2004–5 data.

there may be other barriers to electrification for households besides the availability of electric connection.

Provision of water is another basic infrastructure that seems to vary by state. Households' access to indoor piped water was discussed in Chapter 5, but Table 12.2 provides information about access to water supply at the village level.

This table indicates that the two most important sources of water in rural India are piped water (41per cent) and hand pumps (33 per cent). The states of Himachal Pradesh, Gujarat, and Andhra Pradesh have succeeded in providing access to piped water to more than 80 per cent of the villages. Other states, like Punjab, rely more on a mix of piped water and hand pumps. Piped water is the least common in Orissa, Assam, West Bengal, Uttar Pradesh, Bihar, and Jharkhand.

Besides access to basic infrastructure, the integration of a village into the economy depends on the community's access to banks, post offices, public transportation, phones, and the like. Table 12.3 highlights that with the exception of telephone services most, if not all, states have a long way to go in providing universal access to such facilities in rural areas.

Among the worst connected are the rural areas of Uttar Pradesh, Jharkhand, Madhya Pradesh, Chhattisgarh, and Assam.

Proximity to administrative towns seems to affect the level of development such that the farther away a village is from the district headquarters, the less infrastructure facility it gets. Measuring economic development by counting within the village access to ten infrastructure facilities—electricity,

Table 12.2 Primary Water Source in Village by State

	Piped Water	Tube Well	Hand Pump	Open Well	Covered Well	Other	Total
All India*	40.7	13.4	32.5	8.7	2.0	2.7	100
Jammu and Kashmir	50.0	0.0	20.0	10.0	0.0	20.0	100
Himachal Pradesh	88.5	0.0	5.8	3.9	0.0	1.9	100
Punjab/Chandigarh	36.1	4.9	59.0	0.0	0.0	0.0	100
Haryana	54.4	3.8	30.4	3.8	6.3	1.3	100
Uttar Pradesh	6.7	1.5	88.9	3.0	0.0	0.0	100
Uttarkhand	38.9	0.0	50.0	0.0	0.0	11.1	100
Bihar	1.6	45.9	47.5	3.3	1.6	0.0	100
Jharkhand	3.9	19.2	57.7	19.2	0.0	0.0	100
Rajasthan	31.0	24.1	34.5	6.9	2.3	1.2	100
Madhya Pradesh	13.6	5.9	57.6	17.8	2.5	2.5	100
Chhatishgarh	6.4	6.4	68.1	17.0	0.0	2.1	100
West Bengal	6.3	17.2	62.5	12.5	0.0	1.6	100
Orissa	7.2	56.6	20.5	13.3	0.0	2.4	100
Assam	2.8	88.9	5.6	2.8	0.0	0.0	100
North-East	63.6	6.1	3.0	12.1	0.0	15.2	100
Gujarat, Daman, Dadra	85.7	1.4	12.9	0.0	0.0	0.0	100
Maharashtra/Goa	66.7	2.5	16.7	12.5	0.0	1.7	100
Andhra Pradesh	81.9	6.4	9.6	1.1	0.0	1.1	100
Karnataka	75.4	7.8	3.5	11.3	0.0	2.1	100
Kerala	26.0	6.0	0.0	34.0	32.0	2.0	100
Tamil Nadu/Pondicherry	59.3	13.6	3.4	1.7	3.4	18.6	100

Notes: *Tables present unweighted summary from village questionnaires. These data are nationwide but not nationally representative.
Source: IHDS 2004–5 data.

Table 12.3 Availability of PDS Shops, Banks, Post Offices, Buses, and Phones in the Village

	Public Distribution System Shop	Bank in Village	Post Office in Village	Bus Stop in Village	Landline Phone in Village
All India*	72	30	53	51	79
Jammu and Kashmir	75	40	45	30	85
Himachal Pradesh	46	19	46	58	98
Punjab/Chandigarh	79	48	67	62	98
Haryana	81	47	58	63	100
Uttar Pradesh	79	16	43	19	91
Uttarkhand	35	15	10	10	60
Bihar	67	38	61	39	84
Jharkhand	77	8	15	58	62
Rajasthan	53	22	55	52	82
Madhya Pradesh	51	21	36	39	69
Chhatishgarh	53	8	24	41	57
West Bengal	64	17	52	32	86
Orissa	65	23	42	40	69
Assam	74	8	16	13	76
North-East	67	30	33	48	70
Gujarat, Daman, Dadra	80	34	75	71	88
Maharashtra/Goa	88	39	53	65	91
Andhra Pradesh	93	33	81	68	94
Karnataka	75	35	65	77	96
Kerala	75	64	77	52	82
Tamil Nadu/Pondicherry	83	34	74	74	89

Notes: *Tables present unweighted summary from village questionnaires. These data are nationwide but not nationally representative.
Source: IHDS 2004–5 data.

paved road, *kirana* (grocery) shop, bus stop, landline and mobile access to telephone, post office, police station, bazaar, and bank—we find that villages that are farthest from the district headquarters are the least likely to have access to these development inputs. Figure 12.1 shows a precipitous drop in the number of items available to a village as the distance from district headquarters increases.

Note that in the previous chapters we have described the differences in a variety of human development indicators, such as health, education, and employment opportunities and their relationship to village development. These chapters show that villages with access to at least six of the ten infrastructure facilities described above have considerably greater access to health care, education, and employment opportunities.

Finally, it is worth noting that while many villages have access to various kinds of infrastructure on paper, and often in the form of buildings or bus shelters, the actual provision of services is defunct or unreliable, as evidenced by the case of electricity. For example, in some villages, Public Distribution System (PDS) shops are often closed because of lack of supplies.

EDUCATION IN RURAL INDIA: UNEVEN DEVELOPMENT

India is receiving global recognition for producing savvy engineers, doctors, and other highly trained professionals. Early government investments in high quality medical and engineering schools seems to be paying rich dividends to a section of the population that can be compared with the

Figure 12.1 Number of Infrastructure Items Available by Distance to District Headquarters
Source: IHDS 2004–5 data.

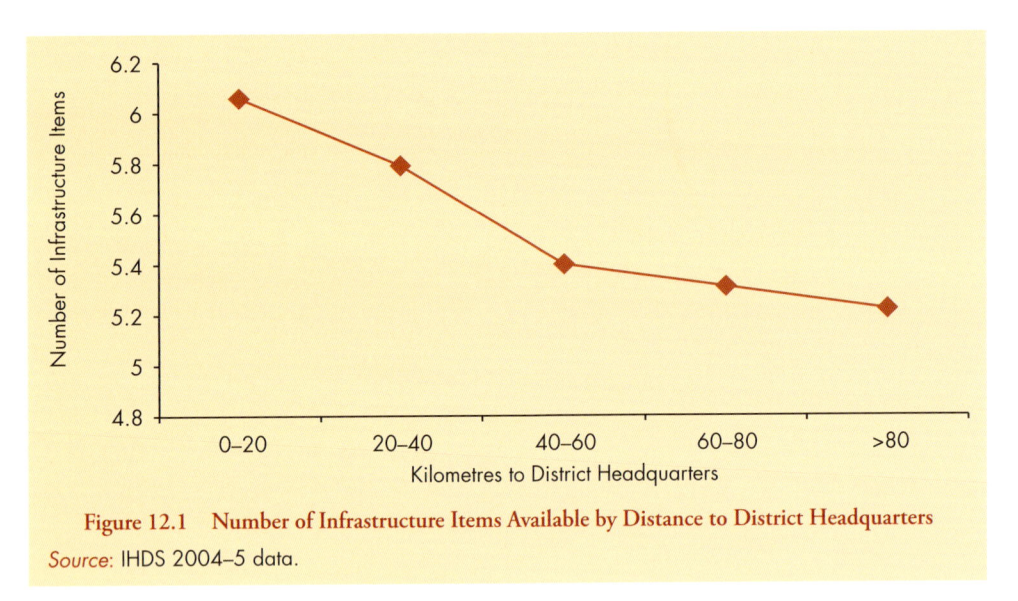

best in the world. In urban areas, there are many excellent educational institutions at the elementary, upper primary, and high school levels. However, as we documented in Chapter 6, the quality of education is highly variable. Only about half the children, aged between 8–11 in rural areas, are able to read a simple paragraph. Many children drop out of the schooling system, either because of a lack of access to schools or poor returns to education in rural areas. The IHDS results presented in Chapter 6 document that a substantial fraction of students completing Standard 5 drop out before completing Standard 10, and this is particularly true in rural areas. This finding may be related to a lack of access to schools in rural areas. Though, almost all villages in India boast of a government primary school, reflected in high primary school enrolment rates documented earlier, as Table 12.4 indicates, this is not true of higher levels of education, particularly secondary schools.

In some cases where government schools are distant, private schools may fill the gap. We documented an increasing number of rural children attending private schools (about 20 per cent). However, private schools are still rare in rural areas, with nearly 60 per cent of the villages not having a private school of any kind. It is important to note that the absence of school from villages is not synonymous with total lack of access to schools. In many instances, even when a school is not located in the village, it may be accessible in a nearby village. Table 12.5 shows the location of educational facilities in the village and within 1–5 km for primary, upper primary, secondary, and higher secondary schools, as well as colleges, whether they are public or private.

In many parts of India, children have access to a primary (Standards 1–5) and upper primary (Standards 5–8) school within walking distance from the village, even if not within the village. This access declines at the secondary level (Standards 9–10).

At higher levels of education (that is, higher secondary and beyond), almost all states fare poorly. Overall, only 13 per cent of villages have access to a government higher secondary school. Kerala leads with 48 per cent of the villages having access to a government higher secondary school, and Punjab follows with 35 per cent.

It is important to note that the absence of school from villages does not imply total lack of access to schools.

If we include access to private higher secondary schools, more than 50 per cent of villages have a high school within 5 km. As Table 12.5 indicates, in Kerala, almost all villages have some type of a high school within 5 km. Punjab and Tamil Nadu also fare quite well, with more than 70 per cent of villages having access to a higher secondary school within 5 km. However, Bihar and Jharkhand fare poorly even when private schools are included.

Dissatisfaction with the public school system is evidenced by a growing trend among households at all levels of income of sending their children to private schools. Table 12.6 documents a mean school index, ranging from 1 to 5, measuring the presence of primary, upper primary, secondary, and higher secondary schools, as well as colleges in rural areas.

These values are listed overall, and separately for government and private schools. While government schools form the majority of educational establishments available, states such as Punjab, Haryana, and Kerala also seem to have a sizeable number of private schools. Ironically, these are also states with the most access to various levels of government schools. With the exception of Uttar Pradesh, all states where private school presence is strong are states where government schools are widely available. This complementarity between private and public systems is a theme to which we shall return when discussing community programmes.

Table 12.4 Access to Government Educational Institutions in the Village

	Per cent Villages with Access to Government...						
	Anganwadi	Primary	Upper Primary	Secondary	Higher Secondary	College	Girls' School
All India*	89	93	60	28	13	2	10
Jammu and Kashmir	85	100	55	25	5	0	30
Himachal Pradesh	77	83	56	40	23	6	2
Punjab/Chandigarh	90	98	66	52	34	5	10
Haryana	96	99	72	58	23	1	34
Uttar Pradesh	86	92	49	9	8	1	6
Uttarkhand	75	85	45	15	10	0	0
Bihar	75	82	66	21	5	5	7
Jharkhand	96	88	50	4	4	0	8
Rajasthan	92	98	69	31	15	1	24
Madhya Pradesh	91	97	65	17	8	1	19
Chhatishgarh	88	96	53	16	12	2	8
West Bengal	86	94	30	29	9	0	5
Orissa	88	90	52	31	6	6	8
Assam	87	95	71	11	8	0	8
North-East	79	85	58	36	15	3	3
Gujarat, Daman, Dadra	91	91	54	24	14	0	14
Maharashtra/Goa	96	97	49	16	5	0	3
Andhra Pradesh	98	100	74	56	11	2	4
Karnataka	96	100	78	20	4	1	4
Kerala	82	75	66	56	48	7	5
Tamil Nadu/Pondicherry	88	82	57	34	26	8	2

Notes: *Tables present unweighted summary from village questionnaires. These data are nationwide but not nationally representative.
Source: IHDS 2004–5 data.

CHALLENGES IN RURAL HEALTH CARE

Access to medical facilities is even more varied than access to schools. Only 70 per cent of villages surveyed by the IHDS have access to some type of medical facility within the village. A distribution of medical facilities is show in Figure 12.2.

Only 52 per cent of villages in this sample have some kind of government medical facility (see Table 12.7).

Unfortunately, in most states, the lack of public medical facilities is not compensated by access to private medical facilities. In about 20 per cent of the villages that are not covered by the government, private clinics fill the need. However, about 30 per cent of villages in India have neither a government nor a private medical facility. One-third of the villages have access to medical facilities offered by both sectors within the village. The most common government facility for medical care in a village is a government health sub-centre.

Sub-centres are typically the first point of contact between government health services and patients and serve a population of about 5,000 individuals. They are expected to be staffed by two health workers. One is a female auxiliary nurse midwife (ANM) who provides immunization, and maternal and child health services. The other is typically a paramedical offering basic medical care along with emergency care while referring major illnesses for physician care to PHCs. Many sub-centres tend to be understaffed. Sub-centres refer patients to a PHC or CHC. Coverage norms vary depending upon geography. In the plains' states, PHCs cover a population of about 30,000, and CHCs cover a population of about 120,000. In general, several trained

Table 12.5 Distance to Nearest Educational Institution (Government or Private)

Per cent Villages with Distance to Nearest Educational Institution (Government or Private)

	Primary In Village	Primary 1–5 Kms	Upper Primary In Village	Upper Primary 1–5 Kms	Secondary In Village	Secondary 1–5 Kms	Higher Secondary In Village	Higher Secondary 1–5 Kms	College In Village	College 1–5 Kms
All India*	97.8	2.2	68.9	26.7	39.0	38.4	17.9	34.4	4.0	13.2
Jammu and Kashmir	100.0	0.0	80.0	20.0	29.4	58.8	7.1	57.1	0.0	28.6
Himachal Pradesh	82.7	17.3	55.8	42.3	28.6	50.0	23.5	29.4	6.1	10.2
Punjab/Chandigarh	100.0	0.0	74.6	23.7	58.6	34.5	40.0	36.7	8.3	8.3
Haryana	100.0	0.0	75.6	23.1	63.6	27.3	26.0	42.5	1.4	16.4
Uttar Pradesh	96.2	3.8	63.4	35.1	23.1	49.3	14.2	49.3	1.5	17.9
Uttarkhand	100.0	0.0	61.1	33.3	27.8	38.9	16.7	38.9	0.0	0.0
Bihar	90.9	9.1	69.0	27.6	22.8	56.1	5.7	35.9	7.0	17.5
Jharkhand	96.0	4.0	76.5	23.5	33.3	33.3	18.2	9.1	0.0	0.0
Rajasthan	100.0	0.0	72.1	25.6	34.9	37.4	16.3	36.3	2.6	2.6
Madhya Pradesh	99.2	0.9	67.8	32.2	19.3	30.7	9.9	26.1	0.9	8.9
Chhatishgarh	100.0	0.0	55.3	44.7	21.3	61.7	12.8	44.7	2.1	8.5
West Bengal	98.4	1.6	36.2	48.3	33.3	56.7	10.2	49.2	0.0	18.6
Orissa	94.0	6.0	56.6	42.2	36.1	48.2	7.3	40.2	6.0	25.3
Assam	100.0	0.0	81.8	15.2	16.1	54.8	10.3	44.8	6.7	33.3
North-East	90.3	9.7	72.4	17.2	56.5	4.4	27.3	18.2	5.6	0.0
Gujarat, Daman, Dadra	98.6	1.4	64.7	19.1	32.4	20.6	17.9	25.4	0.0	10.3
Maharashtra/Goa	100.0	0.0	64.4	28.8	42.6	43.5	12.1	35.3	3.5	13.3
Andhra Pradesh	100.0	0.0	76.6	16.0	59.1	26.9	11.8	15.1	3.3	10.9
Karnataka	100.0	0.0	79.4	15.6	40.7	34.8	8.5	28.7	1.5	11.5
Kerala	100.0	0.0	98.0	0.0	87.5	8.3	83.3	12.5	29.7	16.2
Tamil Nadu/Pondicherry	98.3	1.7	76.5	15.7	53.9	32.7	36.4	41.8	12.7	10.9

Notes: *Tables present unweighted summary from village questionnaires. These data are nationwide but not nationally representative.
Source: IHDS 2004–5 data.

physicians are available in PHCs, with four to six hospital beds and an ability to provide preventive as well as curative services.

Private health services consist of trained allopathic physicians working in major non-profit hospitals or clinics, setting up their own private clinics, and running four to ten bed hospitals or maternity clinics, as well as licensed practitioners with training in ayurvedic or homeopathic medicine. Moreover, many paramedics also set up private practice, sometimes in conjunction with a pharmacy. Although pharmacists are not expected to provide prescription drugs without prescription from a licensed practitioner, most prescribe and sell medication with impunity (see Chapter 7, Box 7.2 for a description of private and government facilities surveyed by the IHDS). At the most elementary level, a private *dai* (midwife) provides help with childbirth as well as sundry illnesses. Most dais are not trained but come from families that have practised midwifery for generations. The percentages of sample villages with access to various forms of health care are provided in Table 12.7.

Sub-centres are poorly equipped and inadequately staffed. Households seem to have little trust in the treatment provided by these sub-centres. As Chapter 7 documents, even when a village has no other medical facility except the sub-centre, less than 30 per cent of individuals with a minor illness such as a cough, cold, or fever use the government facility, and more than 50 per cent travel outside the village to visit a private practitioner. The presence of a PHC or a CHC improves the usage of public facilities.

As documented in Chapter 7, many rural residents travel to a neighbouring village or town to seek medical advice and treatment. The journey often adds an additional

Table 12.6 Index of Government and Private School Access in the Village

	All	Mean School Index Government	Private
All India*	2.73	1.95	0.78
Jammu and Kashmir	2.75	1.85	0.9
Himachal Pradesh	2.56	2.02	0.5
Punjab/Chandigarh	3.92	2.49	1.4
Haryana	4.29	2.52	1.77
Uttar Pradesh	2.74	1.58	1.16
Uttarkhand	2.3	1.55	0.75
Bihar	2.03	1.74	0.29
Jharkhand	2.12	1.46	0.65
Rajasthan	3.08	2.14	0.94
Madhya Pradesh	2.4	1.87	0.53
Chhatishgarh	2.14	1.78	0.37
West Bengal	1.94	1.62	0.32
Orissa	1.98	1.8	0.18
Assam	1.97	1.84	0.13
North-East	2.39	1.93	0.45
Gujarat, Daman, Dadra	2.17	1.87	0.3
Maharashtra/Goa	2.41	1.66	0.75
Andhra Pradesh	3.06	2.41	0.65
Karnataka	2.75	2.01	0.74
Tamil Nadu/Pondicherr	2.8	1.98	0.82
Kerala	4.57	2.44	2.13

Notes: Ranges from 1–5 including presence of primary, upper primary, secondary, higher secondary schools and college.
*Tables present unweighted summary from village questionnaires. These data are nationwide but not nationally representative.
Source: IHDS 2004–5 data.

burden of travel expenditure to medical costs. Rural areas in the southern states have much better coverage than the rest of India (Table 12.7). While Kerala and Tamil Nadu have good coverage, with more than 70–80 per cent of villages having some kind of government medical facility, in Uttarakhand and Chhattisgarh less than 30 per cent of the villages have access to government medical facility within the village.

The IHDS data suggest that access to healthcare in Uttarakhand may be particularly problematic when we look at its lower availability of health facilities (Table 12.7) in combination with its absence of roads and easy access to buses (Table 12.3). However, caution should be exercised in interpreting these findings because the IHDS sample of villages is more limited than the sample of households, and it is difficult to make any generalizations based on this small sample.

Immunization programmes are found in all villages except in Bihar (see Table 12.8).

These programmes deserve special attention in light of the historic division in the Indian health care system. Maternal and child health programmes have usually fallen under the heading of family welfare and trace their origin to family planning programmes. The ANMs who provide immunization also provide family planning services, and their performance has been closely monitored with respect to meeting family planning acceptance targets. While this target-driven approach has been relaxed in recent years, it may well be that

Health Facility	Per cent Villages
Health Sub-centre	43
Primary Health Centre	16
Community Health Centre	3
District Hospital	2
Government Communicable Disease Centre	4
Private—Untrained Doctor	41
Private—Trained Doctor	23
Private Hospital	5
Private Pharmacy	22
Private Maternity Home	2
Private Dai	54
Other Government Medical Facility	4

Figure 12.2 Distribution of Sample Villages by Health Facilities
Source: IHDS 2004–5 data.

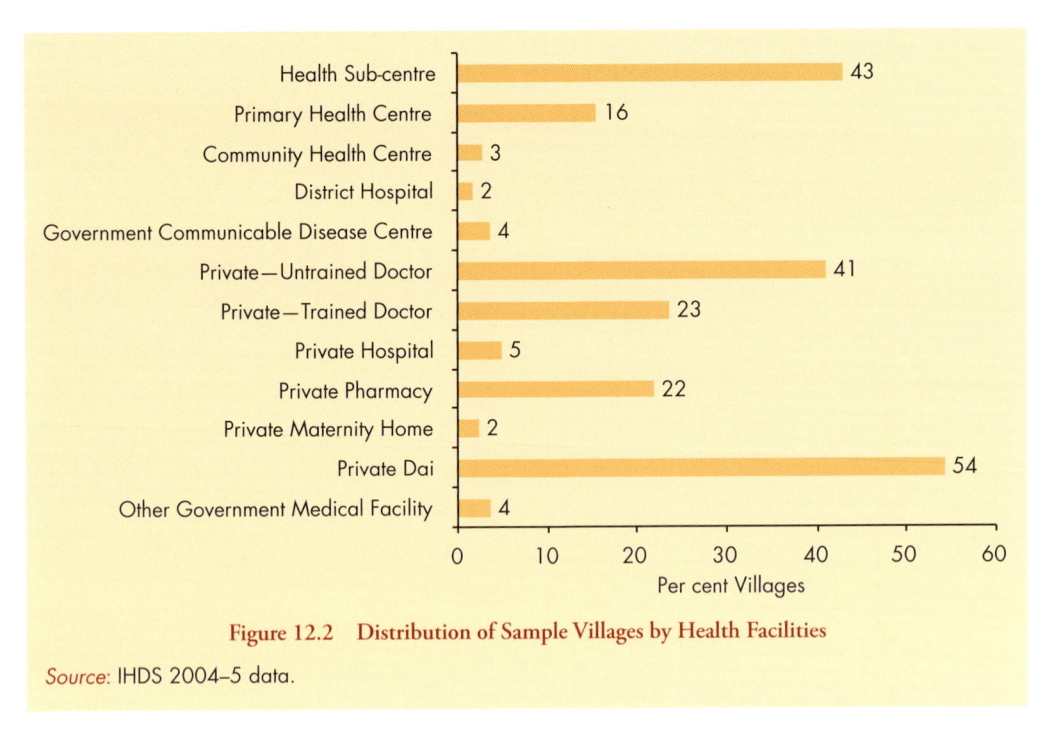

this approach had set a structure for the delivery of immunization services. Nonetheless, even here, while most villages have access to immunization programmes, the actual immunization rates documented in Chapter 8 remain modest, with higher immunization coverage for polio (administered under pulse polio campaigns) than for other immunizations.

Surprisingly, in states like Andhra Pradesh and Kerala that have good government coverage, there is also a strong presence of private medical facilities. However, this is not always the case. States like Tamil Nadu and the states in the North-East, while enjoying fairly high levels of rural access to government medical facilities, have relatively few private medical establishments. On the other hand, states such as Uttarakhand and West Bengal have a much larger presence of private medical facilities than government centres. Among the states leading in the presence of the private sector in rural health care, Punjab (75 per cent), West Bengal (77 per cent), and Kerala (72 per cent) stand out. When we correlate the presence of private facilities with usage presented in Chapter 7, it appears that West Bengal and Punjab document high usage of private facilities. However, in Kerala which has the availability of private as well as public facilities, the use of private facilities for short-term or long-term illnesses is not very high.

Many people rely on private facilities even when they have access to government centres, reflecting greater confidence in the quality and the efficiency of private services. Whether this confidence is well placed remains open to question. Often these private dispensaries are run by untrained doctors. In villages surveyed by the IHDS, less than 25 per cent of the villages have access to private dispensaries with trained doctors. As documented in Table 12.7, about 41 per cent of the villages are served by untrained practitioners. They often treat common colds and fevers, prescribe antibiotics, and treat dehydration by administering oral rehydration therapies. Even some highly developed states like Haryana and Karnataka have a substantial presence of private facilities run by untrained personnel.

While most states have some facility for health care in villages, the facilities are faced with myriad problems ranging from lack of medical and other supplies, to the absence of medical personnel, and general lack of accountability. Drugs, in particular, often tend to be in short supply, and patients are forced to buy their own medication from private pharmacies. Doctors often don't want to live and raise their families in remote villages. Thus, although doctors may be on the payroll, they are often not available. For villagers, then, the option of having access to private untrained personnel may well be better than nothing. In the case of common illnesses, these practitioners seem to cure enough people that they have a relatively thriving practice. However, many untrained practitioners and pharmacies retain their reputations by prescribing antibiotics even for minor illnesses, a practice that may lead to long-term antibiotic resistance and may be harmful to long-term health.

COMMUNITY PROGRAMMES

In recent years, development practitioners have begun to recognize the role of self-help groups and NGOs in mobilizing the community and generating organic potential for development. The Indian government has also recognized this potential and has tried to foster the growth of such

Table 12.7 Per cent of Sample Villages with Different Types of Medical Facilities

	Any Government Facility	Any Private Facility	Type of Govt Facility				Type of Private Facility					
			Sub-centre	Primary Health Centre	Community Health Centre	Government Maternity Centre	Private Doctor Trained	Private Doctor Untrained	Private Hospital	Private Chemist	Private Maternity Home	Private Dai (mid-wife)
All India*	52	52	43	16	3	4	23	41	5	22	2	54
Jammu and Kashmir	50	30	45	10	5	0	5		0	15	0	25
Himachal Pradesh	54	35	27	25	2	2	17	30	0	8	0	56
Punjab/Chandigarh	56	75	49	11	3	5	33	23	3	46	2	87
Haryana	56	85	44	11	0	0	16	64	5	13	3	85
Uttar Pradesh	38	67	36	9	1	1	23	50	3	26	2	55
Uttarkhand	15	50	10	0	5	10	30	66	0	25	0	55
Bihar	49	51	43	10	0	0	16	50	7	30	5	75
Jharkhand	39	54	35	8	0	0	31	46	0	12	0	46
Rajasthan	60	43	48	13	5	7	15	31	3	15	5	68
Madhya Pradesh	38	34	34	6	2	2	13	33	1	10	2	65
Chhatishgarh	22	31	16	10	0	0	0	31	2	4	0	76
West Bengal	49	77	44	11	3	3	17	29	9	23	0	65
Orissa	57	30	46	13	7	6	13	68	0	17	1	32
Assam	34	45	24	11	0	0	8	23	0	42	0	13
North-East	67	15	45	30	9	3	12	45	0	15	0	30
Gujarat, Daman, Dadra	29	65	26	4	0	1	50	9	3	7	0	79
Maharashtra/Goa	50	50	45	15	2	3	42	53	5	30	4	80
Andhra Pradesh	65	71	59	13	4	7	18	19	11	32	7	56
Karnataka	61	40	51	23	2	3	23	68	1	7	1	20
Kerala	80	72	70	66	16	3	57	14	39	70	7	15
Tamil Nadu/Pondicherry	77	37	60	29	0	18	31	30	14	31	5	8

Notes: *Tables present unweighted summary from village questionnaires. These data are nationwide but not nationally representative.
Source: IHDS 2004–5 data.

organizations by providing direct and indirect support to them. In some cases, these voluntary groups work directly with government agencies and help in implementing government programmes. In others, they receive financial aid from the state. Other organizations have chosen not to be co-opted by the state and, instead, operate independently, sometimes as pressure groups working to ensure effective governance.

The IHDS collected information about the existence of a variety of programmes in sample villages. It is important to note that because the key informants were often village functionaries, there is a potential for the overstatement of various programmes. Nonetheless, Table 12.8 provides an interesting portrait of the presence of self-help groups, government programmes, and NGOs.

To the extent that villages are able to promote their own development through the use of self-help groups and non-governmental bodies, they may be able to substitute for, or supplement formal government programmes.

The success of states is often evidenced in the implementation of programmes. Even when there are programmes sponsored by the central government, the success rate and coverage of the programmes vary widely by state. Overall, the southern states stand out in coverage and implementation of government programmes.

However, the IHDS also suggests an interesting puzzle. Development discourse is suffused with an implicit or explicit assumption that when a state fails to reach certain areas or populations, the NGO sector has the ability to fill the vacuum. However, in the IHDS villages, the presence of an NGO sector is not independent of the level of economic development. The IHDS village survey asked about the presence or absence of the following programmes: *Mahila Mandal* (women's organization), youth groups, self-help groups, trade unions/professional groups, credit or savings groups, festival/religious groups, caste associations, development groups or NGOs, agricultural or milk cooperatives, Panchayat Bhavan, *Pani* Panchayat (water cooperative), community centres, and community television sets. Figure 12.3 plots the number of these programmes reflecting social development in a village against infrastructure development discussed earlier (consisting of roads, banks, telephone services, and the like).

The results are striking. Villages that have higher infrastructure development also have greater presence of the community organizations. When we reflect on the nature of the non-governmental sector in India, this is not surprising.

While the development discourse tends to view the voluntary sector as being rooted in local culture, given the symbiotic relationship between the state and the voluntary sector in India, it seems eminently reasonable that the voluntary sector thrives only where state penetration is more effective.

DISCUSSION

The urban–rural divide in indicators of human development has long been recognized. The contribution of this chapter is to focus on variations between villages in levels of infrastructure development. This provides a framework for interpreting the observation throughout this report that villages with higher levels of infrastructure development have far better health and educational outcomes than those with lower levels of development. These villages also have better employment opportunities and higher incomes.

Table 12.8 Per cent of Sample Villages with Access to Different Government Programmes

	Safe Drinking Water	Sanitation/ Toilets	Immun- ization	Midday Meal	Improved Stove	Agricult. Ext.	Micro- Credit	Widow Pensions	Old Age Pensions
All India*	61	55	89	87	35	37	49	87	88
Jammu and Kashmir	70	10	80	75	15	30	30	75	55
Himachal Pradesh	96	75	73	85	31	48	35	92	98
Punjab/Chandigarh	20	38	79	87	30	43	31	80	85
Haryana	67	41	96	89	42	35	46	95	95
Uttar Pradesh	78	78	80	77	44	15	71	93	96
Uttarkhand	61	83	78	83	56	44	22	94	89
Bihar	28	25	56	51	5	18	66	75	95
Jharkhand	12	4	89	77	0	0	15	69	81
Rajasthan	36	33	86	89	18	29	56	89	69
Madhya Pradesh	28	35	94	92	29	37	30	87	93
Chhatishgarh	43	23	92	89	30	30	28	96	98
West Bengal	58	66	56	94	14	11	44	61	92
Orissa	34	30	94	86	16	21	47	95	96
Assam	50	25	100	72	3	11	17	61	78
North-East	49	42	91	55	27	52	42	52	61
Gujarat, Daman, Dadra	60	36	100	99	24	63	23	83	61
Maharashtra/Goa	83	78	99	96	68	62	63	81	80
Andhra Pradesh	87	99	98	97	62	72	65	93	99
Karnataka	87	60	97	98	44	17	50	100	93
Kerala	78	94	100	76	60	82	80	100	100
Tamil Nadu/Pondicherry	83	80	93	97	42	51	66	98	95

Notes: *Tables present unweighted summary from village questionnaires. These data are nationwide but not nationally representative.
Source: IHDS 2004–5 data.

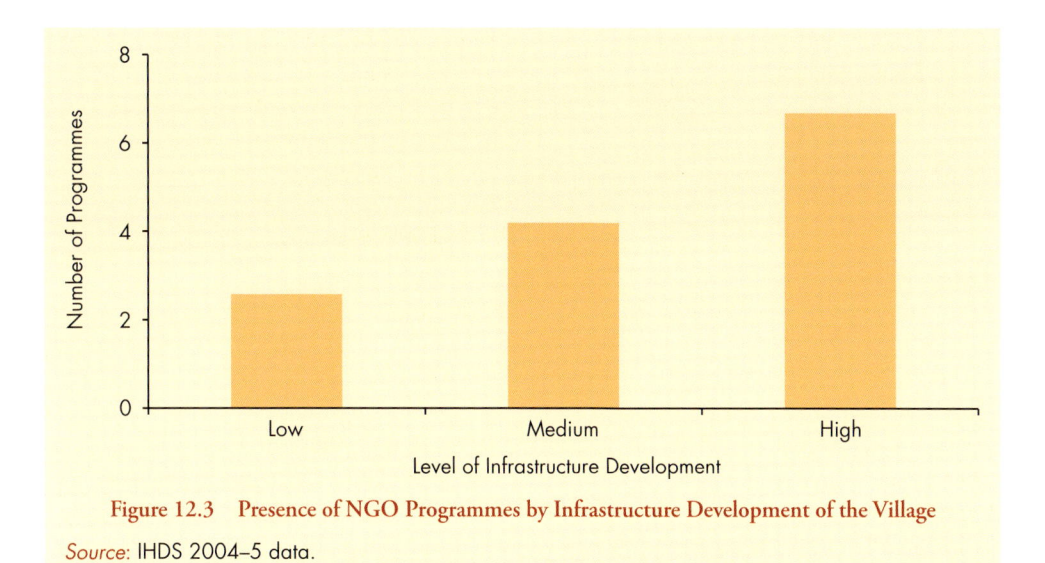

Figure 12.3 Presence of NGO Programmes by Infrastructure Development of the Village
Source: IHDS 2004–5 data.

What makes some villages more fortunate than others? Two factors play an important role: distance to district towns and greater infrastructure development in the state. While much attention has been directed to the economic growth in the six metropolitan cities—Mumbai, New Delhi, Chennai, Bangalore, Kolkata, and Hyderabad—the growth in secondary and tertiary cities has been overlooked. However, these smaller cities—Nasik, Surat, Allahabad, and others—are home to industries and government offices that provide a large number of jobs and serve as engines of growth to nearby rural areas. Thus, villages from which individuals can commute to these district towns become prosperous and manage to lay claims to development funds for road, school, and hospital construction. The second influence is more general. States differ considerably in their history and geography, which shape the level of institutional development. We don't fully understand the forces that have led to these different developmental trajectories. Some arguments suggest that land tenure patterns in colonial India, in which landlords were vested with significant power, had led to low investments in public infrastructure.[2] Others have emphasized differential development of Panchayati Raj institutions.[3] Still others have focused on the role of social movements, such as the anti-caste movement.[4] Regardless of the source, it seems evident that some states have better functioning bureaucracies in which the fruits of development reach far-flung villages, while villages in other states continue to struggle.

These are the villages that appear to be forgotten by the development surge—those that lack paved roads and experience scarcity of public transportation. It is in these poorly developed villages, in which 37 per cent of the IHDS households reside, that we find the lowest levels of human development: low school enrolment, poor learning outcomes, higher infant mortality, and low rates of vaccination. These are the villages where development efforts will have to be concentrated in order to ensure that human development goals are met.

HIGHLIGHTS

- Villages located closer to district towns have greater infrastructure development than those located farther away.
- More than 92 per cent of the IHDS villages have a government primary school within the village, but the availability declines at higher levels of schooling.
- Location of private schools is associated with the location of government schools. States with a better developed public education infrastructure also have a greater availability of private schools.
- Nearly 30 per cent of the IHDS villages have neither a public nor private health care provider within the village.
- Villages with a greater availability of infrastructure also have more access to non-governmental organizations.

---

[2] Banerjee and Iyer (2005).
[3] Rao and Walton (2004).
[4] Omvedt (1993).

Policy Responses

13

Social Safety Nets in India

Public programmes have been designed to assist the poor since the planning process began in 1951. Some have succeeded more than others. Most have evolved over time. Some have been transformed into virtually new programmes. The IHDS investigated several important programmes that existed in 2005:

1. Public Distribution System, in existence since the 1960s, often modified since then, and supplemented in December 2001 by Antyodaya for the poorest of the poor;
2. School assistance, such as free books and uniforms;
3. Midday Meal (MDM) programme which was extended to schools across the nation since the 1990s;
4. Integrated Child Development Services (ICDS), since the mid-1970s;
5. Food for Work Programme started in 2000–1 as part of the Employment Assurance Scheme; and
6. Programmes directed at the elderly, such as the NOAP, Widow Pension, and Annapurna. These programmes have been discussed in Chapter 9 and will not be discussed in detail in this chapter.

Policy debates on these programmes have focused on the related issues of coverage and targeting. The IHDS results address both of these questions. First, how broadly have these programmes been implemented? While critics have sometimes charged that the programmes exist more on paper than in the lives of the poor, the IHDS results show substantial coverage for some programmes, especially the longer established ones. While there is a wide state variation and much unmet need, the results suggest that, over time, programmes do expand to reach a broader array of India. Much remains to be done, but much has been accomplished.

A second, closely related question asks how well the existing level of assistance has targeted those most in need. Sometimes this issue is framed as how much of the unnecessary leakage of benefits has gone to those who are not in need. But targeting is a complicated issue because sometimes the costs of targeting exceed the benefits. Targeting costs are not merely administrative. The more targeted the programme is towards the poor, the weaker the political support for the programme. Benefits that are widely shared have wide public support. Moreover, targeted benefits for the disadvantaged become stigmatized, partly undoing socially what the programme accomplishes economically. In addition, given the complexity of Indian inequality across class, caste, community, and regional lines, targeting inevitably raises politically divisive questions about what types of targeting are legitimate.

On the other hand, the IHDS results suggest that some of the most successful government programmes have a built-in natural targeting that is not so much administratively regulated as determined by selection characteristics of the recipients themselves. Most MDM programmes, for instance, strive for universal coverage that is unregulated by the student's particular economic or social circumstances. Nevertheless, MDM programmes are overwhelmingly programmes for government schools, so many of the more privileged sections rule themselves out by opting for private schools. The PDS programmes have a similar natural selection mechanism that operates at least as effectively as the distinction between below poverty line (BPL) and above poverty line (APL) cards. Wealthier households are simply not interested in the inferior grains provided by the PDS shops and prefer to shop in the less subsidized private market, where they find adequate supplies of good quality grains. Thus, the IHDS results below show that as wealth increases, even BPL cardholders purchase more of their grain in the private market.

THE PDS

Of all the safety net operations, the most far reaching is the PDS. The PDS provides basic items such as rice, wheat, sugar, and non-food items such as kerosene in rationed amounts at below market prices. The programmes originated in the early period after Independence, when food shortages required large imports of food under the *PL-480* grants from the United States. A large network of PDS shops, also known as Fair Price Shops (FPSs), was established. Local traders were enrolled as owners, and households were issued a PDS card with monthly per capita entitlements of food staples. The programme continued with indigenous public resources even after the *PL-480* programme ceased to exist, when India's food production improved. The network of 4.76 lakh FPSs now distributes commodities worth Rs 25,000 cr annually to a large proportion of households across all parts of India.

The PDS has changed both qualitatively and quantitatively since the 1970s. At first, the PDS was confined to urban areas and regions with food deficits. The main emphasis was on price stabilization. Private trade was considered exploitative and the PDS was considered a countervailing power to private trade.

Since the early 1980s, the welfare role of the PDS has gained importance. Nevertheless, in recent times, the PDS was widely criticized, for its failure to reach those living below the poverty line, for whom the programme was intended. Although rural areas were covered in many states in the 1980s, the PDS had an urban bias and large regional inequalities in its operation. An effort was made, therefore, to streamline the PDS by introducing the Targeted Public Distribution System (TPDS) in June 1997. The objective was to help very poor families buy food grains at a reasonably low cost so that they would improve their nutrition standards and attain food security. The new system follows a two-tier subsidized pricing structure, one for BPL families, and another for APL families. The Union Budget 2000–1 announced a monthly allocation of 25 kg of food grains to about 60 million BPL families under the TPDS. The issue price of food grains for BPL families is fixed at 50 per cent of the economic cost that the APL families pay, and all prices are revised by the Food Corporation of India (FCI) from time to time. The total food subsidy (including programmes other than PDS) has significantly increased in real terms over the years.

In order to target the TPDS more towards the poor, the Antyodaya Anna Yojana (AAY) was launched in December 2000. This scheme sought to identify the ten million poorest of the BPL families and provide them each with 25 kg of food grains per month at a fixed price of Rs 2 per kg for wheat, and Rs 3 per kg for rice.

Distribution of PDS Cards

The IHDS finds that 83 per cent of households have a PDS ration card, 85 per cent in rural areas and 79 per cent in towns and cities (see Table A.13.1).[1] The most common reasons cited by respondents for not having a PDS card are bureaucratic difficulties (43 per cent), the household has moved but the card has not been transferred (10 per cent), a PDS card is not needed (9 per cent), it was lost (8 per cent), and a residual, other reasons (30 per cent). Comparisons of different types of households confirm some of these reasons. For example, 45 per cent of households who have moved within the past ten years lack a PDS card, compared with only 15 per cent of households who have lived in their places for at least 20 years. Statewise differences are again large. Low take-up is especially common in new, and more inaccessible, states (for example, 31 per cent of households in Chhattisgarh and 38 per cent in Jharkhand lack PDS cards) and in poor states (for example, 33 per cent in Bihar), corroborating the importance of administrative difficulties in issuing ration cards. The issuing of cards is closer to 100 per cent in Himachal Pradesh, Maharashtra, and Kerala. However, high income households, who have less of a need for a PDS card, actually have slightly higher rates of having a PDS card than the lowest income households. Young households are especially unlikely to have a ration card. Almost one-third (33 per cent) of households lack PDS cards when the oldest man is in his twenties, compared to only 10 per cent of households when the oldest man is 60 or older. Caste and religious differences, however, are small.

Of those with a card, 40 per cent have a BPL card and another 3 per cent have an Antyodaya card. The more useful BPL and Antyodaya cards are more common in rural areas (49 per cent) than in towns and cities (28 per cent)[2] but this is almost entirely a function of greater rural poverty. Income is, not surprisingly, the best predictor of holding a BPL or

---

[1] The IHDS estimates are higher than the NSS estimates (81 per cent rural and 67 per cent urban) perhaps in part because of households' reluctance to report to a government survey that they have an inappropriate BPL card, or even their expectations of acquiring a new one (NSSO 2005c).

[2] These IHDS estimates are also higher than NSS estimates of 36 per cent for rural areas and 18 per cent for urban areas, probably reasons similar to those noted in footnote 1. However, the IHDS and the NSS rank states similarly on BPL card ownership, so the associations reported here are likely to be robust to survey methodology.

Antyodaya card rather than an APL card. Nevertheless, there is often a disturbing mismatch between income and the issuance of BPL cards. A substantial proportion of households in the top three income quintiles have been issued BPL cards, although most are not eligible to receive them. On the other hand, although all those in the bottom quintile and most in the second quintile should have the BPL cards, only 59 per cent and 57 per cent of the bottom two income quintiles have been issued BPL cards.

Some of the discrepancy results from the volatility of annual income. More long range measures of economic position such as household assets (see Chapter 5) also predict BPL cards together with income measures. Figure 13.1 shows BPL cardholding by both annual income and household possessions.

Households that are poor on both measures have the highest rates of BPL cardholding, while those most affluent on both measures have the lowest rate. Nevertheless, 10 per cent of the households in the top quintiles on both measures have a BPL card rather than the more appropriate APL card. Worse, 33 per cent of the households in the poorest quintiles on both measures do not have a BPL card.

Statewise variation also accounts for some of these discrepancies. BPL cards are more commonly issued in the south and in several poor states, especially to households that are poor. Among households with PDS cards, BPL or Antyodaya cards are more common in Jharkhand (64 per cent), Chhattisgarh (67 per cent), and Orissa (70 per cent), but also in Andhra Pradesh (85 per cent) and Karnataka (77 per cent). Punjab and Haryana have few BPL cards, as might be expected, but so do Uttar Pradesh (28 per cent), Rajasthan (28 per cent), and West Bengal (29 per cent). Thus, high and low proportions of BPL cardholders do not exactly follow high and low poverty states.

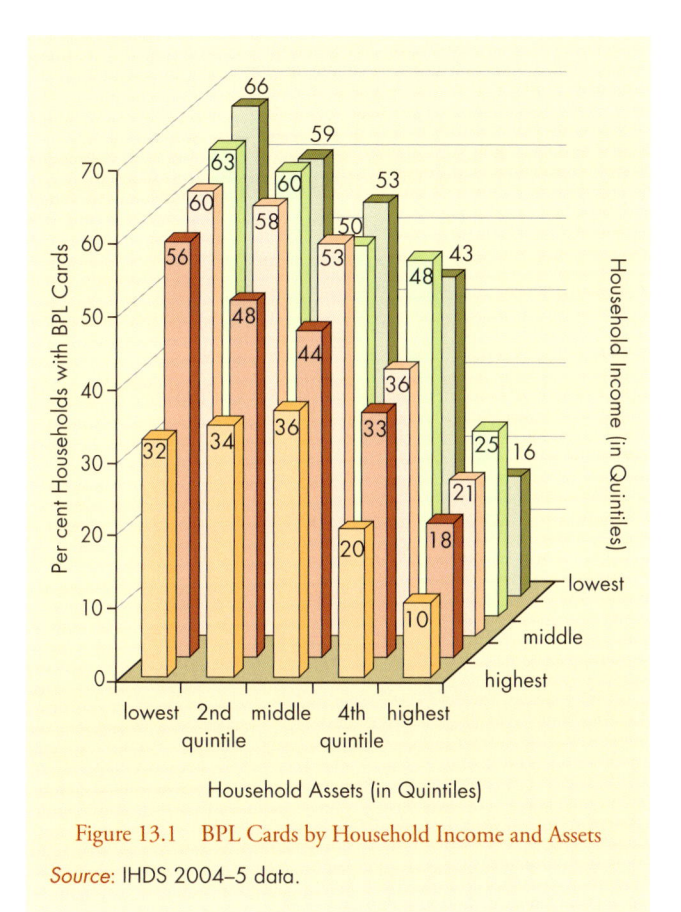

The more disadvantaged social groups are more likely to have BPL cards, partly because they are more often poor. Among Adivasis, 71 per cent who have a ration card have a BPL card, The same is true for 54 per cent of Dalits and 47 per cent of OBCs. Even considering only the lowest income quintile, Adivasis (78 per cent) and Dalits (67 per cent) have higher BPL uptake than forward castes (40 per cent).

Use of PDS Cards

Almost all BPL cardholders used their cards in the previous month (91 per cent) and 73 per cent of APL cardholders used their cards. Most were used for kerosene. Only 55 per cent of BPL or Antyodaya cardholders who consumed rice previous month bought it at a PDS shop and only 13 per cent bought all their rice there (see Table 13.1).

Similarly, only 44 per cent of BPL or Antyodaya cardholders who consume wheat purchased it at a PDS shop, but a larger proportion (28 per cent) bought all their wheat there. APL cardholders rarely used a PDS shop to purchase rice (11 per cent) or wheat (8 per cent) when they consumed those staples. Among BPL or Antyodaya cardholders, 35 per cent who bought sugar used a PDS shop in the previous month, and 21 per cent bought all their sugar there. For APL cardholders, the rates are much lower; 13 per cent bought any sugar and 8 per cent bought all their sugar at a PDS shop.

While the use of PDS shops is determined very much by the type of card a household has been issued, within cardholder types, income still plays a substantial role. The more affluent BPL households go to PDS shops less often for their rice and wheat and rarely for 100 per cent of their needs. Even among the small minority of APL cardholders who use PDS shops for grains, it is most often the poorer APL cardholders.

PDS shops are more sought for kerosene. Among BPL or Antyodaya cardholders who used kerosene in the previous month, 92 per cent bought it at a PDS shop, and 80 per cent purchased all their kerosene there. Even among APL cardholders, 89 per cent who used kerosene bought it at a PDS shop, and 75 per cent bought all their kerosene there. But kerosene is an undifferentiated commodity. Unlike rice or wheat, kerosene purchased at the PDS shop is identical to the kerosene purchased in the market.

Figure 13.1 BPL Cards by Household Income and Assets
Source: IHDS 2004–5 data.

Table 13.1 Use of PDS Shops for Rice, Wheat, Sugar, and Kerosene by Income and Card Type

(in percentage)

	BPL and Antyodaya Cardholders Income Quintiles						APL Cardholders Income Quintiles					
	Poorest	2nd q	Middle	4th q	Affluent	Total	Poorest	2nd q	Middle	4th q	Affluent	Total
Any PDS purchase												
Rice	60	55	56	53	35	55	14	18	14	11	6	11
Wheat	51	45	45	40	27	44	13	12	11	7	5	8
Sugar	34	35	37	36	29	35	16	15	13	14	11	13
Kerosene	93	92	92	91	84	92	91	92	89	89	85	89
100 Per cent PDS purchase												
Rice	16	12	12	11	8	13	6	5	4	3	3	4
Wheat	34	29	27	25	19	28	11	8	8	6	4	7
Sugar	23	20	21	20	16	21	13	11	7	7	5	8
Kerosene	82	79	81	79	74	80	78	75	76	74	72	75

Note: q denotes quintile.
Source: IHDS 2004–5 data.

MIDDAY MEAL PROGRAMME

After Tamil Nadu introduced a successful MDM programme in schools, the National Programme of Nutritional Support to Primary Education was launched across India in 1995. The MDM programme aims to increase primary school attendance and to improve the nutritional status of school children. Generally, the programme serves children aged 6–11. However, some upper primary schools also run the MDM programme, and recent union budgets have made a separate provision for upper primary schools. Under the MDM scheme, cooked meals are to be served during lunchtime in the school, with a calorie value equivalent to 100 gm of wheat or rice per student per school day. In some places, a dry ration is provided to be carried home based on a certain minimum level of school attendance.

The IHDS data reports that 60 per cent of children up to Standard 5 receive midday meals or free grains,[3] 35 per cent receive the full MDM programme, 8 per cent get only *dalia* (broken wheat) for the meal, and 16 per cent are given grains in place of the meal. These programmes are mainly found in government schools. Among private schools, only 8 per cent of primary students participate, compared to 80 per cent at government schools.

Even among government schools, there are large differences by state and urban/rural residence. Coverage is slightly better in rural government schools. Eighty one per cent of rural primary students participate in the MDM programme, but only 70 per cent of primary students in towns and cities do. But state differences are larger. Coverage is almost universal in Himachal Pradesh (95 per cent of government primary students), Karnataka (93 per cent), and Gujarat (91 per cent). Even some poorer states, such as Rajasthan (93 per cent) and Madhya Pradesh (91 per cent) have excellent coverage. On the other hand, coverage is about half or less in Assam (21 per cent of government primary students), Punjab (50 per cent), and Kerala (56 per cent). While the need may be somewhat less in these prosperous states, coverage is also weak in Bihar (53 per cent).

While the PDS is a more targeted programme, the MDM programme is not. Self-selection into government primary schools is the main mechanism determining which children receive midday meals. Within government schools, there are only small differences by household income, education, caste, or religion.

Midday meals are beginning to appear post primary school in some states. Tamil Nadu, Karnataka, and Gujarat have almost full coverage in Standards 6 and 7. In Kerala and Jharkhand, almost half of standard 6 and 7 students get a midday meal. Beyond standard 7, only Tamil Nadu has a substantial MDM programme, although some Jharkhand secondary students also receive midday meals now.

---

[3] The IHDS results are, again, higher than the NSS and again the reason is probably methodological differences. The NSS reports 23 per cent of rural households and 8 per cent of urban households benefit from midday meals (comparable IHDS percentages would be 31 per cent and 15 per cent) [NSSO 2005c]. But the NSS asks only a single question of the household respondent, 'whether anybody in the household received benefits from this and other programmes', whereas IHDS asks a specific question about each child as part of an extended inquiry about school experiences.

THE ICDS

Launched in 1975, the ICDS is a nationwide programme to build nutrition, health, and educational levels among pre-school children, and among expectant and nursing mothers. The ICDS programme provides an integrated set of services, including supplementary nutrition, preschool education, immunization, health check-ups, referral services, and health education, in millions of local *anganwadi* centres. Initially the programme focused on the poor living in backward areas, especially tribal areas and urban slums. However, the ICDS has expanded significantly and is now available to all households, regardless of poverty or caste status. By March 2005, 7.1 lakh anganwadis were reported as operational, serving 4.8 cr children with nutritional services and 2.2 cr children with preschool education.

The IHDS asked one woman in each household, with at least one child born since January 2000, whether she or her children had ever received any ICDS services. This is a smaller sample (10,428), so these estimates have a larger sampling error than estimates based on other statistics reported earlier. Overall, about 35 per cent of households with a child born since 2000 had received some ICDS services, 22 per cent had received maternity related services, and 35 per cent had received services for children. For a 30 year old programme, this is disappointing coverage.

Rural areas have more than twice the coverage of urban areas. Twenty six per cent of rural mothers and 41 per cent of rural children received some ICDS service, compared with 11 per cent of urban mothers and 18 per cent of urban children. Given limited resources, a rural bias is an effective approach. Nevertheless, there is enormous room for expansion, in both urban and rural areas.

State differences reveal great gaps among state governments in how they have been able to mobilize resources to provide ICDS services. In Tamil Nadu, 75 per cent of eligible households participate in ICDS. Only 7 per cent do so in Bihar. Only Tamil Nadu has made a significant impact in towns and cities with 58 per cent of urban households receiving the services. In no other state does urban ICDS coverage reach even 30 per cent. Some wealthy states cover the majority of households (for example, Haryana at 68 per cent), but so do some poor states (for example, Chhattisgarh at 62 per cent and Orissa at 67 per cent). Poor states like Bihar have weak ICDS coverage (7 per cent), but so does rich Punjab (8 per cent).

Compared to the substantial state and urban–rural variation in ICDS services, differences among households are relatively minor. In villages, the poorest fifth of households participate only slightly more (44 per cent) than the highest income fifth (39 per cent), although the difference is greater in urban places (33 per cent versus 12 per cent). In villages, forward castes, OBCs, and Dalits have almost identical ICDS usage (42 per cent), but Adivasis are especially well served (63 per cent). Coverage among minority religions, however, is below the average coverage in rural areas with 28 per cent for Muslims and 16 per cent for other religions. In urban areas, the group differences are much smaller, and Adivasis have lower ICDS coverage (14 per cent) than the urban average (19 per cent). Although the class and group differences are smaller than the state and urban–rural differences, it is reassuring that, in general, the poorer and more disadvantaged sectors have the highest ICDS coverage. Although the ICDS is no longer a targeted programme, the somewhat higher coverage of the poor and disadvantaged reflects the programme's origins.

FOOD FOR WORK AND SAMPOORNA GRAMEEN ROZGAR YOJANA

The Food for Work Programme started in January 2001 as part of the Employment Assurance Scheme in eight drought affected states. It provides wage employment and food supplements for rural infrastructure projects. Preference is given to labour intensive projects, especially those that would help relieve droughts like Water conservation, watershed development, water harvesting, de-silting of village ponds, and construction of rural *kaccha* roads. After the IHDS was fielded, the government greatly expanded its rural employment efforts through the employment guarantee scheme. Results from those efforts are not reflected in the IHDS results.

The IHDS found 330 individuals who reported work under Sampoorna Grameen Rozgar Yojana (SGRY) or food for work programme in the past year. The great majority of these cases (80 per cent) came from Uttar Pradesh, Chhattisgarh, Madhya Pradesh, and Orissa. The typical worker was employed for 30 days and was paid Rs 50 per day.

Almost all SGRY workers are rural, and three-quarters are men. Most (71 per cent) are in the poorest quintile of household assets (although only 34 per cent are in the poorest income quintile, suggesting that current incomes may have benefited from participation by usually poor households). Their educational attainments are remarkably similar to those of most rural workers. Most are 20–49 years old, very similar to the age structure of all rural workers. Adivasis are overrepresented (31 per cent compared to 11 per cent of other rural workers), forward castes (4 per cent compared with 17 per cent of other rural workers), and minority religions (3 per cent compared to 11 per cent of other rural workers) are underrepresented.

TARGETING AND COVERAGE OF BENEFITS

Benefits targeted towards the poor conserve limited resources for those most in need. It would seem, therefore, that targeting should improve programme participation among the poor. On the other hand, universal programmes enjoy widespread public support, so the poor can benefit from the increased supply of government services.

The old age pension and widow pension plans reviewed in Chapter 9 are examples of government programmes explicitly targeted to the poor. The MDM and ICDS programmes are now intended to be universal programmes, while PDS shops fall somewhere between because of their larger benefits for households with BPL cards.

The actual extent of targeting low income groups, however, can depend on many factors beyond the announced policy. Geographic concentration, administrative problems of implementation, and middle class preference for goods and services in the private market can greatly affect the extent to which benefits end up being targeted towards the most needy. A convenient measure of effective targeting is the strength of the relationship between household poverty and programme use. The larger the difference in poverty rates between programme users and non-users, the greater the effective targeting of the programme. We use gamma, a common statistical index of association, to measure this effective targeting. We use the bottom quintile of household assets as the best measure of long-term household poverty. Table 13.2 reports this measure of effective targeting and the extent to which the poor receive benefits from the programme.

The first interesting result to notice is that supposedly universal programmes like MDM are actually more targeted than are purposefully targeted programmes such as food grain distribution through PDS shops. This is attributable to the fact that poorer children attend government schools where MDMs are provided, while wealthier children go to private schools. Similarly ICDS has received greater emphasis in poorer areas with greater concentration of Scheduled Tribes. The most interesting result, however, is that, in general, the poor are best served by non-targeted programmes such as the ICDS and MDM while coverage of the poor is lowest among the most targeted programmes like Food for Work and Old Age Pensions. Although a different selection of programmes would undoubtedly yield somewhat different conclusions, this comparison raises important questions about whether targeting actually works in the interests of the poor.

DISCUSSION

This chapter seeks to analyse that the coverage varies widely across these government programmes and so does the extent to which benefits are related to household poverty, or disadvantaged social position. These two types of variation are related. The broadest programmes (for example, MDM) are least related to a household's economic or social position. Poor households benefit from these programmes, but so do middle income households. In contrast, the most targeted programmes (for example, food for work and the income supplement programmes for the elderly, discussed in Chapter 9) are the smallest. Targeting does not necessarily create more benefits for the poor. Many more poor, and Dalit or Adivasi households benefit from the non-targeted MDM than from the targeted food for work or widows' pension schemes.

Table 13.2 Targeting and Coverage of Government Benefits

(in percentage)

Programme	Population	Coverage: Per cent of Bottom Quintile Who Are Programme Users	Per cent of Programme Users in the Bottom Quintile	Per cent of Programme Non-users in the Bottom Quintile	Effective Targeting: Association of Poverty and Programme Use
Midday meals	Children 6–11	55	36	27	0.218
ICDS	Households with children under 5	35	34	31	0.054
PDS shop: food grains	Households consuming rice or wheat last month	30	29	25	0.106
Old age and widow pension	Individuals 60 years old or older	15	41	22	0.417
SGRY	Rural employed persons in six states	2	76	45	0.580

Source: IHDS 2004–5 data.

SOCIAL SAFETY NETS IN INDIA

HIGHLIGHTS

- Below poverty level PDS cards are most common in households with both low annual income and few household amenities.
- Higher income households use their PDS cards less than low income households, even when they have an (inappropriate) BPL card.
- While almost all (80 per cent) students in government primary schools participate in midday meal programmes, children from urban and higher income families participate less often because they are more often in private schools.
- States differ widely in programme participation, although low participation rates for several programmes are found in both wealthy states (for example, Punjab) and poor states (for example, Bihar).
- Dalits and Adivasis have higher participation in all benefit programmes.
- Programmes that are more effectively targeted to the poor (for example, old-age assistance, food-for-work) often have lower coverage rates for the poor than non-targeted programmes such as midday meals or the ICDS.

Table A.13.1a Access to Social Safety Net Programmes

(in percentage)

	Has Any Card All Households	BPL or Antyodaya (Versus APL) PDS Cardholders	Rice at PDS	Wheat at PDS BPL or Antyodaya Cardholders	Midday Meals Government Primary Students	ICDS Maternal Benefit	ICDS Child Benefit Women (15–49) with a Child Born in Last 5 Years	SGRY or Food for Work Rural Employed[4]	Old Age and Widow Pension 60+
All India	83	43	31	35	80	22	35	0.9	9.0
Age[1]									
15–19							26	44	
20–9	67	48	31	37		24	37	1.3	
30–9	78	45	31	38		18	31	1.1	
40–9	85	45	29	34		17	28	1.2	
50–9	88	40	26	33				0.9	
60–9	89	40	30	31				–	7.6
70–9	90	38	36	37				–	11.4
80+	92	31	32	36				–	10.9
Sex[2]									
Male					79		35	1.2	7.3
Female					80		35	0.6	10.6
Urban/Rural									
Metro urban	81	18	18	21	58	9	12		3.8
Other urban	78	32	33	35	73	12	19		5.8
More developed village	88	47	36	42	83	29	43	0.3	9.4
Less developed village	82	51	26	31	80	23	40	1.3	10.8
Income Quintiles									
Poorest	81	59	36	42	84	25	42	1.2	14.6
2nd Quintile	82	57	30	36	83	25	40	1.6	10.0
Middle	84	50	31	35	77	23	36	0.6	9.1
4th Quintile	86	37	28	32	74	20	32	0.5	6.5
Affluent	84	16	19	22	73	15	24	0.2	4.5
Education[3]									
0 years	82	61	32	35	83	22	37	0.9	11.6
1–4 Std	83	58	32	40	79	28	44	1.2	6.5
5–9 Std	84	47	31	35	80	25	40	1.2	5.4
10–11 Std	84	35	31	38	75	18	28	1.0	3.4
12 Std and some college	84	28	30	38	77	15	26	0.6	3.6
College graduate	83	17	22	26	70	10	14	0.4	1.1

(contd)

(Table A.13.1a contd)

	Has Any Card — All Households	BPL or Antyodaya (Versus APL) — PDS Cardholders	Rice at PDS — BPL or Antyodaya Cardholders	Wheat at PDS — BPL or Antyodaya Cardholders	Midday Meals — Government Primary Students	ICDS Maternal Benefit — Women (15–49) with a Child Born in Last 5 Years	ICDS Child Benefit — Women (15–49) with a Child Born in Last 5 Years	SGRY or Food for Work — Rural Employed[4]	Old Age and Widow Pension 60+
Social group									
Forward caste	84	24	29	28	79	16	29	0.2	5.5
OBC	81	47	32	37	80	22	36	0.8	8.7
Dalit	86	54	32	35	82	26	38	1.1	15.6
Adivasi	79	71	28	43	84	39	58	2.8	12.2
Muslim	84	36	26	29	73	13	24	0.4	4.7
Christian, Sikh, Other	87	23	30	48	57	10	17	0.0	6.1

Notes: [1] Age is the age of the oldest male for ration card columns; age of the mother for ICDS columns; and age of the worker for SGRY or Food-for-Work.

[2] Sex is the sex of the child for midday meals and ICDS; sex of the worker for SGRY/Food-for-Work.

[3] Education is the maximum adult education for ration card columns; education of the mother for midday meals and ICDS; education of the worker for SGRY/Food-for-Work.

[4] The SGRY/Food-for-Work is analysed only for rural Uttar Pradesh, Biihar, Chhattisgarh, Madhya Pradesh, Orissa, and Maharashtra where the programme was active in 2005.

+ refers to 60 or more.

Source: IHDS 2004–5 data.

Table A.13.1b Statewise Access to Social Safety Net Programmes

(in percentage)

	Has Any Card	BPL or Antyodaya (Versus APL)	Rice at PDS	Wheat at PDS	Midday Meals	ICDS Maternal Benefit	ICDS Child Benefit	SGRY or Food for Work	Old Age and Widow Pension
	All Households	PDS Cardholders	BPL or Antyodaya Cardholders		Government Primary Students	Women (15–49) with a Child Born in Last 5 Years		Rural Employed[4]	60+
All India	**83**	**43**	**31**	**35**	**80**	**22**	**35**	**0.9**	**9.0**
States									
Jammu and Kashmir	88	32	49	41	69	13	29		2.2
Himachal Pradesh	97	25	75	62	95	41	50		19.0
Uttarakhand	92	38	57	37	74	17	22		5.6
Punjab	89	5			50	9	8		11.8
Haryana	94	18		4	71	39	68		60.6
Delhi	75	28	16	19	65	10	13		4.6
Uttar Pradesh	83	28	18	16	86	5	10	0.6	5.9
Bihar	67	53	0	0	53	2	7	0.5	10.2
Jharkhand	62	64	9	23	80	34	54		4.7
Rajasthan	96	28	0	27	93	21	32		8.5
Chhattisgarh	69	67	26	46	83	31	62	3.2	10.0
Madhya Pradesh	76	41	29	27	91	27	44	1.4	7.9
North-East	71	46	28	3	59	4	14		15.3
Assam	86	28	4	0	21	6	10		1.7
West Bengal	94	29	4	24	77	16	35		3.1
Orissa	78	70	15	0	87	42	67	1.4	24.8
Gujarat	84	47	20	29	91	13	42		1.9
Maharashtra	90	31	64	66	87	39	52	0.3	4.2
Andhra Pradesh	77	85	40	11	89	32	40		16.3
Karnataka	72	77	61	81	93	39	46		8.6
Kerala	95	38	28	43	56	12	20		6.9
Tamil Nadu	94	51	44	80	85	60	75		3.4

Notes: [1] Age is the age of the oldest adult male for ration card columns; age of the mother for ICDS columns; and age of the worker for SGRY or Food-for-Work.

[2] Sex is the sex of the child for midday meals and ICDS; sex of the worker for SGRY/Food-for-Work.

[3] Education is the maximum adult education for ration card columns; education of the mother for midday meals and ICDS; education of the worker for SGRY/Food-for-Work.

[4] The SGRY/Food-for-Work is analysed only for rural Uttar Pradesh, Biihar, Chhattisgarh, Madhya Pradesh, Orissa, and Maharashtra where the programme was active in 2005.

+ refers to 60 or more.

Source: IHDS 2004–5 data.

14

Conclusion

I was again on a great voyage of discovery and the land of India and the people of India lay spread out before me. India with all her infinite charm and variety began to grow upon me more and more, and yet the more I saw of her, the more I realized how very difficult it was for me or anyone else to grasp the ideas she had embodied… I was also fully aware of the diversities and divisions of Indian life, of classes, castes, religions, races, different degrees of cultural development. Yet I think that a country with a long cultural background and a common outlook on life develops a spirit that is peculiar to it and that is impressed on all its children, however much they may differ among themselves. (Nehru 1946: 58–9)

As we end our journey through Indian social life, we are painfully aware that we have only drawn broad contours of it. Statistics can identify the fundamental bone structure of a body, but they cannot colour it with flesh and blood beauty. However, behind these statistics lie thousands of interviews that our research teams have conducted through the length and breadth of India. We would not be doing justice to the hopes and dreams with which the men, women, and children, who participated in the IHDS spoke to us if we did not add our observations to highlight the vulnerabilities, resolve, and hope of these families.

Since Independence, poverty rates in India have declined substantially, going from 54.9 per cent of people living in poverty in 1973–4 to 27.5 per cent in 2004–5 as measured by the NSS. Vigorous debates about how to count the poor have occupied economists over the past decade,[1] and it is not our intention to add to this debate. Rather, we would like to draw on the IHDS results to focus on two dimensions of vulnerability. First, a segment of the Indian population lives in absolute destitution. In the course of IHDS fieldwork, we visited many homes and were struck by the stark nakedness of some of these homes. Walking into a rural hut with a few pots piled on the floor and a mat laid out in the honour of the visitors made us realize that all the worldly goods of these households were spread before our eyes. Chapter 5 documents that 15 per cent of the households do not possess a cot, 3 per cent do not have two sets of clothing, and 7 per cent do not have footwear for all the household members. The NSS data similarly indicate that 2.6 per cent of rural and 0.6 per cent of urban households report being hungry. This destitution is not evenly spread across Indian society. If we define destitute households as those that do not possess footwear and two sets of clothing for everybody (that is, 7 per cent of the IHDS households), 2 per cent of the forward caste households are destitute, compared with 12 per cent of Dalits and 17 per cent of Adivasis. Similarly, 12 per cent of households in the least developed villages are destitute, compared to less than 1 per cent of those in metropolitan areas. While almost none of the households in Kerala or Himachal Pradesh fall in this category, 33 per cent of the households in Orissa do.

A second aspect of vulnerability that deserves attention is that many families survive at the margins. Illness or natural calamities like droughts or floods can propel them quickly into poverty. These marginal households have few resources to draw on when adversity strikes. While the savings rate may be high for upper income households, 39 per cent of Indian households do not even have a bank account. Seven per cent of IHDS households took a loan in the preceding

---

[1] Deaton and Kozel (2005); Dubey and Gangopadhyay (1998).

five years to deal with a medical emergency, and 6 per cent had to borrow to finance regular consumption. If selling land or jewellery is an indicator of extreme vulnerability, 2 per cent of the households had to sell land and 3 per cent had to sell jewellery to repay loans in the preceding five years.

While recognizing these vulnerabilities, we were deeply humbled by the resolve and creativity shown by the Indian families. Nearly 50 per cent of rural elderly men and 31 per cent of urban elderly men continue to work well into their seventies, a time, when by most standards, they should be able to enjoy retirement. Families continue to provide care and support for each other. Seventy seven per cent of the elderly above 60 years reside with married children, or other relatives. Individuals work hard to patch together livelihoods and often work in whatever jobs they can find. It is not uncommon to see a rural man working for a few days a year on his own farm, a few days as an agricultural labourer in an adjoining farm, and in construction labour during the non-agricultural season, while his wife looks after animals, takes care of agricultural tasks, and engages in sewing, or making pickles to supplement the family income.

However, for us personally, it is the message of hope that is the most striking. Even among households that have seen little of India's much trumpeted 9 per cent economic growth, there is a great desire to ensure that their children will partake in this growth in the decades to come. More than 90 per cent of children aged 6–14 have attended school at some point in their young lives, and 85 per cent were enrolled at the time of the interview. Girls are somewhat less likely to be enrolled, but they are not far behind their brothers now.

In articulating these vulnerabilities, creativity, and hopes of the IHDS households, we seek to encourage a discussion of some persistent challenges facing Indian society in the twenty-first century. Three challenges are particularly noteworthy:

(1) Historical fault lines along gender, caste, and religious boundaries have remained persistent themes throughout this report;
(2) Global forces have widened the disparities between metropolitan cities and forgotten villages, and between states that were already more advanced and those mired in the economic doldrums; and
(3) In spite of some noteworthy achievements, public institutions in most of India have failed in delivering basic services.

CASTE, RELIGION, AND GENDER DISPARITIES

Differences in well-being among social groups are long established, but a variety of contemporary forces have conspired to sustain and sometimes exacerbate these inequalities. Dalits have long laboured at the margins of a society that depends on that labour, but that has often excluded them. Although, some Adivasis in the North-East have fared better, other Adivasis have either lived in such remote locations that they have been left out of the recent economic progress or have been forced to migrate, only to work as low paid labourers. In some cases, such as for OBCs and Muslims, historical disadvantages have been exacerbated by structural shifts. A decline in artisan incomes has affected Muslims disproportionately, while agricultural stagnation has disproportionately affected OBCs, especially. These historical and contemporary forces are manifested in the continuing human developed disparities presented in this report.

In general, the IHDS finds that Adivasis and Dalits are still at the bottom on most indicators of well-being, Muslims and OBCs occupy the middle, and forward caste Hindus and other minority religions are at the top. We see these patterns in a variety of indicators: household incomes and poverty rates, landownership and agricultural incomes, health, and education. These group positions are not immutable, and on some dimensions we see slightly different rankings. For example, Adivasis generally have slightly better health outcomes (that is, reported short-term morbidity and child mortality), probably as a function of living in the North-East, where health care appears to be of higher quality. Similarly, when it comes to education, Muslims are as disadvantaged as Dalits and Adivasis, although their economic well-being is more at par with that of OBCs.

Two aspects of these social group disparities deserve attention. First, much of the inequality seems to emerge from differential access to livelihoods. Salaried jobs pay far more than casual labour or farming. These jobs elude the disadvantaged groups for many reasons. Living in rural areas, having lower education, and arguably having fewer connections for job search, all may play a role. Regardless of the reason, more than three out of ten forward caste and minority religion men have salaried jobs, compared with about two out of ten Muslim, OBC, and Dalit men and even fewer Adivasi men. Dalits and Adivasis are further disadvantaged by not owing land, or owning some, mainly, low productivity land. Not surprisingly, these income differences translate into differences in other indicators of human development.

Second, as if inequalities in the parental generation were not enough, future generations seem doomed to replicate these inequalities because of the continuing differences in education—both in quality and quantity. In spite of the long history of positive discrimination policies—particularly, reservation in college admission—social inequalities begin early in primary schools. Thus, affirmative action remedies are too little and too late by the time students reach the higher secondary level. The IHDS not only documents these substantial disparities in school enrolment, it also uncovers tremendous differences at all levels of skill development. More than two-thirds of children aged 8–11 from forward castes and minority religions can read simple paragraphs, compared with less than half of those from Dalit and Adivasi households. These group differences persist even after we take into account school enrolment, parental education, and income. We know too little about the actual operation of schools to be able to explain these differences, but it is clear that remedial action in primary schools—and perhaps even before then—is needed in order to equalize the playing field. It is particularly worrisome to note that Muslim children are as disadvantaged as Dalit and Adivasi children, although little attention has been paid to religious background as a source of educational disadvantage. At the other end of the skill spectrum, more than a third of forward caste males and more than half of minority religions have some English skills compared to less than a third of OBC males, one in five Muslims, one in five Dalits, and one in seven Adivasis. Differences among women are even greater.

Gender forms another axis along which IHDS found tremendous disparities. The IHDS, the NSS, and the Census record extremely low rates of female labour force participation. Education fails to reduce these differences, with women's labour force disadvantage growing rather than reducing at levels of education up to higher secondary education. When women are in the labour force, they tend to work mostly on family farms or caring for livestock. Even when women engage in paid work, their daily income is only 53 paise per rupee earned by men in rural areas and 68 paise in urban areas.

Women's economic vulnerability is compounded by their social vulnerability. More than 95 per cent of new brides live with their in-laws after marriage, and more than 40 per cent do not have their natal family nearby. Wives, therefore, have few sources of social support and must rely on husbands and in-laws for both financial and social needs. A preference for sons over daughters remains strong, so sex selective abortions result in more male than female births, and once born, girls still experience higher mortality in infancy and childhood.

SPATIAL DISPARITIES

Inequalities between cities and villages, and among rich and poor states, are not new. However, recent economic changes have heightened these disparities. As agriculture has stagnated, urban employment has come to play an even greater role in shaping economic well-being.[2] Moreover, historical accidents as well as state policies have led to higher economic growth in some states than in others, resulting in widening interstate disparities.[3] Political and social differences have also played a role.[4] The result is the striking patterns of spatial inequality the IHDS has found across almost all indicators of human development.

Urban Advantage

Since official poverty lines are set at different levels for urban and rural areas, poverty rates in villages appear quite similar to those in towns or cities. IHDS found rates of 26.5 for rural areas and 23.7 for urban areas, a difference only slightly greater than found in the NSS. For example, the NSS poverty rate for urban areas was 25.7 in urban areas and 28.3 in rural areas.[5] However, limiting our focus to poverty rates obscures other dimensions of locational advantage. Urban areas more often have running water, electricity, and local medical facilities. Hence, even the poorest urban residents have greater access to basic amenities than wealthier rural residents. For example, 83 per cent of urban households in the lowest income quintile have electricity, almost comparable to the 89 per cent electrification of rural households in the top quintile. Teachers and doctors in urban areas are more likely to live close to their work and less likely to be absent, increasing the quality of overall schooling and medical care. This is easily seen in the difference in skill acquisition for children aged 8–11. Among children living in metropolitan areas, 69 per cent can read a simple paragraph, while only 47 per cent of the children in the least developed villages can read.

This report has documented the particularly high urban advantage in human development in the six metropolitan areas—Mumbai, New Delhi, Bangalore, Kolkata, Chennai, and Hyderabad—compared with two- and three-tier cities. Similarly, the rural disadvantage is particularly sharp in the least developed villages. Indians in metropolitan areas seem to live in a totally different universe from their brothers and sisters in the least developed villages. They have higher household incomes (median income of Rs 72,000 versus Rs 20,297). A higher proportion of adults who speak English fluently (16 versus 2 per cent for males) and have some computing skills (19 versus 2 per cent), have a cell phone in the household (24 versus 1 per cent), have a flush toilet (55 versus 7 per cent), have children who have had all basic vaccinations (62 versus 40 per cent), and lower child mortality (31 versus 82 per thousand).

---

[2] Ramaswamy (2007).
[3] Deaton and Drèze (2002).
[4] Chhibber and Nooruddin (2004); Banerjee, Somnathan, and Iyer (2005).
[5] These figures use a uniform recall method. A mixed-recall method yields results that are even closer: 21.8 for rural areas and 21.7 for urban areas.

Regional Disparities

One of the most striking results in this report are the large state differences in almost all indicators of human development (see Box 14.1).

Infant mortality rates in Kerala (estimated at nine in the IHDS) rival those of developed countries. In contrast, those in Uttar Pradesh (estimated at 80 in the IHDS) are substantially higher. Similarly, female literacy rates in the North-East are 81 per cent, about twice the rate in Rajasthan.

Regional disparities in income, education, health, and other dimensions of human development, are well known. However, the causes of these disparities remain poorly understood. Like others who have noted these disparities, we do not attempt to explain them. However, this section highlights the results from preceding chapters that might spur a discussion about how to best understand these differences in order to develop effective public policy.

Several observations are worth noting. Substantial state differences in economic development affect both the

---

Box 14.1 Regional Differences Are Often Larger Than Other Differences

Results presented in this report indicate that on a variety of dimensions of human development, differences between states are often as large, if not larger than, the differences by income, education, urban/rural residence, and caste or religion. Although, some of the state level differences may be due to education, income, or other personal characteristics, contextual factors seem to play an independent role.

State Differences in Selected Indicators

	Households with Electricity 18+ Hours (per cent)	Children Aged 8–11 Can Read (per cent)	Women Aged 15–59 Work (per cent)	Women Married Before 18 (per cent)	Under 5 Mortality (per 1,000)
State					
Lowest	3 (Bihar)	39 (UP)	26 (Punjab)	19 (Kerala)	11 (Kerala)
Highest	99 (Himachal)	83 (Himachal)	79 (Himachal)	86 (Bihar)	116 (Uttar Pradesh)
Difference	96	44	53	–67	105
Income					
Bottom Quantile	45	45	61	70	78
Top Quantile	66	73	30	42	37
Difference	21	28	–31	–28	–41
Social Group					
Dalit	55	44	51	71	94
Forward Castes	64	71	37	49	50
Difference	9	27	–14	–22	–44
Education					
None	41	35	63	75	92
College graduate	67	80	27	7	37
Difference	26	45	–36	–68	–55
Urban/Rural					
Less developed village	38	47	62	70	82
Metropolitan city	90	69	15	38	31
Difference	52	22	–47	–32	–51
Table cross Reference	Appendix Table A.5.1	Appendix Table A.6.4	Appendix Table A.4.1	Appendix Table A.10.1	Appendix Table A.8.1

Source: IHDS 2004–5 data.

availability of work and the wages obtained when work is found. In states where water or soil conditions limit multiple cropping, underemployment is widespread. For example, rural males in Orissa work only 178 days in a year, while those in Punjab work 278 days. Non-agricultural work may take up some of this slack, but rural non-farm employment also varies tremendously by state. Moreover, a state's level of urbanization also influences income and employment, with men in Tamil Nadu having greater access to better paying salaried employment or non-agricultural labour than men in Chhattisgarh. These factors combine to create much higher incomes in some states as compared to others.

Indicators of human development such as school enrolment and infant mortality are often correlated with state income, in part, because individual families in richer states have higher incomes and so are better able to provide school fees and medical care for their own children. But more development creates many spill-over effects that provide the institutions and social climate that benefit poor families in these developed areas. These context effects have a more subtle but pervasive impact. If richer households ensure that their children are vaccinated, even poor children have a lower likelihood of contracting measles or chickenpox because their wealthier friends are vaccinated and if vaccinations become more common as more households acquire the means to access better medical care, the expectations of what parents do for their children change for everyone. Even poor parents may have a greater incentive to ensure that their children attend school if they see widespread availability of better paying jobs requiring some education. When there are enough consumers, the supply of amenities such as cell phones and LPG will be higher than in poor states, with few buyers, thereby improving the chances of even lower income households in these areas to acquire these amenities.

However, state differences in human development are not perfectly arrayed along a single income dimension. The richer north-eastern states have considerably lower vaccination coverage than Orissa, one of the poorest states. The quality of public services and effective governance as well as political commitment, play an important role in shaping human development indicators. In 1991, Gujarat (61 per cent literacy rate) and Himachal Pradesh (64 per cent literacy rate) were more or less at par. By 2001, Himachal Pradesh (76 per cent) had made greater strides than Gujarat (69 per cent). Himachal Pradesh made a conscious decision to invest in primary education, and the results are most clearly seen in skill acquisition by children. The IHDS records that 83 per cent of the children aged 8–11 in Himachal Pradesh are able to read a simple paragraph, better than any other state in the nation, and well beyond the 64 per cent children in Gujarat who can read at that level.

While many of these state differences make sense, given the political economy of the area, some others are not so obvious. In particular, why does social structure differ so markedly across different states? Punjab and Haryana have many similarities, yet some gender norms in the two seem to be quite different. Only 28 per cent of women respondents from Punjab were married before age 18, compared to 56 per cent in Haryana. Eighty six per cent of women in Punjab say that domestic violence would be rare under a set of listed conditions, compared with 67 per cent in Haryana. The female literacy rate is 68 per cent in Punjab but 56 per cent in Haryana, although male literacy rates are similar in both states. Nevertheless, sex ratios at birth are among the most skewed in the nation for both states.

We would also expect similarities in organizational membership between Uttar Pradesh and Bihar. However, only 9 per cent of the households in Uttar Pradesh belong to any organizations, while 63 per cent in Bihar belong to some organization—most frequently a caste association or social organization. History, geography, and religious composition, undoubtedly play a role. Perhaps the prevalence of the Sikh religion in Punjab leads to more egalitarian gender roles on some dimensions,[6] and perhaps a history of caste mobilization in Bihar results in higher rates of associational membership there.

Spatial variation in human development may also be patterned by social influences. Diarrhoea, fever, and respiratory illnesses spread by contact. When some people in a neighbourhood are ill, others are more likely to become ill. When some children receive vaccination and show no adverse effects, other parents may be more willing to have their children vaccinated. When some families shun child marriage for their daughters, it changes the nature of marriage arrangements, and more families recognize that an unmarried 19 year old girl is not doomed to spinsterhood. Social influences are particularly important in shaping attitudes towards institutions, organizational memberships, and social networks. When a self-help group is set up in a village, many families become members, and this can then spread to neighbouring villages.

This report has documented substantial state variation in almost all indicators of human development. For education, both household- and state-level variations are important. But in some cases, state-level differences seem to dwarf individual differences (see Box 13.1). This is particularly so for health outcomes. Reported short-term morbidity, health care, and

---

[6] However, high rates of sex selection in Punjab, resulting in an unfavourable sex ratio, suggest caution against assuming absence of son preference in Punjab.

vaccination rates vary far more between states than between different income or educational groups. These state differences in human development have real implications for the well-being of current residents as well as future prospects for economic growth. In a globalizing economy, industries have more choices in where to locate. States with more electricity, better schools, a more skilled workforce with computer and English capabilities, and better functioning public service delivery systems, will be more likely to attract new industries. Thus, states with greater urban densities have experienced greater employment growth in recent years.[7] The potential for a long-term cycle of lose-lose situations for states with lower levels of human development deserves greater attention in the development discourse.

PUBLIC INSTITUTIONS AND BASIC SERVICES

As we noted at the beginning of this report, independence brought with it a pledge of service, a pledge to fulfil Mahatma Gandhi's dream of wiping every tear from every eye. It also brought a dream of catapulting India into modernity, through central planning. Public services in India were developed around these twin principles. A commitment to the poor or the marginalized, and central planning, with a division of responsibility between the centre and states. Consequently, what has evolved is an elaborate bureaucracy built in part on service delivery to the poor. Serving the poor should not be synonymous with poor quality of service delivery, but in reality, many public institutions seem rife with inefficiency and indifference.

This report has documented the poverty of service delivery in many institutions. Water and electricity remain irregular. Forty three per cent of households with electric connections do not have electricity at least 18 hours per day, 63 per cent of households with piped water do not get water at least three hours per day. Teacher absenteeism in government schools is rampant, and almost a third of children in these schools report having been beaten or pinched in the preceding month. Barely half of children aged 8–11 can read a simple paragraph, and less than half can do two-digit subtractions. About one in six of the government heath centres visited by IHDS interviewers had dirty walls and about one in seven had dirty floors. The doctor/director was absent at the time of the visit in almost one-quarter of the visits. Not surprisingly, government services remain underutilized. The vast majority of sick people, even the poor, rely on private health care. Enrolments in private schools are rapidly rising, even in rural areas.

There is no necessary reason why the public sector must provide poor service. The IHDS has also documented government services working well in many places. At the same time, tremendous strides have been made in capital expenditures on health centres and schools. More than 90 per cent of the IHDS villages had a primary school within the village, and more than half had a government health facility. Government teachers and health care providers are better trained and are generally better paid than most of their counterparts in the private sector. Most of these professionals want to do well, and given the right environment and necessary support, they could realize the dreams of Gandhi and the independence generation. Uncovering why this happens now in only some places is one of the great tasks of future research.

While a variety of experiments with private service delivery are being undertaken, it is difficult to see this as a comprehensive solution for the nation as a whole. The private sector often complements public sector efforts rather than substituting for them. Results from the village assessments show that private schools spring up in states that have better developed systems of government schools, and NGOs seem to gravitate towards areas with better developed infrastructure. Hence, the provision of higher quality public services seems an essential steppingstone towards improving human development.

This completes our report, reflecting a voyage of discovery across different dimensions of human development, using rich resources of survey data. We trust we have been able to give some voice to the thousands of people who cooperated in making this possible. But we realize also that a review such as this only begins to tap the possibilities of the IHDS. The survey is unique in asking about such a broad spectrum of issues affecting the Indian people. We have necessarily treated these issues sequentially, and have only occasionally been able to exploit the IHDS advantage of investigating links across issues. The sheer quantity of topics raised in the IHDS means that this review could only begin to analyse how each aspect of human development is patterned across the great diversity of India. Continuing research with this data, our own and that of others, will reveal even more interesting linkages that help us understand how human development is progressing. But we hope that these initial efforts reported here will have justified the IHDS's broad approach in bringing together such a diverse set of topics. Like Nehru, we recognize the complexity of the challenges and the diversity of the people, but that recognition is incomplete without an attempt to also understand some of the unity across that diversity.

---

[7] Ramaswamy (2007).

Appendix I—IHDS: The Design

One of the most important goals of this research is to deepen our understanding of human development in India. Unlike the large body of empirical literature that relies on aggregated secondary data for analysis of human development issues, in this study we have used data from the IHDS 2005, administered to a nationally representative sample of households. This appendix describes our data collection and sample selection methods, assesses the quality of data, and provides an overview of the data analysis techniques used in the preceding chapters. The authors of this monograph are designers and organizers of this survey. Data collection for this survey was supported by two grants (RØ1HDØ41455 and RØ1HDØ46166) from the US National Institutes of Child Health and Human Development with supplementary funding from the World Bank.

A survey that encompasses a full range of human development issues faces practical challenges, not encountered by more limited focus projects. Every issue, from questionnaire design, to data cleaning, to statistical analysis, is complicated by the decision to broaden the range of the human development issues addressed. The analytic gains are substantial, but the practical costs are also real. After a careful consideration of these issues it was decided to field the IHDS to over 41,000 households residing in rural and urban areas, selected from 33 states and union territories. The sample extends to 384 out of 593 districts identified in the 2001 Census. While financial and management limitations precluded inclusion of all districts in the sample, the selection of 384 out of 593 districts allows for a highly diverse sample. All states and union territories are included in the sample, with the exception of Andaman and Nicobar Islands, and Lakshadweep. These two contain less than 0.05 per cent of India's population and their island location, as well as requirement of special permits to visit some parts, make them difficult to survey.

The IHDS benefited from a rich history of survey research in India, generally, and from NCAER and its collaborating institutions, in particular. The questionnaire design was borrowed, as needed, from Indian and international household surveys. Some of the important Indian sources include the NSSs, the *NFHSs*, and the 1994 Human Development Profile of India. International sources include five countries and the Status of Women and Fertility Survey, the World Bank Living Standard Measurement Surveys, and Indonesian and Malaysian Family Life Surveys. Organization of fieldwork and oversight was in the capable hands of professionals with a generation of practical experience, culled from a wide variety of surveys. Data cleaning and analysis enlisted a small army of personnel with well developed, often obsessive, attention to detail. At its best, most of this work is invisible, thus, permitting the analyst and the reader to focus on the central research questions. But the success of those analyses and the validity of their conclusions depend on the competent execution of the survey itself. This chapter reviews the major issues of that execution.

SAMPLING

The IHDS is a nationally representative survey of 41,554 urban and rural households. It covers all states and union territories of India, with the exception of Andaman, Nicobar, and Lakshadweep islands. These households are spread across 33 states and union territories, 384 districts, 1,503 villages and 971 urban blocks, located in 276 towns and cities. Districtwise coverage for total, rural, and urban sample is shown in Figures AI.1, AI.2 and AI.3.

These 41,554 households include 215,754 individuals. Statewise distribution of sampled households and individuals is presented in Table AI.1.

Villages and urban blocks (comprising of 150–200 households) formed the primary sampling unit (PSU) from which the households were selected. Urban and rural PSUs were selected using a different design. In order to draw a random sample of urban households, all urban areas in a state were listed in the order of their size with number of blocks drawn from each urban area allocated based on probability proportional to size. Once the numbers of blocks for each urban area were determined, the enumeration blocks were selected randomly with help from the Registrar General of India. From these Census Enumeration Blocks of about 150–200 households, a complete household listing was conducted and household samples of 15 households per block were selected.

The rural sample contains about half the households that were interviewed initially by NCAER in 1993–4 in a survey titled Human Development Profile of India (HDPI),[1] and the other half of the samples were drawn from both districts surveyed in HDPI as well as from the districts located in the states and union territories not covered in HDPI. The original HDPI was a stratified random sample of 33,230 households,

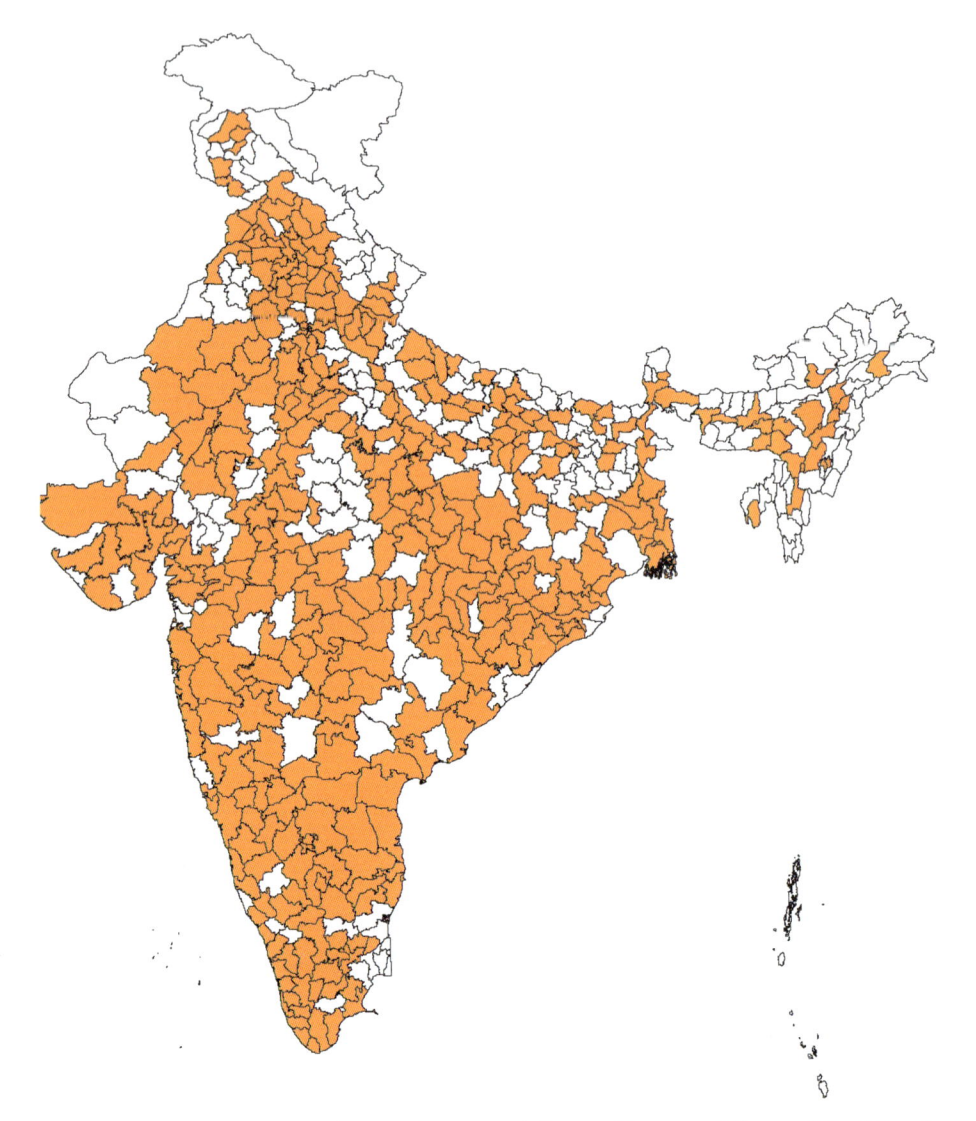

Figure AI.1   India Human Development Survey 2005, District Coverage—Urban and Rural Sample
Source: IHDS 2004–5.

[1] Shariff (1999).

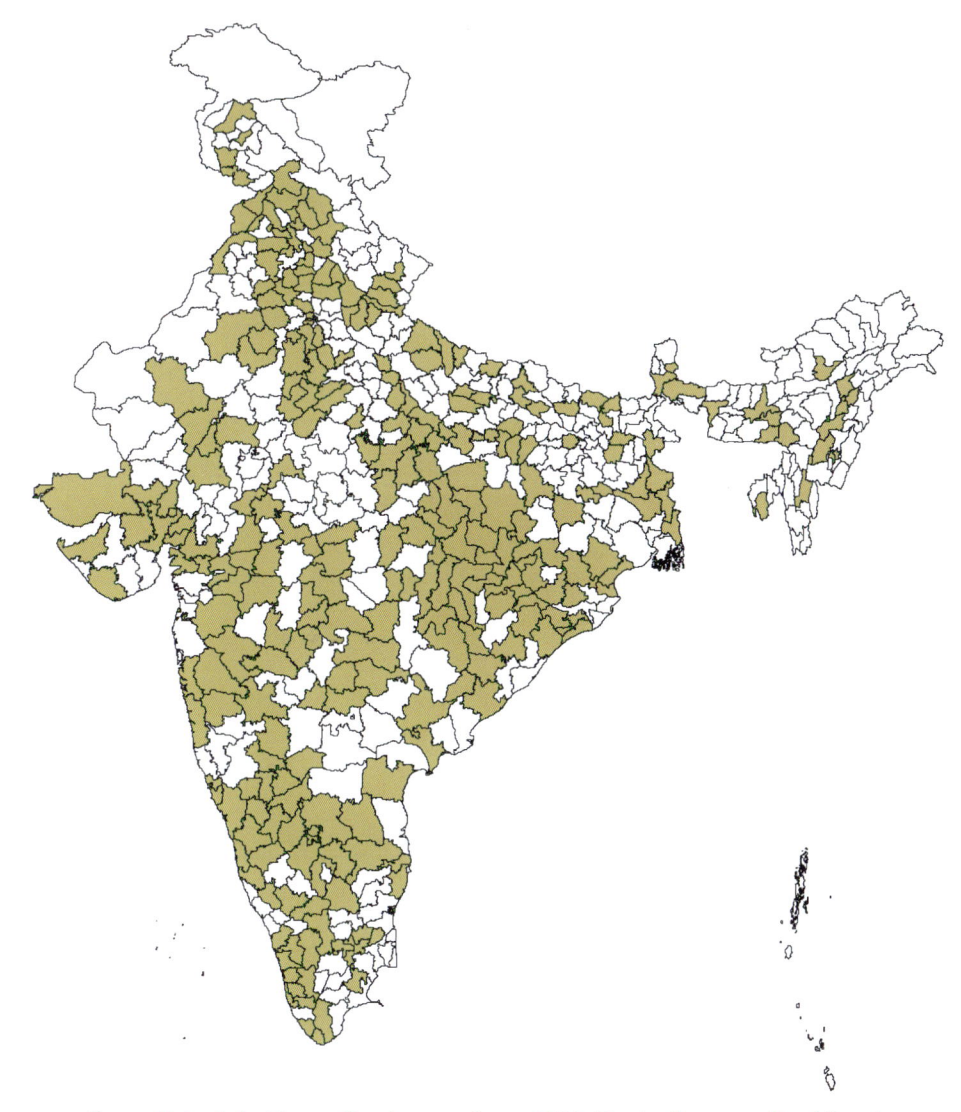

Figure AI.2 India Human Development Survey 2005, District Coverage—Rural Sample

Source: IHDS 2004–5.

located in 16 major states, 195 districts, and 1,765 villages. In states where the 1993–4 survey was conducted and re-contact details were available, 13,593 households were randomly selected for re-interview in 2005.

After a gap of 11–12 years, about 82 per cent of the households were contactable for re-interview, resulting in a resurvey of 11,153 original households, as well as 2,440 households which were separated from these root households, but were still living in the village. Distribution of the sample is described in Figure AI.4.

In order to check the representativeness of the sample, in each district, where re-interviews were conducted, two fresh villages were randomly selected using the probability proportional to size technique. In the villages selected for survey in this manner, 20 randomly selected households were interviewed. Comparing the panel sample with this randomly selected refresher sample, allows us to determine whether this panel sample is overrepresented among certain segments of the society. Table AI.2 compares the characteristics of the re-interview sample with the refresher sample for the districts where any re-interviews took place.

The comparison suggests that on most variables of interest such as caste, religion, education, and economic status, the re-interviewed sample does not differ substantially from the fresh sample.

Additionally 3,993 rural households were randomly selected from the states where the 1993–4 survey was not conducted, or where re-contact information was not available. This approach to combining a randomly selected panel sample, while refreshing it, with another random sample has been used in a variety of surveys including the Panel Study of Income Dynamics in the US and Malaysian Family Life

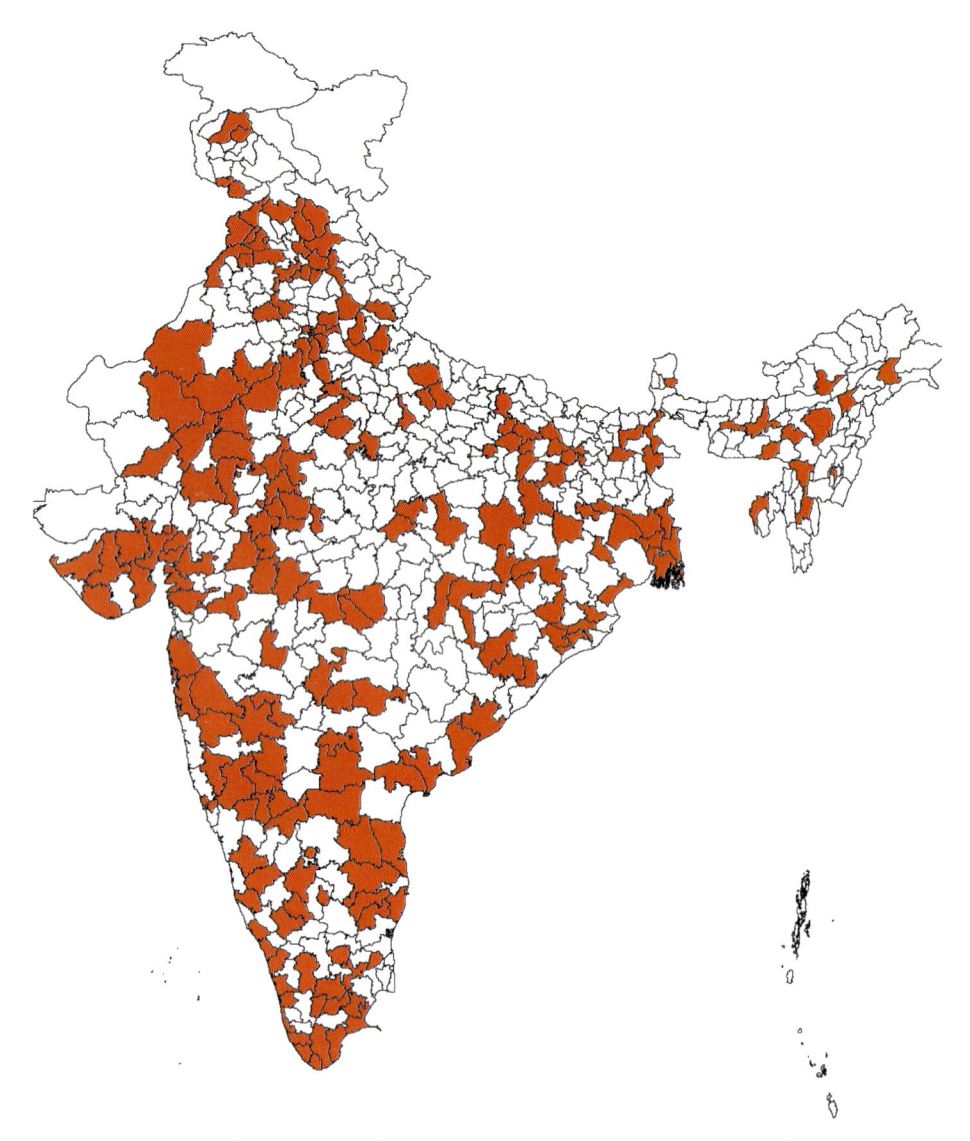

Figure AI.3 India Human Development Survey 2005, District Coverage—Urban Sample
Source: IHDS 2004–5.

Survey.[2] However, given the potential for significant sampling and non-sampling errors, we present a detailed analysis of the quality of IHDS data below.

COMPARATIVE RESULTS

IHDS was not intended to provide national nor, certainly, statewise estimates of levels of human development outcomes. There are already many excellent Indian surveys that fill that mission. The main purpose of IHDS is to provide a means for gaining insight by analysing the relationships among these human development outcomes and the connections between human development and its background causes.

Nevertheless, it is useful to compare IHDS estimates of human development levels with estimates from other more narrowly focused surveys that usually have larger sample sizes and smaller sampling errors. The NSSs and the *NFHSs* are obvious comparisons because of their excellent quality and wide use. The Indian Census provides another useful reference. The Census and these surveys differ not only in their objectives and design, but their question wording, sampling design, coding decisions, and government sponsorship, all of which should be expected to provoke somewhat different answers from respondents, and yield different frequencies (Table AI.3).

[2] Leslie Kish and Alastair Scott were the first to describe the probability sampling procedures which are designed to optimize the reselection or retention of sample units during a transition from an old to a new sample design. A description of this can be found in 'Retaining units after changing strata and probabilities', in the *Journal of the American Statistical Association*, Vol. 667, Number 335, Applications Section, September 1971.

Table AI.1 Statewise Distribution of IHDS Sample

	Disctrict in 2001 Census	Included in IHDS Districts	Included in IHDS Urban Areas	Included in IHDS Blocks	Included in IHDS Villages	Households Surveyed Rural	Households Surveyed Urban	Households Surveyed Total	Individuals Surveyed Rural	Individuals Surveyed Urban	Individuals Surveyed Total
Jammu and Kashmir	14	5	5	21	20	400	315	715	2,528	1,702	4,230
Himachal Pradesh	12	9	7	21	52	1,057	315	1,372	5,663	1,503	7,166
Punjab	17	13	11	36	61	1,033	560	1,593	6,202	2,831	9,033
Chandigarh	1	1	1	6	0	0	90	90	0	383	383
Uttaranchal	13	6	3	9	20	309	149	458	1,757	736	2,493
Haryana	19	14	6	18	79	1,350	268	1,618	8,112	1,291	9,403
Delhi	9	10	7	56	6	60	900	960	329	4,291	4,620
Rajasthan	32	23	17	60	88	1,590	895	2,485	9,663	4,805	14,468
Uttar Pradesh	70	43	24	75	138	2,389	1,123	3,512	14,966	6,499	21,465
Bihar	37	17	10	31	61	965	465	1,430	5,950	2,856	8,806
Sikkim	4	1	1	3	3	60	45	105	293	212	505
Arunachal Pradesh	13	1	1	3	6	120	45	165	623	209	832
Nagaland	8	4	1	2	5	100	30	130	480	84	564
Manipur	9	3	1	3	3	60	45	105	359	239	598
Mizoram	8	1	1	3	3	60	45	105	263	239	502
Tripura	4	2	1	3	7	184	45	229	818	190	1,008
Meghalaya	7	3	1	3	6	116	45	161	505	250	755
Assam	23	8	7	21	38	699	318	1,017	3,286	1,404	4,690
West Bengal	18	14	21	75	66	1,247	1,133	2,380	6,170	4,788	10,958
Jharkhand	18	6	9	27	26	519	405	924	2,913	2,095	5,008
Orissa	30	26	13	40	84	1,464	600	2,064	7,710	2,886	10,596
Chhattisgarh	16	15	6	18	49	905	270	1,175	4,833	1,377	6,210
Madhya Pradesh	45	31	13	42	121	2,177	628	2,805	12,392	3,409	15,801
Gujarat	25	17	14	60	70	1,167	911	2,078	5,926	4,234	10,160
Diu and Daman	2	2	0	0	3	60	0	60	281	0	281
Dadra and Nagar Haveli	1	1	0	0	3	60	0	60	315	0	315
Maharashtra	35	27	18	75	115	2,078	1,125	3,203	10,881	5,721	16,602
Andhra Pradesh	23	19	18	60	94	1,526	909	2,435	6,669	3,992	10,661
Karnataka	27	26	21	78	144	2,832	1,189	4,021	14,184	5,675	19,859
Goa	2	2	1	3	6	100	65	165	475	307	782
Lakshadweep	1	0	0	0	0	0	0	0	0	0	0
Kerala	14	12	14	42	61	1,089	642	1,731	4,892	3,089	7,981
Tamil Nadu	30	21	22	74	62	898	1,200	2,098	3,691	4,855	8,546
Pondicherry	4	1	1	3	3	60	45	105	245	228	473
Andaman and Nicobar	2	0	0	0	0	0	0	0	0	0	0
Total	593	384	276	971	1503	26,734	14,820	41,554	1,43,374	72,380	2,15,754

Source: IHDS 2004–5 data.

Table AI.2 Comparison of New and Re-interview Rural Sample in Districts Where Any Re-interviews Took Place

	New Sample	Re-interview Sample
Individual Characteristics		
Age		
0–4	10	9
5–9	12	11
10–14	12	13
15–19	10	10
20–9	17	16
30–9	14	13
40–59	17	18
60+	8	9
Sex		
Male	51	51
Female	49	49
Education		
Illiterate	44	44
1–4 Std	17	17
5–9 Std	27	27
10–11 Std	6	7
12 Some college	3	3
College graduate	2	2
Household Characteristics		
Social group		
Forward Caste Hindu	16	18
OBC	38	35
Dalit	23	26
Adivasi	12	10
Muslim	9	9
Christian, Sikh, Jain	2	2
Place of Residence		
Metro	0	0
Other urban	1	1
More developed village	50	45
Less developed village	49	54
Maximum Adult Education		
Iliterate	30	29
1–4 Std	10	10

(contd)

(Table AI.2 contd)

	New Sample	Re-interview Sample
5–9 Std	34	33
10–11 Std	11	12
12 Some college	8	8
College graduate	7	8
Household Income		
Negative—Rs 999	3	3
1st Quintile (Rs 1,000–14,000)	27	23
2nd Qunitile (Rs 14,001–22,950)	24	23
3rd Quintile (Rs 22,951–36,097)	19	21
4th Qunitile (Rs 36,098–69,000)	17	18
5th Qunitile (Rs 69,001+)	10	12

Source: IHDS 2004–5 data.

However, a comparison of IHDS data with the NSS (2004–5), *NFHS-III* (2005–6) and Census (2001) presented in Table AI.3 provides considerable reassurance about the robustness of IHDS data. IHDS sample distribution on urban residence, caste, and religion is remarkably similar to NSS and *NFHS-III*, although all three surveys (IHDS, NSS, and *NFHS*) have a higher proportion of households claiming Scheduled Caste status than enumerated in Census. The IHDS has a slightly higher proportion of households falling in Scheduled Caste category and slightly lower proportion in Scheduled Tribe category than NSS or *NFHS*. On other variables of interest, we find literacy and school enrolment in IHDS to be very similar to that in NSS. On work participation rate for males, IHDS falls in between NSS and Census estimates. However, given the special effort made to obtain estimates of women's unpaid work, it is not surprising that IHDS estimates for women's work participation are higher than both NSS and the Census. Family size estimates range from 4.7 in NSS to 5.3 in the Census. The average family size in IHDS was 5.2. Of particular interest is the poverty rate estimated at 25.7 per cent by IHDS, close to 27.5 per cent estimated by NSS. The IHDS records a higher proportion of households owning TV, using electricity and LPG gas than the NSS, possibly due to differences in question wording. But on most other variables, the IHDS results seem to be fairly consistent with the results from other surveys.

However, it is important to note that these broad similarities between IHDS data and other data sources do not remain quite so robust when we look at sub-national levels. Hence, we caution the readers about over interpreting IHDS estimates for statewise or other smaller samples. The IHDS sample sizes are large enough to investigate the general patterns that determine human development outcomes, but if readers desire a precise point estimate of the level of some particular indicator for a sub-sample of the Indian population, they are better referred to sources such as the NSS or the Census.

QUESTIONNAIRE DESIGN

The 100 pages of questions used in IHDS were carefully selected from items successfully administered in previous surveys in India and other developing countries, although some were modified after fielding these in the pre-testing of IHDS questionnaire. Some topics on which IHDS has special perspective (for example, marriage and gender relations) required the development of a new set of questions. But all questions, even those adopted from previous work, went through rigorous pre-testing and screening. The final

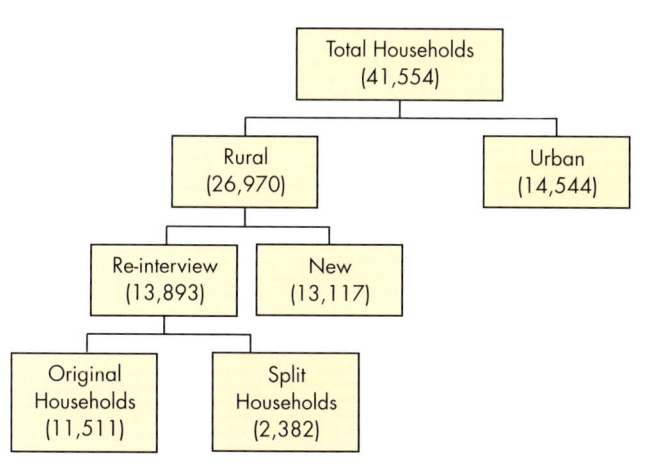

Figure AI.4 Sample Distribution

Note: 276 households were selected as rural but became urban by 2001, bringing the total of urban households to 14,820.

Source: IHDS 2004–5 data.

Table AI.3 Comparison of IHDS Estimates with Other Data Sources

	IHDS 2004–5	NFHS–III 2005–6	NSS 2004–5	Census 2001
Urban	26	31	25	28
Per cent literate				
Age 5+	67	67	66	NA
Age 7+	68	69	67	65
Caste				
Other Backward Classes	42	40	41	NA
Scheduled Castes	21	19	20	16
Scheduled Tribes	7	8	9	8
Other	30	32	31	NA
Religion				
Hindu	80	82	82	81
Muslim	14	13	13	13
Christian	2	3	2	2
Sikh	2	2	2	2
Buddhist	1	1	1	1
Jain	1	1	1	1
Others	2	1	1	1
Per cent currently in school (age 5–14)	80	NA	83	NA
Knowledge of AIDS (women)	54	61	NA	NA
Work participation rate for males	53	NA	55	52
Work participation rate for females	32	NA	29	26
Average family size	5	5	5	5
Number of children ever born to women (age 40–4)	4	4	NA	NA
Number of children ever born to women (age 45–9)	4	4	NA	NA
Per cent women married (age 15–49)	73	75	76	77
Per cent women married (all ages)	48	47	48	48
Per cent electricity	72	68	65	56
Per cent piped water	40	25	41	37
TV ownership (colour or b/w)	48	(Colour) 25	37	24
LPG use	33	25	22	18
Per cent flush toilets	23	NA	19	18
Per cent poor	26	NA	27	NA

Note: NA—not available due to potential measurement errors and/or small sample sizes.
Source: IHDS 2004–5 data.

questionnaires were the result of a careful, often painful, process of selection and revision in order to keep the questions understandable by respondents as well as the interview length manageable, with an eye on minimizing their burden as far as possible, without sacrificing the required detail.

Some parts of the questionnaire attempted to replicate other works as precisely as possible in order to maximize comparability. The consumption questions used for calculation of poverty incidence in Chapter 3, for instance, were copied from the short form of the consumption module developed for NSS employment/unemployment survey. The 61st Round NSS survey was administered in 2004–5, allowing us to test the reliability of the IHDS estimates. One goal of IHDS was to compare a household's relative position on this much used consumption index with data on income and on household amenities, two other measures of economic position. Comparability required replicating the NSS measures as far as possible.

Other parts of the interview borrowed substantially from past work, but had to be adapted to the IHDS format. Reading, writing, and arithmetic tests were developed in conjunction with PRATHAM, although adapted for IHDS use. Since PRATHAM's *Annual Status of Education Report* was prepared in 2005, once again, this allows for considerable data quality evaluation and comparability.

Some often used questions had to be replaced by alternatives that our respondents found more understandable. The social network questions used in analysis, reported in Chapter 13, for example, first used a relational format—with whom do you talk when you seek advice—but were changed to a more direct, although less common positional format—do you know anyone in … which our respondents found easier to answer (and proved to be far more easily coded for analysis).

Some questions, even those used in many previous surveys, proved too ambiguous in pre-testing and had to be deleted altogether because no suitable alternative could be devised. For example, a question on interpersonal trust, one of the most widely cited questions around the globe, asked, 'Would you say that most people can be trusted, or that you need to be careful in dealing with people?' Too many of our pre-test respondents asserted, not unreasonably, that both propositions were true and they could not choose between them.

Where the survey questions are somewhat novel or phrased differently from other comparable surveys, this is clearly identified in relevant discussion of these results. The survey made specific effort at obtaining information on women's and children's work. Building on work done by the International Labour Organisation as well as time allocation studies done in India, special effort was made to determine women's and children's participation in caring for livestock, or in farm related activities. The resultant increase in netting women's work participation is discussed in detail in Chapter 4.

The questions finally fielded in IHDS were organized into two separate questionnaires, household and women. The household questionnaires were administered to the individual most knowledgeable about income and expenditure, frequently the male head of the household. The questionnaire for health and education was administered to a woman in the household, most often the spouse of the household head. Each interview required between 45 minutes and an hour-and-a-half to complete, a length that seemed the outer limits of what we could reasonably ask from our respondents. Questions on fertility, marriage, and gender relations in the households were addressed to an ever-married woman between 15–49 in the household. If no household member could fit the criteria, that portion of the questionnaire was skipped (about 19 per cent of all households). If the household had more than one ever-married woman between 15–49, one woman was selected randomly to answer those questions.

Because IHDS recognizes that all human development is nurtured within a local and institutional context, separate questionnaires were developed to measure village characteristics and to assess the functioning of up to two schools and two medical facilities located within the selected villages. In cases where there were no school and/or medical facilities within the selected village, the nearest school(s) and medical facility or facilities were surveyed. The data generated in the village, school, and medical facilities forms the basis of analysis carried out in Chapter 13.

FIELDWORK

The survey questions were originally drafted in English. However, given the multilingual diversity of India and large disparities in literacy levels, the questionnaires were then translated into Hindi for pre-testing, and then, after revisions, translated from the Hindi and English versions into 11 additional languages. The questionnaires translated in other languages were again pre-tested during training in the respective areas before these were used by the field teams to gather the information.

Fieldwork was performed by 25 agencies throughout the country, selected for their experience with administering large scale scientific surveys. A list of these collaborating organizations is included in Appendix II. The length and diversity of IHDS required more extensive training than is needed for single topic surveys. The NCAER staff, assisted by researchers from the University of Maryland, organized 11 two-week training sessions across the country, each for 15–50 interviewers. Classroom reviews of each questionnaire section alternated with supervised field experience. In addition to written interviewer manuals, training films were developed in which interviewers could see actual survey administration.

Once trained, interviewers went into the field typically in teams of five, two pairs of male and female interviewers and a team leader. The team leader was responsible for supervising and assisting with the household interviews and usually conducted the village, school, and medical facility interviews. After arriving at a PSU, the team would contact local leaders to describe the survey, secure permissions, and develop a map of the area. Urban neighbourhoods and new villages selected in IHDS first required creation of a sampling frame. Large villages were divided into hamlets, or sections within the village, and two opposite sections were randomly selected for complete canvassing. Villages interviewed in the 1994 HDPI did not require canvassing and sampling, but the previous households had to be tracked, each member accounted for, and split households located.

Once the sample had been drawn or the 1993–4 HDPI households located, pairs of interviewers began arranging interviews. After obtaining consent, the household roster was filled out in duplicate. Separate households were defined as people living under one roof and sharing the same kitchen. Joint families often required specific probing since two married brothers might share the same dwelling but maintain separate kitchens and food budgets. Absent family members had to be identified as either temporarily absent household members (that is, living outside the household for less than six months), or residents of other households (for example, students living in nearby towns to pursue their education).

Once the household roster was completed, the two copies were divided between the two interviewers, and the female interviewer then completed the education and health questionnaire, usually with the help from a senior woman in the household. If the household included more than one eligible woman for the marriage and fertility sections, one was selected using a standard random number procedure. After completing the two main household interviews, the interviewers administered the learning tests to any child in the age group 8–11 years, and his/her height and weight measurements were taken. Often, more than one visit was needed to complete all sections of the household interview.

Completed interviews were checked by the team supervisor, rechecked by the agency coordinator and sent to NCAER headquarters in New Delhi, where editing staff again reviewed the skip patterns, looked for missing data, and checked coding. These multilevel reviews enabled prompt identification of problems and feedback to the interview teams. The NCAER also maintained its own field staff in each state for random re-interview checks for data quality and for troubleshooting of problems encountered by interview teams. Phone contact between agency field staff and NCAER headquarters also resolved many issues before they became major problems.

Data entry was centralized at NCAER's New Delhi offices and was undertaken as completed interviews arrived. The questionnaire form was mostly self-coded for ease of data entry. The 1,400 variables from the household interview were checked for consistency (for example, no five-year old mothers of three children) and problems resolved by consulting the originally filled questionnaire, or occasionally telephone calls back to the interview site. The main data files are publicly available for downloading and further analyses by all interested scholars. IHDS should become a premier resource for understanding the complexities of the human development process.

PUBLIC USE DATA

Data from IHDS 2005 are publicly available for free download from http://www.icpsr.umich.edu/cocoon/DSDR/STUDY/22626.xml. More information about the survey is available at www.ihds.umd.edu.

Appendix II—Chapter Organization and Definition of Variables

CHAPTER ORGANIZATION

Each of the chapters in this book reviews a major topic within the ambit of human development: income, education, health, social integration, and so on. Each topic has some issues specific to it (for example, marriage relations in Chapter 10). A few issues span more than one topic. For example, privatization is discussed in Chapters 4, 6, and 7. But as discussed in the introduction, a principal integrating theme is to review how these human development outcomes vary across a common set of social and economic determinants. Individual outcomes (for example, wages, employment, and morbidity) are compared along three characteristics of those individuals:

1. Gender
2. Age
3. Own education (adults only)

All individual and household outcomes are compared across five regional and household characteristics:

1. States
2. Rural–urban residence
3. Household income
4. Household educational level[1]
5. Religious and caste social group

The following section describes how each of these eight indicators is constructed, their distribution across India, and relationship with the other indicators. The sample distributions and interrelationships are presented in Table AII.1.

BACKGROUND CHARACTERISTICS

Gender

Each of the individual characteristics (that is, gender, age, and education) was reported by the main household respondent. This results in some imprecision pertaining to age and education, including the usual age heaping at round figure ages (20, 30, and so on). Some corrections have been made based on other information in the survey (for example, birth histories) but for comparisons of most human development outcomes, even imprecise measures are sufficient to reveal the strong patterns.

Measurement problems are not an issue for gender, although difficulties in locating transient and homeless populations may result in an undercount of men. India is well known for its imbalanced sex ratios and missing women. The IHDS also recorded fewer females than males, especially among the younger age groups, for whom the effects of sex selective abortions have become more apparent. The dynamics of gender inequality underlying these imbalanced

---

[1] Household educational level is used only for household level outcomes since individual outcomes are compared against the individual's own education.

Table AII.1 Sample Distribution Along Individual and Household Background Characteristics

	Rural	Urban	Total
Individual Characteristics			
Age			
0–4	10	8	9
5–9	12	10	11
10–14	12	11	12
15–19	10	11	10
20–9	16	19	17
30–9	13	15	14
40–59	18	20	18
60+	9	7	8
Sex			
Male	51	51	51
Female	49	49	49
Education			
Illiterate	44	26	39
1–4 Std	17	14	16
5–9 Std	27	30	28
10–11 Std	6	12	8
12 Some college	3	8	5
College graduate	2	10	4
Household Characteristics			
Social Group			
Forward Caste Hindu	16	31	21
OBC	38	31	36
Dalit	24	17	22
Adivasi	10	3	8
Muslim	10	14	11
Christian, Sikh, Jain	2	4	3
Place of Residence			
Metro		26	8
Other urban		74	21
More developed village	48		34
Less developed village	52		37
Maximum Adult Education in Household			
Illiterate	29	10	24
1–4 Std	10	5	8
5–9 Std	33	28	32

(contd)

(Table AII.1 contd)

	Rural	Urban	Total
10–11 Std	12	17	14
12 Some college	8	13	10
College graduate	8	27	13
Household Income			
Negative Rs 999	3	1	2
1st Quintile (Rs 1,000–14,000)	25	6	20
2nd Quintile (Rs 14,001–22,950)	23	10	19
3rd Quintile (Rs 22,951–36,097)	20	19	20
4th Quintile (Rs 36,098–69,000)	17	26	20
5th Quintile (Rs 69,001+)	12	38	19

Source: IHDS 2004–5 data.

sex ratios are examined in Chapters 8 and 10. Because women and men live in the same households, they don't differ greatly on household characteristics (although, somewhat more women live in low income households). Individual differences are substantial, however, as will be seen throughout the remaining chapters. Men average 5.1 years of education, for instance, compared to women's 3.6 years.

Age

India's fertility decline is fairly recent, so India is still a young country. Forty five per cent of IHDS household members are under 21. The young are somewhat more concentrated in poorer states, where the fertility decline has been the weakest, and in poorer households. There are more elderly (age 60 or more) in states with an early fertility decline (for example, Kerala), or where out-migration of the working age population leaves a higher concentration of the elderly (for example, Himachal Pradesh). Their well-being receives attention in Chapter 9. Age is inversely correlated with years of schooling since education has expanded manifold since independence. This correlation needs to be kept in mind in evaluating some tables since several human development outcomes tend to increase with both more education, and older ages.

Education

Education is one of the most consistent predictors of favourable human development outcomes. Everything from incomes to health to social connections is higher among the better educated. Because of educational expansion, India has many highly qualified graduates whose future is promising. The country also still has many illiterates whose struggles are often poorly rewarded. The tables that follow divide years of education into groups, according to the school system's natural break points. More than two in five adults have had no schooling. A small group, 9 per cent, started primary school without finishing. Over a quarter of adults finished primary school without completing secondary school. Almost a quarter of adults, however, have completed their 10th Standard. Ten per cent finished at that level, 6 per cent finished higher secondary school, and 7 per cent are college graduates.

Higher levels of education are more common among every advantaged group. Urban residents are more educated than rural residents. High income households have more educated members than poor households. Forward castes and non-Muslim minority religions have considerably more education, on an average, than other groups while Dalits and Adivasis have the least. Some of the many advantages of urban, affluent, forward castes result from their higher education, but some part of their higher education results from their many other advantages.

States

Regional inequalities have provoked a growing debate as parts of India have grown especially rapidly in recent years. Differences across states are a recurring theme in IHDS results, often overwhelming differences by class and social group. But there are limitations to the extent of state differences that can be reliably reported. The survey was fielded in thirty three states and union territories.

Sample sizes vary substantially across these states and territories (see Table AI.1). Care must always be taken not to rely too heavily on the position of any one state in the distribution of state outcomes. Sampling errors almost always overlap between states with similar positions on any human development measure. Rather, much of the usefulness of state differences is to observe the pattern of state differences, rich versus poor, north versus south, and high versus low education.

While we report statewise results even for some samples that are quite small (for example, Uttarakhand), some of the union territories and states have samples too small to reliably report separate results. Therefore, these smaller samples had to be combined with neighbouring areas for reporting purposes (for example, Goa with Maharashtra). All the smaller north-eastern states (Arunachal Pradesh, Manipur, Meghalaya, Tripura, and so on) are reported as a single entity. These states share some common features, but are quite heterogeneous on many other dimensions. The other smaller states and territories were combined with larger neighbours, Chandigarh with Punjab, Daman and Diu, and Dadra and Nagar Haveli with Gujarat, Goa with Maharashtra, and, Pondicherry with Tamil Nadu. The Delhi sample is large enough to report separately for most purposes, but the rural sample in Delhi is based on only seven semi-urban villages, so Delhi is not reported separately for agricultural and other rural totals.

This organization leaves 22 'states' that are compared in each of the main chapters. For consistency, they are always reported in the same order rather than, for instance, from high to low on any outcome. Development is one common, but far from universal pattern distinguishing the 22 states. Urbanization, income, and education, is a coherent package that distinguishes states like Delhi and Kerala from states like Orissa and Jharkhand. There are exceptions, even within this development cluster, but it will be useful to think of this as one (among several) organizing principle for regional inequalities. However, other outcomes demonstrate quite a different pattern. Some social groups have strong state associations (for example, Muslims in Jammu and Kashmir; Christians in the North-East) but these are not usually development related (although tribal population more often reside in rural, less developed states and Sikhs in the wealthy Punjab). Some dimensions of gender inequality also cross-cut development levels. For example, unbalanced sex ratios are found in wealthy Punjab and poor Uttar Pradesh while more balanced sex ratios are found in affluent Kerala and poorer Orissa. The lesson here is that development levels are an important, but not the only dimension along which states in India differ.

Rural–Urban Residence

Village to city differences are a second type of regional inequality generally thought to be growing in recent years. Urban residents have higher incomes, their children stay in school longer, and when sick they have better access to medical care. While India has been slowly urbanizing throughout the last century, the pace of urbanization is only modest by world standards. In 2005, India had forty one urban areas with over a million population, while China had ninety five. Villages still hold much staying power, and even urban migrants maintain ties with their native villages. The perception of growing rural–urban disparities could threaten this stability.

The IHDS uses the Census 2001 definitions which classify as urban, places with a population of 5,000 or more and where most male employment is outside agriculture.[2] According to the 2001 Census, 28 per cent of India was urban. The IHDS slightly over sampled (34 per cent) urban areas but all analyses have been weighted back to the Census proportions.

Both urban and rural areas encompass great diversity. India's major metropolitan areas are the global cities. Mumbai's Bollywood is familiar to most of the world, Bangalore's IT industry, and Chennai's call centres daily influence the lives of millions of people outside India. At the other end of the spectrum, thousands of small towns are barely distinguishable from large villages. To capture these differences, IHDS reports urban results in two categories. The six largest metropolitan areas[3] (Mumbai, Kolkata, Delhi, Chennai, Hyderabad, and Bangalore) account for 7 per cent and all the other urban areas combined account for 21 per cent. Similarly, some villages have substantial infrastructure, paved roads with easy access to urban centres, postal and telephone connections, electricity to power lights, and televisions. Others lack most of the conveniences of modern life and can be reached only by narrow footpaths. In some cases one even has to use unconventional means like camel or boat. The IHDS divides villages into two approximately equal groups according to an index of infrastructural development described in the Chapter 12. The more developed villages generally appear closer to urban areas on most human development outcomes.

As discussed in Chapters 2 and 6, town, and especially metropolitan households, have higher incomes and education than rural households. This conflation of causal influences

---

[2] The official Census definition of an urban area is (a) All statutory places with a municipality, corporation, cantonment board, or notified town area committee, etc., or (b) A place satisfying the following three criteria simultaneously: i) a minimum population of 5,000, ii) at least 75 per cent of male working population engaged in non-agricultural pursuits, and iii) a density of population of at least 400 per sq. km (1,000 per sq. mile).

[3] The IHDS loosely follows the Census definitions of Urban Agglomeration which include areas outside the official municipal boundaries, but which are integrated into the urban core. All urban residents in districts identified as part of the urban agglomeration are counted as living in the metropolitan area. Census rules do not allow urban agglomerations to cross state boundaries, but we have included Gurgaon (Haryana), Ghaziabad, and Gautam Buddha Nagar (Uttar Pradesh) districts with the Delhi metropolitan area.

will often require that we look jointly at residence and socio-economic position in the chapters that follow to sort out which aspects of human development are specifically related to urbanization and which are a result of greater affluence and education. Urban areas also differ on their caste and religious composition. Forward castes and minority religions are especially concentrated in urban areas. Dalits and, especially, Adivasis are more rural.

Income

The IHDS is one of the first major Indian survey to measure detailed income. The NSS measures consumption expenditures and the *NFHS* measures the ownership of consumer goods. The IHDS measured these too. Each provides a somewhat different aspect of economic position, but is closely related. The details of their measurement and their inter-relationships are described in Chapters 2 and 5. The IHDS measure of income is summed across over 50 separate components including wages and salaries, net farm income, family business net income, property, and pension incomes.

The average Indian household had an annual income of Rs 27,857 in 2004. But because some households earned much more than this median, the mean was Rs 47,804. For all tables, households are divided into five quintiles with cutting points at 14,000, 22,950, 36,098, and 69,000. A small number of households (2 per cent) reported negative or very low incomes because of agricultural or business losses. Although these households are undergoing current economic distress, in many other ways (for example, consumer goods owned, educational levels, and so on) they appear more like moderate income households rather than poor households in the bottom quintile. They have, therefore, been excluded from the income tables, but are included in other analyses.

The income quintiles used throughout these reports do not vary across urban and rural areas, or across states, and, consequently, they do not adjust for price differences. Urban–rural price differences can be as large as 15 per cent.

Household Education

Many of the human development outcomes described in the previous chapters benefit the entire household. An indoor water tap, access to nearby medical clinics, and connections to government officials are resources the entire household can take advantage of. To see how these advantages are related to educational levels, the tables use a measure of the highest adult (that is, age 21 or older) education in the household, when appropriate.[4] The same schooling categories are used as for individual education, but the distribution is higher. Only a quarter of Indian households have no adult without any formal education, but 37 per cent have an adult who has matriculated, 10th Standard, or gone further. At the top, 13 per cent of households have an adult with a college degree. This measure of household education is associated with the same advantages as individual education. Urban residence, higher incomes, and forward castes are more common in well educated households. Note that the household educational attainment is greater than the individual one since household level education is based on highest education for any household member.

Social Groups

Perhaps no other country in the world offers such a rich diversity of religions, castes, ethnic, and linguistic identities, as it is found in India. Any useable grouping for a review of human development is bound to ignore important distinctions that the people themselves would never overlook. The tables here follow a six-fold classification:

1. Forward Castes
2. Other Backward Castes (OBC)
3. Dalits (Scheduled Castes)
4. Adivasis (Scheduled Tribes)
5. Muslims
6. Other Minority Religions (Christians, Sikhs, Buddhists, Jains)

The obvious question for such a scheme is where one classifies Muslim OBCs, Christian Adivasis, Sikh Dalits, and other groups, that easily fit more than one category. Muslim OBCs differ from Hindu OBCs and from other Muslims on most human development outcomes, and, likewise, for Christian Adivasis, Sikh Dalits, and other groups. Independent religion and caste classifications would avoid these ambiguities, but would create too many categories for the compact presentation needed here. The compromise result is this six category scheme described in Figure AII.1. More detailed classifications are available from the public data for analysts requiring more precision. Our construction of socio-religious categories has two major implications that must be kept in mind. First, 2,014 Muslim families, who classify themselves as OBCs form about 4.6 per cent of the total population, are included with Muslims rather than OBCs. Second, the inclusion of Christian, Sikh, and Buddhist Scheduled Caste families with Dalits and Adivasis, according to their self-classification, reduces the group classified as other minority religions from 6.29 per cent of the total population to 2.70 per cent (Figure AII.1).

---

[4] In households without any adult 21 years or older, the highest education is substituted.

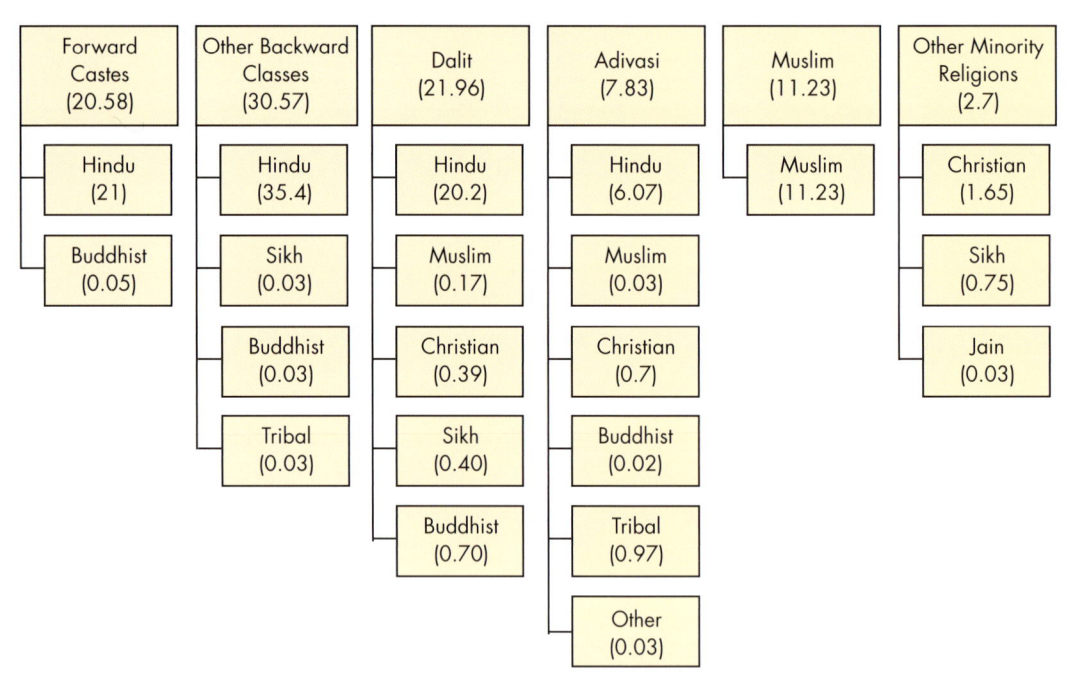

```
Forward Castes (20.58)          Other Backward Classes (30.57)    Dalit (21.96)         Adivasi (7.83)        Muslim (11.23)    Other Minority Religions (2.7)
    |                                |                                |                        |                    |                     |
  Hindu (21)                      Hindu (35.4)                    Hindu (20.2)            Hindu (6.07)          Muslim (11.23)       Christian (1.65)
    |                                |                                |                        |                                          |
  Buddhist (0.05)                 Sikh (0.03)                     Muslim (0.17)           Muslim (0.03)                              Sikh (0.75)
                                     |                                |                        |                                          |
                                  Buddhist (0.03)                 Christian (0.39)        Christian (0.7)                            Jain (0.03)
                                     |                                |                        |
                                  Tribal (0.03)                   Sikh (0.40)             Buddhist (0.02)
                                                                      |                        |
                                                                  Buddhist (0.70)         Tribal (0.97)
                                                                                               |
                                                                                          Other (0.03)
```

Figure AII.1 Socio-religious Group Categorization (in percentage)

Note: 276 households were selected as rural but became urban by 2001, bringing the total of urban households to 14,820.
Source: IHDS 2004–5 data.

Religion and caste classifications are based on the main respondent's self-identification. Self-identification yields somewhat different information from official data which use detailed but statewise government schedules. The official schedules often miss migrants from other states. Self-identification also encourages marginal groups to claim scheduled caste or tribe membership in order to qualify for government reservations. As a result the IHDS ends up with somewhat higher proportions of the population as Dalits and Adivasis than the Census figures, and slightly higher than the NSS.

The groups differ greatly on almost every measure of economic and social standing. Forward castes and non-Muslim minority religions are more urban, educated, and wealthy. Dalits and Adivasis are more often rural, illiterate, and poor. The OBCs are somewhere in between, but usually closer to Dalits than to forward castes. Muslims are also somewhere in between, but much closer to Dalits in education, closer to forward castes in urbanization, and in between on incomes, but slightly better off than the OBCs. These groups differ also on most of the human development outcomes we review in the previous chapters. Sometimes these differences are a result of the economic, educational, and regional differences, but sometimes some group differences remain even when comparing otherwise equivalent households.

Bibliography

Abbas, A.A. and G.J. Walker (1986). 'Determinants of the Utilization of Maternal and Child Health Services in Jordan', *International Journal of Epidemiology*, 15(3): 404–7.

Abdelrahman, A.I. and S.P. Morgan (1987). 'Socioeconomic and Institutional Correlates of Family Formation: Khartoum, Sudan, 1945–75', *Journal of Marriage and the Family*, 49(2): 401–12.

Abler, D.G., G.S. Tolley, and G.S. Kirpalani (1994). *Technical Change and Income Distribution in Indian Agriculture*, Boulder, Colorado, Westview Press.

Acharya, M. and L. Bennett (1983). *Women and Subsistence Sector: Economic Participation and Household Decision Making in Nepal*, World Bank Staff Working Papers No. 526, Washington DC, World Bank.

Adams, A. and S. Castle (1994). 'Gender Relations and Social Dynamics' in G. Sen and A. Germain (eds), Population Policies Reconsidered: Health, Empowerment, and Rights. Boston, Harvard School of Public Health.

Adams, B.N. (2004). 'Families and Family Study in International Perspective', *Journal of Marriage and the Family*, 66(5): 1076–88.

Adnett, N. (2004). 'Private-Sector Provision of Schooling: An Economic Assessment', *Comparative Education*, 40(3): 385–99.

Aga Khan Foundation (2007). *Non-state Providers and Public-Private-Community Partnerships in Education—Contributions towards Achieving EFA: A Critical Review of Challenges, Opportunities and Issues*, Background paper for EFA *Global Monitoring Report 2008*.

Agarwal, B. (1994). *A Field of One's Own: Gender and Land Rights in South Asia*, Cambridge, Cambridge University Press.

Agarwala, R. and S.M. Lynch (2006). 'Refining the Measurement of Women's Autonomy: An International Application of a Multidimensional Construct', *Social Forces*, 84(4): 2077–99.

Agarwala, S.N. (1957). 'The Age at Marriage in India', *Population Index*, 23(2): 96–107.

Aghion, P. and J.G. Williamson (1998). *Growth, Inequality and Globalization: Theory, History and Policy*. Cambridge, Cambridge University Press.

Agnes, F. (1999). *Law and Gender Inequality: The Politics of Women's Rights in India*, New Delhi, Oxford University Press.

Ahluwalia, M.S. (1978). *Rural Poverty in India: 1956–57 to 1973–74*, World Bank Staff Working Paper, Washington DC.

Ahmed, A.U. (2004). *Impact of Feeding Children in School: Evidence from Bangladesh*, Washington DC, International Food Policy Research Institute.

——— (2005). *Comparing Food and Cash Incentives for Schooling in Bangladesh*, Washington DC, International Food Policy Research Institute.

Ainsworth, J.W. (2002). 'Why Does It Take a Village? The Mediation of Neighbourhood Effects on Educational Achievement', *Social Forces*, 81(1): 117–52.

Alam, M. and S.N. Mishra (1998). 'Structural Reforms and Employment Issues in India: A Case of Industrial Labor', *Indian Journal of Labour Economics,* 41(2): 71–92.

Alcázar, L., F.H. Rogers, N. Chaudhury, J. Hammer, M. Kremer, and K. Muralidharan (2006). 'Why are Teachers Absent? Probing Service Delivery in Peruvian Primary Schools', *International Journal of Educational Research*, 45(3): 117–36.

Alderman, H., J.R. Behrman, D.R. Ross, and R. Sabot (1996). 'Decomposing the Gender Gap in Cognitive Skills in a Poor Rural Economy', *The Journal of Human Resources*, 31(1): 229–54.

Alderman, H., P.F. Orazem, and E.M. Paterno (2001). 'School Quality, School Cost, and the Public/Private School Choices of Low-Income Households in Pakistan', *The Journal of Human Resources*, 36(2): 304–26.

Altonji, J.G., F. Hayashi, and L.J. Kotlikoff (1992). 'Is the Extended Family Altruistically Linked? Direct Tests Using Micro Data', *The American Economic Association*, 82 (5): 1177–98.

Anand, S. (1991). *Poverty and Human Development in Asia and The Pacific*, New York, United Nations Development Programme, pp. 1–39.

Anand, S. and A. Sen (1993). 'Human Development Index: Methodology and Measurement,' Human Development Report Office, Occasional Paper 12, New York, United Nations Development Programme.

——— (2000). 'The Income Component of the Human Development Index', *Journal of Human Development, 2000*, 1(1): 88–106.

Andersen, R.M. (1995). 'Revisiting the Behavioral Model and Access to Medical Care: Does it Matter?', *Journal of Health and Social Behavior*, 36(1): 1–10.

Angrist, J., E. Bettinger, E. Bloom, E. King, and M. Kremer (2002). 'Vouchers for Private Schooling in Colombia: Evidence from a

Randomized Natural Experiment', *The American Economic Review*, 92(5): 1535–58.

Anitha, B.K. (2000). *Village, Caste and Education*, Delhi, Rawat Publication.

Anker, R. (1998). *Gender and Jobs: Sex Segregation of Occupations in the World*, Geneva, International Labour Office.

Aradhya, N. and A. Kashyap (2006). *The 'Fundamentals': Right to Education in India*, Bangalore, Books for Change.

Araujo, M.C. and N. Schady (2006). *Cash Transfers, Conditions, School Enrollment, and Child Work: Evidence from a Randomized Experiment in Ecuador*, Washington DC, World Bank. (Policy Research Working Paper, 3930).

Arnold, F., M.K. Choe, and T.K. Roy (1998). 'Son Preference, the Family-Building Process and Child Mortality in India', *Population Studies*, 52(3): 301–15.

Arrow, K., S. Bowles, and S. Durlauf (2000). *Meritocracy and Economic Ineqaulity*, Princeton, Princeton University Press.

Arum, R. (2000). 'Schools and Communities: Ecological and Institutional Dimensions', *Annual Review of Sociology*, 26: 395–418.

Arya, S. and A. Roy (eds) (2006). *Poverty, Gender and Migration*, New Delhi, Sage Publications.

Asian Development Bank [ADB] (2007). *Key Indicators 2007: Inequality in Asia*, Manila, ADB.

Bailey, F.G. (1957). *Caste and Economic Frontier*, Manchester, Manchester University Press.

Bairagi, R. (1986). 'Food Crisis, Nutrition, and Female Children in Rural Bangladesh', *Population and Development Review*, 12(2): 307–15.

Bajos, N. and J. Marquet (2000). 'Research on HIV Sexual Risk: Social Relations-Based Approach in a Cross-Cultural Perspective', *Social Science & Medicine*, 50(11): 1533–46.

Balk, D. (1997). 'Defying Gender Norms in Rural Bangladesh: A Social Demographic Analysis', *Population Studies*, 51(2): 153–72.

Ban, R. and V. Rao (2008). 'Tokenism or Agency? The Impact of Women's Reservations on Village Democracies in South India', *Economic Development and Cultural Change*, 56: 501–30.

Bandura, A. (1993). 'Perceived Self Efficacy in Cognitive Development and Functioning', *Educational Psychologist*, (28): 117–48.

Banerjee, A. and L. Iyer (2005). 'History, Institutions, and Economic Performance: The Legacy of Colonial Land Tenure Systems in India', *The American Economic Review*, 95(4): 1190–1213.

Banerjee, A., S. Rohini, and L. Iyer (2005). 'History, Social Divisions and Public Goods in Rural India', *Journal of the European Economic Association*, 3(2–3): 639–47.

Banerjee, A.V., S. Cole, E. Duflo, and L. Linden (2007). 'Remedying Education: Evidence from Two Randomized Experiments in India', *Quarterly Journal of Economics*, 122(3): 1235–64.

Banerjee, A., R. Somnathan, and L. Iyer (2005). 'History, Social Divisions and Public Goods in Rural India', *Journal of the European Economic Association* 3(2–3): pp. 639–47.

Bardhan, P. (1984). *Land, Labor and Rural Poverty*, New York, Columbia University Press.

——— (1973). 'The Incidence of Rural Poverty in the Sixties', *Economic and Political Weekly*, February : 245–54.

Bardhan, P.K. and T.N. Srinivasan (1974). *Poverty and Income Distribution in India*, Calcutta, Statistical Publishing Society.

Barnes, D.F. (ed.) (2007). *The Challenge of Rural Electrification: Strategies for Developing countries*. Washington DC: Resources for the Future Press.

Barnes, D.F. and M. Sen (2004). *The Impact of Energy on Women's Lives in Rural India*. Washington DC. The World Bank.

Basant, R. and A. Shariff (eds) (2009). *Oxford Handbook of Muslims in India: Empirical and Policy Perspectives*. New Delhi, Oxford University Press.

Basu, A. (1998). 'Appropriating Gender', in P. Jeffrey and A. Basu (eds), *Appropriating Gender: Women's Activism and Politicized Religion in South Asia*. New York, Routledge.

Basu, A.M. (1990). 'Cultural Influences on Health Care Use: Two Regional Groups in India', *Studies in Family Planning*, 21(5): 275–86.

——— (1993). 'Cultural Influences on the Timing of First Births in India: Large Differences that add up to Little Difference'. *Population Studies*, 47(1): 85–95.

Basu, A.M. and G.B. Koolwal (2005). 'Two Concepts of Female Empowerment: Some Leads from DHS Data on Women's Status and Reproductive Health', in S. Kishor (ed.), *A Focus on Gender: Collected Papers on Gender using DHS Data*. Calverton Maryland, ORC Macro: pp. 15–54.

Basu, K. (1994). *Agrarian Questions*, New Delhi, Oxford University Press.

——— (ed.) (2007). *Oxford Companion to Economics in India*. New Delhi, Oxford University Press.

Bayly, S. (1999). *Caste, Society and Politics in India from the Eighteenth Century to The Modern Age*, Cambridge, Cambridge University Press.

Bedi, A.S. and J.H.Y. Edwards (2002). 'The Impact of School Quality on Earnings and Educational Returns: Evidence from a Low-Income Country', *Journal of Development Economics*, 68: 157–85.

Beegle, K. (2008). 'Health Facility and School Surveys in the Indonesia Family Life Survey', in S. Amin, J. Das, and M. Goldstein (eds), *Are You Being Served? New Tools for Measuring Service Delivery*. Washington DC: The World Bank: pp. 343–64.

Beegle, K., E. Frankenberg, and D. Thomas (2001). 'Bargaining Power within Couples and Use of Prenatal and Delivery Care in Indonesia', *Studies in Family Planning*, 32(2): 130–46.

Bella, N. and H. Mputu (2004). 'Dropout in Primary and Secondary: A Global Issue and an Obstacle to the Achievement of the Education for All Goals', *The International Journal on School Disaffection*, 2(2): 14–30.

Berman, J. (1974). *Patronage and Exploitation: Changing Agrarian Relations in South Gujarat, India*, Berkelely, California, University of California Press.

Berreman, G. D. (1991). 'The Brahmanical view of Caste' in D. Gupta (ed.), *Social Stratification*. New Delhi, Oxford University Press.

Besley, T. and R. Burgess (2000). 'Land Reform, Poverty Reduction, and Growth: Evidence from India', *Quarterly Journal of Economics*, 115(2): 389–430.

Beteille, A. (1969). *Castes: Old and New, Essays in Social Structure and Social Stratification*, Bombay, Asia Publishing House.

——— (1990). 'Race, Caste and Gender', *Man*, 25(3): 489–504.

——— (1992a). 'Caste and Family: In Representations of Indian Society', *Anthropology Today*, 8(1): 13–18.

——— (1992b). *The Backward Classes in Contemporary India*, New Delhi, Oxford University Press.

——— (1996). *Caste, Class and Power: Changing Patterns of Stratification in a Tanjore Village*, New Delhi, Oxford University Press.

Bhagwati, J. (1993). *India in Transition: Freeing the Economy*, Oxford, Clarendon Press.

Bhalla, Surjit, Singh (2002). 'Growth and Poverty in India—Myth and Reality', in Govinda Rao (ed.), *Poverty and Public Policy: Essays in Honour of Raja Chelliah* (forthcoming).

Bhargava, A. (2006). 'Desired Family Size, Family Planning and Fertility in Ethiopia', *Journal of Biosocial Science*, 39: 367–81.

Bhasin, V. (2007). 'Status of Tribal Women in India', *Studies on Home and Community Science*, 1(1): 1–16.

Bliss, C. and N. Stern (1976). *Economic Aspects of the Connection Between Productivity and Consumption*, University of Essex, Department of Economics, Discussion Paper No. 67, October.

Bloch, F., V. Rao, and S. Desai (2004). 'Wedding Celebrations as Conspicuous Consumption: Signaling Social Status in Rural India.' *The Journal of Human Resources*, 39(3): 675–95.

Blyn, G. (1966). *Agricultural Trends in India 1891–1947: Output, Availability and Productivity*, Philadelphia, University of Pennsylvania Press.

Boserup, E. (1970). *Woman's Role in Economic Development*, London, George Allen and Unwin.

——— (1976). 'Environment, Population, and Technology in Primitive Societies', *Population and Development Review*, 2(1): 21–36.

Boyden, J., B. Ling, and W. Myers (1998). *What Works for Working Children?* Stockholm and Florence, Italy, Rädda Barnen and UNICEF, International Child Development Centre.

Breman, J. (2007). *Poverty Regime in Village India*, New Delhi, Oxford University Press.

Brett, E.A. (1993). 'Voluntary Agencies as Development Organizations: Theorizing the Problem of Efficiency and Accountability', *Development and Change*, 24: 269–303.

Briscoe, J. (1984). 'Water Supply and Health in Developing Countries: Selective Primary Health Care Revisited', *American Journal of Public Health*, 74: 1009–13.

Broehl Jr, W.G., (1978). *The Village Entrepreneur: Change Agents in India's Rural Development*, Cambridge, Mass., Harvard University Press.

Brown, B.B. (1983). 'The Impact of Male Labour Migration on Women in Botswana', *African Affairs*, 82(328): 367–88.

Brown, S. and K. Taylor (2005). *Household Debt and Financial Assets: Evidence from Great Britain, Germany and the United States*, Discussion Papers in Economics 05/5, Department of Economics, University of Leicester.

Buvinic, M., M.A. Lycette, and W.P. McGreevey (eds) (1983). Women and Poverty in the Third World, Baltimore, The Johns Hopkins University Press.

Byers, T.J. (1998). *The Indian Economy: Major Debates Since Independence*, New Delhi, Oxford University Press.

——— (1998). *The State, Development Planning and Liberalisation in India*, New Delhi, Oxford University Press.

Cameron, L.A., J.M. Dowling, and C.Worswick (2001). 'Education and Labor Market Participation of Women in Asia: Evidence from Five Countries', *Economic Development and Cultural Change*, 49(3): 460–77.

Cassen, R. and V. Joshi (1995). *India: The Future of Economic Reform*, New Delhi, Oxford University Press.

Census of India (2001a). *Atlas of Indian Household Amenities and Assets*, www.geodemo.net/cs2/.../atlasamenities2001/...atlas/atlas.html.

——— (2001b). *Tables on Houses, Household Amenities and Assets Vol. 3*, www.nuepa.org/libdoc/nbm.html.

Chatterjee, G.S. and N. Bhattacharya (1974). 'Between State Variations in Consumer Prices and Per Capital Household Expenditure', in T.N. Srinivasan and P.K. Bardhan (eds), *Poverty and Income Distribution in India*, Calcutta, Statistical Publishing Society.

Chaudhuri, P. (1993). 'Changing Perception of Poverty in India: State and Poverty', *The Indian Journal of Statistics*, 55(3): 310–21.

Chaudhury, N., J. Hammer, M. Kremer, K. Muralidharan, and F. Halsey Rogers (2006). 'Missing in Action: Teacher and Health Worker Absence in Developing Countries', *Journal of Economic Perspectives*, 20: 91–116.

Chen, D.H.C. (2004). *Gender Equality and Economic Development: The Role for Information and Communication Technologies*, Washington DC, World Bank.

Chen, M.A. (2000). *Perpetual Mourning: Widowhood in Rural India*. New York, Oxford University Press.

Chhibbar, Y.P. (1968). *From Caste to Class: A Study of the Indian Middle Classes*, New Delhi, Associated Publishing House.

Chhiber, V. (2003). *Locked in Place: State Building and Late Industrialization in India*. Princeton, New Jersey, Princeton University Press.

Chibber, P. and I. Nooruddin (2004). 'Do Party Systems Count? The Number of Parties and Government Performance in the Indian States', in *Comparative Political Studies*, 37: pp. 152–87.

Cigno, A., F. Rosati, and L. Guarcello (2002). 'Does Globalization Increase Child Labor?', *World Development*, 30 (9): 1579–89.

Coady, D.P. (2004). *Designing And Evaluating Social Safety Nets: Theory, Evidence, and Policy Conclusions*, Discussion Paper No. 172, Washington DC, International Food Policy Research Institute.

Crompton, R. and K. Sanderson (1990). *Gendered Jobs and Social Change*, London, Unwin Hyman.

Crook, N. and T. Dyson (1982). 'Urbanization in India: Results of the 1981 Census', *Population and Development Review*, 8(1): 145–55.

Dandekar, V.M. (1996). *Indian Economy 1947–92: Population Poverty and Employment*, New Delhi, Sage Publications.

Dandekar, V.M. and N. Rath (1971). 'Poverty in India-1: Dimensions and Trends', *Economic and Political Weekly*, January: 25–146.

Dantwala, M.L. (1950). 'India's Progress in Agrarian Reforms', *Far Eastern Survey*, 19(22): 239–44.

Das Gupta, M. (1995). 'Life Course Perspectives on Women's Autonomy and Health Outcomes', *American Anthropologist*, 97(3): 481–91.

——— (1997). 'Socio-Economic Status and Clustering of Child Deaths in Rural Punjab', *Population Studies*, 51(2): 191–202.

Das, J., J. Hammer, and K. Leonard (2008). 'The Quality of Medical Advice in Low-Income Countries', *Journal of Economic Perspectives*, 22: 93–114.

Das, M.B. (2005). 'Muslim Women's Low Labour Force Participation in India: Some Structural Explanations', in Z. Hasan and R. Menon (eds), *In A Minority: Essays on Muslim Women in India*, New Delhi, Oxford University Press.

Das, M.B. and P.V. Datta (2007). *Does Caste Matter for Wages in the Indian Labor Market?*, Washington DC, World Bank.

Das, V. (ed.) (2003). *Handbook of Indian Sociology*. New Delhi, Oxford University Press.

Datt, G. and M. Ravallion (1998). 'Why Have Some Indian States Done Better Than Others at Reducing Rural Poverty?', *Economica*, 65(257): 17–38.

de Haan, A. and B. Rogly (eds) (2002). *Labour Mobility and Rural Society*, London, Frank Cass.

De Janvry, A. and K. Subbarao (1986). *Agricultural Price Policy and Income Distribution in India*, New Delhi, Oxford University Press.

Deaton, A. (2003). 'Adjusted Indian Poverty Estimates for 1999–2000', *Economic and Political Weekly*, (January 25): 322–6.

Deaton, A. and J. Drèze (2002). 'Poverty and Inequality in India', *Economic and Political Weekly*, 37(36): 3729.

Deaton, A. and V. Kozel (2005). 'Data and Dogma: The Great Indian Poverty Debate', *World Bank Research Observer*, 20: 177–99.

Dehejia, R.H. and R. Gatti (2002). *Child Labor: The Role of Income Variability and Access to Credit Across Countries*', NBER Working Paper No. 9018, Cambridge, Mass., National Bureau of Economic Research.

Deolalikar, A. (2005). *Attaining the Millenium Development Goals in India*, New Delhi, Oxford University Press for The World Bank.

Desai, M.J. (1991). 'Human Development: Concepts and Measurements', *European Economic Review*, 35: 350–7.

Desai, S. (1994). *Gender Inequalities and Demographic Behavior in India*. New York, The Population Council.

——— (2007). 'Middle Class', in K. Basu (ed.), *Oxford Companion to Economics in India*. New Delhi, Oxford University Press.

Desai, S. and M.B. Das (2004). 'Is Employment Driving India's Growth Surge?', *Economic and Political Weekly*, 39: 345–51.

Desai, S. and V. Kulkarni (2008). 'Changing Educational Inequalities in India: In The Context of Affirmative Action', *Demography*, 45(2): 245–70.

Desai, S., A. Dubey, R. Vanneman, and R. Banerjee (2009). 'Private Schooling in India: A New Educational Landscape', in S. Bery, B. Bossworth, and A. Panagariya (eds), *India Policy Forum Vol. 5*, Washington DC and New Delhi, Brookings Institution and Sage.

Desai, S., C.D. Adams, and A. Dubey (2009). 'Segmented Schooling: Inequalities in Primary Education,' in K. Newman and S. Thorat, (eds), *Blocked by Caste: Discrimination and Social Exclusion in Modern India*. New Delhi, Oxford University Press.

Deshpande, A. (2000). 'Does Caste Still Define Disparity? A Look at Inequality in Kerala, India', *The American Economic Review*, 90(2): 322–5.

——— (2007). 'Overlapping Identities under Liberalization: Gender and Caste in India', *Economic Development and Cultural Change*, 55(4): 735–60.

Deshpande, R.S. (2003). *Current Land Policy Issues in India*, Geneva, Food and Agricultural Organisation.

Dev, S.M. and C. Ravi (2007). 'Poverty and Inequality: All-India and States, 1983–2005', *Economic and Political Weekly*, 42(6): 509–21.

Dijkstra, G.A. and L. Hanmer (2000). 'Measuring Socio-Economic Gender Inequality, Towards an Alternative to the UNDP Gender-Related Development Index', *Feminist Economics*, 6(2): 41–75.

Dirks, N.B. (1997). 'Recasting Tamil Society: The Politics of Caste and Race in Contemporary Southern India', in C. J. Fuller (ed.), *Caste Today*, New Delhi, Oxford University Press, pp 263–95.

Dixon, P. and J. Tooley (2005). 'The Regulation of Private Schools Serving Low-Income Families in Andhra Pradesh, India', *The Review of Austrian Economics*, 18(1): 29–54.

Drèze, J. and G.G. Kingdon (2001). 'School Participation in Rural India', *Journal of Development Economics*, 5: 1–24.

Drèze, J. and M. Murthi (2001). 'Fertility, Education, and Development: Evidence from India', *Population and Development Review*, 27(1): 33–63.

Dubey, A. and S. Gangopadhyay (1998). 'Counting the Poor: Where are the Poor in India?', *Sarvekshana Analytical Report No. 1*, Department of Statistics, Government of India, pp. 8–119.

Dubey, A., R. Palmer-Jones, and K. Sen (2006). 'Surplus Labour, Social Structure and Rural to Urban Migration: Evidence from Indian Data', *European Journal of Development Economics*, 18(1): 86–104.

Dumont, L. (1980). *Homo Hierarchicus: The Caste System and its Implications*, Chicago, University of Chicago Press.

Dutt, G. and M. Ravallion (1998). 'Agricultural Productivity and Rural Poverty in India', *Journal of Development Studies*, 34(4):62–85.

Foster, A.D. and M.R. Rosenzweig (2002). 'Household Division and Rural Economic Growth', *The Review of Economic Studies*, 69(4): 839–69.

Frankel, F. (1971). *India's Green Revolution: Economic Gains and Political Costs*, Princeton, New Jersey, Princeton University Press.

Fuller, C.J. (1997). *Caste Today*, New Delhi, Oxford University Press.

Gangolli, L.V., R. Duggal, and A. Shukla (2005). *Review of Health Care in India*. Mumbai, Centre for Enquiry into Health and Allied Themes.

Ghose, Ajit K. (2004). 'The Employment Challenge in India', *Economic and Political Weekly*, 39(48): 5106–16.

Ghurye, G.S. (1950). *Caste and Class in India*, Bombay, Popular Book Depot.

Gore, C., G. Rodgers, and J. Figueiredo (1995). *Social Exclusion: Rhetoric, Reality, Responses*, Geneva, International Institute for Labour Studies.

Goswami, O. (1984). 'Agriculture in Slump: The Peasant Economy of East and North Bengal in the 1930s', *Indian Economic and Social History Review*, 21(3).

Government of India [GoI] (2002). *National Human Development Report 2001*, Planning Commission, Government of India, New Delhi, Oxford University Press.

——— (2006). *Social, Economic and Educational Status of the Muslim Community in India*. New Delhi: Government of India.

——— (2007). *Annual Report of Ministry of Home Affairs (2006–07)*, New Delhi, MHA.

——— (2007). *Tenth Five Year Plan 2002–2007, Volume II*. Planning Commission, New Delhi.

Grootaert, C. and R. Kanbur (1995). 'Child Labour: An Economic Perspective', *International Labour Review*, 134(2): 187–203.

Grosh, M. and P. Glewwe (2000). *Designing Household Survey Questionnaires for Developing Countries: Lessons from 15 Years of the Living Standards Measurement Study*, Washington DC, World Bank.

Guha, R. and J.P. Parry (1999). *Institutions and Inequalities: Essays in Honour of Andre Beteille*, New Delhi, Oxford University Press.

Gulati, L. (1993). *In the Absence of their Men: The Impact of Male Migration on Women*, New Delhi, Sage Publications.

Haq, M.U. (1997). *Human Development in South Asia 1997*, Karachi, Oxford University Press.

Himanshu (2007). 'Recent Trends in Poverty and Inequality: Some Preliminary Results', *Economic and Political Weekly*, 42(6):497–508.

Imai, K. (2003). *The Employment Guarantee Scheme as a Social Safety Net—Poverty Dynamics and Poverty Alleviation*, Department of Economics Working Paper Series, No. 149. Oxford, Oxford University.

International Institute for Population Science and O.R.C. Macro (2000). *National Family Health Survey (NFHS-2), 1998–99: India*. Mumbai, IIPS.

International Institute for Population Sciences and Macro International (2007). *National Family Health Survey (NFHS-3) 2005–2006, India: Volume 1*, Mumbai, IIPS.

International Labour Organisation [ILO] (2003). *Decent Work in Agriculture*, Geneva: International Labour Office.

Jaffrelot, C. (2000). 'The Rise of the Other Backward Classes in the Hindi Belt', *The Journal of Asian Studies*, 59(1): 86–108.

Johnson, D.S., T.M. Smeeding, and B.B. Torrey (2005). 'Economic Inequality Through the Prisms of Income and Consumption', *Monthly Labor Review*, 128(4): 11–24.

Joshi, V, and I.M.D. Little (1996). *India's Economic Reforms, 1991–2001*, Oxford, Clarendon Press.

Kabeer, N. (2001). 'Safety Nets and Opportunity Ladders: Addressing Vulnerability and Enhancing Productivity in South Asia', *Development Policy Review*, 20(5): 589–614.

Khan, A.A. and F.S. Bidabadi (2004). 'Livestock Revolution in India: Its Impact and Policy Response', *South Asia Research*, 24(2): 99–122.

Kishor, S. (1993). 'May God Give Sons to All: Gender and Child Mortality in India'. *American Sociological Review*, 58(2): 247–65.

——— (2005). 'Gender in the Demographic and Health Surveys', in S. Kishor (ed.), *A Focus on Gender: Collected Papers on Gender using DHS Data*. Calverton Maryland, ORC Macro: pp. 1–7.

Kochar, A. (2001). *Emerging Challenges for Indian Education Policy*, Center for Research on Economic Development and Policy Reform, Working Paper No. 97.

Krishnaswamy, K.S. (1990). *Poverty and Income Distribution*, New Delhi, Oxford University Press for Sameeksha Trust.

Kulkarni, P.M. (2009). 'Human Development Differentials Among Social Groups', in A. Shariff and M. Krishnaraj (eds), *States, Markets and Inequalities: Human Development in Rural India*. New Delhi, Orient Longman.

Kumar, D. (1962). 'Caste and Landlessness in South India', *Comparative Studies in Society and History*, 4(3): 337–63.

Kuznets, S. (1955). 'Economic Growth and Income Inequality', *American Economic Review*, 45: 1–28.

Lanjouw, P. and R. Murgai (2009). 'Poverty Decline, Agricultural Wages, and Nonfarm Employment in Rural India: 1983–2004', *The Journal of the International Association of Agricultural Economics* 40(2): 243–63.

Liebig, P.S. and S.I. Rajan (eds) (2003). *An Aging India: Perspectives, Prospects and Policies*. Binghamton, NY, Howarth Press.

Lin, N. (2001). *Social Capital: A Theory of Social Structure and Action*. Cambridge, Cambridge University Press.

Malhotra, A., R. Vanneman, and S. Kishor (1995). Fertility, Dimensions of Patriarchy, and Development in India. *Population and Development Review*, 21(2): 281–305.

Malik, S. (1979). *Social Integration of Scheduled Castes*, New Delhi, Abhinav Publications.

Meenakshi, J.V., R. Ray, and S. Gupta (2000). 'Estimates of Poverty for SC, ST, and Female Headed Households', *Economic and Political Weekly*, 2748–54.

Mendelsohn, O. and M. Vicziany (1998). *The Untouchables: Subordination, Poverty and the State in Modern India*. Cambridge, Cambridge University Press.

Mensch, B., S. Singh, and J. Casterline (2005). 'Trends in the Timing of First Marriage among Men and Women in the Developing World', in C.B. Lloyd, J. Behrman, N.P. Stromquist and B. Cohen (eds), *The Changing Transitions to Adulthood in Developing Countries: Selected Studies*. Washington DC, National Academies Press.

Metcalf, T.R. (1967). 'Landlords Without Land: The U.P. Zamindars Today', *Pacific Affairs*, 40(1/2): 5–18.

Mohanty, M. (2006). 'Social Inequality, Labour Market Dynamics and Reservation', *Economic and Political Weekly*, 41: 3777–89.

Moneer, A. (2004). 'Ageing, Old Age Income Security and Reforms: An Exploration of Indian Situation', *Economic and Political Weekly*, 39(33): 3731–40.

——— (2005). 'South Asian Elderly: ADL and IADL Statuses of the Elderly in India: A Preliminary Investigation', Population Research Centre, Institute of Economic Growth, Delhi, April (mimeo).

Muralidharan, K. and M. Kremer (2008). 'Public and Private Schools in Rural India', in R. Chakrabarti and P. Petersen (eds), *School Choice International: Exploring Public Private Partnerships*. Cambridge, Mass, MIT Press, Vol. 2008: pp. 91–110.

National Academy (1997). *Reproductive Health in Developing Countries: Expanding Dimensions, Building Solutions*, Washington DC, National Academy Press.

National Sample Survey Organisation [NSSO] (1992). *Operational Land Holdings in India. Report 407*. Ministry of Planning and Programme Implementation, Government of India, New Delhi.

——— (2003). *Some Aspects of operational Land Holdings in India, Report 492*. Government of India, New Delhi.

——— (2004). *Morbidity, Health Care and the Condition of the Aged. Report 507. Report 494*. Government of India, New Delhi

——— (2005a). *Employment and Unemployment Situation in India. Report 515 (Part 1)*. Government of India, New Delhi.

——— (2005b). *Level and Pattern of Consumer Expenditure. Report 508. Government of India*, New Delhi.

——— (2005c). *Public Distribution System and Other Source of Households Consumption. Report 510 (Vol. I and II)*. Government of India, New Delhi.

——— (2006a). *Employment and Unemployment Situation in India, 2004–05 (Part-I)*, New Delhi, Government of India.

——— (2006b). *Some Aspects of Operational Land Holdings in India: 2002–03*, Report 492. Ministry of Planning and Programme Implementation, Government of India, New Delhi.

Navaneetham, K. and A. Dharmalingam (2002). Utilization of Maternal Health Care Services in Southern India. *Social Science and Medicine*, 55(10): 1849.

Nehru, Jawaharlal (1946). *The Discovery of India*. New Delhi, Oxford University Press: pp. 58–9.

——— (2003). *The Essential Writings of Jawaharlal Nehru*. New Delhi, Oxford University Press

Oberoi, P. (1998). *Family, Kinship and Marriage in India*. Delhi, Oxford India Paperbacks.

Omvedt, G. (1993). *Reinventing Revolution: New Social Movements and the Socialist Tradition in India*. Armonk, New York, M.E. Sharpe.

Pallikadavath, S., M. Foss, and R.W. Stones (2004). 'Antenatal Care: Provision and Inequality in Rural North India', *Social Science and Medicine*, 59(6): 1147–58.

Palmer-Jones R.W. and A. Dubey (2005). 'Poverty Counts in India since 1983: New Poverty Counts and Robust Poverty Comparisons', *Artha Vijnana*, 47(3–4): 287–328.

——— (2005). 'Prices, Price Indexes and Poverty Counts in India During the 1980s and 19980s: From Unit Value CPIs to Poverty Lines', *Artha Vijnana*, 47(3–4): 259–86.

Palmer-Jones, R. and K. Sen (2001). *On India's Poverty Puzzles and Statistics of Poverty*. pp. 211–17.

——— (2003). 'What Has Luck Got To Do With It? A Regional Analysis of Poverty and Agricultural Growth in Rural India', *Journal of Development Studies*, 40(1): 1–31.

Palmer-Jones, R. and K. Sen (2006). 'It's Where You Are That Matters; The Spatial Determinants of Rural Poverty in India', *Agricultural Economics*, 34(1): 1–14.

Paris, T., A. Singh, J. Luis, and M. Hossain (2005). 'Labour Outmigration, Livelihood of Rice Farming Households and Women Left Behind: A Case Study in Eastern Uttar Pradesh', *Economic and Political Weekly*, 40(25): 2522–9.

Patnaik, U., Z. Hassan, and T.V. Sathyamurthy (1995). *Aspects of the Farmer's Movement in Uttar Pradesh in the Context of Uneven Capitalist Development in Indian Agriculture*, New Delhi, Oxford University Press.

PRATHAM (2005). *Annual Status of Education Report*. New Delhi, Pratham Documentation Center, Pratham.

Raj, K.N., N. Bhattacharya, S. Guha, and S. Padhi (1985). *Essays on the Commercialization of Indian Agriculture*, New Delhi, Oxford University Press.

Ram, R. (2006). 'Further Examination of The Cross-country Association Between Income Inequality and Population Health', *Social Science and Medicine*, 62(3).

Ramaswamy, K.V. (2007). 'Regional Dimension of Growth and Employment', *Economic and Political Weekly*, 42(49): 47–56.

Rao, A. (2003). *Gender and Caste: Issues in Contemporary Indian Feminism*, New Delhi, Kali for Women.

Rao, V. and M. Walton (2004). *Culture and Public Action*, Stanford, Stanford University Press.

Ravallion, M. and B. Bidani (1994). 'How Robust is a Poverty Profile?', *World Bank Economic Review*, 8: 75–102.

Ravallion, M. and G. Datt (2002). 'Why Has Economic Growth Been More Pro-Poor in Some States of India Than Others?', *Journal of Development Economics*, 68: 381–400.

Ravallion, Martin (1992). *Poverty Comparisons, A Guide to Concepts and Methods, Living Standards Measurement Study*, Working Paper 88, Washington DC, World Bank.

Sen, A. (2000). 'A Decade of Human Development', *Journal of Human Development*, 1(1): 17–23.

Sen, A. and Himanshu (2004). 'Poverty and Inequality in India-1', *Economic and Political Weekly*, (September): 4247–63.

——— (2004). 'Poverty and Inequality in India-2', *Economic and Political Weekly*, (September): 4361–75.

Sen, A.K. (1999). *Development as Freedom*, Oxford, Oxford University Press.

Shah, G., H. Mander, S. Thorat, S. Deshpande, and A. Baviskar (2006). *Untouchability in Rural India*, New Delhi, Sage Publications.

Shariff, A. (1999). *India Human Development Report*, New Delhi, Oxford University Press.

Shariff, A. and M. Krishnaraj (eds) (2007). *State, Markets and Inequalities: Human Development in Rural India*. New Delhi, Orient-Longman.

Sharma, K. L. (1999). *Social Inequality in India: Profiles of Caste, Class and Social Mobility*, Jaipur, Rawat Publications.

Sharma, U. (1980). *Women, Work and Property in North-West India*, New York, Tavistock.

Shivkumar, A.K. (1994). 'Human Development Index for Indian States', *Economic and Political Weekly*, 26: 2343–5.

Srinivas, M.N. (1957). 'Caste in Modern India', *The Journal of Asian Studies*, 16(4): 529–48.
——— (1987). *The Dominant Caste and Other Essays*, New Delhi, Oxford India Paperbacks.
Subbarao, K., A. Bonnerjee, S. Carvalho, K. Ezemenari, C. Graham, and A. Thompson (1997). *Safety Net Programmes and Poverty Reduction: Lessons from Cross-Country Experience*, Washington DC, World Bank.
Sujatha, K. and R. Govinda (2002). *Education among Scheduled Tribes*, New Delhi, Oxford University Press.
Sundar, N. (1999). 'The Indian Census, Identity and Inequality', in R. Guha and J. Perry (eds), *Institutions and Inequalities: Essays in Honour of Andre Beteille*. New Delhi, Oxford University Press, pp. 100–27.
Sundaram, K. and S. Tendulkar (2003). 'Poverty in India in the 1990s: Revised Results for All-India and 15 Major States for 1993–94', *Economic and Political Weekly*, (November): 4865–72.
——— (2004). 'The Poor in the Indian Labor Force: Challenges from 1990s', *Economic and Political Weekly*, 39: 5125–32.
Swaminathan, M. (1998). 'Economic Growth and the Persistence of Child Labor: Evidence from an Indian City', *World Development*, 26(8): 1513–28.
——— (2000). *Weakening Welfare: The Public Distribution of Food in India*. New Delhi, LeftWord Books.
Tendulkar, S., K. Sundaram, and L.R. Jain (2003a). 'Poverty Has Declined in the 1990s: A Resolution of Comparability Problems in NSS Consumer Expenditure Data', *Economic and Political Weekly*, (January): 327–37.
——— (2003b). 'Poverty in India in the 1990s: An Analysis of Changes in 15 Major State', *Economic and Political Weekly* (5 April): 1385–93.
The Planning Commission (2009). *Report of the Expert Group to Review the Methodology for Estimation of Poverty*. New Delhi, Government of India.
The Probe Team (1999). *Public Report on Basic Education in India*, New Delhi, Oxford University Press.
Thorat, S. and K. Newman (eds) (2009). *Blocked by Caste: Economic Discrimination in Modern India*. New Delhi, Oxford University Press.
Thorat, S. and P. Attewell (2007). 'The Legacy of Social Exclusion: A Correspondence Study of Job Discrimination in India', *Economic and Political Weekly*, 42(41).
Tomlinson, B.R. (1979). *The Political Economy of the Raj 1914–1947: The Economics of Decolonization in India*, London, The Macmillan Press Ltd.
——— (1993). *The Economy of Modern India, 1860–1970*, Cambridge, Cambridge University Press.
Tourangeau, R. and T. W. Smith (1996). 'Asking Sensitive Questions: The Impact of Data Collection Mode, Question Format, and Question Context', *The Public Opinion Quarterly*, 60(2): 275–304.
United Nations Development Programme [UNDP] (1999). 'Reinventing Global Governance for Humanity and Equity', in *Human Development Report 1999*, Oxford, Oxford University Press.
——— (2004). 'Cultural Liberty in Today's Diverse World', in *Human Development Report 2004*, Oxford, Oxford University Press.
——— (2006). *Beyond Scarcity: Power, Poverty and the Global Water Crisis*, New York, Oxford University Press.
United Nations Development Programme [UNDP] (2007). 'Fighting Climate Change: Human Solidarity in a Divided World', in *Human Development Report 2007/2008*, New York, Palgrave Macmillan.
——— (2007). *Human Development Report 2007/2008*. New York, Palgrave Macmillan.
United Nations Educational, Scientific and Cultural Organization [UNESCO] (1960). *Convention against Discrimination in Education*, Adopted by the General Conference at its Eleventh Session, Paris, 14 December 1960. Paris, UNESCO.
Vaidyanathan, A. (1992). 'Poverty and Economy: the Regional Dimension', in B. Harriss, S. Guhan, and R.H. Cassen (eds), *Poverty in India*, Oxford: Oxford University Press, pp. 58–75.
——— (1994). 'Employment Situation in India: the Emerging Perspective', *Economic and Political Weekly*, 59(50): 3147–56.
Vaishnavi, S.D. and U. Dash (2009). 'Catastrophic Payments for Health Care among Households in Urban Tamil Nadu, India', *Journal of International Development*, 21(2): 169–84.
Vanneman, R., C. Adams, and A. Dubey (2007). *Is It Worth Measuring Income in Developing Countries?*, Annual Meeting of the Population Association of America, New York.
Visaria, L., S. Jejeebhoy, and T. Merrick (1999). 'From Family Planning to Reproductive Health: Challenges Facing India', *International Family Planning Perspectives*, 25 (Supplement): 44–9.
Visaria, P. and B.S. Minhas (1990). 'Evolving an Employment Policy for the 1990s: What Do the Data Tell Us?', *Economic and Political Weekly*, 26(15): 969–79
World Bank (1997). *World Development Report, 1997: The State in a Changing World*, Oxford, Oxford University Press.
——— (2002a). *A Sourcebook for Poverty Reduction Strategies*, Washington DC, World Bank.
——— (2002b). *Bangladesh: Progress in Poverty Reduction*, Background Paper Bangladesh Development Forum, Paris, March, Washington DC, World Bank.
——— (2004). *World Development Report: Making Services Work for the Poor*, Washington DC, Oxford University Press and World Bank.
World Health Organization [WHO] (2001). *Private Sector Involvement in City Health Systems*, Proceedings of a WHO conference meeting 14–16 February, Dunedin, New Zealand. http://www.who.int
——— (2002). 'Active Ageing: a Policy Framework', WHO/NMH/NPH/02.8, Geneva, WHO, Contribution of WHO to the Second World Assembly on Ageing, Madrid, April 2002.
——— (2006). *Fuel for Life: Household Energy and Health*, Geneva, WHO.
World Health Report (2002). 'Reducing Risks, Promoting Healthy Life', Geneva, WHO, http//:www.who.int/whr/2002/en/.